MAINTAINING the PROMISES... DAILY

Passing on the Program...

Step 10

Pan Fellowship

© Copyright 2008 by HP Publishing (UK) Ltd
63 Shepherds Court
LONDON W12-8PW
England

44+(0)208 740 8567
www.hppublishing.com
www.hpretreats.org

First Edition

This edition was printed in the United Kingdom

ISBN 978-0-9556930-4-5

Our thanks and gratitude to Alcoholics Anonymous for the gift they have given to the world of the Twelve Steps. This volume has been compiled using quotes from 13 of AA's copyrighted books and from the experience in life, both in and out of Alcoholics Anonymous, of those working the "Programme," which we recognise as the Steps. This material has been reprinted for the ease and speed of study during a Pan-Fellowship Retreat.

WE STRONGLY SUGGEST THAT EACH INDIVIDUAL WISHING TO BETTER UNDERSTAND THE 12 STEPS DO AS WE HAVE DONE AND PURCHASE AND STUDY ALL THE BOOKS OF ALCOHOLICS ANONYMOUS:

Alcoholics Anonymous
The Twelve Steps and Twelve Traditions
As Bill Sees It
The Language of the Heart
Came to Believe
The Best of the Grapevine
Dr. Bob and the Good Oldtimers
Experience, Strength, and Hope
Pass it On—Bill Wilson and the AA Message
Daily Reflections
The Home Group: Heartbeat of AA
AA Comes of Age
Living Sober

ALL THAT WE HAVE ATTEMPTED TO DO IS, TO FIND, AND "PULL OUT," THE EXPERIENCE OF THE 12 STEPS FROM THE MANY LIVES OF THOSE WHO CONTRIBUTED TO THE 13 BOOKS.

In an attempt to honour and accent the lessons and information found in these texts we have often made **bold**, *italicized*, and <u>underlined</u> these 1,000 quotes from that material. In a further attempt to keep the material true to its original writing the use of these quotes often causes this written material to switch personal pronoun. Often the writing will switch from first person, to second person, to third person and back again, all within the same paragraph. The text also changes gender rather frequently. It is our intention to increase our own and the reader's depth of understanding of the 12 Steps of Alcoholics Anonymous. It really is an amazing programme.

Quotes are printed from Alcoholics Anonymous material as mentioned above.

TABLE OF CONTENTS

Chapter		Page
	Introduction	i
1	PRAYERS AND QUOTES	1
	Opening Prayer	3
	Serenity Prayer	4
	Third Step Prayer	4
	Seventh Step Prayer	4
	Prayer of Saint Francis of Assisi	5
	Prayer for Open-Mindedness	5
	Thy Will Be Done	5
2	DISTURBANCE CONTROL—STEWARDSHIP	7
	Three Types of Step Ten	12
	(1) The Spot Check Inventory	12
	Formula for Spot-Check Inventory	14
	(2) The Balance Sheet	16
	When We Retire at Night	17
	On Gratitude	17
	(3) Annual or Semi-Annual House-Cleaning	18
	The Principle of Step Ten	19
3	366 BALANCE SHEETS	21
4	HOW TO ANSWER FOURTH COLUMN QUESTIONS	391
	Selfish/Self-Centred/Self-Seeking	393
	Dishonesty	394
	Fears	395
	Blame (Responsible)	396
	Decisions	397
	Our Part	400
5	140 INVENTORY FORMS	401
6	THE PRINCIPLES...	545
	THE REFERENCES...	551
	CONTACT US	**556**

INTRODUCTION

It is our desire that as many people as possible realise the power and wisdom encapsulated in the Twelve Steps and use this material to maintain the Promises of the Programme with Step 10's. We have been using these methods for many years now. They have never failed to bring about relief, for those of us who have looked deep within our souls to see our part in the creation of our life's problems. Our mental, emotional, psychological, physical, and spiritual relief has been immense. We trust the reader who chooses this daily path will find the same. We **can** choose to be **"happy, joyous and free".** [1]

The programme tells us that, **"The ...answer lies in a constant effort to practice all of the ...Twelve Steps. Persistence will cause this to sink in and affect that unconscious from where the trouble stems."** [2]

The true sign that we have real sobriety, defined later, as **a peaceful, calm, contented, sedate and well-balanced life;** is how we live our lives outside "the rooms". If we are demonstrating anger in or out of meetings we have not truly gained the *Promises*. The ability to work the Programme in the meetings of our many fellowships is easier than outside in our Relationships, Family, and Work lives. The Buddhists call this type of spirituality, **cloistered virtue.** It does not create a **bridge to normal living.**

The **bridge IS the Programme.** Our experience shows that, even when **sober,** without a strong, powerful Programme we become as crazy as we ever were; if we don't relapse or take a sojourn into other addictions. In *Addictions Anonymous* and the *Pan-Fellowship* members have find that once one addiction is "handled" with the Steps another would rear its ugly head. Remember, in the Pan-Fellowship our definition of sobriety is: **a peaceful, calm, contented, sedate and well-balanced life.**

Our father programme tells us that, **"the roads to recovery are many; that any story or theory of recovery from one who has trod the highway is bound to contain much truth."** [3] We trust we'll find this material to be a source of discussion and investigation of the **Maintenance Steps.**

This material is the voice of a great many members from a great many sources. **"We have also adopted procedures from a number of other sources, some very old, but all quite standard, well-known, and simple, if not easy."** [4]

INTRODUCTION

We don't have all the answers, **"Consequently, the full individual liberty to practice any creed or principle or therapy whatever should be a first consideration for us all. Let us not, therefore, pressure anyone with our individual or even our collective views. Let us instead accord each other the respect and love that is due to every human being as he tries to make his way toward the light. Let us always try to be inclusive rather than exclusive..."** [5]

This material takes about as deep a practice of Step 10, and makes as wide an application, as we are aware of at this time. Many have chosen to broaden their commitment to these processes through these pages. All other material found herein is based on practical experience from the lives of fellow addicts. They have found peace of mind and contented sanity and sobriety by the planned way of spiritual life set forth in the Twelve Steps and Maintained by the last three.

Our Programs are not accountable to any organised religion, medicine, or psychology. We have, however, drawn therapeutic practices from each of these disciplines, moulding them into a "design for living".

Spiritual concepts must be embraced, but these practises do not involve organised religion. Although we must believe in a Higher Power, it is our privilege to interpret it according to our own understanding.

We must acquire honesty, humility and appreciation to eliminate self-centredness and keep our peace and emotional sobriety. For those of us who are willing to accept the 12 Step Programme as a means of recovery from any addiction, we recommend a close study of any and all experience, found in any of the many programs, of these Steps. Don't just read them; study them *repeatedly*. We have done this with AA's material and continue to find as much information as possible to broaden our knowledge of these processes. These many programs have worked out methods that have proved to be sound and effective in the lives of millions.

We will use the words "our addiction" whenever possible throughout this material; with the understanding that once we have quit our primary addiction we find that we have many others that pop up. Our experience shows that the programme of these Twelve Steps works no matter what the "addiction." *We further suggest the definition of addiction as, "anything that we do that we cannot seem to stop doing on our own steam."* This would include things like overeating, smoking, gambling, co-dependence, worrying, etc, not forgetting sexual behaviour, anger or rage, self harming, worry and much else.

Chapter 1

Prayers and Quotes to Remember

PRAYERS AND QUOTES TO REMEMBER

*Opening Prayer**

We are here to develop and maintain a conscious contact with a *Power Greater than Ourselves*. It has been said that where two or more are gathered together in the name of Good, there this Higher Power would be in the midst. We believe that It is here with us now. We believe this is something It would have us do, and that we have It's blessing.

We pledge our honesty, open mindedness, and willingness to work these Steps, searching our hearts and minds for weaknesses and errors, that we may be free.

We believe that within each of us there is a unique connection to God and that we are real partners with It in this business of living, *accepting our full responsibilities* and certain that the rewards are freedom and growth and happiness.

For this we are grateful. We ask at all times to be guided, as we maintain conscious contact with God, finding new ways of living our gratitude.

And so it is. Amen

*This opening prayer is taken from what was called the "Al-Anon Prayer" in Southern California. It is updated in contemporary language; the gender has been removed and it specifically refers to the "Steps."

PRAYERS AND QUOTES

Step Eleven conveys to us that it, **"surely means that we ought to look toward God's perfection as our guide rather than as a goal to be reached in any foreseeable time."** [6]

There are many spiritual paths. The important thing is to **"be quick to see where religious people are right." "We are only operating a spiritual kindergarten in which people are enabled to get over drinking** (and other addictions) **and find the grace to go on living to better effect. Each man's theology has to be his own quest, his own affair."** [7]

But like this member, **"I centre my thoughts on a Higher Power. I... surrender all to this power within me... May the steps I take today strengthen my words and deeds."** [8]

SERENITY PRAYER:

When we first enter the programme one of the first prayers we learn is the Serenity Prayer. **"God grant me the Serenity to accept the things I cannot change; the Courage to change the things I can; and the Wisdom to know the difference."** [9]

IN STEP THREE WE PRAY:

"God I offer myself to Thee to build with me and to do with me as Thou wilt. Relieve me of the bondage of self that I may better do Thy will. Take away my difficulties, that victory over them may bear witness to those I would help of Thy Power, Thy Love, and Thy Way of life. May I do Thy will always!" [10]

IN STEP SEVEN WE *HUMBLY ASKED*:

"My creator, I am now willing that you should have all of me good and bad. I pray that you now remove from me every single defect of character, which stands in the way of usefulness to you and my fellows. Grant me strength as I go out from here to do your bidding. Amen" [1][11]

---

[1] The meaning of Amen is, and so be it. If uncomfortable saying amen say and so it is or and so be it. But either way get that prayer is a proclamation not a petition.

TO REMEMBER

NOW, IN STEP ELEVEN – *"knowledge of Gods will for us..."*

The Prayer of St. Francis of Assisi

"Lord, make me a channel of thy peace—that where there is hatred, I may bring love—that where there is wrong, I may bring the spirit of forgiveness—that where there is discord, I may bring harmony—that where there is error, I may bring truth—that where there is doubt, I may bring faith—that where there is despair, I may bring hope—that where there are shadows, I may bring light—that where there is sadness, I may bring joy. Lord, grant that I may seek rather to comfort than to be comforted—to understand, than to be understood, to love, than to be loved. For it is by self-forgetting that one finds. It is by forgiving that one is forgiven. It is by dying that one awakens to Eternal Life." [12]

PRAYER FOR OPEN-MINDEDNESS

The following prayer, paraphrased from *Share* magazine (the UK's AA magazine), it was recommended to a Sponsee for use when things weren't going as planned.

"Dear God, please have me set aside everything I think I know about _____(Blank)_____ so that I may be open to a new experience."

"THY WILL BE DONE". [13]

We often pray: *"How can I best serve Thee—Thy will (not mine) be done."* [14] Or more simply put: *"Thy will be done".*[15] True prayer must be *"Thy will, not mine, be done."* [16] But the implication relative to the Will of God in this prayer is not a submission to the inevitability of evil, bad, or limitation; we pray in the knowledge that the will of God is always Good.

STEP 10

Chapter 2

Disturbance Control

Stewardship

(Excerpted from the book Deep Soul Cleansing)

DISTURBANCE CONTROL—STEWARDSHIP
STEP TEN

"<u>Continued</u> To Take Personal Inventory and When We Were Wrong Promptly Admitted It."[17]

We must remember what we have learned from the previous Nine Steps: gaining Power in our lives means taking responsibility for our own emotions, comfort, feelings and conduct. **"When we approach Step Ten we commence to put our...way of living to practical use, day by day, in fair weather or foul. Then comes the acid test: can we stay sober, keep in emotional balance, and live, to good purpose, under all conditions?"**[18] Always we keep at the forefront of our minds the collective knowledge that sobriety, defined as just not drinking or using is in itself not enough: **"at Step Ten, we had begun to get a basis for daily living, and we keenly realised that we would need to continue taking personal inventory."**[19]

Often as we go through our day the only thing that has happened is someone has made a stupid remark. After which, our emotions have been affected to the extreme and we fume. This is where Step 10 comes in.

"Step Ten...suggests we continue to take personal inventory and continue to set right any new mistakes as we go along. We vigorously commenced this way of living as we cleaned up the past. We have entered the world of the Spirit. Our next function is to grow in understanding and effectiveness. This is not an overnight matter. It should continue for a lifetime."[20] **"'Resentment is** (still) **the Number One offender.' It is a primary cause of relapses."**[21]

"We react sanely and normally, and we find that this has happened automatically. We will see that our new attitude...has been given us without any thought or effort on our part. It just comes! That is the miracle of it. We are not fighting it, neither are we avoiding temptation. We feel as though we had been placed in a position of neutrality—safe and protected...the problem has been removed. It does not exist for us. We are neither cocky nor are we afraid. That is our experience. That is how we react so long as we keep in fit spiritual condition. (We find this to be true with any problem on which we thoroughly work the 12 Step process.)

"It is easy to let up on the spiritual programme of action and rest on our laurels. We are headed for trouble if we do."[22] But we can maintain our **"emotional sobriety. If we examine every disturbance we have, great or small, we will find at the root of it**

DISTURBANCE CONTROL

some unhealthy dependency and its consequence unhealthy demand. Let us, with God's help, continually surrender these hobbling demands. Then we can be set free to live and love; we may then be able to Twelve Step others into emotional sobriety."[23]

WE MUST NOT **"REST ON OUR LAURELS"** NO MATTER HOW MUCH WE ARE TEMPTED TO DO SO. If we do we risk losing what we have gained. **"We learned that if we were seriously disturbed, our first need was to quiet that disturbance, regardless of whom or what we thought caused it."**[24] We are no longer victims of other people's behaviour. We're free and we are going to remain that way. We can and will maintain the Promises we have now gained by working all of the types of Tenth Steps suggested below. We have **"to continue to take inventory every day if expect to get well and stay well."**[25]

"A business which takes no regular inventory usually goes broke."[26] Our new found "business of living" is no different. Our inventories often contain errors: **"Of course, my self-analysis has frequently been faulty. Sometimes I've failed to share my defects with the right people; at other times, I've confessed their defects, rather than my own; and at still other times, my confession of defects has been more in the nature of loud complaints about my circumstances and my problems.**[27] This is the reason why written inventory always works better than doing it in our heads.

"Long ago I was lucky enough to see that I'd have to keep up my self-analysis or else blow my top completely. Though driven by stark necessity, this continuous self-revelation—to myself and others—was rough medicine to take. But years of repetition has made this job far easier."[28] **"If we go on growing, our attitudes and actions toward security—emotional security and financial security—commence to change profoundly. Our demand for emotional security, for our own way, had constantly thrown us into unworkable relations with other people."**[29]

We must always keep in mind that **"The first requirement is that we be convinced that any life run on self-will can hardly be a success."**[30] Therefore any inventory involves a similar surrender to that in the first three Steps. We at least acknowledge that we must write inventory at the end of each day. It is amazing that no matter how long we are around: **"Some of us have tried to hold on to our old ideas and the result was nil until we let go absolutely."**[31] Eventually most of us learn that **"the more we fought and tried to have our own way, the worse matters got."**[32]

STEWARDSHIP

This process is about gaining a measure of control over our life. As another member put it: **"I have no control over some of the things that happen in my life, but with the help of God I can now choose how I will respond."**[33] The best way of understanding Step Ten and Eleven, is to see them as a daily practice of all the previous Steps, One to Nine, simultaneously. All the processes used in those Steps will be duplicated in Step Ten at some point. Remember that our Step Four Inventory was **"but the beginning of a life long practice."**[34] A practice where, **"I place the principles of spirituality ahead of judging, fault-finding, and criticism."**[35]

"Perhaps life, as it has a way of doing, suddenly hands us a great big lump that we can't begin to swallow, let alone digest."[36] **"Mental and emotional difficulties are sometimes very hard to take while we are trying to maintain sobriety... Adversity gives us more opportunity to grow than does comfort or success."**[37]

In the book Deep Soul Cleansing, in the chapter on the Fourth Step, we talked about a "ONE POUND WEIGHT," (found on 130.4-6) and how the longer you hold it the heavier it gets. The same is true with resentments (or "disturbances"). Our task now is to practice letting go of it more quickly, before there is damage to ourselves or our relationships. Whatever disturbing burdens we pick up today, let's release them as soon as possible. We must not get unduly emotional about this work. We only desire the truth that will set us free. Remember that **"inventory is a fact-finding and fact-facing process. It is an effort to discover the truth... We took stock honestly."**[38] That is what this Step is all about, facts not emotions.

The cry of the "self-satisfied" is often, **"'Well, I'm sober and I'm happy. What more can I want or do? I'm fine the way I am.' We know** (from our own experience) **that the price of such self-satisfaction is an inevitable backslide, punctuated at some point by a very rude awakening. We have to grow or else deteriorate. For us, the 'status quo' can only be for today, never tomorrow. Change we must; we cannot stand still...**

"We have come to believe that (the) **recovery Steps and Traditions do represent the approximate truths which we need for our particular purpose. The more we practice them, the more we like them.**

"While we need not alter our truths, we surely improve their application to ourselves...and to our relation with the world around us. We can constantly Step up 'the practice of these principles in all our affairs.

DISTURBANCE CONTROL

"Let us continue to take our inventory... searching out our flaws and confessing them freely. Let us devote ourselves to the repair of all faulty relations that may exist, whether within or without."[39]

THREE TYPES OF TENTH STEPS

FIRST IS THE **"'SPOT-CHECK' INVENTORY"**[40]

"Although all inventories are alike in principle, the time factor does distinguish one from another. There's the "spot-check" inventory, taken at any time of the day, whenever we find ourselves <u>tangled up</u>."[41]

"Before we ask what a "spot-check" inventory is, let's look at the kind of setting in which such an inventory can do its work.

"It is a spiritual axiom that every time we are disturbed, <u>no matter what the cause,</u> there is something wrong with us. If somebody hurts us and we are sore, <u>we are in the wrong also</u>."[42]

"When I get upset, cross-grained and out of tune with my fellow man I know that I am out of tune with God. Searching where I have been at fault, it is not hard to discover and get right again."[43] Where we use our inventory process this becomes patently clear. After each "disturbance" we want to be able to look back and say: *"I knew something was terribly wrong, and the reason had to lie within myself."*[44] But it is likely that we will resist this fact. Old habits die hard. This is why we need to remind ourselves of it on a daily basis.

We found that: *"Acceptance was the Answer."* *"Acceptance is the answer to all my problems today. When I am <u>disturbed</u>, it is because I find some person, place, thing, or situation—some fact of my life—unacceptable to me, and I can find no serenity until I accept that person, place, thing, or situation as being exactly the way it is supposed to be at this moment. Nothing, absolutely nothing, happens in God's world by mistake...unless I accept life completely on life's terms, I cannot be happy. <u>I need to concentrate not so much on what needs to be changed in the world as on what needs to be changed in me and in my attitudes</u>."*[45]

"But are there no exceptions to this rule? What about "justifiable" anger? If somebody cheats us, aren't we entitled to be angry? Can't we be properly angry with self-righteous folk?"[46]

STEWARDSHIP

The answer to each of these questions is an emphatic and resounding **No!** Venting our anger is not OK, nor should it be repressed, stuffing it down and not dealing with it. ***"We have found that justified anger ought to be left to those better qualified to handle it... It mattered little whether our resentments were justified or not... As we saw it, our wrath was always justified. Anger, the occasional luxury of more balanced people, could keep us on an emotional orgy indefinitely."***[47] ***"It will become more and more evident as we go forward that it is pointless to become angry, or get hurt by people who, like us, are suffering from the pains of growing up."***[48]

"Many religions and philosophies urge us to get rid of anger in order to find a happier life. Yet a great number of people are certain that bottling up anger is very bad for emotional health, that we should get our hostility out in some way, or it will 'poison' our insides by turning inward toward ourselves, thus leading to deep depression."[49] We agree that anger needs to be dealt with but do not agree that it is healthy to "get it out." Punching pillows or using soft batons and hitting things may be effective for some, but we believe that it is at best a temporary measure, and if we do not deal with the root causes we will graduate from punching the pillow to more destructive behaviour.

"The minute... I... (feel) sorrow for myself, or... hurt by, or resentful towards anyone, I am in horrible danger."[50] ***"Here is a look at some of the shapes and colours anger seems at times to arrive in:***

"Intolerance	*Snobbishness*	*Tension*	*Distrust*
"Contempt	*Rigidity*	*Sarcasm*	*Anxiety*
"Envy	*Cynicism*	*Self-pity*	*Suspicion*
"Jealousy	*Hatred*	*Discontent*	*Malice*
(Frustration)	(Self-righteousness)	(Injustice)	(Hurt)
(Betrayal)		(Fear)	

"Many of us believe anger is frequently an outgrowth of fear... Perhaps 'justifiable' resentment is the trickiest of all to handle... Even if we actually have been treated shabbily or unjustly, resentment is a luxury... we cannot afford. For us, <u>all</u> anger is self-destructive...

"It's also remarkably effective, when we begin to get teed off at something, to pick up the phone and talk about it to our sponsor."[51]

DISTURBANCE CONTROL

We have found that: **"Other kinds of disturbances—jealousy, envy, self-pity, or hurt pride—did the same thing."**[52] All lead to anger. So what do we do about these "feelings?" **"A 'spot-check' inventory taken in the midst of such disturbances can be of very great help in quieting stormy emotions. Today's spot check finds its chief application to situations which arise in each day's march... The quick inventory is aimed at our daily ups and downs, especially those where people or new events throw us off balance and tempt us to make mistakes."**[53] There will be time later, at the end of the day, to more permanently repair and bolster our emotional and spiritual states.

"Simply repressing, glossing over, or damming up anger rarely (if ever) **seems advisable. Instead, we try to learn not to act <u>on</u> it, but to do something <u>about</u> it."**[54] **"Continue to take personal inventory and when we are wrong we promptly admit it."**[55] Does not the earlier statement say clearly that if our feelings are hurt we are <u>always</u> in the wrong also? This being so, we must be diligent. What we have found is that an outburst of anger is long after the events that loaded us to explode. Then it can be the most trivial thing that triggers the anger. If we were to look back over the days, weeks, even months and years before an eruption we would find many examples of times we mistakenly thought we could hold it together and we stuffed our feelings.

We want to re-establish a point. When we speak of not having an angry flare-up we do not mean that we stuff our feelings, we mean to deal with them in a healthy and powerful way through the use of the process suggested in the Steps, early in the cycle of upset. Besides, **"The positive value of righteous indignation is theoretical... It leaves every one of us open to the rationalisation that we may be as angry as we like provided we can claim to be righteous about it."**[56] Our experience demonstrates that even one well nursed "bad apple" of belief—this time, "I am right!" is enough to make the whole Spiritual barrel of ripe, delicious, desirable and wonderful "Apples"(the promises) of our lives to turn rotten.

FORMULA FOR SPOT-CHECK INVENTORY

There is a formula in the "Big Book" of *Alcoholics Anonymous* for a Spot Check Inventory and the maintenance of the promises gained from the previous Nine Steps. It suggests that we:

"Continue to watch for selfishness, dishonesty, resentment, and fear ("every time we are disturbed"[57]**). When these crop up...**
1) **"We ask God at once to remove them.**

STEWARDSHIP

2) *"We discuss them with someone immediately and*
3) *"Make amends quickly if we have harmed anyone.*
4) *"Then we resolutely [2] turn our thoughts to someone we can help.*[58]

"Love and tolerance of others is our code. And we have ceased fighting anything or anyone—even alcohol (or any of our addictions). *For by this time sanity will have returned."*[59] Notice that fear—that *"evil and corroding thread"*[60] still crops up in our lives. What do we do about it? We treat it exactly the same as any other "disturbance," crediting it with no more power than it possesses, which is none at all. Most of us want to be courageous and in order to become so we must recognise that:

"Courage is resistance to fear, mastery of fear—not absence of fear."—Mark Twain

The way to conquer fear is by remembering that *"we are now on a different basis; the basis of trusting and relying upon God. We trust infinite God rather than finite selves."*[61] And we act accordingly. *"Now and then we fall under heavy criticism. When we are angered and hurt, it's difficult not to retaliate in kind. Yet we can restrain ourselves* (using this process) *and then probe ourselves, asking whether our critics were really right* (later that evening as seen ahead). *If so, we can admit our defects to them. This usually clears the air for mutual understanding."*[62] Our bottom line experience is that, *"Nothing pays like restraint of tongue and pen."*[63] Or, given today's technology, it pays to refrain from clicking on the send button. *"The most heated bit of letter-writing can be a wonderful safety valve—providing the wastebasket is somewhere nearby."*[64]

EXPERIENCE SHOWS THIS IS A BAND-AID—A PLASTER—USED ONLY FOR EMERGENCY TREATMENT ON THE "BATTLEFIELD OF LIFE."

"We are sure God wants us to be happy, joyous, and free. We cannot subscribe to the belief that this life is a vale of tears, though it was once that for many of us."[65] Life tends to be a "battlefield" because we make it one. *"It is clear that we made our own misery. God didn't do it."*[66] So how do we heal these battle scars <u>permanently</u>? The answer lies in the other two types of Tenth Steps.

---

[2] **Resolutely** = with determination, boldly, without vacillating, without shrinking, with firm purpose or purposefully, with resolve.

DISTURBANCE CONTROL

SECOND IS THE **"DAILY BALANCE SHEET"**

"There's the one we take at day's end, when we review the happenings of the hours just passed. Here we cast a balance sheet, crediting ourselves with things well done, and chalking up debits where due."[67]

If, during the course of the day, we have acquired any resentment, we write a four-column inventory on them. That way the wound attended to with the **"Spot Check Inventory"** (temporary band-aide) can be permanently healed with this process and amends made where necessary. Remember that **"all inventories are alike in principle"**[68] therefore, the four column format is always appropriate.

It is always the same with disturbance and resentment; we still think we're right. While **"admitting he may be somewhat at fault, he is sure that other people are more to blame."**[69] You would think that some day we would stop trying to be right, wouldn't you? In any situation where we believe things to be a certain way, we ask ourselves: "Is there another way this could be?" And we keep asking ourselves the question, until we have at least ten other possibilities. Then the odds are we are wrong, ten-to-one. We are not mind readers; thus it is a waste of time and mental acuity. Besides, is it really our business? **"So I don't just take the inventory at night—I take it continually throughout the day... For me,** (it) **has become a way of life."**[70]

We are working towards a life where we spend our time looking at **our** motives and plans and schemes. Those we can correct. Instead of attempting to "correct" others like we do; often, **"We 'constructively criticise' someone who needed it, when our real motive was to win a useless argument... We sometimes hurt those we love because they need to be 'taught' a lesson, when we really mean to punish."**[71] Even if it were true that we wanted to sincerely 'help' them, you would think that by now we would see that this never works. Besides, we need to decide whether we want a loving relationship or be their unsolicited "teacher." The **"Twelve Steps continually remind us of the stark need for ego deflation."**[72] **"Learning daily to spot, admit, and correct these flaws is the essence of character-building and good life."**[73]

We have created a simple and straightforward form for this purpose. It is suggested that **"When evening comes, perhaps just before going to sleep, many of us draw up a balance sheet for the day."**[74] **"Here we need only recognise that we did act or think badly, to visualise how we might have done better, and resolve** *with God's help to carry these lessons over into tomorrow, making, of course, any amends still neglected.*"[75]

WHEN WE RETIRE AT NIGHT

This work is completed with our Daily Prayer and Meditation as suggested in the *Big Book*: **"When we retire at night, we constructively review our day. Were we resentful, selfish, dishonest or afraid? Do we owe an apology? Have we kept something to ourselves, which should be discussed with another person at once? Were we kind and loving toward all? What could we have done better? Were we thinking of ourselves most of the time? Or; were we thinking of what we could do for others, of what we could pack into the stream of life? But we must be careful not to drift into worry, remorse or morbid reflection, for that would diminish our usefulness to others. After making our review we ask God's forgiveness and inquire what corrective measures should be taken?"**[76] The form which follows is taken directly from this paragraph.

This being a spiritual programme which needs constant attention, here is where we take our 'spiritual temperature,' if you will. A wise man told us that if we want to know how far we are away from God, we find out where we stand in our relationships. If the answer is that we are in conflict, we are far off. If we are at peace, we are close to God. A member from Sydney, Australia put it another way: **"The depth of our anxiety measures the distance we are from God."**[77]

Many members also practice keeping a journal, and this is said to be a very good technique for reviewing our day. This practice will also help us with our inventories when we go on our annual or semi-annual retreats. Basically, writing almost always helps.

ON GRATITUDE AND A GRATITUDE LIST

Writing a gratitude list seems to some of us like a labour intensive task but can bring great rewards if practised. There are some that suggest we write one on a daily basis. It is extremely difficult to be both miserable and grateful at the same time.

"It took several years, but I learned to be grateful for my alcoholism and the programme of recovery it forced me into, for all the things that had happened to me and for me, for a life today that transcends and far exceeds anything I had previously known. I could not have that today if I had not experienced all the yesterdays."[78]

DISTURBANCE CONTROL

"When we retire at night we constructively review our day."[79] In this process we must always remember that: ***"Love and tolerance of others is our code."***[80] ***"And we have ceased fighting anything and anyone—even alcohol."***[81]

After completing our "Daily Balance Sheet," we do any column work that is indicated. Otherwise there will be a constant build up of "twinges" that have not been handled, creating more and more "disturbance." As stated earlier, all inventories are basically the same, so we work a four column inventory on any type of disturbance. It comes as no surprise that this daily inventory is a Balance Sheet; this is exactly what we are looking for; balance, equanimity, our place as one among many, neither better than nor worse than anyone else: ***"Every human being, no matter what his attitudes for good or evil, is a part of the Divine spiritual economy. Therefore, each of us has his place, and I cannot see that God intends to exalt one over another."***[82]

THIRD is the ***"Annual or Semi-Annual House-Cleaning"***

Many of our programme friends go on a yearly retreat to tend to this important ***"House-Cleaning"*** (basically a renewal of the Steps). If we have survived for many years without relapsing, we may finally work all the Steps again. Like this member from Oklahoma ***"I reviewed my entire life—the years before...and the twelve years in AA...For the first time in my life, it grew quite clear to me that I was an utter, complete, 100-percent, dyed-in-the-wool louse. I was so self-centred, so full of ego, that I had all but destroyed myself. During the years...I had learned little more than to 'keep the plug in the jug.' I had neglected to try to work <u>all</u> the Twelve Steps of the programme."***[83] ***"Yes, I did go back and start all over on the Twelve Steps, and I felt the wonder of other discoveries—about myself and my Higher Power. I would have felt these years ago had I but followed the programme and had I been, as the Big Book states, 'willing to go to any length to get it.'"***[84]

"Then there are those occasions when alone, or in the company of our sponsor or spiritual advisor, we make a careful review of our progress since the last time. Many...go in for annual or semi-annual house-cleanings. Many of us also like the experience of an occasional retreat from the outside world where we quieten down for an undisturbed day or so of self-overhaul and meditation."[85]

STEWARDSHIP

Many of us have foolishly tried to work Step Tens in our heads, without putting them *in writing*: *"Admitting to God, to ourselves, **AND** another human being the exact nature of our wrongs."*[86] We then learned the hard way that: *"In actual practice, we usually find a solitary self-appraisal insufficient."*[87]

Though our decisions and choices were the cause of much of our problems in life we don't use that as an excuse not to be decisive in the present. *"We lose the fear of making decisions, great or small, as we realise that should our choice prove wrong we can, if we will, learn from the experience. Should our decision be the right one, we can* (and are careful to) *thank God for giving us the courage and the grace that caused us so to act."*[88] Remember, it is our intention today to be conscious of our choices and decisions.

"All of my family and loved ones, all of my friends, are nearer and dearer to me than ever before; and I have literally dozens of new friends."[89] We *want* to have, and *"develop the best possible relations with every human being we know."*[90] *"I know the purpose of life: The purpose of life is to create and the by-product is happiness. To create: Everyone does it, some at the instinct level, and others in the arts. My personal definition...includes every waking activity of the human being; to have a creative attitude toward things is a more exact meaning, to live and deal with other human beings creatively, which to me means seeing the God in them, and respecting and worshiping this God."*[91] It is our responsibility, no matter what the other person is doing, to see the God in everyone.

We've come a long way. Let's not lose our momentum now. The so called "Pink Cloud" can be maintained with careful stewardship. *"The secret of fulfilling my potential is acknowledging my limitations and believing that time is a gift, not a threat."*[92] To repeat what was said earlier: *"The idea that we can be possessively loving of a few, can ignore the many, and can continue to fear or hate anybody has to be abandoned."*[93]

THE PRINCIPLE OF STEP TEN

Stewardship

The so-called "maintenance Steps" of the programme begin with Step Ten, teaching us perseverance and **stewardship**. Whereas perseverance is just plain "keeping on, keeping on"; **stewardship** is realising the need for a maintenance programme to keep the "Promises" we gained through working the previous Nine Steps. Dr. Bob said that *"we are **stewards** of what we have."*[94] We look after what we have been given.

Chapter 3

366 Balance Sheets

BALANCE SHEETS

A SIMPLE DAILY PROGRAMME

A simple (if not easy) daily programme follows, which, in part, we lay out in a form. We have experienced that this daily "work" is not nearly as hard as not doing it. We have found that life without the spiritual awakening this programme offers is difficult to say the least. The way we have been living our lives hasn't worked. Why we would be satisfied with mediocre sobriety, or sobriety defined as just not using our substance of choice, is a great mystery. We, as addicts, have spent most of our lives with what we call the *more* diseases. What ever felt good we would go to any lengths to acquire and repeat, whether it *really* gave us what we were looking for or not.

There is a phrase in the "Big Book" that many of us in these 12 Step Programmes are familiar with which says: **"With all the earnestness at our command, we beg of you to be fearless and thorough from the very start."** [95] But how many of us heed this plea?

In this writer's past 40 years of experience in and out of the rooms, and to my chagrin, from my own personal experience, a "sober" life of being just ok today is not enough. It has been found that there is no way to just stand still. We eventually go backward without daily, conscious effort. Each time we employ the simple tools we have so generously been given in these 12 Step programmes life *is* easier. Therefore, what we thought was going to be relentless effort, is actually a piece of cake compared to the enormous struggle to then get out of the pain we create *not* working the programme today. One day at a time.

We have had over 200 participants in a retreat, which is more like a 12 Step boot camp, designed to make clear the benefits of the Steps. We all see at that retreat that it is possible, just like any habit, to create a new more useful way of life. It does take working this programme, one day at a time, and that means today, not tomorrow or yesterday. The ones that have stuck to it have wonderfully dramatic life changing experiences. Nearly all of the participants have had the experience of realising that the tools for our life are in our hands.

This programme is about resolving relationships, with others, with a Higher Power, which solves our relationship with ourselves. Within a working relationship we never look for what we can get, but only what we can joyfully give. It is here we learn the truth that sets us free; that *giving and receiving are the same thing*. Real love is about honouring who someone really is and wanting what is best for *them*. It involves trust, patience, compassion and forgiveness. It is about the big picture and putting our hurts aside. This is accomplished through the Steps.

A SIMPLE PROGRAMME

Love *never* fails. We are speaking about the love that doesn't judge, the love where we allow each other space to grow, the love that looks beyond appearances. In order to receive this kind of love we must be willing to give it.

Living the spiritual life means following the principles at all times: when we are hurt, when we are stuck in traffic, when we lose our job, etc. We have the tools in our programme. What we have learned through the Steps is that we have choices. We can continue living according to our past decisions and beliefs or make new choices.

One truly liberating fact is it is never too late to begin. Wherever we are in our life at this moment there is no better time to begin living joyfully and peacefully. No matter what has gone before, today is a new day and the slate can be wiped clean and Step Tens assist in that daily effort. Inasmuch as we are always creating our experience of life, something we learned on our Fourth Step, why not create the life experience we desire instead of one that we don't want.

The more we work towards our unfolding, the less we experience our unravelling. In a study on the spiritual exercise of baby boomers, it was reported that as they matured, it was learned that spirituality must be a continual practice, and not a quick fix. For most of us, change happens incrementally rather than of the "flash of light variety." Those of us that have experience that more dramatic form of awakening can report as they did that; unfortunately, we don't overcome years of conditioning in an instance.

However, who among us doesn't long for an easy solution. But, try as we may, a short period of prayer and meditation, a single workshop (or series for that matter), or even one of our retreats won't bring us permanent relief. If we want our lives to be different we must be willing to do the daily work of changing our faulty beliefs, mistaken habits, destructive patterns, and childish decisions.

Spiritual depth does not come easily. There is no greater feeling than the spiritual awakening of our consciousness. Our daily effort is rewarded with the realisation of our unity with one another and with the Universe Itself; so, for fear of being redundant, **"with all the earnestness at our command, we beg of you to be fearless and thorough from the very start."** [96]

BALANCE SHEETS

Day _____ Month _____ Year _____

Food

Breakfast		
Lunch		
Dinner		
Snack		
Exercise		

Money

Item	Amount
Total Spent Today	
Quality of Life Today	%

Litres Water _____ Hours Sleep _____

When we retire at night we constructively review our day. We remember we have ceased fighting anything and anyone—love and tolerance of others is our code.

We Draw Up a Balance Sheet

The "Negative Side" (-)	The "Positive Side" (+)
Were we resentful?	Have we stayed clean of our addiction today?
Were we selfish?	Were we kind?
Were we dishonest?	Were we loving toward all?
Were we afraid?	What did we pack into life?
Have we kept something to ourselves?	Did we pray and meditate?
Were we thinking of ourselves most of the time?	Did we call someone we could help today?
Were we "disturbed" today?	Did we think of how we could help others?
Do we owe an apology? And if so to whom?	Did we study literature today?
What could we have done better?	Did we go to a meeting today?
Did we blame our feelings on someone else?	Did we call our sponsor today?
Do we need to write 10th Step on something?	Did we do anything that is improved over our past?

Journal—Gratitude List—Tomorrows Action Plan

_____
_____
_____
_____
_____

BALANCE SHEETS

Day _____ Month _____ Year _____

Food		Money	
Breakfast		Item	Amount
Lunch			
Dinner			
Snack			
Exercise			
		Total Spent Today	
Litres Water Hours Sleep		Quality of Life Today	%

When we retire at night we constructively review our day. We remember we have ceased fighting anything and anyone—love and tolerance of others is our code.

We Draw Up a Balance Sheet

The "Negative Side" (-)	The "Positive Side" (+)
Were we resentful?	Have we stayed clean of our addiction today?
Were we selfish?	Were we kind?
Were we dishonest?	Were we loving toward all?
Were we afraid?	What did we pack into life?
Have we kept something to ourselves?	Did we pray and meditate?
Were we thinking of ourselves most of the time?	Did we call someone we could help today?
Were we "disturbed" today?	Did we think of how we could help others?
Do we owe an apology? And if so to whom?	Did we study literature today?
What could we have done better?	Did we go to a meeting today?
Did we blame our feelings on someone else?	Did we call our sponsor today?
Do we need to write 10th Step on something?	Did we do anything that is improved over our past?

Journal—Gratitude List—Tomorrows Action Plan

BALANCE SHEETS

Day _____ Month _____ Year _____

Food

Breakfast		
Lunch		
Dinner		
Snack		
Exercise		

Money

Item		Amount
Total Spent Today		

Litres Water	Hours Sleep	Quality of Life Today	%

When we retire at night we constructively review our day. We remember we have ceased fighting anything and anyone—love and tolerance of others is our code.

We Draw Up a Balance Sheet

The "Negative Side" (-)	The "Positive Side" (+)
Were we resentful?	Have we stayed clean of our addiction today?
Were we selfish?	Were we kind?
Were we dishonest?	Were we loving toward all?
Were we afraid?	What did we pack into life?
Have we kept something to ourselves?	Did we pray and meditate?
Were we thinking of ourselves most of the time?	Did we call someone we could help today?
Were we "disturbed" today?	Did we think of how we could help others?
Do we owe an apology? And if so to whom?	Did we study literature today?
What could we have done better?	Did we go to a meeting today?
Did we blame our feelings on someone else?	Did we call our sponsor today?
Do we need to write 10th Step on something?	Did we do anything that is improved over our past?

Journal—Gratitude List—Tomorrows Action Plan

STEP 10

BALANCE SHEETS

Day _____ Month _____ Year _____

Food

Breakfast	
Lunch	
Dinner	
Snack	
Exercise	
Litres Water	Hours Sleep

Money

Item	Amount
Total Spent Today	
Quality of Life Today	%

When we retire at night we constructively review our day. We remember we have ceased fighting anything and anyone—love and tolerance of others is our code.

We Draw Up a Balance Sheet

The "Negative Side" (-)	The "Positive Side" (+)
Were we resentful?	Have we stayed clean of our addiction today?
Were we selfish?	Were we kind?
Were we dishonest?	Were we loving toward all?
Were we afraid?	What did we pack into life?
Have we kept something to ourselves?	Did we pray and meditate?
Were we thinking of ourselves most of the time?	Did we call someone we could help today?
Were we "disturbed" today?	Did we think of how we could help others?
Do we owe an apology? And if so to whom?	Did we study literature today?
What could we have done better?	Did we go to a meeting today?
Did we blame our feelings on someone else?	Did we call our sponsor today?
Do we need to write 10th Step on something?	Did we do anything that is improved over our past?

Journal—Gratitude List—Tomorrows Action Plan

MAINTAINING THE PROMISES...DAILY

BALANCE SHEETS

Day _____ Month _____ Year _____

Food		Money	
Breakfast		Item	Amount
Lunch			
Dinner			
Snack			
Exercise			
		Total Spent Today	
Litres Water Hours Sleep		Quality of Life Today	%

When we retire at night we constructively review our day. We remember we have ceased fighting anything and anyone—love and tolerance of others is our code.

We Draw Up a Balance Sheet

The "Negative Side" (-)	The "Positive Side" (+)
Were we resentful?	Have we stayed clean of our addiction today?
Were we selfish?	Were we kind?
Were we dishonest?	Were we loving toward all?
Were we afraid?	What did we pack into life?
Have we kept something to ourselves?	Did we pray and meditate?
Were we thinking of ourselves most of the time?	Did we call someone we could help today?
Were we "disturbed" today?	Did we think of how we could help others?
Do we owe an apology? And if so to whom?	Did we study literature today?
What could we have done better?	Did we go to a meeting today?
Did we blame our feelings on someone else?	Did we call our sponsor today?
Do we need to write 10th Step on something?	Did we do anything that is improved over our past?

Journal—Gratitude List—Tomorrows Action Plan

STEP 10

BALANCE SHEETS

Day _____ Month _____ Year _____

Food		Money	
Breakfast		Item	Amount
Lunch			
Dinner			
Snack			
Exercise			
		Total Spent Today	
Litres Water _____ Hours Sleep _____		Quality of Life Today	%

When we retire at night we constructively review our day. We remember we have ceased fighting anything and anyone—love and tolerance of others is our code.

We Draw Up a Balance Sheet

The "Negative Side" (-)	The "Positive Side" (+)
Were we resentful?	Have we stayed clean of our addiction today?
Were we selfish?	Were we kind?
Were we dishonest?	Were we loving toward all?
Were we afraid?	What did we pack into life?
Have we kept something to ourselves?	Did we pray and meditate?
Were we thinking of ourselves most of the time?	Did we call someone we could help today?
Were we "disturbed" today?	Did we think of how we could help others?
Do we owe an apology? And if so to whom?	Did we study literature today?
What could we have done better?	Did we go to a meeting today?
Did we blame our feelings on someone else?	Did we call our sponsor today?
Do we need to write 10th Step on something?	Did we do anything that is improved over our past?

Journal—Gratitude List—Tomorrows Action Plan

BALANCE SHEETS

Day _____ Month _____ Year _____

Food

Breakfast		
Lunch		
Dinner		
Snack		
Exercise		
Litres Water ____ Hours Sleep ____		

Money

Item	Amount
Total Spent Today	
Quality of Life Today	%

When we retire at night we constructively review our day. We remember we have ceased fighting anything and anyone—love and tolerance of others is our code.

We Draw Up a Balance Sheet

The "Negative Side" (-)	The "Positive Side" (+)
Were we resentful?	Have we stayed clean of our addiction today?
Were we selfish?	Were we kind?
Were we dishonest?	Were we loving toward all?
Were we afraid?	What did we pack into life?
Have we kept something to ourselves?	Did we pray and meditate?
Were we thinking of ourselves most of the time?	Did we call someone we could help today?
Were we "disturbed" today?	Did we think of how we could help others?
Do we owe an apology? And if so to whom?	Did we study literature today?
What could we have done better?	Did we go to a meeting today?
Did we blame our feelings on someone else?	Did we call our sponsor today?
Do we need to write 10th Step on something?	Did we do anything that is improved over our past?

Journal—Gratitude List—Tomorrows Action Plan

_____
_____
_____
_____
_____
_____

STEP 10

BALANCE SHEETS

Day _____ Month _____ Year _____

Food		Money	
Breakfast		Item	Amount
Lunch			
Dinner			
Snack			
Exercise			
		Total Spent Today	
Litres Water _____ Hours Sleep _____		Quality of Life Today	%

When we retire at night we constructively review our day. We remember we have ceased fighting anything and anyone—love and tolerance of others is our code.

We Draw Up a Balance Sheet

The "Negative Side" (-)	The "Positive Side" (+)
Were we resentful?	Have we stayed clean of our addiction today?
Were we selfish?	Were we kind?
Were we dishonest?	Were we loving toward all?
Were we afraid?	What did we pack into life?
Have we kept something to ourselves?	Did we pray and meditate?
Were we thinking of ourselves most of the time?	Did we call someone we could help today?
Were we "disturbed" today?	Did we think of how we could help others?
Do we owe an apology? And if so to whom?	Did we study literature today?
What could we have done better?	Did we go to a meeting today?
Did we blame our feelings on someone else?	Did we call our sponsor today?
Do we need to write 10th Step on something?	Did we do anything that is improved over our past?

Journal—Gratitude List—Tomorrows Action Plan

BALANCE SHEETS

Day _____ Month _____ Year _____

Food

Breakfast		
Lunch		
Dinner		
Snack		
Exercise		
Litres Water	Hours Sleep	

Money

Item		Amount
Total Spent Today		
Quality of Life Today		%

When we retire at night we constructively review our day. We remember we have ceased fighting anything and anyone—love and tolerance of others is our code.

We Draw Up a Balance Sheet

The "Negative Side" (-)	The "Positive Side" (+)
Were we resentful?	Have we stayed clean of our addiction today?
Were we selfish?	Were we kind?
Were we dishonest?	Were we loving toward all?
Were we afraid?	What did we pack into life?
Have we kept something to ourselves?	Did we pray and meditate?
Were we thinking of ourselves most of the time?	Did we call someone we could help today?
Were we "disturbed" today?	Did we think of how we could help others?
Do we owe an apology? And if so to whom?	Did we study literature today?
What could we have done better?	Did we go to a meeting today?
Did we blame our feelings on someone else?	Did we call our sponsor today?
Do we need to write 10th Step on something?	Did we do anything that is improved over our past?

Journal—Gratitude List—Tomorrows Action Plan

_____
_____
_____
_____
_____
_____
_____

STEP 10

BALANCE SHEETS

Day _____ Month _____ Year_____

Food		Money	
Breakfast		Item	Amount
Lunch			
Dinner			
Snack			
Exercise			
		Total Spent Today	
Litres Water	Hours Sleep	Quality of Life Today	%

When we retire at night we constructively review our day. We remember we have ceased fighting anything and anyone—love and tolerance of others is our code.

We Draw Up a Balance Sheet

The "Negative Side" (-)	The "Positive Side" (+)
Were we resentful?	Have we stayed clean of our addiction today?
Were we selfish?	Were we kind?
Were we dishonest?	Were we loving toward all?
Were we afraid?	What did we pack into life?
Have we kept something to ourselves?	Did we pray and meditate?
Were we thinking of ourselves most of the time?	Did we call someone we could help today?
Were we "disturbed" today?	Did we think of how we could help others?
Do we owe an apology? And if so to whom?	Did we study literature today?
What could we have done better?	Did we go to a meeting today?
Did we blame our feelings on someone else?	Did we call our sponsor today?
Do we need to write 10th Step on something?	Did we do anything that is improved over our past?

Journal—Gratitude List—Tomorrows Action Plan

BALANCE SHEETS

Day _____ Month _____ Year _____

Food

Breakfast		Item	Amount
Lunch			
Dinner			
Snack			
Exercise			
		Total Spent Today	
Litres Water Hours Sleep		Quality of Life Today	%

When we retire at night we constructively review our day. We remember we have ceased fighting anything and anyone—love and tolerance of others is our code.

We Draw Up a Balance Sheet

The "Negative Side" (-)	The "Positive Side" (+)
Were we resentful?	Have we stayed clean of our addiction today?
Were we selfish?	Were we kind?
Were we dishonest?	Were we loving toward all?
Were we afraid?	What did we pack into life?
Have we kept something to ourselves?	Did we pray and meditate?
Were we thinking of ourselves most of the time?	Did we call someone we could help today?
Were we "disturbed" today?	Did we think of how we could help others?
Do we owe an apology? And if so to whom?	Did we study literature today?
What could we have done better?	Did we go to a meeting today?
Did we blame our feelings on someone else?	Did we call our sponsor today?
Do we need to write 10th Step on something?	Did we do anything that is improved over our past?

Journal—Gratitude List—Tomorrows Action Plan

_____
_____
_____
_____
_____
_____

STEP 10

BALANCE SHEETS

Day _____ Month _____ Year _____

Food		Money		
Breakfast		Item		Amount
Lunch				
Dinner				
Snack				
Exercise				
		Total Spent Today		
Litres Water	Hours Sleep	Quality of Life Today		%

When we retire at night we constructively review our day. We remember we have ceased fighting anything and anyone—love and tolerance of others is our code.

We Draw Up a Balance Sheet

The "Negative Side" (−)	The "Positive Side" (+)
Were we resentful?	Have we stayed clean of our addiction today?
Were we selfish?	Were we kind?
Were we dishonest?	Were we loving toward all?
Were we afraid?	What did we pack into life?
Have we kept something to ourselves?	Did we pray and meditate?
Were we thinking of ourselves most of the time?	Did we call someone we could help today?
Were we "disturbed" today?	Did we think of how we could help others?
Do we owe an apology? And if so to whom?	Did we study literature today?
What could we have done better?	Did we go to a meeting today?
Did we blame our feelings on someone else?	Did we call our sponsor today?
Do we need to write 10th Step on something?	Did we do anything that is improved over our past?

Journal—Gratitude List—Tomorrows Action Plan

BALANCE SHEETS

Day _____ Month _____ Year _____

Food

Breakfast		
Lunch		
Dinner		
Snack		
Exercise		
Litres Water	Hours Sleep	

Money

Item		Amount
Total Spent Today		
Quality of Life Today		%

When we retire at night we constructively review our day. We remember we have ceased fighting anything and anyone—love and tolerance of others is our code.

We Draw Up a Balance Sheet

The "Negative Side" (-)	The "Positive Side" (+)
Were we resentful?	Have we stayed clean of our addiction today?
Were we selfish?	Were we kind?
Were we dishonest?	Were we loving toward all?
Were we afraid?	What did we pack into life?
Have we kept something to ourselves?	Did we pray and meditate?
Were we thinking of ourselves most of the time?	Did we call someone we could help today?
Were we "disturbed" today?	Did we think of how we could help others?
Do we owe an apology? And if so to whom?	Did we study literature today?
What could we have done better?	Did we go to a meeting today?
Did we blame our feelings on someone else?	Did we call our sponsor today?
Do we need to write 10th Step on something?	Did we do anything that is improved over our past?

Journal—Gratitude List—Tomorrows Action Plan

STEP 10

BALANCE SHEETS

Day _____ Month _____ Year _____

Food		Money	
Breakfast		Item	Amount
Lunch			
Dinner			
Snack			
Exercise			
		Total Spent Today	
Litres Water Hours Sleep		Quality of Life Today	%

When we retire at night we constructively review our day. We remember we have ceased fighting anything and anyone—love and tolerance of others is our code.

We Draw Up a Balance Sheet

The "Negative Side" (-)	The "Positive Side" (+)
Were we resentful?	Have we stayed clean of our addiction today?
Were we selfish?	Were we kind?
Were we dishonest?	Were we loving toward all?
Were we afraid?	What did we pack into life?
Have we kept something to ourselves?	Did we pray and meditate?
Were we thinking of ourselves most of the time?	Did we call someone we could help today?
Were we "disturbed" today?	Did we think of how we could help others?
Do we owe an apology? And if so to whom?	Did we study literature today?
What could we have done better?	Did we go to a meeting today?
Did we blame our feelings on someone else?	Did we call our sponsor today?
Do we need to write 10th Step on something?	Did we do anything that is improved over our past?

Journal—Gratitude List—Tomorrows Action Plan

MAINTAINING THE PROMISES...DAILY

BALANCE SHEETS

Day _____ Month _____ Year_____

Food		Money		
Breakfast		Item		Amount
Lunch				
Dinner				
Snack				
Exercise				
		Total Spent Today		
Litres Water	Hours Sleep	Quality of Life Today		%

When we retire at night we constructively review our day. We remember we have ceased fighting anything and anyone—love and tolerance of others is our code.

We Draw Up a Balance Sheet

The "Negative Side" (-)	The "Positive Side" (+)
Were we resentful?	Have we stayed clean of our addiction today?
Were we selfish?	Were we kind?
Were we dishonest?	Were we loving toward all?
Were we afraid?	What did we pack into life?
Have we kept something to ourselves?	Did we pray and meditate?
Were we thinking of ourselves most of the time?	Did we call someone we could help today?
Were we "disturbed" today?	Did we think of how we could help others?
Do we owe an apology? And if so to whom?	Did we study literature today?
What could we have done better?	Did we go to a meeting today?
Did we blame our feelings on someone else?	Did we call our sponsor today?
Do we need to write 10th Step on something?	Did we do anything that is improved over our past?

Journal—Gratitude List—Tomorrows Action Plan

STEP 10

BALANCE SHEETS

Day _____ Month _____ Year _____

Food		Money	
Breakfast		Item	Amount
Lunch			
Dinner			
Snack			
Exercise			
		Total Spent Today	
Litres Water	Hours Sleep	Quality of Life Today	%

When we retire at night we constructively review our day. We remember we have ceased fighting anything and anyone—love and tolerance of others is our code.

We Draw Up a Balance Sheet

The "Negative Side" (-)	The "Positive Side" (+)
Were we resentful?	Have we stayed clean of our addiction today?
Were we selfish?	Were we kind?
Were we dishonest?	Were we loving toward all?
Were we afraid?	What did we pack into life?
Have we kept something to ourselves?	Did we pray and meditate?
Were we thinking of ourselves most of the time?	Did we call someone we could help today?
Were we "disturbed" today?	Did we think of how we could help others?
Do we owe an apology? And if so to whom?	Did we study literature today?
What could we have done better?	Did we go to a meeting today?
Did we blame our feelings on someone else?	Did we call our sponsor today?
Do we need to write 10th Step on something?	Did we do anything that is improved over our past?

Journal—Gratitude List—Tomorrows Action Plan

BALANCE SHEETS

Day _____ Month _____ Year _____

Food

Food		Money	
Breakfast		Item	Amount
Lunch			
Dinner			
Snack			
Exercise			
		Total Spent Today	
Litres Water	Hours Sleep	Quality of Life Today	%

When we retire at night we constructively review our day. We remember we have ceased fighting anything and anyone—love and tolerance of others is our code.

We Draw Up a Balance Sheet

The "Negative Side" (-)	The "Positive Side" (+)
Were we resentful?	Have we stayed clean of our addiction today?
Were we selfish?	Were we kind?
Were we dishonest?	Were we loving toward all?
Were we afraid?	What did we pack into life?
Have we kept something to ourselves?	Did we pray and meditate?
Were we thinking of ourselves most of the time?	Did we call someone we could help today?
Were we "disturbed" today?	Did we think of how we could help others?
Do we owe an apology? And if so to whom?	Did we study literature today?
What could we have done better?	Did we go to a meeting today?
Did we blame our feelings on someone else?	Did we call our sponsor today?
Do we need to write 10th Step on something?	Did we do anything that is improved over our past?

Journal—Gratitude List—Tomorrows Action Plan

STEP 10

BALANCE SHEETS

Day _____ Month _____ Year _____

Food		Money	
Breakfast		Item	Amount
Lunch			
Dinner			
Snack			
Exercise			
		Total Spent Today	
Litres Water	Hours Sleep	Quality of Life Today	%

When we retire at night we constructively review our day. We remember we have ceased fighting anything and anyone—love and tolerance of others is our code.

We Draw Up a Balance Sheet

The "Negative Side" (−)	The "Positive Side" (+)
Were we resentful?	Have we stayed clean of our addiction today?
Were we selfish?	Were we kind?
Were we dishonest?	Were we loving toward all?
Were we afraid?	What did we pack into life?
Have we kept something to ourselves?	Did we pray and meditate?
Were we thinking of ourselves most of the time?	Did we call someone we could help today?
Were we "disturbed" today?	Did we think of how we could help others?
Do we owe an apology? And if so to whom?	Did we study literature today?
What could we have done better?	Did we go to a meeting today?
Did we blame our feelings on someone else?	Did we call our sponsor today?
Do we need to write 10th Step on something?	Did we do anything that is improved over our past?

Journal—Gratitude List—Tomorrows Action Plan

BALANCE SHEETS

Day _____ Month _____ Year_____

Food

Breakfast		
Lunch		
Dinner		
Snack		
Exercise		

Money

Item		Amount
Total Spent Today		

Litres Water	Hours Sleep	Quality of Life Today	%

When we retire at night we constructively review our day. We remember we have ceased fighting anything and anyone—love and tolerance of others is our code.

We Draw Up a Balance Sheet

The "Negative Side" (-)	The "Positive Side" (+)
Were we resentful?	Have we stayed clean of our addiction today?
Were we selfish?	Were we kind?
Were we dishonest?	Were we loving toward all?
Were we afraid?	What did we pack into life?
Have we kept something to ourselves?	Did we pray and meditate?
Were we thinking of ourselves most of the time?	Did we call someone we could help today?
Were we "disturbed" today?	Did we think of how we could help others?
Do we owe an apology? And if so to whom?	Did we study literature today?
What could we have done better?	Did we go to a meeting today?
Did we blame our feelings on someone else?	Did we call our sponsor today?
Do we need to write 10th Step on something?	Did we do anything that is improved over our past?

Journal—Gratitude List—Tomorrows Action Plan

STEP 10

BALANCE SHEETS

Day _____ Month _____ Year _____

Food		Money	
Breakfast		Item	Amount
Lunch			
Dinner			
Snack			
Exercise			
		Total Spent Today	
Litres Water Hours Sleep		Quality of Life Today	%

When we retire at night we constructively review our day. We remember we have ceased fighting anything and anyone—love and tolerance of others is our code.

We Draw Up a Balance Sheet

The "Negative Side" (-)	The "Positive Side" (+)
Were we resentful?	Have we stayed clean of our addiction today?
Were we selfish?	Were we kind?
Were we dishonest?	Were we loving toward all?
Were we afraid?	What did we pack into life?
Have we kept something to ourselves?	Did we pray and meditate?
Were we thinking of ourselves most of the time?	Did we call someone we could help today?
Were we "disturbed" today?	Did we think of how we could help others?
Do we owe an apology? And if so to whom?	Did we study literature today?
What could we have done better?	Did we go to a meeting today?
Did we blame our feelings on someone else?	Did we call our sponsor today?
Do we need to write 10th Step on something?	Did we do anything that is improved over our past?

Journal—Gratitude List—Tomorrows Action Plan

BALANCE SHEETS

Day _____ Month _____ Year_____

Food

Breakfast	
Lunch	
Dinner	
Snack	
Exercise	
Litres Water _____ Hours Sleep _____	

Money

Item	Amount
Total Spent Today	
Quality of Life Today	%

When we retire at night we constructively review our day. We remember we have ceased fighting anything and anyone—love and tolerance of others is our code.

We Draw Up a Balance Sheet

The "Negative Side" (-)	The "Positive Side" (+)
Were we resentful?	Have we stayed clean of our addiction today?
Were we selfish?	Were we kind?
Were we dishonest?	Were we loving toward all?
Were we afraid?	What did we pack into life?
Have we kept something to ourselves?	Did we pray and meditate?
Were we thinking of ourselves most of the time?	Did we call someone we could help today?
Were we "disturbed" today?	Did we think of how we could help others?
Do we owe an apology? And if so to whom?	Did we study literature today?
What could we have done better?	Did we go to a meeting today?
Did we blame our feelings on someone else?	Did we call our sponsor today?
Do we need to write 10th Step on something?	Did we do anything that is improved over our past?

Journal—Gratitude List—Tomorrows Action Plan

STEP 10

BALANCE SHEETS

Day _____ Month _____ Year _____

Food		Money	
Breakfast		Item	Amount
Lunch			
Dinner			
Snack			
Exercise			
		Total Spent Today	
Litres Water	Hours Sleep	Quality of Life Today	%

When we retire at night we constructively review our day. We remember we have ceased fighting anything and anyone—love and tolerance of others is our code.

We Draw Up a Balance Sheet

The "Negative Side" (-)	The "Positive Side" (+)
Were we resentful?	Have we stayed clean of our addiction today?
Were we selfish?	Were we kind?
Were we dishonest?	Were we loving toward all?
Were we afraid?	What did we pack into life?
Have we kept something to ourselves?	Did we pray and meditate?
Were we thinking of ourselves most of the time?	Did we call someone we could help today?
Were we "disturbed" today?	Did we think of how we could help others?
Do we owe an apology? And if so to whom?	Did we study literature today?
What could we have done better?	Did we go to a meeting today?
Did we blame our feelings on someone else?	Did we call our sponsor today?
Do we need to write 10th Step on something?	Did we do anything that is improved over our past?

Journal—Gratitude List—Tomorrows Action Plan

BALANCE SHEETS

Day _____ Month _____ Year _____

Food		Money	
Breakfast		Item	Amount
Lunch			
Dinner			
Snack			
Exercise			
		Total Spent Today	
Litres Water	Hours Sleep	Quality of Life Today	%

When we retire at night we constructively review our day. We remember we have ceased fighting anything and anyone—love and tolerance of others is our code.

We Draw Up a Balance Sheet

The "Negative Side" (-)	The "Positive Side" (+)
Were we resentful?	Have we stayed clean of our addiction today?
Were we selfish?	Were we kind?
Were we dishonest?	Were we loving toward all?
Were we afraid?	What did we pack into life?
Have we kept something to ourselves?	Did we pray and meditate?
Were we thinking of ourselves most of the time?	Did we call someone we could help today?
Were we "disturbed" today?	Did we think of how we could help others?
Do we owe an apology? And if so to whom?	Did we study literature today?
What could we have done better?	Did we go to a meeting today?
Did we blame our feelings on someone else?	Did we call our sponsor today?
Do we need to write 10th Step on something?	Did we do anything that is improved over our past?

Journal—Gratitude List—Tomorrows Action Plan

STEP 10

BALANCE SHEETS

Day _____ Month _____ Year _____

Food		Money	
Breakfast		Item	Amount
Lunch			
Dinner			
Snack			
Exercise			
		Total Spent Today	
Litres Water	Hours Sleep	Quality of Life Today	%

When we retire at night we constructively review our day. We remember we have ceased fighting anything and anyone—love and tolerance of others is our code.

We Draw Up a Balance Sheet

The "Negative Side" (−)	The "Positive Side" (+)
Were we resentful?	Have we stayed clean of our addiction today?
Were we selfish?	Were we kind?
Were we dishonest?	Were we loving toward all?
Were we afraid?	What did we pack into life?
Have we kept something to ourselves?	Did we pray and meditate?
Were we thinking of ourselves most of the time?	Did we call someone we could help today?
Were we "disturbed" today?	Did we think of how we could help others?
Do we owe an apology? And if so to whom?	Did we study literature today?
What could we have done better?	Did we go to a meeting today?
Did we blame our feelings on someone else?	Did we call our sponsor today?
Do we need to write 10th Step on something?	Did we do anything that is improved over our past?

Journal—Gratitude List—Tomorrows Action Plan

BALANCE SHEETS

Day _____ Month _____ Year _____

Food		Money	
Breakfast		Item	Amount
Lunch			
Dinner			
Snack			
Exercise			
		Total Spent Today	
Litres Water _____ Hours Sleep _____		Quality of Life Today	%

When we retire at night we constructively review our day. We remember we have ceased fighting anything and anyone—love and tolerance of others is our code.

We Draw Up a Balance Sheet

The "Negative Side" (-)	The "Positive Side" (+)
Were we resentful?	Have we stayed clean of our addiction today?
Were we selfish?	Were we kind?
Were we dishonest?	Were we loving toward all?
Were we afraid?	What did we pack into life?
Have we kept something to ourselves?	Did we pray and meditate?
Were we thinking of ourselves most of the time?	Did we call someone we could help today?
Were we "disturbed" today?	Did we think of how we could help others?
Do we owe an apology? And if so to whom?	Did we study literature today?
What could we have done better?	Did we go to a meeting today?
Did we blame our feelings on someone else?	Did we call our sponsor today?
Do we need to write 10th Step on something?	Did we do anything that is improved over our past?

Journal—Gratitude List—Tomorrows Action Plan

STEP 10

BALANCE SHEETS

Day _____ Month _____ Year_____

Food		Money	
Breakfast		Item	Amount
Lunch			
Dinner			
Snack			
Exercise			
		Total Spent Today	
Litres Water	Hours Sleep	Quality of Life Today	%

When we retire at night we constructively review our day. We remember we have ceased fighting anything and anyone—love and tolerance of others is our code.

We Draw Up a Balance Sheet

The "Negative Side" (-)	The "Positive Side" (+)
Were we resentful?	Have we stayed clean of our addiction today?
Were we selfish?	Were we kind?
Were we dishonest?	Were we loving toward all?
Were we afraid?	What did we pack into life?
Have we kept something to ourselves?	Did we pray and meditate?
Were we thinking of ourselves most of the time?	Did we call someone we could help today?
Were we "disturbed" today?	Did we think of how we could help others?
Do we owe an apology? And if so to whom?	Did we study literature today?
What could we have done better?	Did we go to a meeting today?
Did we blame our feelings on someone else?	Did we call our sponsor today?
Do we need to write 10th Step on something?	Did we do anything that is improved over our past?

Journal—Gratitude List—Tomorrows Action Plan

BALANCE SHEETS

Day _____ Month _____ Year _____

Food

Breakfast	
Lunch	
Dinner	
Snack	
Exercise	
Litres Water Hours Sleep	

Money

Item	Amount
Total Spent Today	
Quality of Life Today	%

When we retire at night we constructively review our day. We remember we have ceased fighting anything and anyone—love and tolerance of others is our code.

We Draw Up a Balance Sheet

The "Negative Side" (-)	The "Positive Side" (+)
Were we resentful?	Have we stayed clean of our addiction today?
Were we selfish?	Were we kind?
Were we dishonest?	Were we loving toward all?
Were we afraid?	What did we pack into life?
Have we kept something to ourselves?	Did we pray and meditate?
Were we thinking of ourselves most of the time?	Did we call someone we could help today?
Were we "disturbed" today?	Did we think of how we could help others?
Do we owe an apology? And if so to whom?	Did we study literature today?
What could we have done better?	Did we go to a meeting today?
Did we blame our feelings on someone else?	Did we call our sponsor today?
Do we need to write 10th Step on something?	Did we do anything that is improved over our past?

Journal—Gratitude List—Tomorrows Action Plan

STEP 10

BALANCE SHEETS

Day _____ Month _____ Year _____

Food		Money	
Breakfast		Item	Amount
Lunch			
Dinner			
Snack			
Exercise			
		Total Spent Today	
Litres Water	Hours Sleep	Quality of Life Today	%

When we retire at night we constructively review our day. We remember we have ceased fighting anything and anyone—love and tolerance of others is our code.

We Draw Up a Balance Sheet

The "Negative Side" (-)	The "Positive Side" (+)
Were we resentful?	Have we stayed clean of our addiction today?
Were we selfish?	Were we kind?
Were we dishonest?	Were we loving toward all?
Were we afraid?	What did we pack into life?
Have we kept something to ourselves?	Did we pray and meditate?
Were we thinking of ourselves most of the time?	Did we call someone we could help today?
Were we "disturbed" today?	Did we think of how we could help others?
Do we owe an apology? And if so to whom?	Did we study literature today?
What could we have done better?	Did we go to a meeting today?
Did we blame our feelings on someone else?	Did we call our sponsor today?
Do we need to write 10th Step on something?	Did we do anything that is improved over our past?

Journal—Gratitude List—Tomorrows Action Plan

_____

_____

_____

_____

_____

_____

BALANCE SHEETS

Day _____ Month _____ Year _____

Food		Money	
Breakfast		Item	Amount
Lunch			
Dinner			
Snack			
Exercise			
		Total Spent Today	
Litres Water _____ Hours Sleep _____		Quality of Life Today	%

When we retire at night we constructively review our day. We remember we have ceased fighting anything and anyone—love and tolerance of others is our code.

We Draw Up a Balance Sheet

The "Negative Side" (-)	The "Positive Side" (+)
Were we resentful?	Have we stayed clean of our addiction today?
Were we selfish?	Were we kind?
Were we dishonest?	Were we loving toward all?
Were we afraid?	What did we pack into life?
Have we kept something to ourselves?	Did we pray and meditate?
Were we thinking of ourselves most of the time?	Did we call someone we could help today?
Were we "disturbed" today?	Did we think of how we could help others?
Do we owe an apology? And if so to whom?	Did we study literature today?
What could we have done better?	Did we go to a meeting today?
Did we blame our feelings on someone else?	Did we call our sponsor today?
Do we need to write 10th Step on something?	Did we do anything that is improved over our past?

Journal—Gratitude List—Tomorrows Action Plan

STEP 10

BALANCE SHEETS

Day _____ Month _____ Year _____

Food

Breakfast			
Lunch			
Dinner			
Snack			
Exercise			
Litres Water	Hours Sleep		

Money

Item		Amount
Total Spent Today		
Quality of Life Today		%

When we retire at night we constructively review our day. We remember we have ceased fighting anything and anyone—love and tolerance of others is our code.

We Draw Up a Balance Sheet

The "Negative Side" (-)	The "Positive Side" (+)
Were we resentful?	Have we stayed clean of our addiction today?
Were we selfish?	Were we kind?
Were we dishonest?	Were we loving toward all?
Were we afraid?	What did we pack into life?
Have we kept something to ourselves?	Did we pray and meditate?
Were we thinking of ourselves most of the time?	Did we call someone we could help today?
Were we "disturbed" today?	Did we think of how we could help others?
Do we owe an apology? And if so to whom?	Did we study literature today?
What could we have done better?	Did we go to a meeting today?
Did we blame our feelings on someone else?	Did we call our sponsor today?
Do we need to write 10th Step on something?	Did we do anything that is improved over our past?

Journal—Gratitude List—Tomorrows Action Plan

BALANCE SHEETS

Day _____ Month _____ Year _____

Food

Breakfast		
Lunch		
Dinner		
Snack		
Exercise		
Litres Water ____ Hours Sleep ____		

Money

Item	Amount
Total Spent Today	
Quality of Life Today	%

When we retire at night we constructively review our day. We remember we have ceased fighting anything and anyone—love and tolerance of others is our code.

We Draw Up a Balance Sheet

The "Negative Side" (-)	The "Positive Side" (+)
Were we resentful?	Have we stayed clean of our addiction today?
Were we selfish?	Were we kind?
Were we dishonest?	Were we loving toward all?
Were we afraid?	What did we pack into life?
Have we kept something to ourselves?	Did we pray and meditate?
Were we thinking of ourselves most of the time?	Did we call someone we could help today?
Were we "disturbed" today?	Did we think of how we could help others?
Do we owe an apology? And if so to whom?	Did we study literature today?
What could we have done better?	Did we go to a meeting today?
Did we blame our feelings on someone else?	Did we call our sponsor today?
Do we need to write 10th Step on something?	Did we do anything that is improved over our past?

Journal—Gratitude List—Tomorrows Action Plan

STEP 10

BALANCE SHEETS

Day _____ Month _____ Year _____

Food		Money	
Breakfast		Item	Amount
Lunch			
Dinner			
Snack			
Exercise			
		Total Spent Today	
Litres Water Hours Sleep		Quality of Life Today	%

When we retire at night we constructively review our day. We remember we have ceased fighting anything and anyone—love and tolerance of others is our code.

We Draw Up a Balance Sheet

The "Negative Side" (-)	The "Positive Side" (+)
Were we resentful?	Have we stayed clean of our addiction today?
Were we selfish?	Were we kind?
Were we dishonest?	Were we loving toward all?
Were we afraid?	What did we pack into life?
Have we kept something to ourselves?	Did we pray and meditate?
Were we thinking of ourselves most of the time?	Did we call someone we could help today?
Were we "disturbed" today?	Did we think of how we could help others?
Do we owe an apology? And if so to whom?	Did we study literature today?
What could we have done better?	Did we go to a meeting today?
Did we blame our feelings on someone else?	Did we call our sponsor today?
Do we need to write 10th Step on something?	Did we do anything that is improved over our past?

Journal—Gratitude List—Tomorrows Action Plan

BALANCE SHEETS

Day _____ Month _____ Year _____

Food		Money	
Breakfast		Item	Amount
Lunch			
Dinner			
Snack			
Exercise			
		Total Spent Today	
Litres Water _____ Hours Sleep _____		Quality of Life Today	%

When we retire at night we constructively review our day. We remember we have ceased fighting anything and anyone—love and tolerance of others is our code.

We Draw Up a Balance Sheet

The "Negative Side" (-)	The "Positive Side" (+)
Were we resentful?	Have we stayed clean of our addiction today?
Were we selfish?	Were we kind?
Were we dishonest?	Were we loving toward all?
Were we afraid?	What did we pack into life?
Have we kept something to ourselves?	Did we pray and meditate?
Were we thinking of ourselves most of the time?	Did we call someone we could help today?
Were we "disturbed" today?	Did we think of how we could help others?
Do we owe an apology? And if so to whom?	Did we study literature today?
What could we have done better?	Did we go to a meeting today?
Did we blame our feelings on someone else?	Did we call our sponsor today?
Do we need to write 10th Step on something?	Did we do anything that is improved over our past?

Journal—Gratitude List—Tomorrows Action Plan

STEP 10

BALANCE SHEETS

Day _____ Month _____ Year _____

Food		Money	
Breakfast		Item	Amount
Lunch			
Dinner			
Snack			
Exercise			
		Total Spent Today	
Litres Water	Hours Sleep	Quality of Life Today	%

When we retire at night we constructively review our day. We remember we have ceased fighting anything and anyone—love and tolerance of others is our code.

We Draw Up a Balance Sheet

The "Negative Side" (-)	The "Positive Side" (+)
Were we resentful?	Have we stayed clean of our addiction today?
Were we selfish?	Were we kind?
Were we dishonest?	Were we loving toward all?
Were we afraid?	What did we pack into life?
Have we kept something to ourselves?	Did we pray and meditate?
Were we thinking of ourselves most of the time?	Did we call someone we could help today?
Were we "disturbed" today?	Did we think of how we could help others?
Do we owe an apology? And if so to whom?	Did we study literature today?
What could we have done better?	Did we go to a meeting today?
Did we blame our feelings on someone else?	Did we call our sponsor today?
Do we need to write 10th Step on something?	Did we do anything that is improved over our past?

Journal—Gratitude List—Tomorrows Action Plan

BALANCE SHEETS

Day _____ Month _____ Year_____

Food		Money	
Breakfast		Item	Amount
Lunch			
Dinner			
Snack			
Exercise			
		Total Spent Today	
Litres Water Hours Sleep		Quality of Life Today	%

When we retire at night we constructively review our day. We remember we have ceased fighting anything and anyone—love and tolerance of others is our code.

We Draw Up a Balance Sheet

The "Negative Side" (−)	The "Positive Side" (+)
Were we resentful?	Have we stayed clean of our addiction today?
Were we selfish?	Were we kind?
Were we dishonest?	Were we loving toward all?
Were we afraid?	What did we pack into life?
Have we kept something to ourselves?	Did we pray and meditate?
Were we thinking of ourselves most of the time?	Did we call someone we could help today?
Were we "disturbed" today?	Did we think of how we could help others?
Do we owe an apology? And if so to whom?	Did we study literature today?
What could we have done better?	Did we go to a meeting today?
Did we blame our feelings on someone else?	Did we call our sponsor today?
Do we need to write 10th Step on something?	Did we do anything that is improved over our past?

Journal—Gratitude List—Tomorrows Action Plan

STEP 10

BALANCE SHEETS

Day _____ Month _____ Year _____

Food		Money	
Breakfast		Item	Amount
Lunch			
Dinner			
Snack			
Exercise			
		Total Spent Today	
Litres Water Hours Sleep		Quality of Life Today	%

When we retire at night we constructively review our day. We remember we have ceased fighting anything and anyone—love and tolerance of others is our code.

We Draw Up a Balance Sheet

The "Negative Side" (-)	The "Positive Side" (+)
Were we resentful?	Have we stayed clean of our addiction today?
Were we selfish?	Were we kind?
Were we dishonest?	Were we loving toward all?
Were we afraid?	What did we pack into life?
Have we kept something to ourselves?	Did we pray and meditate?
Were we thinking of ourselves most of the time?	Did we call someone we could help today?
Were we "disturbed" today?	Did we think of how we could help others?
Do we owe an apology? And if so to whom?	Did we study literature today?
What could we have done better?	Did we go to a meeting today?
Did we blame our feelings on someone else?	Did we call our sponsor today?
Do we need to write 10th Step on something?	Did we do anything that is improved over our past?

Journal—Gratitude List—Tomorrows Action Plan

BALANCE SHEETS

Day _____ Month _____ Year _____

Food		Money	
Breakfast		Item	Amount
Lunch			
Dinner			
Snack			
Exercise			
		Total Spent Today	
Litres Water _____ Hours Sleep _____		Quality of Life Today	%

When we retire at night we constructively review our day. We remember we have ceased fighting anything and anyone—love and tolerance of others is our code.

We Draw Up a Balance Sheet

The "Negative Side" (-)	The "Positive Side" (+)
Were we resentful?	Have we stayed clean of our addiction today?
Were we selfish?	Were we kind?
Were we dishonest?	Were we loving toward all?
Were we afraid?	What did we pack into life?
Have we kept something to ourselves?	Did we pray and meditate?
Were we thinking of ourselves most of the time?	Did we call someone we could help today?
Were we "disturbed" today?	Did we think of how we could help others?
Do we owe an apology? And if so to whom?	Did we study literature today?
What could we have done better?	Did we go to a meeting today?
Did we blame our feelings on someone else?	Did we call our sponsor today?
Do we need to write 10th Step on something?	Did we do anything that is improved over our past?

Journal—Gratitude List—Tomorrows Action Plan

STEP 10

BALANCE SHEETS

Day _____ Month _____ Year_____

Food		Money	
Breakfast		Item	Amount
Lunch			
Dinner			
Snack			
Exercise			
		Total Spent Today	
Litres Water	Hours Sleep	Quality of Life Today	%

When we retire at night we constructively review our day. We remember we have ceased fighting anything and anyone—love and tolerance of others is our code.

We Draw Up a Balance Sheet

The "Negative Side" (-)	The "Positive Side" (+)
Were we resentful?	Have we stayed clean of our addiction today?
Were we selfish?	Were we kind?
Were we dishonest?	Were we loving toward all?
Were we afraid?	What did we pack into life?
Have we kept something to ourselves?	Did we pray and meditate?
Were we thinking of ourselves most of the time?	Did we call someone we could help today?
Were we "disturbed" today?	Did we think of how we could help others?
Do we owe an apology? And if so to whom?	Did we study literature today?
What could we have done better?	Did we go to a meeting today?
Did we blame our feelings on someone else?	Did we call our sponsor today?
Do we need to write 10th Step on something?	Did we do anything that is improved over our past?

Journal—Gratitude List—Tomorrows Action Plan

BALANCE SHEETS

Day _____ Month _____ Year _____

Food		Money	
Breakfast		Item	Amount
Lunch			
Dinner			
Snack			
Exercise			
		Total Spent Today	
Litres Water _____ Hours Sleep _____		Quality of Life Today	%

When we retire at night we constructively review our day. We remember we have ceased fighting anything and anyone—love and tolerance of others is our code.

We Draw Up a Balance Sheet

The "Negative Side" (-)	The "Positive Side" (+)
Were we resentful?	Have we stayed clean of our addiction today?
Were we selfish?	Were we kind?
Were we dishonest?	Were we loving toward all?
Were we afraid?	What did we pack into life?
Have we kept something to ourselves?	Did we pray and meditate?
Were we thinking of ourselves most of the time?	Did we call someone we could help today?
Were we "disturbed" today?	Did we think of how we could help others?
Do we owe an apology? And if so to whom?	Did we study literature today?
What could we have done better?	Did we go to a meeting today?
Did we blame our feelings on someone else?	Did we call our sponsor today?
Do we need to write 10th Step on something?	Did we do anything that is improved over our past?

Journal—Gratitude List—Tomorrows Action Plan

STEP 10

BALANCE SHEETS

Day _____ Month _____ Year _____

Food		Money	
Breakfast		Item	Amount
Lunch			
Dinner			
Snack			
Exercise			
		Total Spent Today	
Litres Water Hours Sleep		Quality of Life Today	%

When we retire at night we constructively review our day. We remember we have ceased fighting anything and anyone—love and tolerance of others is our code.

We Draw Up a Balance Sheet

The "Negative Side" (-)	The "Positive Side" (+)
Were we resentful?	Have we stayed clean of our addiction today?
Were we selfish?	Were we kind?
Were we dishonest?	Were we loving toward all?
Were we afraid?	What did we pack into life?
Have we kept something to ourselves?	Did we pray and meditate?
Were we thinking of ourselves most of the time?	Did we call someone we could help today?
Were we "disturbed" today?	Did we think of how we could help others?
Do we owe an apology? And if so to whom?	Did we study literature today?
What could we have done better?	Did we go to a meeting today?
Did we blame our feelings on someone else?	Did we call our sponsor today?
Do we need to write 10th Step on something?	Did we do anything that is improved over our past?

Journal—Gratitude List—Tomorrows Action Plan

BALANCE SHEETS

Day _____ Month _____ Year _____

Food		Money	
Breakfast		Item	Amount
Lunch			
Dinner			
Snack			
Exercise			
		Total Spent Today	
Litres Water	Hours Sleep	Quality of Life Today	%

When we retire at night we constructively review our day. We remember we have ceased fighting anything and anyone—love and tolerance of others is our code.

We Draw Up a Balance Sheet

The "Negative Side" (-)	The "Positive Side" (+)
Were we resentful?	Have we stayed clean of our addiction today?
Were we selfish?	Were we kind?
Were we dishonest?	Were we loving toward all?
Were we afraid?	What did we pack into life?
Have we kept something to ourselves?	Did we pray and meditate?
Were we thinking of ourselves most of the time?	Did we call someone we could help today?
Were we "disturbed" today?	Did we think of how we could help others?
Do we owe an apology? And if so to whom?	Did we study literature today?
What could we have done better?	Did we go to a meeting today?
Did we blame our feelings on someone else?	Did we call our sponsor today?
Do we need to write 10th Step on something?	Did we do anything that is improved over our past?

Journal—Gratitude List—Tomorrows Action Plan

STEP 10

BALANCE SHEETS

Day _____ Month _____ Year _____

Food		Money	
Breakfast		Item	Amount
Lunch			
Dinner			
Snack			
Exercise			
		Total Spent Today	
Litres Water _____ Hours Sleep _____		Quality of Life Today	%

When we retire at night we constructively review our day. We remember we have ceased fighting anything and anyone—love and tolerance of others is our code.

We Draw Up a Balance Sheet

The "Negative Side" (-)	The "Positive Side" (+)
Were we resentful?	Have we stayed clean of our addiction today?
Were we selfish?	Were we kind?
Were we dishonest?	Were we loving toward all?
Were we afraid?	What did we pack into life?
Have we kept something to ourselves?	Did we pray and meditate?
Were we thinking of ourselves most of the time?	Did we call someone we could help today?
Were we "disturbed" today?	Did we think of how we could help others?
Do we owe an apology? And if so to whom?	Did we study literature today?
What could we have done better?	Did we go to a meeting today?
Did we blame our feelings on someone else?	Did we call our sponsor today?
Do we need to write 10th Step on something?	Did we do anything that is improved over our past?

Journal—Gratitude List—Tomorrows Action Plan

BALANCE SHEETS

Day _____ Month _____ Year _____

Food		Money	
Breakfast		Item	Amount
Lunch			
Dinner			
Snack			
Exercise			
		Total Spent Today	
Litres Water	Hours Sleep	Quality of Life Today	%

When we retire at night we constructively review our day. We remember we have ceased fighting anything and anyone—love and tolerance of others is our code.

We Draw Up a Balance Sheet

The "Negative Side" (-)	The "Positive Side" (+)
Were we resentful?	Have we stayed clean of our addiction today?
Were we selfish?	Were we kind?
Were we dishonest?	Were we loving toward all?
Were we afraid?	What did we pack into life?
Have we kept something to ourselves?	Did we pray and meditate?
Were we thinking of ourselves most of the time?	Did we call someone we could help today?
Were we "disturbed" today?	Did we think of how we could help others?
Do we owe an apology? And if so to whom?	Did we study literature today?
What could we have done better?	Did we go to a meeting today?
Did we blame our feelings on someone else?	Did we call our sponsor today?
Do we need to write 10th Step on something?	Did we do anything that is improved over our past?

Journal—Gratitude List—Tomorrows Action Plan

STEP 10

BALANCE SHEETS

Day _____ Month _____ Year _____

Food		Money	
Breakfast		Item	Amount
Lunch			
Dinner			
Snack			
Exercise			
		Total Spent Today	
Litres Water Hours Sleep		Quality of Life Today	%

When we retire at night we constructively review our day. We remember we have ceased fighting anything and anyone—love and tolerance of others is our code.

We Draw Up a Balance Sheet

The "Negative Side" (-)	The "Positive Side" (+)
Were we resentful?	Have we stayed clean of our addiction today?
Were we selfish?	Were we kind?
Were we dishonest?	Were we loving toward all?
Were we afraid?	What did we pack into life?
Have we kept something to ourselves?	Did we pray and meditate?
Were we thinking of ourselves most of the time?	Did we call someone we could help today?
Were we "disturbed" today?	Did we think of how we could help others?
Do we owe an apology? And if so to whom?	Did we study literature today?
What could we have done better?	Did we go to a meeting today?
Did we blame our feelings on someone else?	Did we call our sponsor today?
Do we need to write 10th Step on something?	Did we do anything that is improved over our past?

Journal—Gratitude List—Tomorrows Action Plan

BALANCE SHEETS

Day _____ Month _____ Year _____

Food		Money	
Breakfast		Item	Amount
Lunch			
Dinner			
Snack			
Exercise			
		Total Spent Today	
Litres Water ____ Hours Sleep ____		Quality of Life Today	%

When we retire at night we constructively review our day. We remember we have ceased fighting anything and anyone—love and tolerance of others is our code.

We Draw Up a Balance Sheet

The "Negative Side" (-)	The "Positive Side" (+)
Were we resentful?	Have we stayed clean of our addiction today?
Were we selfish?	Were we kind?
Were we dishonest?	Were we loving toward all?
Were we afraid?	What did we pack into life?
Have we kept something to ourselves?	Did we pray and meditate?
Were we thinking of ourselves most of the time?	Did we call someone we could help today?
Were we "disturbed" today?	Did we think of how we could help others?
Do we owe an apology? And if so to whom?	Did we study literature today?
What could we have done better?	Did we go to a meeting today?
Did we blame our feelings on someone else?	Did we call our sponsor today?
Do we need to write 10th Step on something?	Did we do anything that is improved over our past?

Journal—Gratitude List—Tomorrows Action Plan

STEP 10

BALANCE SHEETS

Day _____ Month _____ Year _____

Food

Breakfast	
Lunch	
Dinner	
Snack	
Exercise	
Litres Water	Hours Sleep

Money

Item	Amount
Total Spent Today	
Quality of Life Today	%

When we retire at night we constructively review our day. We remember we have ceased fighting anything and anyone—love and tolerance of others is our code.

We Draw Up a Balance Sheet

The "Negative Side" (-)	The "Positive Side" (+)
Were we resentful?	Have we stayed clean of our addiction today?
Were we selfish?	Were we kind?
Were we dishonest?	Were we loving toward all?
Were we afraid?	What did we pack into life?
Have we kept something to ourselves?	Did we pray and meditate?
Were we thinking of ourselves most of the time?	Did we call someone we could help today?
Were we "disturbed" today?	Did we think of how we could help others?
Do we owe an apology? And if so to whom?	Did we study literature today?
What could we have done better?	Did we go to a meeting today?
Did we blame our feelings on someone else?	Did we call our sponsor today?
Do we need to write 10th Step on something?	Did we do anything that is improved over our past?

Journal—Gratitude List—Tomorrows Action Plan

BALANCE SHEETS

Day _____ Month _____ Year _____

Food		Money	
Breakfast		Item	Amount
Lunch			
Dinner			
Snack			
Exercise			
		Total Spent Today	
Litres Water	Hours Sleep	Quality of Life Today	%

When we retire at night we constructively review our day. We remember we have ceased fighting anything and anyone—love and tolerance of others is our code.

We Draw Up a Balance Sheet

The "Negative Side" (-)	The "Positive Side" (+)
Were we resentful?	Have we stayed clean of our addiction today?
Were we selfish?	Were we kind?
Were we dishonest?	Were we loving toward all?
Were we afraid?	What did we pack into life?
Have we kept something to ourselves?	Did we pray and meditate?
Were we thinking of ourselves most of the time?	Did we call someone we could help today?
Were we "disturbed" today?	Did we think of how we could help others?
Do we owe an apology? And if so to whom?	Did we study literature today?
What could we have done better?	Did we go to a meeting today?
Did we blame our feelings on someone else?	Did we call our sponsor today?
Do we need to write 10th Step on something?	Did we do anything that is improved over our past?

Journal—Gratitude List—Tomorrows Action Plan

STEP 10

BALANCE SHEETS

Day _____ Month _____ Year _____

Food		Money	
Breakfast		Item	Amount
Lunch			
Dinner			
Snack			
Exercise			
		Total Spent Today	
Litres Water	Hours Sleep	Quality of Life Today	%

When we retire at night we constructively review our day. We remember we have ceased fighting anything and anyone—love and tolerance of others is our code.

We Draw Up a Balance Sheet

The "Negative Side" (-)	The "Positive Side" (+)
Were we resentful?	Have we stayed clean of our addiction today?
Were we selfish?	Were we kind?
Were we dishonest?	Were we loving toward all?
Were we afraid?	What did we pack into life?
Have we kept something to ourselves?	Did we pray and meditate?
Were we thinking of ourselves most of the time?	Did we call someone we could help today?
Were we "disturbed" today?	Did we think of how we could help others?
Do we owe an apology? And if so to whom?	Did we study literature today?
What could we have done better?	Did we go to a meeting today?
Did we blame our feelings on someone else?	Did we call our sponsor today?
Do we need to write 10th Step on something?	Did we do anything that is improved over our past?

Journal—Gratitude List—Tomorrows Action Plan

BALANCE SHEETS

Day _____ Month _____ Year_____

Food		Money	
Breakfast		Item	Amount
Lunch			
Dinner			
Snack			
Exercise			
		Total Spent Today	
Litres Water	Hours Sleep	Quality of Life Today	%

When we retire at night we constructively review our day. We remember we have ceased fighting anything and anyone—love and tolerance of others is our code.

We Draw Up a Balance Sheet

The "Negative Side" (-)	The "Positive Side" (+)
Were we resentful?	Have we stayed clean of our addiction today?
Were we selfish?	Were we kind?
Were we dishonest?	Were we loving toward all?
Were we afraid?	What did we pack into life?
Have we kept something to ourselves?	Did we pray and meditate?
Were we thinking of ourselves most of the time?	Did we call someone we could help today?
Were we "disturbed" today?	Did we think of how we could help others?
Do we owe an apology? And if so to whom?	Did we study literature today?
What could we have done better?	Did we go to a meeting today?
Did we blame our feelings on someone else?	Did we call our sponsor today?
Do we need to write 10th Step on something?	Did we do anything that is improved over our past?

Journal—Gratitude List—Tomorrows Action Plan

STEP 10

BALANCE SHEETS

Day _____ Month _____ Year _____

Food		Money	
Breakfast		Item	Amount
Lunch			
Dinner			
Snack			
Exercise			
		Total Spent Today	
Litres Water	Hours Sleep	Quality of Life Today	%

When we retire at night we constructively review our day. We remember we have ceased fighting anything and anyone—love and tolerance of others is our code.

We Draw Up a Balance Sheet

The "Negative Side" (-)	The "Positive Side" (+)
Were we resentful?	Have we stayed clean of our addiction today?
Were we selfish?	Were we kind?
Were we dishonest?	Were we loving toward all?
Were we afraid?	What did we pack into life?
Have we kept something to ourselves?	Did we pray and meditate?
Were we thinking of ourselves most of the time?	Did we call someone we could help today?
Were we "disturbed" today?	Did we think of how we could help others?
Do we owe an apology? And if so to whom?	Did we study literature today?
What could we have done better?	Did we go to a meeting today?
Did we blame our feelings on someone else?	Did we call our sponsor today?
Do we need to write 10th Step on something?	Did we do anything that is improved over our past?

Journal—Gratitude List—Tomorrows Action Plan

MAINTAINING THE PROMISES...DAILY

BALANCE SHEETS

Day _____ Month _____ Year _____

Food

Breakfast		
Lunch		
Dinner		
Snack		
Exercise		
Litres Water _____ Hours Sleep _____		

Money

Item	Amount
Total Spent Today	
Quality of Life Today	%

When we retire at night we constructively review our day. We remember we have ceased fighting anything and anyone—love and tolerance of others is our code.

We Draw Up a Balance Sheet

The "Negative Side" (-)	The "Positive Side" (+)
Were we resentful?	Have we stayed clean of our addiction today?
Were we selfish?	Were we kind?
Were we dishonest?	Were we loving toward all?
Were we afraid?	What did we pack into life?
Have we kept something to ourselves?	Did we pray and meditate?
Were we thinking of ourselves most of the time?	Did we call someone we could help today?
Were we "disturbed" today?	Did we think of how we could help others?
Do we owe an apology? And if so to whom?	Did we study literature today?
What could we have done better?	Did we go to a meeting today?
Did we blame our feelings on someone else?	Did we call our sponsor today?
Do we need to write 10th Step on something?	Did we do anything that is improved over our past?

Journal—Gratitude List—Tomorrows Action Plan

STEP 10

BALANCE SHEETS

Day _____ Month _____ Year _____

Food		Money	
Breakfast		Item	Amount
Lunch			
Dinner			
Snack			
Exercise			
		Total Spent Today	
Litres Water	Hours Sleep	Quality of Life Today	%

When we retire at night we constructively review our day. We remember we have ceased fighting anything and anyone—love and tolerance of others is our code.

We Draw Up a Balance Sheet

The "Negative Side" (-)	The "Positive Side" (+)
Were we resentful?	Have we stayed clean of our addiction today?
Were we selfish?	Were we kind?
Were we dishonest?	Were we loving toward all?
Were we afraid?	What did we pack into life?
Have we kept something to ourselves?	Did we pray and meditate?
Were we thinking of ourselves most of the time?	Did we call someone we could help today?
Were we "disturbed" today?	Did we think of how we could help others?
Do we owe an apology? And if so to whom?	Did we study literature today?
What could we have done better?	Did we go to a meeting today?
Did we blame our feelings on someone else?	Did we call our sponsor today?
Do we need to write 10th Step on something?	Did we do anything that is improved over our past?

Journal—Gratitude List—Tomorrows Action Plan

BALANCE SHEETS

Day _____ Month _____ Year _____

Food		Money	
Breakfast		Item	Amount
Lunch			
Dinner			
Snack			
Exercise			
		Total Spent Today	
Litres Water Hours Sleep		Quality of Life Today	%

When we retire at night we constructively review our day. We remember we have ceased fighting anything and anyone—love and tolerance of others is our code.

We Draw Up a Balance Sheet

The "Negative Side" (-)	The "Positive Side" (+)
Were we resentful?	Have we stayed clean of our addiction today?
Were we selfish?	Were we kind?
Were we dishonest?	Were we loving toward all?
Were we afraid?	What did we pack into life?
Have we kept something to ourselves?	Did we pray and meditate?
Were we thinking of ourselves most of the time?	Did we call someone we could help today?
Were we "disturbed" today?	Did we think of how we could help others?
Do we owe an apology? And if so to whom?	Did we study literature today?
What could we have done better?	Did we go to a meeting today?
Did we blame our feelings on someone else?	Did we call our sponsor today?
Do we need to write 10th Step on something?	Did we do anything that is improved over our past?

Journal—Gratitude List—Tomorrows Action Plan

STEP 10

BALANCE SHEETS

Day _____ Month _____ Year _____

Food		Money		
Breakfast		Item		Amount
Lunch				
Dinner				
Snack				
Exercise				
		Total Spent Today		
Litres Water	Hours Sleep	Quality of Life Today		%

When we retire at night we constructively review our day. We remember we have ceased fighting anything and anyone—love and tolerance of others is our code.

We Draw Up a Balance Sheet

The "Negative Side" (-)	The "Positive Side" (+)
Were we resentful?	Have we stayed clean of our addiction today?
Were we selfish?	Were we kind?
Were we dishonest?	Were we loving toward all?
Were we afraid?	What did we pack into life?
Have we kept something to ourselves?	Did we pray and meditate?
Were we thinking of ourselves most of the time?	Did we call someone we could help today?
Were we "disturbed" today?	Did we think of how we could help others?
Do we owe an apology? And if so to whom?	Did we study literature today?
What could we have done better?	Did we go to a meeting today?
Did we blame our feelings on someone else?	Did we call our sponsor today?
Do we need to write 10th Step on something?	Did we do anything that is improved over our past?

Journal—Gratitude List—Tomorrows Action Plan

BALANCE SHEETS

Day _____ Month _____ Year _____

Food

Breakfast	
Lunch	
Dinner	
Snack	
Exercise	

Litres Water	Hours Sleep

Money

Item	Amount
Total Spent Today	
Quality of Life Today	%

When we retire at night we constructively review our day. We remember we have ceased fighting anything and anyone—love and tolerance of others is our code.

We Draw Up a Balance Sheet

The "Negative Side" (-)	The "Positive Side" (+)
Were we resentful?	Have we stayed clean of our addiction today?
Were we selfish?	Were we kind?
Were we dishonest?	Were we loving toward all?
Were we afraid?	What did we pack into life?
Have we kept something to ourselves?	Did we pray and meditate?
Were we thinking of ourselves most of the time?	Did we call someone we could help today?
Were we "disturbed" today?	Did we think of how we could help others?
Do we owe an apology? And if so to whom?	Did we study literature today?
What could we have done better?	Did we go to a meeting today?
Did we blame our feelings on someone else?	Did we call our sponsor today?
Do we need to write 10th Step on something?	Did we do anything that is improved over our past?

Journal—Gratitude List—Tomorrows Action Plan

STEP 10

BALANCE SHEETS

Day _____ Month _____ Year _____

Food		Money	
Breakfast		Item	Amount
Lunch			
Dinner			
Snack			
Exercise			
		Total Spent Today	
Litres Water	Hours Sleep	Quality of Life Today	%

When we retire at night we constructively review our day. We remember we have ceased fighting anything and anyone—love and tolerance of others is our code.

We Draw Up a Balance Sheet

The "Negative Side" (-)	The "Positive Side" (+)
Were we resentful?	Have we stayed clean of our addiction today?
Were we selfish?	Were we kind?
Were we dishonest?	Were we loving toward all?
Were we afraid?	What did we pack into life?
Have we kept something to ourselves?	Did we pray and meditate?
Were we thinking of ourselves most of the time?	Did we call someone we could help today?
Were we "disturbed" today?	Did we think of how we could help others?
Do we owe an apology? And if so to whom?	Did we study literature today?
What could we have done better?	Did we go to a meeting today?
Did we blame our feelings on someone else?	Did we call our sponsor today?
Do we need to write 10th Step on something?	Did we do anything that is improved over our past?

Journal—Gratitude List—Tomorrows Action Plan

BALANCE SHEETS

Day _____ Month _____ Year_____

Food		Money	
Breakfast		Item	Amount
Lunch			
Dinner			
Snack			
Exercise			
		Total Spent Today	
Litres Water	Hours Sleep	Quality of Life Today	%

When we retire at night we constructively review our day. We remember we have ceased fighting anything and anyone—love and tolerance of others is our code.

We Draw Up a Balance Sheet

The "Negative Side" (-)	The "Positive Side" (+)
Were we resentful?	Have we stayed clean of our addiction today?
Were we selfish?	Were we kind?
Were we dishonest?	Were we loving toward all?
Were we afraid?	What did we pack into life?
Have we kept something to ourselves?	Did we pray and meditate?
Were we thinking of ourselves most of the time?	Did we call someone we could help today?
Were we "disturbed" today?	Did we think of how we could help others?
Do we owe an apology? And if so to whom?	Did we study literature today?
What could we have done better?	Did we go to a meeting today?
Did we blame our feelings on someone else?	Did we call our sponsor today?
Do we need to write 10th Step on something?	Did we do anything that is improved over our past?

Journal—Gratitude List—Tomorrows Action Plan

STEP 10

BALANCE SHEETS

Day _____ Month _____ Year _____

Food		Money	
Breakfast		Item	Amount
Lunch			
Dinner			
Snack			
Exercise			
		Total Spent Today	
Litres Water	Hours Sleep	Quality of Life Today	%

When we retire at night we constructively review our day. We remember we have ceased fighting anything and anyone—love and tolerance of others is our code.

We Draw Up a Balance Sheet

The "Negative Side" (-)	The "Positive Side" (+)
Were we resentful?	Have we stayed clean of our addiction today?
Were we selfish?	Were we kind?
Were we dishonest?	Were we loving toward all?
Were we afraid?	What did we pack into life?
Have we kept something to ourselves?	Did we pray and meditate?
Were we thinking of ourselves most of the time?	Did we call someone we could help today?
Were we "disturbed" today?	Did we think of how we could help others?
Do we owe an apology? And if so to whom?	Did we study literature today?
What could we have done better?	Did we go to a meeting today?
Did we blame our feelings on someone else?	Did we call our sponsor today?
Do we need to write 10th Step on something?	Did we do anything that is improved over our past?

Journal—Gratitude List—Tomorrows Action Plan

BALANCE SHEETS

Day _____ Month _____ Year _____

Food		Money	
Breakfast		Item	Amount
Lunch			
Dinner			
Snack			
Exercise			
		Total Spent Today	
Litres Water	Hours Sleep	Quality of Life Today	%

When we retire at night we constructively review our day. We remember we have ceased fighting anything and anyone—love and tolerance of others is our code.

We Draw Up a Balance Sheet

The "Negative Side" (-)	The "Positive Side" (+)
Were we resentful?	Have we stayed clean of our addiction today?
Were we selfish?	Were we kind?
Were we dishonest?	Were we loving toward all?
Were we afraid?	What did we pack into life?
Have we kept something to ourselves?	Did we pray and meditate?
Were we thinking of ourselves most of the time?	Did we call someone we could help today?
Were we "disturbed" today?	Did we think of how we could help others?
Do we owe an apology? And if so to whom?	Did we study literature today?
What could we have done better?	Did we go to a meeting today?
Did we blame our feelings on someone else?	Did we call our sponsor today?
Do we need to write 10th Step on something?	Did we do anything that is improved over our past?

Journal—Gratitude List—Tomorrows Action Plan

STEP 10

BALANCE SHEETS

Day _____ Month _____ Year _____

Food		Money	
Breakfast		Item	Amount
Lunch			
Dinner			
Snack			
Exercise			
		Total Spent Today	
Litres Water	Hours Sleep	Quality of Life Today	%

When we retire at night we constructively review our day. We remember we have ceased fighting anything and anyone—love and tolerance of others is our code.

We Draw Up a Balance Sheet

The "Negative Side" (-)	The "Positive Side" (+)
Were we resentful?	Have we stayed clean of our addiction today?
Were we selfish?	Were we kind?
Were we dishonest?	Were we loving toward all?
Were we afraid?	What did we pack into life?
Have we kept something to ourselves?	Did we pray and meditate?
Were we thinking of ourselves most of the time?	Did we call someone we could help today?
Were we "disturbed" today?	Did we think of how we could help others?
Do we owe an apology? And if so to whom?	Did we study literature today?
What could we have done better?	Did we go to a meeting today?
Did we blame our feelings on someone else?	Did we call our sponsor today?
Do we need to write 10th Step on something?	Did we do anything that is improved over our past?

Journal—Gratitude List—Tomorrows Action Plan

BALANCE SHEETS

Day _____ Month _____ Year _____

Food		Money	
Breakfast		Item	Amount
Lunch			
Dinner			
Snack			
Exercise			
		Total Spent Today	
Litres Water	Hours Sleep	Quality of Life Today	%

When we retire at night we constructively review our day. We remember we have ceased fighting anything and anyone—love and tolerance of others is our code.

We Draw Up a Balance Sheet

The "Negative Side" (-)	The "Positive Side" (+)
Were we resentful?	Have we stayed clean of our addiction today?
Were we selfish?	Were we kind?
Were we dishonest?	Were we loving toward all?
Were we afraid?	What did we pack into life?
Have we kept something to ourselves?	Did we pray and meditate?
Were we thinking of ourselves most of the time?	Did we call someone we could help today?
Were we "disturbed" today?	Did we think of how we could help others?
Do we owe an apology? And if so to whom?	Did we study literature today?
What could we have done better?	Did we go to a meeting today?
Did we blame our feelings on someone else?	Did we call our sponsor today?
Do we need to write 10th Step on something?	Did we do anything that is improved over our past?

Journal—Gratitude List—Tomorrows Action Plan

STEP 10

BALANCE SHEETS

Day _____ Month _____ Year _____

Food		Money	
Breakfast		Item	Amount
Lunch			
Dinner			
Snack			
Exercise			
		Total Spent Today	
Litres Water Hours Sleep		Quality of Life Today	%

When we retire at night we constructively review our day. We remember we have ceased fighting anything and anyone—love and tolerance of others is our code.

We Draw Up a Balance Sheet

The "Negative Side" (-)	The "Positive Side" (+)
Were we resentful?	Have we stayed clean of our addiction today?
Were we selfish?	Were we kind?
Were we dishonest?	Were we loving toward all?
Were we afraid?	What did we pack into life?
Have we kept something to ourselves?	Did we pray and meditate?
Were we thinking of ourselves most of the time?	Did we call someone we could help today?
Were we "disturbed" today?	Did we think of how we could help others?
Do we owe an apology? And if so to whom?	Did we study literature today?
What could we have done better?	Did we go to a meeting today?
Did we blame our feelings on someone else?	Did we call our sponsor today?
Do we need to write 10th Step on something?	Did we do anything that is improved over our past?

Journal—Gratitude List—Tomorrows Action Plan

BALANCE SHEETS

Day _____ Month _____ Year_____

Food

Breakfast		
Lunch		
Dinner		
Snack		
Exercise		

Money

Item		Amount
Total Spent Today		

Litres Water	Hours Sleep	Quality of Life Today	%

When we retire at night we constructively review our day. We remember we have ceased fighting anything and anyone—love and tolerance of others is our code.

We Draw Up a Balance Sheet

The "Negative Side" (-)	The "Positive Side" (+)
Were we resentful?	Have we stayed clean of our addiction today?
Were we selfish?	Were we kind?
Were we dishonest?	Were we loving toward all?
Were we afraid?	What did we pack into life?
Have we kept something to ourselves?	Did we pray and meditate?
Were we thinking of ourselves most of the time?	Did we call someone we could help today?
Were we "disturbed" today?	Did we think of how we could help others?
Do we owe an apology? And if so to whom?	Did we study literature today?
What could we have done better?	Did we go to a meeting today?
Did we blame our feelings on someone else?	Did we call our sponsor today?
Do we need to write 10th Step on something?	Did we do anything that is improved over our past?

Journal—Gratitude List—Tomorrows Action Plan

STEP 10

BALANCE SHEETS

Day _____ Month _____ Year _____

Food

Breakfast	
Lunch	
Dinner	
Snack	
Exercise	

Money

Item	Amount
Total Spent Today	

Litres Water	Hours Sleep	Quality of Life Today	%

When we retire at night we constructively review our day. We remember we have ceased fighting anything and anyone—love and tolerance of others is our code.

We Draw Up a Balance Sheet

The "Negative Side" (−)	The "Positive Side" (+)
Were we resentful?	Have we stayed clean of our addiction today?
Were we selfish?	Were we kind?
Were we dishonest?	Were we loving toward all?
Were we afraid?	What did we pack into life?
Have we kept something to ourselves?	Did we pray and meditate?
Were we thinking of ourselves most of the time?	Did we call someone we could help today?
Were we "disturbed" today?	Did we think of how we could help others?
Do we owe an apology? And if so to whom?	Did we study literature today?
What could we have done better?	Did we go to a meeting today?
Did we blame our feelings on someone else?	Did we call our sponsor today?
Do we need to write 10th Step on something?	Did we do anything that is improved over our past?

Journal—Gratitude List—Tomorrows Action Plan

BALANCE SHEETS

Day _____ Month _____ Year _____

Food		Money	
Breakfast		Item	Amount
Lunch			
Dinner			
Snack			
Exercise			
		Total Spent Today	
Litres Water Hours Sleep		Quality of Life Today	%

When we retire at night we constructively review our day. We remember we have ceased fighting anything and anyone—love and tolerance of others is our code.

We Draw Up a Balance Sheet

The "Negative Side" (-)	The "Positive Side" (+)
Were we resentful?	Have we stayed clean of our addiction today?
Were we selfish?	Were we kind?
Were we dishonest?	Were we loving toward all?
Were we afraid?	What did we pack into life?
Have we kept something to ourselves?	Did we pray and meditate?
Were we thinking of ourselves most of the time?	Did we call someone we could help today?
Were we "disturbed" today?	Did we think of how we could help others?
Do we owe an apology? And if so to whom?	Did we study literature today?
What could we have done better?	Did we go to a meeting today?
Did we blame our feelings on someone else?	Did we call our sponsor today?
Do we need to write 10th Step on something?	Did we do anything that is improved over our past?

Journal—Gratitude List—Tomorrows Action Plan

STEP 10

BALANCE SHEETS

Day _____ Month _____ Year _____

Food		Money		
Breakfast		Item		Amount
Lunch				
Dinner				
Snack				
Exercise				
		Total Spent Today		
Litres Water	Hours Sleep	Quality of Life Today		%

When we retire at night we constructively review our day. We remember we have ceased fighting anything and anyone—love and tolerance of others is our code.

We Draw Up a Balance Sheet

The "Negative Side" (-)	The "Positive Side" (+)
Were we resentful?	Have we stayed clean of our addiction today?
Were we selfish?	Were we kind?
Were we dishonest?	Were we loving toward all?
Were we afraid?	What did we pack into life?
Have we kept something to ourselves?	Did we pray and meditate?
Were we thinking of ourselves most of the time?	Did we call someone we could help today?
Were we "disturbed" today?	Did we think of how we could help others?
Do we owe an apology? And if so to whom?	Did we study literature today?
What could we have done better?	Did we go to a meeting today?
Did we blame our feelings on someone else?	Did we call our sponsor today?
Do we need to write 10th Step on something?	Did we do anything that is improved over our past?

Journal—Gratitude List—Tomorrows Action Plan

BALANCE SHEETS

Day _____ Month _____ Year _____

Food		Money	
Breakfast		Item	Amount
Lunch			
Dinner			
Snack			
Exercise			
		Total Spent Today	
Litres Water	Hours Sleep	Quality of Life Today	%

When we retire at night we constructively review our day. We remember we have ceased fighting anything and anyone—love and tolerance of others is our code.

We Draw Up a Balance Sheet

The "Negative Side" (-)	The "Positive Side" (+)
Were we resentful?	Have we stayed clean of our addiction today?
Were we selfish?	Were we kind?
Were we dishonest?	Were we loving toward all?
Were we afraid?	What did we pack into life?
Have we kept something to ourselves?	Did we pray and meditate?
Were we thinking of ourselves most of the time?	Did we call someone we could help today?
Were we "disturbed" today?	Did we think of how we could help others?
Do we owe an apology? And if so to whom?	Did we study literature today?
What could we have done better?	Did we go to a meeting today?
Did we blame our feelings on someone else?	Did we call our sponsor today?
Do we need to write 10th Step on something?	Did we do anything that is improved over our past?

Journal—Gratitude List—Tomorrows Action Plan

STEP 10

BALANCE SHEETS

Day _____ Month _____ Year _____

Food		Money	
Breakfast		Item	Amount
Lunch			
Dinner			
Snack			
Exercise			
		Total Spent Today	
Litres Water	Hours Sleep	Quality of Life Today	%

When we retire at night we constructively review our day. We remember we have ceased fighting anything and anyone—love and tolerance of others is our code.

We Draw Up a Balance Sheet

The "Negative Side" (−)	The "Positive Side" (+)
Were we resentful?	Have we stayed clean of our addiction today?
Were we selfish?	Were we kind?
Were we dishonest?	Were we loving toward all?
Were we afraid?	What did we pack into life?
Have we kept something to ourselves?	Did we pray and meditate?
Were we thinking of ourselves most of the time?	Did we call someone we could help today?
Were we "disturbed" today?	Did we think of how we could help others?
Do we owe an apology? And if so to whom?	Did we study literature today?
What could we have done better?	Did we go to a meeting today?
Did we blame our feelings on someone else?	Did we call our sponsor today?
Do we need to write 10th Step on something?	Did we do anything that is improved over our past?

Journal—Gratitude List—Tomorrows Action Plan

MAINTAINING THE PROMISES...DAILY

BALANCE SHEETS

Day _____ Month _____ Year _____

Food		Money	
Breakfast		Item	Amount
Lunch			
Dinner			
Snack			
Exercise			
		Total Spent Today	
Litres Water _____ Hours Sleep _____		Quality of Life Today	%

When we retire at night we constructively review our day. We remember we have ceased fighting anything and anyone—love and tolerance of others is our code.

We Draw Up a Balance Sheet

The "Negative Side" (-)	The "Positive Side" (+)
Were we resentful?	Have we stayed clean of our addiction today?
Were we selfish?	Were we kind?
Were we dishonest?	Were we loving toward all?
Were we afraid?	What did we pack into life?
Have we kept something to ourselves?	Did we pray and meditate?
Were we thinking of ourselves most of the time?	Did we call someone we could help today?
Were we "disturbed" today?	Did we think of how we could help others?
Do we owe an apology? And if so to whom?	Did we study literature today?
What could we have done better?	Did we go to a meeting today?
Did we blame our feelings on someone else?	Did we call our sponsor today?
Do we need to write 10th Step on something?	Did we do anything that is improved over our past?

Journal—Gratitude List—Tomorrows Action Plan

STEP 10

BALANCE SHEETS

Day _____ Month _____ Year _____

Food		Money	
Breakfast		Item	Amount
Lunch			
Dinner			
Snack			
Exercise			
		Total Spent Today	
Litres Water	Hours Sleep	Quality of Life Today	%

When we retire at night we constructively review our day. We remember we have ceased fighting anything and anyone—love and tolerance of others is our code.

We Draw Up a Balance Sheet

The "Negative Side" (-)	The "Positive Side" (+)
Were we resentful?	Have we stayed clean of our addiction today?
Were we selfish?	Were we kind?
Were we dishonest?	Were we loving toward all?
Were we afraid?	What did we pack into life?
Have we kept something to ourselves?	Did we pray and meditate?
Were we thinking of ourselves most of the time?	Did we call someone we could help today?
Were we "disturbed" today?	Did we think of how we could help others?
Do we owe an apology? And if so to whom?	Did we study literature today?
What could we have done better?	Did we go to a meeting today?
Did we blame our feelings on someone else?	Did we call our sponsor today?
Do we need to write 10th Step on something?	Did we do anything that is improved over our past?

Journal—Gratitude List—Tomorrows Action Plan

BALANCE SHEETS

Day _____ Month _____ Year _____

Food		Money	
Breakfast		Item	Amount
Lunch			
Dinner			
Snack			
Exercise			
		Total Spent Today	
Litres Water ____ Hours Sleep ____		Quality of Life Today	%

When we retire at night we constructively review our day. We remember we have ceased fighting anything and anyone—love and tolerance of others is our code.

We Draw Up a Balance Sheet

The "Negative Side" (-)	The "Positive Side" (+)
Were we resentful?	Have we stayed clean of our addiction today?
Were we selfish?	Were we kind?
Were we dishonest?	Were we loving toward all?
Were we afraid?	What did we pack into life?
Have we kept something to ourselves?	Did we pray and meditate?
Were we thinking of ourselves most of the time?	Did we call someone we could help today?
Were we "disturbed" today?	Did we think of how we could help others?
Do we owe an apology? And if so to whom?	Did we study literature today?
What could we have done better?	Did we go to a meeting today?
Did we blame our feelings on someone else?	Did we call our sponsor today?
Do we need to write 10th Step on something?	Did we do anything that is improved over our past?

Journal—Gratitude List—Tomorrows Action Plan

STEP 10

BALANCE SHEETS

Day _____ Month _____ Year _____

Food		Money	
Breakfast		Item	Amount
Lunch			
Dinner			
Snack			
Exercise			
		Total Spent Today	
Litres Water	Hours Sleep	Quality of Life Today	%

When we retire at night we constructively review our day. We remember we have ceased fighting anything and anyone—love and tolerance of others is our code.

We Draw Up a Balance Sheet

The "Negative Side" (-)	The "Positive Side" (+)
Were we resentful?	Have we stayed clean of our addiction today?
Were we selfish?	Were we kind?
Were we dishonest?	Were we loving toward all?
Were we afraid?	What did we pack into life?
Have we kept something to ourselves?	Did we pray and meditate?
Were we thinking of ourselves most of the time?	Did we call someone we could help today?
Were we "disturbed" today?	Did we think of how we could help others?
Do we owe an apology? And if so to whom?	Did we study literature today?
What could we have done better?	Did we go to a meeting today?
Did we blame our feelings on someone else?	Did we call our sponsor today?
Do we need to write 10th Step on something?	Did we do anything that is improved over our past?

Journal—Gratitude List—Tomorrows Action Plan

BALANCE SHEETS

Day _____ Month _____ Year _____

Food

Breakfast		
Lunch		
Dinner		
Snack		
Exercise		
Litres Water	Hours Sleep	

Money

Item	Amount
Total Spent Today	
Quality of Life Today	%

When we retire at night we constructively review our day. We remember we have ceased fighting anything and anyone—love and tolerance of others is our code.

We Draw Up a Balance Sheet

The "Negative Side" (-)	The "Positive Side" (+)
Were we resentful?	Have we stayed clean of our addiction today?
Were we selfish?	Were we kind?
Were we dishonest?	Were we loving toward all?
Were we afraid?	What did we pack into life?
Have we kept something to ourselves?	Did we pray and meditate?
Were we thinking of ourselves most of the time?	Did we call someone we could help today?
Were we "disturbed" today?	Did we think of how we could help others?
Do we owe an apology? And if so to whom?	Did we study literature today?
What could we have done better?	Did we go to a meeting today?
Did we blame our feelings on someone else?	Did we call our sponsor today?
Do we need to write 10th Step on something?	Did we do anything that is improved over our past?

Journal—Gratitude List—Tomorrows Action Plan

STEP 10

BALANCE SHEETS

Day _____ Month _____ Year _____

Food		Money	
Breakfast		Item	Amount
Lunch			
Dinner			
Snack			
Exercise			
		Total Spent Today	
Litres Water	Hours Sleep	Quality of Life Today	%

When we retire at night we constructively review our day. We remember we have ceased fighting anything and anyone—love and tolerance of others is our code.

We Draw Up a Balance Sheet

The "Negative Side" (-)	The "Positive Side" (+)
Were we resentful?	Have we stayed clean of our addiction today?
Were we selfish?	Were we kind?
Were we dishonest?	Were we loving toward all?
Were we afraid?	What did we pack into life?
Have we kept something to ourselves?	Did we pray and meditate?
Were we thinking of ourselves most of the time?	Did we call someone we could help today?
Were we "disturbed" today?	Did we think of how we could help others?
Do we owe an apology? And if so to whom?	Did we study literature today?
What could we have done better?	Did we go to a meeting today?
Did we blame our feelings on someone else?	Did we call our sponsor today?
Do we need to write 10th Step on something?	Did we do anything that is improved over our past?

Journal—Gratitude List—Tomorrows Action Plan

_____
_____
_____
_____
_____
_____

BALANCE SHEETS

Day _____ Month _____ Year _____

Food		Money	
Breakfast		Item	Amount
Lunch			
Dinner			
Snack			
Exercise			
		Total Spent Today	
Litres Water	Hours Sleep	Quality of Life Today	%

When we retire at night we constructively review our day. We remember we have ceased fighting anything and anyone—love and tolerance of others is our code.

We Draw Up a Balance Sheet

The "Negative Side" (-)	The "Positive Side" (+)
Were we resentful?	Have we stayed clean of our addiction today?
Were we selfish?	Were we kind?
Were we dishonest?	Were we loving toward all?
Were we afraid?	What did we pack into life?
Have we kept something to ourselves?	Did we pray and meditate?
Were we thinking of ourselves most of the time?	Did we call someone we could help today?
Were we "disturbed" today?	Did we think of how we could help others?
Do we owe an apology? And if so to whom?	Did we study literature today?
What could we have done better?	Did we go to a meeting today?
Did we blame our feelings on someone else?	Did we call our sponsor today?
Do we need to write 10th Step on something?	Did we do anything that is improved over our past?

Journal—Gratitude List—Tomorrows Action Plan

BALANCE SHEETS

Day _____ Month _____ Year _____

Food		Money	
Breakfast		Item	Amount
Lunch			
Dinner			
Snack			
Exercise			
		Total Spent Today	
Litres Water Hours Sleep		Quality of Life Today	%

When we retire at night we constructively review our day. We remember we have ceased fighting anything and anyone—love and tolerance of others is our code.

We Draw Up a Balance Sheet

The "Negative Side" (-)	The "Positive Side" (+)
Were we resentful?	Have we stayed clean of our addiction today?
Were we selfish?	Were we kind?
Were we dishonest?	Were we loving toward all?
Were we afraid?	What did we pack into life?
Have we kept something to ourselves?	Did we pray and meditate?
Were we thinking of ourselves most of the time?	Did we call someone we could help today?
Were we "disturbed" today?	Did we think of how we could help others?
Do we owe an apology? And if so to whom?	Did we study literature today?
What could we have done better?	Did we go to a meeting today?
Did we blame our feelings on someone else?	Did we call our sponsor today?
Do we need to write 10th Step on something?	Did we do anything that is improved over our past?

Journal—Gratitude List—Tomorrows Action Plan

BALANCE SHEETS

Day _____ Month _____ Year _____

Food		Money	
Breakfast		Item	Amount
Lunch			
Dinner			
Snack			
Exercise			
		Total Spent Today	
Litres Water	Hours Sleep	Quality of Life Today	%

When we retire at night we constructively review our day. We remember we have ceased fighting anything and anyone—love and tolerance of others is our code.

We Draw Up a Balance Sheet

The "Negative Side" (-)	The "Positive Side" (+)
Were we resentful?	Have we stayed clean of our addiction today?
Were we selfish?	Were we kind?
Were we dishonest?	Were we loving toward all?
Were we afraid?	What did we pack into life?
Have we kept something to ourselves?	Did we pray and meditate?
Were we thinking of ourselves most of the time?	Did we call someone we could help today?
Were we "disturbed" today?	Did we think of how we could help others?
Do we owe an apology? And if so to whom?	Did we study literature today?
What could we have done better?	Did we go to a meeting today?
Did we blame our feelings on someone else?	Did we call our sponsor today?
Do we need to write 10th Step on something?	Did we do anything that is improved over our past?

Journal—Gratitude List—Tomorrows Action Plan

STEP 10

BALANCE SHEETS

Day _____ Month _____ Year _____

Food		Money	
Breakfast		Item	Amount
Lunch			
Dinner			
Snack			
Exercise			
		Total Spent Today	
Litres Water	Hours Sleep	Quality of Life Today	%

When we retire at night we constructively review our day. We remember we have ceased fighting anything and anyone—love and tolerance of others is our code.

We Draw Up a Balance Sheet

The "Negative Side" (-)	The "Positive Side" (+)
Were we resentful?	Have we stayed clean of our addiction today?
Were we selfish?	Were we kind?
Were we dishonest?	Were we loving toward all?
Were we afraid?	What did we pack into life?
Have we kept something to ourselves?	Did we pray and meditate?
Were we thinking of ourselves most of the time?	Did we call someone we could help today?
Were we "disturbed" today?	Did we think of how we could help others?
Do we owe an apology? And if so to whom?	Did we study literature today?
What could we have done better?	Did we go to a meeting today?
Did we blame our feelings on someone else?	Did we call our sponsor today?
Do we need to write 10th Step on something?	Did we do anything that is improved over our past?

Journal—Gratitude List—Tomorrows Action Plan

MAINTAINING THE PROMISES...DAILY

BALANCE SHEETS

Day _____ Month _____ Year _____

Food		Money	
Breakfast		Item	Amount
Lunch			
Dinner			
Snack			
Exercise			
		Total Spent Today	
Litres Water _____ Hours Sleep _____		Quality of Life Today	%

When we retire at night we constructively review our day. We remember we have ceased fighting anything and anyone—love and tolerance of others is our code.

We Draw Up a Balance Sheet

The "Negative Side" (-)	The "Positive Side" (+)
Were we resentful?	Have we stayed clean of our addiction today?
Were we selfish?	Were we kind?
Were we dishonest?	Were we loving toward all?
Were we afraid?	What did we pack into life?
Have we kept something to ourselves?	Did we pray and meditate?
Were we thinking of ourselves most of the time?	Did we call someone we could help today?
Were we "disturbed" today?	Did we think of how we could help others?
Do we owe an apology? And if so to whom?	Did we study literature today?
What could we have done better?	Did we go to a meeting today?
Did we blame our feelings on someone else?	Did we call our sponsor today?
Do we need to write 10th Step on something?	Did we do anything that is improved over our past?

Journal—Gratitude List—Tomorrows Action Plan

STEP 10

BALANCE SHEETS

Day _____ Month _____ Year _____

Food		Money	
Breakfast		Item	Amount
Lunch			
Dinner			
Snack			
Exercise			
		Total Spent Today	
Litres Water	Hours Sleep	Quality of Life Today	%

When we retire at night we constructively review our day. We remember we have ceased fighting anything and anyone—love and tolerance of others is our code.

We Draw Up a Balance Sheet

The "Negative Side" (-)	The "Positive Side" (+)
Were we resentful?	Have we stayed clean of our addiction today?
Were we selfish?	Were we kind?
Were we dishonest?	Were we loving toward all?
Were we afraid?	What did we pack into life?
Have we kept something to ourselves?	Did we pray and meditate?
Were we thinking of ourselves most of the time?	Did we call someone we could help today?
Were we "disturbed" today?	Did we think of how we could help others?
Do we owe an apology? And if so to whom?	Did we study literature today?
What could we have done better?	Did we go to a meeting today?
Did we blame our feelings on someone else?	Did we call our sponsor today?
Do we need to write 10th Step on something?	Did we do anything that is improved over our past?

Journal—Gratitude List—Tomorrows Action Plan

BALANCE SHEETS

Day _____ Month _____ Year _____

Food		Money	
Breakfast		Item	Amount
Lunch			
Dinner			
Snack			
Exercise			
		Total Spent Today	
Litres Water	Hours Sleep	Quality of Life Today	%

When we retire at night we constructively review our day. We remember we have ceased fighting anything and anyone—love and tolerance of others is our code.

We Draw Up a Balance Sheet

The "Negative Side" (-)	The "Positive Side" (+)
Were we resentful?	Have we stayed clean of our addiction today?
Were we selfish?	Were we kind?
Were we dishonest?	Were we loving toward all?
Were we afraid?	What did we pack into life?
Have we kept something to ourselves?	Did we pray and meditate?
Were we thinking of ourselves most of the time?	Did we call someone we could help today?
Were we "disturbed" today?	Did we think of how we could help others?
Do we owe an apology? And if so to whom?	Did we study literature today?
What could we have done better?	Did we go to a meeting today?
Did we blame our feelings on someone else?	Did we call our sponsor today?
Do we need to write 10th Step on something?	Did we do anything that is improved over our past?

Journal—Gratitude List—Tomorrows Action Plan

STEP 10

BALANCE SHEETS

Day _____ Month _____ Year _____

Food		Money	
Breakfast		Item	Amount
Lunch			
Dinner			
Snack			
Exercise			
		Total Spent Today	
Litres Water _____ Hours Sleep _____		Quality of Life Today	%

When we retire at night we constructively review our day. We remember we have ceased fighting anything and anyone—love and tolerance of others is our code.

We Draw Up a Balance Sheet

The "Negative Side" (-)	The "Positive Side" (+)
Were we resentful?	Have we stayed clean of our addiction today?
Were we selfish?	Were we kind?
Were we dishonest?	Were we loving toward all?
Were we afraid?	What did we pack into life?
Have we kept something to ourselves?	Did we pray and meditate?
Were we thinking of ourselves most of the time?	Did we call someone we could help today?
Were we "disturbed" today?	Did we think of how we could help others?
Do we owe an apology? And if so to whom?	Did we study literature today?
What could we have done better?	Did we go to a meeting today?
Did we blame our feelings on someone else?	Did we call our sponsor today?
Do we need to write 10th Step on something?	Did we do anything that is improved over our past?

Journal—Gratitude List—Tomorrows Action Plan

BALANCE SHEETS

Day _____ Month _____ Year _____

Food		Money	
Breakfast		Item	Amount
Lunch			
Dinner			
Snack			
Exercise			
		Total Spent Today	
Litres Water	Hours Sleep	Quality of Life Today	%

When we retire at night we constructively review our day. We remember we have ceased fighting anything and anyone—love and tolerance of others is our code.

We Draw Up a Balance Sheet

The "Negative Side" (-)	The "Positive Side" (+)
Were we resentful?	Have we stayed clean of our addiction today?
Were we selfish?	Were we kind?
Were we dishonest?	Were we loving toward all?
Were we afraid?	What did we pack into life?
Have we kept something to ourselves?	Did we pray and meditate?
Were we thinking of ourselves most of the time?	Did we call someone we could help today?
Were we "disturbed" today?	Did we think of how we could help others?
Do we owe an apology? And if so to whom?	Did we study literature today?
What could we have done better?	Did we go to a meeting today?
Did we blame our feelings on someone else?	Did we call our sponsor today?
Do we need to write 10th Step on something?	Did we do anything that is improved over our past?

Journal—Gratitude List—Tomorrows Action Plan

STEP 10

BALANCE SHEETS

Day _____ Month _____ Year _____

Food		Money		
Breakfast		Item		Amount
Lunch				
Dinner				
Snack				
Exercise				
		Total Spent Today		
Litres Water	Hours Sleep	Quality of Life Today		%

When we retire at night we constructively review our day. We remember we have ceased fighting anything and anyone—love and tolerance of others is our code.

We Draw Up a Balance Sheet

The "Negative Side" (−)	The "Positive Side" (+)
Were we resentful?	Have we stayed clean of our addiction today?
Were we selfish?	Were we kind?
Were we dishonest?	Were we loving toward all?
Were we afraid?	What did we pack into life?
Have we kept something to ourselves?	Did we pray and meditate?
Were we thinking of ourselves most of the time?	Did we call someone we could help today?
Were we "disturbed" today?	Did we think of how we could help others?
Do we owe an apology? And if so to whom?	Did we study literature today?
What could we have done better?	Did we go to a meeting today?
Did we blame our feelings on someone else?	Did we call our sponsor today?
Do we need to write 10th Step on something?	Did we do anything that is improved over our past?

Journal—Gratitude List—Tomorrows Action Plan

BALANCE SHEETS

Day _____ Month _____ Year _____

Food

Breakfast		
Lunch		
Dinner		
Snack		
Exercise		
Litres Water ____ Hours Sleep ____		

Money

Item	Amount
Total Spent Today	
Quality of Life Today	%

When we retire at night we constructively review our day. We remember we have ceased fighting anything and anyone—love and tolerance of others is our code.

We Draw Up a Balance Sheet

The "Negative Side" (-)	The "Positive Side" (+)
Were we resentful?	Have we stayed clean of our addiction today?
Were we selfish?	Were we kind?
Were we dishonest?	Were we loving toward all?
Were we afraid?	What did we pack into life?
Have we kept something to ourselves?	Did we pray and meditate?
Were we thinking of ourselves most of the time?	Did we call someone we could help today?
Were we "disturbed" today?	Did we think of how we could help others?
Do we owe an apology? And if so to whom?	Did we study literature today?
What could we have done better?	Did we go to a meeting today?
Did we blame our feelings on someone else?	Did we call our sponsor today?
Do we need to write 10th Step on something?	Did we do anything that is improved over our past?

Journal—Gratitude List—Tomorrows Action Plan

STEP 10

BALANCE SHEETS

Day _____ Month _____ Year _____

Food		Money	
Breakfast		Item	Amount
Lunch			
Dinner			
Snack			
Exercise			
		Total Spent Today	
Litres Water	Hours Sleep	Quality of Life Today	%

When we retire at night we constructively review our day. We remember we have ceased fighting anything and anyone—love and tolerance of others is our code.

We Draw Up a Balance Sheet

The "Negative Side" (-)	The "Positive Side" (+)
Were we resentful?	Have we stayed clean of our addiction today?
Were we selfish?	Were we kind?
Were we dishonest?	Were we loving toward all?
Were we afraid?	What did we pack into life?
Have we kept something to ourselves?	Did we pray and meditate?
Were we thinking of ourselves most of the time?	Did we call someone we could help today?
Were we "disturbed" today?	Did we think of how we could help others?
Do we owe an apology? And if so to whom?	Did we study literature today?
What could we have done better?	Did we go to a meeting today?
Did we blame our feelings on someone else?	Did we call our sponsor today?
Do we need to write 10th Step on something?	Did we do anything that is improved over our past?

Journal—Gratitude List—Tomorrows Action Plan

BALANCE SHEETS

Day _____ Month _____ Year _____

Food		Money	
Breakfast		Item	Amount
Lunch			
Dinner			
Snack			
Exercise			
		Total Spent Today	
Litres Water	Hours Sleep	Quality of Life Today	%

When we retire at night we constructively review our day. We remember we have ceased fighting anything and anyone—love and tolerance of others is our code.

We Draw Up a Balance Sheet

The "Negative Side" (-)	The "Positive Side" (+)
Were we resentful?	Have we stayed clean of our addiction today?
Were we selfish?	Were we kind?
Were we dishonest?	Were we loving toward all?
Were we afraid?	What did we pack into life?
Have we kept something to ourselves?	Did we pray and meditate?
Were we thinking of ourselves most of the time?	Did we call someone we could help today?
Were we "disturbed" today?	Did we think of how we could help others?
Do we owe an apology? And if so to whom?	Did we study literature today?
What could we have done better?	Did we go to a meeting today?
Did we blame our feelings on someone else?	Did we call our sponsor today?
Do we need to write 10th Step on something?	Did we do anything that is improved over our past?

Journal—Gratitude List—Tomorrows Action Plan

STEP 10

BALANCE SHEETS

Day _____ Month _____ Year _____

Food		Money	
Breakfast		Item	Amount
Lunch			
Dinner			
Snack			
Exercise			
		Total Spent Today	
Litres Water _____ Hours Sleep _____		Quality of Life Today	%

When we retire at night we constructively review our day. We remember we have ceased fighting anything and anyone—love and tolerance of others is our code.

We Draw Up a Balance Sheet

The "Negative Side" (-)	The "Positive Side" (+)
Were we resentful?	Have we stayed clean of our addiction today?
Were we selfish?	Were we kind?
Were we dishonest?	Were we loving toward all?
Were we afraid?	What did we pack into life?
Have we kept something to ourselves?	Did we pray and meditate?
Were we thinking of ourselves most of the time?	Did we call someone we could help today?
Were we "disturbed" today?	Did we think of how we could help others?
Do we owe an apology? And if so to whom?	Did we study literature today?
What could we have done better?	Did we go to a meeting today?
Did we blame our feelings on someone else?	Did we call our sponsor today?
Do we need to write 10th Step on something?	Did we do anything that is improved over our past?

Journal—Gratitude List—Tomorrows Action Plan

BALANCE SHEETS

Day _____ Month _____ Year _____

Food		Money	
Breakfast		Item	Amount
Lunch			
Dinner			
Snack			
Exercise			
		Total Spent Today	
Litres Water	Hours Sleep	Quality of Life Today	%

When we retire at night we constructively review our day. We remember we have ceased fighting anything and anyone—love and tolerance of others is our code.

We Draw Up a Balance Sheet

The "Negative Side" (-)	The "Positive Side" (+)
Were we resentful?	Have we stayed clean of our addiction today?
Were we selfish?	Were we kind?
Were we dishonest?	Were we loving toward all?
Were we afraid?	What did we pack into life?
Have we kept something to ourselves?	Did we pray and meditate?
Were we thinking of ourselves most of the time?	Did we call someone we could help today?
Were we "disturbed" today?	Did we think of how we could help others?
Do we owe an apology? And if so to whom?	Did we study literature today?
What could we have done better?	Did we go to a meeting today?
Did we blame our feelings on someone else?	Did we call our sponsor today?
Do we need to write 10th Step on something?	Did we do anything that is improved over our past?

Journal—Gratitude List—Tomorrows Action Plan

STEP 10

BALANCE SHEETS

Day _____ Month _____ Year _____

Food		Money	
Breakfast		Item	Amount
Lunch			
Dinner			
Snack			
Exercise			
		Total Spent Today	
Litres Water	Hours Sleep	Quality of Life Today	%

When we retire at night we constructively review our day. We remember we have ceased fighting anything and anyone—love and tolerance of others is our code.

We Draw Up a Balance Sheet

The "Negative Side" (-)	The "Positive Side" (+)
Were we resentful?	Have we stayed clean of our addiction today?
Were we selfish?	Were we kind?
Were we dishonest?	Were we loving toward all?
Were we afraid?	What did we pack into life?
Have we kept something to ourselves?	Did we pray and meditate?
Were we thinking of ourselves most of the time?	Did we call someone we could help today?
Were we "disturbed" today?	Did we think of how we could help others?
Do we owe an apology? And if so to whom?	Did we study literature today?
What could we have done better?	Did we go to a meeting today?
Did we blame our feelings on someone else?	Did we call our sponsor today?
Do we need to write 10th Step on something?	Did we do anything that is improved over our past?

Journal—Gratitude List—Tomorrows Action Plan

BALANCE SHEETS

Day _____ Month _____ Year _____

Food		Money	
Breakfast		Item	Amount
Lunch			
Dinner			
Snack			
Exercise			
		Total Spent Today	
Litres Water ____ Hours Sleep ____		Quality of Life Today	%

When we retire at night we constructively review our day. We remember we have ceased fighting anything and anyone—love and tolerance of others is our code.

We Draw Up a Balance Sheet

The "Negative Side" (-)	The "Positive Side" (+)
Were we resentful?	Have we stayed clean of our addiction today?
Were we selfish?	Were we kind?
Were we dishonest?	Were we loving toward all?
Were we afraid?	What did we pack into life?
Have we kept something to ourselves?	Did we pray and meditate?
Were we thinking of ourselves most of the time?	Did we call someone we could help today?
Were we "disturbed" today?	Did we think of how we could help others?
Do we owe an apology? And if so to whom?	Did we study literature today?
What could we have done better?	Did we go to a meeting today?
Did we blame our feelings on someone else?	Did we call our sponsor today?
Do we need to write 10th Step on something?	Did we do anything that is improved over our past?

Journal—Gratitude List—Tomorrows Action Plan

STEP 10

BALANCE SHEETS

Day _____ Month _____ Year _____

Food		Money	
Breakfast		Item	Amount
Lunch			
Dinner			
Snack			
Exercise			
		Total Spent Today	
Litres Water	Hours Sleep	Quality of Life Today	%

When we retire at night we constructively review our day. We remember we have ceased fighting anything and anyone—love and tolerance of others is our code.

We Draw Up a Balance Sheet

The "Negative Side" (-)	The "Positive Side" (+)
Were we resentful?	Have we stayed clean of our addiction today?
Were we selfish?	Were we kind?
Were we dishonest?	Were we loving toward all?
Were we afraid?	What did we pack into life?
Have we kept something to ourselves?	Did we pray and meditate?
Were we thinking of ourselves most of the time?	Did we call someone we could help today?
Were we "disturbed" today?	Did we think of how we could help others?
Do we owe an apology? And if so to whom?	Did we study literature today?
What could we have done better?	Did we go to a meeting today?
Did we blame our feelings on someone else?	Did we call our sponsor today?
Do we need to write 10th Step on something?	Did we do anything that is improved over our past?

Journal—Gratitude List—Tomorrows Action Plan

BALANCE SHEETS

Day _____ Month _____ Year _____

Food		Money	
Breakfast		Item	Amount
Lunch			
Dinner			
Snack			
Exercise			
		Total Spent Today	
Litres Water	Hours Sleep	Quality of Life Today	%

When we retire at night we constructively review our day. We remember we have ceased fighting anything and anyone—love and tolerance of others is our code.

We Draw Up a Balance Sheet

The "Negative Side" (-)	The "Positive Side" (+)
Were we resentful?	Have we stayed clean of our addiction today?
Were we selfish?	Were we kind?
Were we dishonest?	Were we loving toward all?
Were we afraid?	What did we pack into life?
Have we kept something to ourselves?	Did we pray and meditate?
Were we thinking of ourselves most of the time?	Did we call someone we could help today?
Were we "disturbed" today?	Did we think of how we could help others?
Do we owe an apology? And if so to whom?	Did we study literature today?
What could we have done better?	Did we go to a meeting today?
Did we blame our feelings on someone else?	Did we call our sponsor today?
Do we need to write 10th Step on something?	Did we do anything that is improved over our past?

Journal—Gratitude List—Tomorrows Action Plan

STEP 10

BALANCE SHEETS

Day _____ Month _____ Year _____

Food

Breakfast	

Lunch	

Dinner	

Snack	

Exercise	

Litres Water	Hours Sleep

Money

Item	Amount
Total Spent Today	
Quality of Life Today	%

When we retire at night we constructively review our day. We remember we have ceased fighting anything and anyone—love and tolerance of others is our code.

We Draw Up a Balance Sheet

The "Negative Side" (-)	The "Positive Side" (+)
Were we resentful?	Have we stayed clean of our addiction today?
Were we selfish?	Were we kind?
Were we dishonest?	Were we loving toward all?
Were we afraid?	What did we pack into life?
Have we kept something to ourselves?	Did we pray and meditate?
Were we thinking of ourselves most of the time?	Did we call someone we could help today?
Were we "disturbed" today?	Did we think of how we could help others?
Do we owe an apology? And if so to whom?	Did we study literature today?
What could we have done better?	Did we go to a meeting today?
Did we blame our feelings on someone else?	Did we call our sponsor today?
Do we need to write 10th Step on something?	Did we do anything that is improved over our past?

Journal—Gratitude List—Tomorrows Action Plan

BALANCE SHEETS

Day _____ Month _____ Year _____

Food		Money	
Breakfast		Item	Amount
Lunch			
Dinner			
Snack			
Exercise			
		Total Spent Today	
Litres Water Hours Sleep		Quality of Life Today	%

When we retire at night we constructively review our day. We remember we have ceased fighting anything and anyone—love and tolerance of others is our code.

We Draw Up a Balance Sheet

The "Negative Side" (-)	The "Positive Side" (+)
Were we resentful?	Have we stayed clean of our addiction today?
Were we selfish?	Were we kind?
Were we dishonest?	Were we loving toward all?
Were we afraid?	What did we pack into life?
Have we kept something to ourselves?	Did we pray and meditate?
Were we thinking of ourselves most of the time?	Did we call someone we could help today?
Were we "disturbed" today?	Did we think of how we could help others?
Do we owe an apology? And if so to whom?	Did we study literature today?
What could we have done better?	Did we go to a meeting today?
Did we blame our feelings on someone else?	Did we call our sponsor today?
Do we need to write 10th Step on something?	Did we do anything that is improved over our past?

Journal—Gratitude List—Tomorrows Action Plan

STEP 10

BALANCE SHEETS

Day _____ Month _____ Year _____

Food		Money	
Breakfast		Item	Amount
Lunch			
Dinner			
Snack			
Exercise			
		Total Spent Today	
Litres Water	Hours Sleep	Quality of Life Today	%

When we retire at night we constructively review our day. We remember we have ceased fighting anything and anyone—love and tolerance of others is our code.

We Draw Up a Balance Sheet

The "Negative Side" (−)	The "Positive Side" (+)
Were we resentful?	Have we stayed clean of our addiction today?
Were we selfish?	Were we kind?
Were we dishonest?	Were we loving toward all?
Were we afraid?	What did we pack into life?
Have we kept something to ourselves?	Did we pray and meditate?
Were we thinking of ourselves most of the time?	Did we call someone we could help today?
Were we "disturbed" today?	Did we think of how we could help others?
Do we owe an apology? And if so to whom?	Did we study literature today?
What could we have done better?	Did we go to a meeting today?
Did we blame our feelings on someone else?	Did we call our sponsor today?
Do we need to write 10th Step on something?	Did we do anything that is improved over our past?

Journal—Gratitude List—Tomorrows Action Plan

BALANCE SHEETS

Day _____ Month _____ Year_____

Food		Money	
Breakfast		Item	Amount
Lunch			
Dinner			
Snack			
Exercise			
		Total Spent Today	
Litres Water	Hours Sleep	Quality of Life Today	%

When we retire at night we constructively review our day. We remember we have ceased fighting anything and anyone—love and tolerance of others is our code.

We Draw Up a Balance Sheet

The "Negative Side" (-)	The "Positive Side" (+)
Were we resentful?	Have we stayed clean of our addiction today?
Were we selfish?	Were we kind?
Were we dishonest?	Were we loving toward all?
Were we afraid?	What did we pack into life?
Have we kept something to ourselves?	Did we pray and meditate?
Were we thinking of ourselves most of the time?	Did we call someone we could help today?
Were we "disturbed" today?	Did we think of how we could help others?
Do we owe an apology? And if so to whom?	Did we study literature today?
What could we have done better?	Did we go to a meeting today?
Did we blame our feelings on someone else?	Did we call our sponsor today?
Do we need to write 10th Step on something?	Did we do anything that is improved over our past?

Journal—Gratitude List—Tomorrows Action Plan

STEP 10

BALANCE SHEETS

Day _____ Month _____ Year _____

Food		Money	
Breakfast		Item	Amount
Lunch			
Dinner			
Snack			
Exercise			
		Total Spent Today	
Litres Water	Hours Sleep	Quality of Life Today	%

When we retire at night we constructively review our day. We remember we have ceased fighting anything and anyone—love and tolerance of others is our code.

We Draw Up a Balance Sheet

The "Negative Side" (-)	The "Positive Side" (+)
Were we resentful?	Have we stayed clean of our addiction today?
Were we selfish?	Were we kind?
Were we dishonest?	Were we loving toward all?
Were we afraid?	What did we pack into life?
Have we kept something to ourselves?	Did we pray and meditate?
Were we thinking of ourselves most of the time?	Did we call someone we could help today?
Were we "disturbed" today?	Did we think of how we could help others?
Do we owe an apology? And if so to whom?	Did we study literature today?
What could we have done better?	Did we go to a meeting today?
Did we blame our feelings on someone else?	Did we call our sponsor today?
Do we need to write 10th Step on something?	Did we do anything that is improved over our past?

Journal—Gratitude List—Tomorrows Action Plan

MAINTAINING THE PROMISES...DAILY

BALANCE SHEETS

Day _____ Month _____ Year _____

Food

Breakfast	
Lunch	
Dinner	
Snack	
Exercise	
Litres Water	Hours Sleep

Money

Item	Amount
Total Spent Today	
Quality of Life Today	%

When we retire at night we constructively review our day. We remember we have ceased fighting anything and anyone—love and tolerance of others is our code.

We Draw Up a Balance Sheet

The "Negative Side" (-)	The "Positive Side" (+)
Were we resentful?	Have we stayed clean of our addiction today?
Were we selfish?	Were we kind?
Were we dishonest?	Were we loving toward all?
Were we afraid?	What did we pack into life?
Have we kept something to ourselves?	Did we pray and meditate?
Were we thinking of ourselves most of the time?	Did we call someone we could help today?
Were we "disturbed" today?	Did we think of how we could help others?
Do we owe an apology? And if so to whom?	Did we study literature today?
What could we have done better?	Did we go to a meeting today?
Did we blame our feelings on someone else?	Did we call our sponsor today?
Do we need to write 10th Step on something?	Did we do anything that is improved over our past?

Journal—Gratitude List—Tomorrows Action Plan

STEP 10

BALANCE SHEETS

Day _____ Month _____ Year _____

Food		Money	
Breakfast		Item	Amount
Lunch			
Dinner			
Snack			
Exercise			
		Total Spent Today	
Litres Water	Hours Sleep	Quality of Life Today	%

When we retire at night we constructively review our day. We remember we have ceased fighting anything and anyone—love and tolerance of others is our code.

We Draw Up a Balance Sheet

The "Negative Side" (-)	The "Positive Side" (+)
Were we resentful?	Have we stayed clean of our addiction today?
Were we selfish?	Were we kind?
Were we dishonest?	Were we loving toward all?
Were we afraid?	What did we pack into life?
Have we kept something to ourselves?	Did we pray and meditate?
Were we thinking of ourselves most of the time?	Did we call someone we could help today?
Were we "disturbed" today?	Did we think of how we could help others?
Do we owe an apology? And if so to whom?	Did we study literature today?
What could we have done better?	Did we go to a meeting today?
Did we blame our feelings on someone else?	Did we call our sponsor today?
Do we need to write 10th Step on something?	Did we do anything that is improved over our past?

Journal—Gratitude List—Tomorrows Action Plan

BALANCE SHEETS

Day _____ Month _____ Year _____

Food

Breakfast		

Money

Item		Amount

Lunch			

Dinner			

Snack			

Exercise			
		Total Spent Today	
Litres Water	Hours Sleep	Quality of Life Today	%

When we retire at night we constructively review our day. We remember we have ceased fighting anything and anyone—love and tolerance of others is our code.

We Draw Up a Balance Sheet

The "Negative Side" (-)	The "Positive Side" (+)
Were we resentful?	Have we stayed clean of our addiction today?
Were we selfish?	Were we kind?
Were we dishonest?	Were we loving toward all?
Were we afraid?	What did we pack into life?
Have we kept something to ourselves?	Did we pray and meditate?
Were we thinking of ourselves most of the time?	Did we call someone we could help today?
Were we "disturbed" today?	Did we think of how we could help others?
Do we owe an apology? And if so to whom?	Did we study literature today?
What could we have done better?	Did we go to a meeting today?
Did we blame our feelings on someone else?	Did we call our sponsor today?
Do we need to write 10th Step on something?	Did we do anything that is improved over our past?

Journal—Gratitude List—Tomorrows Action Plan

STEP 10

BALANCE SHEETS

Day _____ Month _____ Year _____

Food		Money	
Breakfast		Item	Amount
Lunch			
Dinner			
Snack			
Exercise			
		Total Spent Today	
Litres Water	Hours Sleep	Quality of Life Today	%

When we retire at night we constructively review our day. We remember we have ceased fighting anything and anyone—love and tolerance of others is our code.

We Draw Up a Balance Sheet

The "Negative Side" (-)	The "Positive Side" (+)
Were we resentful?	Have we stayed clean of our addiction today?
Were we selfish?	Were we kind?
Were we dishonest?	Were we loving toward all?
Were we afraid?	What did we pack into life?
Have we kept something to ourselves?	Did we pray and meditate?
Were we thinking of ourselves most of the time?	Did we call someone we could help today?
Were we "disturbed" today?	Did we think of how we could help others?
Do we owe an apology? And if so to whom?	Did we study literature today?
What could we have done better?	Did we go to a meeting today?
Did we blame our feelings on someone else?	Did we call our sponsor today?
Do we need to write 10th Step on something?	Did we do anything that is improved over our past?

Journal—Gratitude List—Tomorrows Action Plan

BALANCE SHEETS

Day _____ Month _____ Year _____

Food

Breakfast		
Lunch		
Dinner		
Snack		
Exercise		
Litres Water	Hours Sleep	

Money

Item	Amount
Total Spent Today	
Quality of Life Today	%

When we retire at night we constructively review our day. We remember we have ceased fighting anything and anyone—love and tolerance of others is our code.

We Draw Up a Balance Sheet

The "Negative Side" (-)	The "Positive Side" (+)
Were we resentful?	Have we stayed clean of our addiction today?
Were we selfish?	Were we kind?
Were we dishonest?	Were we loving toward all?
Were we afraid?	What did we pack into life?
Have we kept something to ourselves?	Did we pray and meditate?
Were we thinking of ourselves most of the time?	Did we call someone we could help today?
Were we "disturbed" today?	Did we think of how we could help others?
Do we owe an apology? And if so to whom?	Did we study literature today?
What could we have done better?	Did we go to a meeting today?
Did we blame our feelings on someone else?	Did we call our sponsor today?
Do we need to write 10th Step on something?	Did we do anything that is improved over our past?

Journal—Gratitude List—Tomorrows Action Plan

STEP 10

BALANCE SHEETS

Day _____ Month _____ Year _____

Food		Money	
Breakfast		Item	Amount
Lunch			
Dinner			
Snack			
Exercise			
		Total Spent Today	
Litres Water Hours Sleep		Quality of Life Today	%

When we retire at night we constructively review our day. We remember we have ceased fighting anything and anyone—love and tolerance of others is our code.

We Draw Up a Balance Sheet

The "Negative Side" (-)	The "Positive Side" (+)
Were we resentful?	Have we stayed clean of our addiction today?
Were we selfish?	Were we kind?
Were we dishonest?	Were we loving toward all?
Were we afraid?	What did we pack into life?
Have we kept something to ourselves?	Did we pray and meditate?
Were we thinking of ourselves most of the time?	Did we call someone we could help today?
Were we "disturbed" today?	Did we think of how we could help others?
Do we owe an apology? And if so to whom?	Did we study literature today?
What could we have done better?	Did we go to a meeting today?
Did we blame our feelings on someone else?	Did we call our sponsor today?
Do we need to write 10th Step on something?	Did we do anything that is improved over our past?

Journal—Gratitude List—Tomorrows Action Plan

MAINTAINING THE PROMISES...DAILY

BALANCE SHEETS

Day _____ Month _____ Year_____

Food		Money	
Breakfast		Item	Amount
Lunch			
Dinner			
Snack			
Exercise			
		Total Spent Today	
Litres Water — Hours Sleep		Quality of Life Today	%

When we retire at night we constructively review our day. We remember we have ceased fighting anything and anyone—love and tolerance of others is our code.

We Draw Up a Balance Sheet

The "Negative Side" (−)	The "Positive Side" (+)
Were we resentful?	Have we stayed clean of our addiction today?
Were we selfish?	Were we kind?
Were we dishonest?	Were we loving toward all?
Were we afraid?	What did we pack into life?
Have we kept something to ourselves?	Did we pray and meditate?
Were we thinking of ourselves most of the time?	Did we call someone we could help today?
Were we "disturbed" today?	Did we think of how we could help others?
Do we owe an apology? And if so to whom?	Did we study literature today?
What could we have done better?	Did we go to a meeting today?
Did we blame our feelings on someone else?	Did we call our sponsor today?
Do we need to write 10th Step on something?	Did we do anything that is improved over our past?

Journal—Gratitude List—Tomorrows Action Plan

STEP 10

BALANCE SHEETS

Day _____ Month _____ Year _____

Food		Money	
Breakfast		Item	Amount
Lunch			
Dinner			
Snack			
Exercise			
		Total Spent Today	
Litres Water Hours Sleep		Quality of Life Today	%

When we retire at night we constructively review our day. We remember we have ceased fighting anything and anyone—love and tolerance of others is our code.

We Draw Up a Balance Sheet

The "Negative Side" (-)	The "Positive Side" (+)
Were we resentful?	Have we stayed clean of our addiction today?
Were we selfish?	Were we kind?
Were we dishonest?	Were we loving toward all?
Were we afraid?	What did we pack into life?
Have we kept something to ourselves?	Did we pray and meditate?
Were we thinking of ourselves most of the time?	Did we call someone we could help today?
Were we "disturbed" today?	Did we think of how we could help others?
Do we owe an apology? And if so to whom?	Did we study literature today?
What could we have done better?	Did we go to a meeting today?
Did we blame our feelings on someone else?	Did we call our sponsor today?
Do we need to write 10th Step on something?	Did we do anything that is improved over our past?

Journal—Gratitude List—Tomorrows Action Plan

BALANCE SHEETS

Day _____ Month _____ Year _____

Food		Money	
Breakfast		Item	Amount
Lunch			
Dinner			
Snack			
Exercise			
		Total Spent Today	
Litres Water Hours Sleep		Quality of Life Today	%

When we retire at night we constructively review our day. We remember we have ceased fighting anything and anyone—love and tolerance of others is our code.

We Draw Up a Balance Sheet

The "Negative Side" (-)	The "Positive Side" (+)
Were we resentful?	Have we stayed clean of our addiction today?
Were we selfish?	Were we kind?
Were we dishonest?	Were we loving toward all?
Were we afraid?	What did we pack into life?
Have we kept something to ourselves?	Did we pray and meditate?
Were we thinking of ourselves most of the time?	Did we call someone we could help today?
Were we "disturbed" today?	Did we think of how we could help others?
Do we owe an apology? And if so to whom?	Did we study literature today?
What could we have done better?	Did we go to a meeting today?
Did we blame our feelings on someone else?	Did we call our sponsor today?
Do we need to write 10th Step on something?	Did we do anything that is improved over our past?

Journal—Gratitude List—Tomorrows Action Plan

STEP 10

BALANCE SHEETS

Day _____ Month _____ Year _____

Food		Money	
Breakfast		Item	Amount
Lunch			
Dinner			
Snack			
Exercise			
		Total Spent Today	
Litres Water	Hours Sleep	Quality of Life Today	%

When we retire at night we constructively review our day. We remember we have ceased fighting anything and anyone—love and tolerance of others is our code.

We Draw Up a Balance Sheet

The "Negative Side" (-)	The "Positive Side" (+)
Were we resentful?	Have we stayed clean of our addiction today?
Were we selfish?	Were we kind?
Were we dishonest?	Were we loving toward all?
Were we afraid?	What did we pack into life?
Have we kept something to ourselves?	Did we pray and meditate?
Were we thinking of ourselves most of the time?	Did we call someone we could help today?
Were we "disturbed" today?	Did we think of how we could help others?
Do we owe an apology? And if so to whom?	Did we study literature today?
What could we have done better?	Did we go to a meeting today?
Did we blame our feelings on someone else?	Did we call our sponsor today?
Do we need to write 10th Step on something?	Did we do anything that is improved over our past?

Journal—Gratitude List—Tomorrows Action Plan

BALANCE SHEETS

Day _____ Month _____ Year_____

Food		Money	
Breakfast		Item	Amount
Lunch			
Dinner			
Snack			
Exercise			
		Total Spent Today	
Litres Water Hours Sleep		Quality of Life Today	%

When we retire at night we constructively review our day. We remember we have ceased fighting anything and anyone—love and tolerance of others is our code.

We Draw Up a Balance Sheet

The "Negative Side" (-)	The "Positive Side" (+)
Were we resentful?	Have we stayed clean of our addiction today?
Were we selfish?	Were we kind?
Were we dishonest?	Were we loving toward all?
Were we afraid?	What did we pack into life?
Have we kept something to ourselves?	Did we pray and meditate?
Were we thinking of ourselves most of the time?	Did we call someone we could help today?
Were we "disturbed" today?	Did we think of how we could help others?
Do we owe an apology? And if so to whom?	Did we study literature today?
What could we have done better?	Did we go to a meeting today?
Did we blame our feelings on someone else?	Did we call our sponsor today?
Do we need to write 10th Step on something?	Did we do anything that is improved over our past?

Journal—Gratitude List—Tomorrows Action Plan

STEP 10

BALANCE SHEETS

Day _____ Month _____ Year _____

Food

Breakfast		Money	
		Item	Amount
Lunch			
Dinner			
Snack			
Exercise			
		Total Spent Today	
Litres Water	Hours Sleep	Quality of Life Today	%

When we retire at night we constructively review our day. We remember we have ceased fighting anything and anyone—love and tolerance of others is our code.

We Draw Up a Balance Sheet

The "Negative Side" (-)	The "Positive Side" (+)
Were we resentful?	Have we stayed clean of our addiction today?
Were we selfish?	Were we kind?
Were we dishonest?	Were we loving toward all?
Were we afraid?	What did we pack into life?
Have we kept something to ourselves?	Did we pray and meditate?
Were we thinking of ourselves most of the time?	Did we call someone we could help today?
Were we "disturbed" today?	Did we think of how we could help others?
Do we owe an apology? And if so to whom?	Did we study literature today?
What could we have done better?	Did we go to a meeting today?
Did we blame our feelings on someone else?	Did we call our sponsor today?
Do we need to write 10th Step on something?	Did we do anything that is improved over our past?

Journal—Gratitude List—Tomorrows Action Plan

BALANCE SHEETS

Day _____ Month _____ Year _____

Food		Money	
Breakfast		Item	Amount
Lunch			
Dinner			
Snack			
Exercise			
		Total Spent Today	
Litres Water ___ Hours Sleep ___		Quality of Life Today	%

When we retire at night we constructively review our day. We remember we have ceased fighting anything and anyone—love and tolerance of others is our code.

We Draw Up a Balance Sheet

The "Negative Side" (-)	The "Positive Side" (+)
Were we resentful?	Have we stayed clean of our addiction today?
Were we selfish?	Were we kind?
Were we dishonest?	Were we loving toward all?
Were we afraid?	What did we pack into life?
Have we kept something to ourselves?	Did we pray and meditate?
Were we thinking of ourselves most of the time?	Did we call someone we could help today?
Were we "disturbed" today?	Did we think of how we could help others?
Do we owe an apology? And if so to whom?	Did we study literature today?
What could we have done better?	Did we go to a meeting today?
Did we blame our feelings on someone else?	Did we call our sponsor today?
Do we need to write 10th Step on something?	Did we do anything that is improved over our past?

Journal—Gratitude List—Tomorrows Action Plan

STEP 10

BALANCE SHEETS

Day _____ Month _____ Year _____

Food		Money	
Breakfast		Item	Amount
Lunch			
Dinner			
Snack			
Exercise			
		Total Spent Today	
Litres Water Hours Sleep		Quality of Life Today	%

When we retire at night we constructively review our day. We remember we have ceased fighting anything and anyone—love and tolerance of others is our code.

We Draw Up a Balance Sheet

The "Negative Side" (-)	The "Positive Side" (+)
Were we resentful?	Have we stayed clean of our addiction today?
Were we selfish?	Were we kind?
Were we dishonest?	Were we loving toward all?
Were we afraid?	What did we pack into life?
Have we kept something to ourselves?	Did we pray and meditate?
Were we thinking of ourselves most of the time?	Did we call someone we could help today?
Were we "disturbed" today?	Did we think of how we could help others?
Do we owe an apology? And if so to whom?	Did we study literature today?
What could we have done better?	Did we go to a meeting today?
Did we blame our feelings on someone else?	Did we call our sponsor today?
Do we need to write 10th Step on something?	Did we do anything that is improved over our past?

Journal—Gratitude List—Tomorrows Action Plan

BALANCE SHEETS

Day _____ Month _____ Year _____

Food		Money	
Breakfast		Item	Amount
Lunch			
Dinner			
Snack			
Exercise			
		Total Spent Today	
Litres Water	Hours Sleep	Quality of Life Today	%

When we retire at night we constructively review our day. We remember we have ceased fighting anything and anyone—love and tolerance of others is our code.

We Draw Up a Balance Sheet

The "Negative Side" (-)	The "Positive Side" (+)
Were we resentful?	Have we stayed clean of our addiction today?
Were we selfish?	Were we kind?
Were we dishonest?	Were we loving toward all?
Were we afraid?	What did we pack into life?
Have we kept something to ourselves?	Did we pray and meditate?
Were we thinking of ourselves most of the time?	Did we call someone we could help today?
Were we "disturbed" today?	Did we think of how we could help others?
Do we owe an apology? And if so to whom?	Did we study literature today?
What could we have done better?	Did we go to a meeting today?
Did we blame our feelings on someone else?	Did we call our sponsor today?
Do we need to write 10th Step on something?	Did we do anything that is improved over our past?

Journal—Gratitude List—Tomorrows Action Plan

STEP 10

BALANCE SHEETS

Day _____ Month _____ Year _____

Food		Money	
Breakfast		Item	Amount
Lunch			
Dinner			
Snack			
Exercise			
		Total Spent Today	
Litres Water	Hours Sleep	Quality of Life Today	%

When we retire at night we constructively review our day. We remember we have ceased fighting anything and anyone—love and tolerance of others is our code.

We Draw Up a Balance Sheet

The "Negative Side" (-)	The "Positive Side" (+)
Were we resentful?	Have we stayed clean of our addiction today?
Were we selfish?	Were we kind?
Were we dishonest?	Were we loving toward all?
Were we afraid?	What did we pack into life?
Have we kept something to ourselves?	Did we pray and meditate?
Were we thinking of ourselves most of the time?	Did we call someone we could help today?
Were we "disturbed" today?	Did we think of how we could help others?
Do we owe an apology? And if so to whom?	Did we study literature today?
What could we have done better?	Did we go to a meeting today?
Did we blame our feelings on someone else?	Did we call our sponsor today?
Do we need to write 10th Step on something?	Did we do anything that is improved over our past?

Journal—Gratitude List—Tomorrows Action Plan

BALANCE SHEETS

Day _____ Month _____ Year _____

Food		Money	
Breakfast		Item	Amount
Lunch			
Dinner			
Snack			
Exercise			
		Total Spent Today	
Litres Water	Hours Sleep	Quality of Life Today	%

When we retire at night we constructively review our day. We remember we have ceased fighting anything and anyone—love and tolerance of others is our code.

We Draw Up a Balance Sheet

The "Negative Side" (-)	The "Positive Side" (+)
Were we resentful?	Have we stayed clean of our addiction today?
Were we selfish?	Were we kind?
Were we dishonest?	Were we loving toward all?
Were we afraid?	What did we pack into life?
Have we kept something to ourselves?	Did we pray and meditate?
Were we thinking of ourselves most of the time?	Did we call someone we could help today?
Were we "disturbed" today?	Did we think of how we could help others?
Do we owe an apology? And if so to whom?	Did we study literature today?
What could we have done better?	Did we go to a meeting today?
Did we blame our feelings on someone else?	Did we call our sponsor today?
Do we need to write 10th Step on something?	Did we do anything that is improved over our past?

Journal—Gratitude List—Tomorrows Action Plan

STEP 10

BALANCE SHEETS

Day _____ Month _____ Year _____

Food		Money	
Breakfast		Item	Amount
Lunch			
Dinner			
Snack			
Exercise			
		Total Spent Today	
Litres Water _____ Hours Sleep _____		Quality of Life Today	%

When we retire at night we constructively review our day. We remember we have ceased fighting anything and anyone—love and tolerance of others is our code.

We Draw Up a Balance Sheet

The "Negative Side" (-)	The "Positive Side" (+)
Were we resentful?	Have we stayed clean of our addiction today?
Were we selfish?	Were we kind?
Were we dishonest?	Were we loving toward all?
Were we afraid?	What did we pack into life?
Have we kept something to ourselves?	Did we pray and meditate?
Were we thinking of ourselves most of the time?	Did we call someone we could help today?
Were we "disturbed" today?	Did we think of how we could help others?
Do we owe an apology? And if so to whom?	Did we study literature today?
What could we have done better?	Did we go to a meeting today?
Did we blame our feelings on someone else?	Did we call our sponsor today?
Do we need to write 10th Step on something?	Did we do anything that is improved over our past?

Journal—Gratitude List—Tomorrows Action Plan

_____
_____
_____
_____
_____
_____

BALANCE SHEETS

Day _____ Month _____ Year _____

Food		Money	
Breakfast		Item	Amount
Lunch			
Dinner			
Snack			
Exercise			
		Total Spent Today	
Litres Water _____ Hours Sleep _____		Quality of Life Today	%

When we retire at night we constructively review our day. We remember we have ceased fighting anything and anyone—love and tolerance of others is our code.

We Draw Up a Balance Sheet

The "Negative Side" (-)	The "Positive Side" (+)
Were we resentful?	Have we stayed clean of our addiction today?
Were we selfish?	Were we kind?
Were we dishonest?	Were we loving toward all?
Were we afraid?	What did we pack into life?
Have we kept something to ourselves?	Did we pray and meditate?
Were we thinking of ourselves most of the time?	Did we call someone we could help today?
Were we "disturbed" today?	Did we think of how we could help others?
Do we owe an apology? And if so to whom?	Did we study literature today?
What could we have done better?	Did we go to a meeting today?
Did we blame our feelings on someone else?	Did we call our sponsor today?
Do we need to write 10th Step on something?	Did we do anything that is improved over our past?

Journal—Gratitude List—Tomorrows Action Plan

STEP 10

BALANCE SHEETS

Day _____ Month _____ Year _____

Food		Money	
Breakfast		Item	Amount
Lunch			
Dinner			
Snack			
Exercise			
		Total Spent Today	
Litres Water _____ Hours Sleep _____		Quality of Life Today	%

When we retire at night we constructively review our day. We remember we have ceased fighting anything and anyone—love and tolerance of others is our code.

We Draw Up a Balance Sheet

The "Negative Side" (-)	The "Positive Side" (+)
Were we resentful?	Have we stayed clean of our addiction today?
Were we selfish?	Were we kind?
Were we dishonest?	Were we loving toward all?
Were we afraid?	What did we pack into life?
Have we kept something to ourselves?	Did we pray and meditate?
Were we thinking of ourselves most of the time?	Did we call someone we could help today?
Were we "disturbed" today?	Did we think of how we could help others?
Do we owe an apology? And if so to whom?	Did we study literature today?
What could we have done better?	Did we go to a meeting today?
Did we blame our feelings on someone else?	Did we call our sponsor today?
Do we need to write 10th Step on something?	Did we do anything that is improved over our past?

Journal—Gratitude List—Tomorrows Action Plan

BALANCE SHEETS

Day _____ Month _____ Year _____

Food		Money	
Breakfast		Item	Amount
Lunch			
Dinner			
Snack			
Exercise			
		Total Spent Today	
Litres Water Hours Sleep		Quality of Life Today	%

When we retire at night we constructively review our day. We remember we have ceased fighting anything and anyone—love and tolerance of others is our code.

We Draw Up a Balance Sheet

The "Negative Side" (-)	The "Positive Side" (+)
Were we resentful?	Have we stayed clean of our addiction today?
Were we selfish?	Were we kind?
Were we dishonest?	Were we loving toward all?
Were we afraid?	What did we pack into life?
Have we kept something to ourselves?	Did we pray and meditate?
Were we thinking of ourselves most of the time?	Did we call someone we could help today?
Were we "disturbed" today?	Did we think of how we could help others?
Do we owe an apology? And if so to whom?	Did we study literature today?
What could we have done better?	Did we go to a meeting today?
Did we blame our feelings on someone else?	Did we call our sponsor today?
Do we need to write 10th Step on something?	Did we do anything that is improved over our past?

Journal—Gratitude List—Tomorrows Action Plan

STEP 10

BALANCE SHEETS

Day _____ Month _____ Year _____

Food		Money	
Breakfast		Item	Amount
Lunch			
Dinner			
Snack			
Exercise			
		Total Spent Today	
Litres Water	Hours Sleep	Quality of Life Today	%

When we retire at night we constructively review our day. We remember we have ceased fighting anything and anyone—love and tolerance of others is our code.

We Draw Up a Balance Sheet

The "Negative Side" (-)	The "Positive Side" (+)
Were we resentful?	Have we stayed clean of our addiction today?
Were we selfish?	Were we kind?
Were we dishonest?	Were we loving toward all?
Were we afraid?	What did we pack into life?
Have we kept something to ourselves?	Did we pray and meditate?
Were we thinking of ourselves most of the time?	Did we call someone we could help today?
Were we "disturbed" today?	Did we think of how we could help others?
Do we owe an apology? And if so to whom?	Did we study literature today?
What could we have done better?	Did we go to a meeting today?
Did we blame our feelings on someone else?	Did we call our sponsor today?
Do we need to write 10th Step on something?	Did we do anything that is improved over our past?

Journal—Gratitude List—Tomorrows Action Plan

BALANCE SHEETS

Day _____ Month _____ Year _____

Food		Money		
Breakfast		Item		Amount
Lunch				
Dinner				
Snack				
Exercise				
		Total Spent Today		
Litres Water	Hours Sleep	Quality of Life Today		%

When we retire at night we constructively review our day. We remember we have ceased fighting anything and anyone—love and tolerance of others is our code.

We Draw Up a Balance Sheet

The "Negative Side" (-)	The "Positive Side" (+)
Were we resentful?	Have we stayed clean of our addiction today?
Were we selfish?	Were we kind?
Were we dishonest?	Were we loving toward all?
Were we afraid?	What did we pack into life?
Have we kept something to ourselves?	Did we pray and meditate?
Were we thinking of ourselves most of the time?	Did we call someone we could help today?
Were we "disturbed" today?	Did we think of how we could help others?
Do we owe an apology? And if so to whom?	Did we study literature today?
What could we have done better?	Did we go to a meeting today?
Did we blame our feelings on someone else?	Did we call our sponsor today?
Do we need to write 10th Step on something?	Did we do anything that is improved over our past?

Journal—Gratitude List—Tomorrows Action Plan

STEP 10

BALANCE SHEETS

Day _____ Month _____ Year _____

Food		Money	
Breakfast		Item	Amount
Lunch			
Dinner			
Snack			
Exercise			
		Total Spent Today	
Litres Water Hours Sleep		Quality of Life Today	%

When we retire at night we constructively review our day. We remember we have ceased fighting anything and anyone—love and tolerance of others is our code.

We Draw Up a Balance Sheet

The "Negative Side" (-)	The "Positive Side" (+)
Were we resentful?	Have we stayed clean of our addiction today?
Were we selfish?	Were we kind?
Were we dishonest?	Were we loving toward all?
Were we afraid?	What did we pack into life?
Have we kept something to ourselves?	Did we pray and meditate?
Were we thinking of ourselves most of the time?	Did we call someone we could help today?
Were we "disturbed" today?	Did we think of how we could help others?
Do we owe an apology? And if so to whom?	Did we study literature today?
What could we have done better?	Did we go to a meeting today?
Did we blame our feelings on someone else?	Did we call our sponsor today?
Do we need to write 10th Step on something?	Did we do anything that is improved over our past?

Journal—Gratitude List—Tomorrows Action Plan

BALANCE SHEETS

Day _____ Month _____ Year _____

Food

Breakfast		
Lunch		
Dinner		
Snack		
Exercise		
Litres Water	Hours Sleep	

Money

Item	Amount
Total Spent Today	
Quality of Life Today	%

When we retire at night we constructively review our day. We remember we have ceased fighting anything and anyone—love and tolerance of others is our code.

We Draw Up a Balance Sheet

The "Negative Side" (-)	The "Positive Side" (+)
Were we resentful?	Have we stayed clean of our addiction today?
Were we selfish?	Were we kind?
Were we dishonest?	Were we loving toward all?
Were we afraid?	What did we pack into life?
Have we kept something to ourselves?	Did we pray and meditate?
Were we thinking of ourselves most of the time?	Did we call someone we could help today?
Were we "disturbed" today?	Did we think of how we could help others?
Do we owe an apology? And if so to whom?	Did we study literature today?
What could we have done better?	Did we go to a meeting today?
Did we blame our feelings on someone else?	Did we call our sponsor today?
Do we need to write 10th Step on something?	Did we do anything that is improved over our past?

Journal—Gratitude List—Tomorrows Action Plan

BALANCE SHEETS

Day _____ Month _____ Year _____

Food

Breakfast		Money	
		Item	Amount
Lunch			
Dinner			
Snack			
Exercise			
		Total Spent Today	
Litres Water	Hours Sleep	Quality of Life Today	%

When we retire at night we constructively review our day. We remember we have ceased fighting anything and anyone—love and tolerance of others is our code.

We Draw Up a Balance Sheet

The "Negative Side" (−)	The "Positive Side" (+)
Were we resentful?	Have we stayed clean of our addiction today?
Were we selfish?	Were we kind?
Were we dishonest?	Were we loving toward all?
Were we afraid?	What did we pack into life?
Have we kept something to ourselves?	Did we pray and meditate?
Were we thinking of ourselves most of the time?	Did we call someone we could help today?
Were we "disturbed" today?	Did we think of how we could help others?
Do we owe an apology? And if so to whom?	Did we study literature today?
What could we have done better?	Did we go to a meeting today?
Did we blame our feelings on someone else?	Did we call our sponsor today?
Do we need to write 10th Step on something?	Did we do anything that is improved over our past?

Journal—Gratitude List—Tomorrows Action Plan

MAINTAINING THE PROMISES...DAILY

BALANCE SHEETS

Day _____ Month _____ Year_____

Food		Money	
Breakfast		Item	Amount
Lunch			
Dinner			
Snack			
Exercise			
		Total Spent Today	
Litres Water Hours Sleep		Quality of Life Today	%

When we retire at night we constructively review our day. We remember we have ceased fighting anything and anyone—love and tolerance of others is our code.

We Draw Up a Balance Sheet

The "Negative Side" (-)	The "Positive Side" (+)
Were we resentful?	Have we stayed clean of our addiction today?
Were we selfish?	Were we kind?
Were we dishonest?	Were we loving toward all?
Were we afraid?	What did we pack into life?
Have we kept something to ourselves?	Did we pray and meditate?
Were we thinking of ourselves most of the time?	Did we call someone we could help today?
Were we "disturbed" today?	Did we think of how we could help others?
Do we owe an apology? And if so to whom?	Did we study literature today?
What could we have done better?	Did we go to a meeting today?
Did we blame our feelings on someone else?	Did we call our sponsor today?
Do we need to write 10th Step on something?	Did we do anything that is improved over our past?

Journal—Gratitude List—Tomorrows Action Plan

STEP 10

BALANCE SHEETS

Day _____ Month _____ Year _____

Food		Money	
Breakfast		Item	Amount
Lunch			
Dinner			
Snack			
Exercise			
		Total Spent Today	
Litres Water	Hours Sleep	Quality of Life Today	%

When we retire at night we constructively review our day. We remember we have ceased fighting anything and anyone—love and tolerance of others is our code.

We Draw Up a Balance Sheet

The "Negative Side" (−)	The "Positive Side" (+)
Were we resentful?	Have we stayed clean of our addiction today?
Were we selfish?	Were we kind?
Were we dishonest?	Were we loving toward all?
Were we afraid?	What did we pack into life?
Have we kept something to ourselves?	Did we pray and meditate?
Were we thinking of ourselves most of the time?	Did we call someone we could help today?
Were we "disturbed" today?	Did we think of how we could help others?
Do we owe an apology? And if so to whom?	Did we study literature today?
What could we have done better?	Did we go to a meeting today?
Did we blame our feelings on someone else?	Did we call our sponsor today?
Do we need to write 10th Step on something?	Did we do anything that is improved over our past?

Journal—Gratitude List—Tomorrows Action Plan

BALANCE SHEETS

Day _____ Month _____ Year_____

Food		Money	
Breakfast		Item	Amount
Lunch			
Dinner			
Snack			
Exercise			
		Total Spent Today	
Litres Water	Hours Sleep	Quality of Life Today	%

When we retire at night we constructively review our day. We remember we have ceased fighting anything and anyone—love and tolerance of others is our code.

We Draw Up a Balance Sheet

The "Negative Side" (-)	The "Positive Side" (+)
Were we resentful?	Have we stayed clean of our addiction today?
Were we selfish?	Were we kind?
Were we dishonest?	Were we loving toward all?
Were we afraid?	What did we pack into life?
Have we kept something to ourselves?	Did we pray and meditate?
Were we thinking of ourselves most of the time?	Did we call someone we could help today?
Were we "disturbed" today?	Did we think of how we could help others?
Do we owe an apology? And if so to whom?	Did we study literature today?
What could we have done better?	Did we go to a meeting today?
Did we blame our feelings on someone else?	Did we call our sponsor today?
Do we need to write 10th Step on something?	Did we do anything that is improved over our past?

Journal—Gratitude List—Tomorrows Action Plan

STEP 10

BALANCE SHEETS

Day _____ Month _____ Year _____

Food		Money	
Breakfast		Item	Amount
Lunch			
Dinner			
Snack			
Exercise			
		Total Spent Today	
Litres Water Hours Sleep		Quality of Life Today	%

When we retire at night we constructively review our day. We remember we have ceased fighting anything and anyone—love and tolerance of others is our code.

We Draw Up a Balance Sheet

The "Negative Side" (-)	The "Positive Side" (+)
Were we resentful?	Have we stayed clean of our addiction today?
Were we selfish?	Were we kind?
Were we dishonest?	Were we loving toward all?
Were we afraid?	What did we pack into life?
Have we kept something to ourselves?	Did we pray and meditate?
Were we thinking of ourselves most of the time?	Did we call someone we could help today?
Were we "disturbed" today?	Did we think of how we could help others?
Do we owe an apology? And if so to whom?	Did we study literature today?
What could we have done better?	Did we go to a meeting today?
Did we blame our feelings on someone else?	Did we call our sponsor today?
Do we need to write 10th Step on something?	Did we do anything that is improved over our past?

Journal—Gratitude List—Tomorrows Action Plan

BALANCE SHEETS

Day _____ Month _____ Year _____

Food		Money	
Breakfast		Item	Amount
Lunch			
Dinner			
Snack			
Exercise			
		Total Spent Today	
Litres Water _____ Hours Sleep _____		Quality of Life Today	%

When we retire at night we constructively review our day. We remember we have ceased fighting anything and anyone—love and tolerance of others is our code.

We Draw Up a Balance Sheet

The "Negative Side" (-)	The "Positive Side" (+)
Were we resentful?	Have we stayed clean of our addiction today?
Were we selfish?	Were we kind?
Were we dishonest?	Were we loving toward all?
Were we afraid?	What did we pack into life?
Have we kept something to ourselves?	Did we pray and meditate?
Were we thinking of ourselves most of the time?	Did we call someone we could help today?
Were we "disturbed" today?	Did we think of how we could help others?
Do we owe an apology? And if so to whom?	Did we study literature today?
What could we have done better?	Did we go to a meeting today?
Did we blame our feelings on someone else?	Did we call our sponsor today?
Do we need to write 10th Step on something?	Did we do anything that is improved over our past?

Journal—Gratitude List—Tomorrows Action Plan

STEP 10

BALANCE SHEETS

Day _____ Month _____ Year _____

Food

Breakfast	
Lunch	
Dinner	
Snack	
Exercise	
Litres Water	Hours Sleep

Money

Item	Amount
Total Spent Today	
Quality of Life Today	%

When we retire at night we constructively review our day. We remember we have ceased fighting anything and anyone—love and tolerance of others is our code.

We Draw Up a Balance Sheet

The "Negative Side" (-)	The "Positive Side" (+)
Were we resentful?	Have we stayed clean of our addiction today?
Were we selfish?	Were we kind?
Were we dishonest?	Were we loving toward all?
Were we afraid?	What did we pack into life?
Have we kept something to ourselves?	Did we pray and meditate?
Were we thinking of ourselves most of the time?	Did we call someone we could help today?
Were we "disturbed" today?	Did we think of how we could help others?
Do we owe an apology? And if so to whom?	Did we study literature today?
What could we have done better?	Did we go to a meeting today?
Did we blame our feelings on someone else?	Did we call our sponsor today?
Do we need to write 10th Step on something?	Did we do anything that is improved over our past?

Journal—Gratitude List—Tomorrows Action Plan

BALANCE SHEETS

Day _____ Month _____ Year _____

Food

Breakfast		Money	
		Item	Amount
Lunch			
Dinner			
Snack			
Exercise			
		Total Spent Today	
Litres Water	Hours Sleep	Quality of Life Today	%

When we retire at night we constructively review our day. We remember we have ceased fighting anything and anyone—love and tolerance of others is our code.

We Draw Up a Balance Sheet

The "Negative Side" (-)	The "Positive Side" (+)
Were we resentful?	Have we stayed clean of our addiction today?
Were we selfish?	Were we kind?
Were we dishonest?	Were we loving toward all?
Were we afraid?	What did we pack into life?
Have we kept something to ourselves?	Did we pray and meditate?
Were we thinking of ourselves most of the time?	Did we call someone we could help today?
Were we "disturbed" today?	Did we think of how we could help others?
Do we owe an apology? And if so to whom?	Did we study literature today?
What could we have done better?	Did we go to a meeting today?
Did we blame our feelings on someone else?	Did we call our sponsor today?
Do we need to write 10th Step on something?	Did we do anything that is improved over our past?

Journal—Gratitude List—Tomorrows Action Plan

STEP 10

BALANCE SHEETS

Day _____ Month _____ Year _____

Food

Breakfast		
Lunch		
Dinner		
Snack		
Exercise		
Litres Water	Hours Sleep	

Money

Item		Amount
Total Spent Today		
Quality of Life Today		%

When we retire at night we constructively review our day. We remember we have ceased fighting anything and anyone—love and tolerance of others is our code.

We Draw Up a Balance Sheet

The "Negative Side" (−)	The "Positive Side" (+)
Were we resentful?	Have we stayed clean of our addiction today?
Were we selfish?	Were we kind?
Were we dishonest?	Were we loving toward all?
Were we afraid?	What did we pack into life?
Have we kept something to ourselves?	Did we pray and meditate?
Were we thinking of ourselves most of the time?	Did we call someone we could help today?
Were we "disturbed" today?	Did we think of how we could help others?
Do we owe an apology? And if so to whom?	Did we study literature today?
What could we have done better?	Did we go to a meeting today?
Did we blame our feelings on someone else?	Did we call our sponsor today?
Do we need to write 10th Step on something?	Did we do anything that is improved over our past?

Journal—Gratitude List—Tomorrows Action Plan

BALANCE SHEETS

Day _____ Month _____ Year _____

Food

Breakfast		
Lunch		
Dinner		
Snack		
Exercise		
Litres Water	Hours Sleep	

Money

Item	Amount
Total Spent Today	
Quality of Life Today	%

When we retire at night we constructively review our day. We remember we have ceased fighting anything and anyone—love and tolerance of others is our code.

We Draw Up a Balance Sheet

The "Negative Side" (-)	The "Positive Side" (+)
Were we resentful?	Have we stayed clean of our addiction today?
Were we selfish?	Were we kind?
Were we dishonest?	Were we loving toward all?
Were we afraid?	What did we pack into life?
Have we kept something to ourselves?	Did we pray and meditate?
Were we thinking of ourselves most of the time?	Did we call someone we could help today?
Were we "disturbed" today?	Did we think of how we could help others?
Do we owe an apology? And if so to whom?	Did we study literature today?
What could we have done better?	Did we go to a meeting today?
Did we blame our feelings on someone else?	Did we call our sponsor today?
Do we need to write 10th Step on something?	Did we do anything that is improved over our past?

Journal—Gratitude List—Tomorrows Action Plan

STEP 10

BALANCE SHEETS

Day _____ Month _____ Year _____

Food		Money	
Breakfast		Item	Amount
Lunch			
Dinner			
Snack			
Exercise			
		Total Spent Today	
Litres Water	Hours Sleep	Quality of Life Today	%

When we retire at night we constructively review our day. We remember we have ceased fighting anything and anyone—love and tolerance of others is our code.

We Draw Up a Balance Sheet

The "Negative Side" (-)	The "Positive Side" (+)
Were we resentful?	Have we stayed clean of our addiction today?
Were we selfish?	Were we kind?
Were we dishonest?	Were we loving toward all?
Were we afraid?	What did we pack into life?
Have we kept something to ourselves?	Did we pray and meditate?
Were we thinking of ourselves most of the time?	Did we call someone we could help today?
Were we "disturbed" today?	Did we think of how we could help others?
Do we owe an apology? And if so to whom?	Did we study literature today?
What could we have done better?	Did we go to a meeting today?
Did we blame our feelings on someone else?	Did we call our sponsor today?
Do we need to write 10th Step on something?	Did we do anything that is improved over our past?

Journal—Gratitude List—Tomorrows Action Plan

MAINTAINING THE PROMISES...DAILY

BALANCE SHEETS

Day _____ Month _____ Year _____

Food		Money	
Breakfast		Item	Amount
Lunch			
Dinner			
Snack			
Exercise			
		Total Spent Today	
Litres Water Hours Sleep		Quality of Life Today	%

When we retire at night we constructively review our day. We remember we have ceased fighting anything and anyone—love and tolerance of others is our code.

We Draw Up a Balance Sheet

The "Negative Side" (-)	The "Positive Side" (+)
Were we resentful?	Have we stayed clean of our addiction today?
Were we selfish?	Were we kind?
Were we dishonest?	Were we loving toward all?
Were we afraid?	What did we pack into life?
Have we kept something to ourselves?	Did we pray and meditate?
Were we thinking of ourselves most of the time?	Did we call someone we could help today?
Were we "disturbed" today?	Did we think of how we could help others?
Do we owe an apology? And if so to whom?	Did we study literature today?
What could we have done better?	Did we go to a meeting today?
Did we blame our feelings on someone else?	Did we call our sponsor today?
Do we need to write 10th Step on something?	Did we do anything that is improved over our past?

Journal—Gratitude List—Tomorrows Action Plan

STEP 10

BALANCE SHEETS

Day _____ Month _____ Year _____

Food		Money	
Breakfast		Item	Amount
Lunch			
Dinner			
Snack			
Exercise			
		Total Spent Today	
Litres Water	Hours Sleep	Quality of Life Today	%

When we retire at night we constructively review our day. We remember we have ceased fighting anything and anyone—love and tolerance of others is our code.

We Draw Up a Balance Sheet

The "Negative Side" (-)	The "Positive Side" (+)
Were we resentful?	Have we stayed clean of our addiction today?
Were we selfish?	Were we kind?
Were we dishonest?	Were we loving toward all?
Were we afraid?	What did we pack into life?
Have we kept something to ourselves?	Did we pray and meditate?
Were we thinking of ourselves most of the time?	Did we call someone we could help today?
Were we "disturbed" today?	Did we think of how we could help others?
Do we owe an apology? And if so to whom?	Did we study literature today?
What could we have done better?	Did we go to a meeting today?
Did we blame our feelings on someone else?	Did we call our sponsor today?
Do we need to write 10th Step on something?	Did we do anything that is improved over our past?

Journal—Gratitude List—Tomorrows Action Plan

BALANCE SHEETS

Day _____ Month _____ Year _____

Food		Money	
Breakfast		Item	Amount
Lunch			
Dinner			
Snack			
Exercise			
		Total Spent Today	
Litres Water	Hours Sleep	Quality of Life Today	%

When we retire at night we constructively review our day. We remember we have ceased fighting anything and anyone—love and tolerance of others is our code.

We Draw Up a Balance Sheet

The "Negative Side" (-)	The "Positive Side" (+)
Were we resentful?	Have we stayed clean of our addiction today?
Were we selfish?	Were we kind?
Were we dishonest?	Were we loving toward all?
Were we afraid?	What did we pack into life?
Have we kept something to ourselves?	Did we pray and meditate?
Were we thinking of ourselves most of the time?	Did we call someone we could help today?
Were we "disturbed" today?	Did we think of how we could help others?
Do we owe an apology? And if so to whom?	Did we study literature today?
What could we have done better?	Did we go to a meeting today?
Did we blame our feelings on someone else?	Did we call our sponsor today?
Do we need to write 10th Step on something?	Did we do anything that is improved over our past?

Journal—Gratitude List—Tomorrows Action Plan

STEP 10

BALANCE SHEETS

Day _____ Month _____ Year _____

Food

Breakfast		
Lunch		
Dinner		
Snack		
Exercise		
Litres Water	Hours Sleep	

Money

Item		Amount
Total Spent Today		
Quality of Life Today		%

When we retire at night we constructively review our day. We remember we have ceased fighting anything and anyone—love and tolerance of others is our code.

We Draw Up a Balance Sheet

The "Negative Side" (-)	The "Positive Side" (+)
Were we resentful?	Have we stayed clean of our addiction today?
Were we selfish?	Were we kind?
Were we dishonest?	Were we loving toward all?
Were we afraid?	What did we pack into life?
Have we kept something to ourselves?	Did we pray and meditate?
Were we thinking of ourselves most of the time?	Did we call someone we could help today?
Were we "disturbed" today?	Did we think of how we could help others?
Do we owe an apology? And if so to whom?	Did we study literature today?
What could we have done better?	Did we go to a meeting today?
Did we blame our feelings on someone else?	Did we call our sponsor today?
Do we need to write 10th Step on something?	Did we do anything that is improved over our past?

Journal—Gratitude List—Tomorrows Action Plan

BALANCE SHEETS

Day _____ Month _____ Year _____

Food		Money	
Breakfast		Item	Amount
Lunch			
Dinner			
Snack			
Exercise			
		Total Spent Today	
Litres Water	Hours Sleep	Quality of Life Today	%

When we retire at night we constructively review our day. We remember we have ceased fighting anything and anyone—love and tolerance of others is our code.

We Draw Up a Balance Sheet

The "Negative Side" (-)	The "Positive Side" (+)
Were we resentful?	Have we stayed clean of our addiction today?
Were we selfish?	Were we kind?
Were we dishonest?	Were we loving toward all?
Were we afraid?	What did we pack into life?
Have we kept something to ourselves?	Did we pray and meditate?
Were we thinking of ourselves most of the time?	Did we call someone we could help today?
Were we "disturbed" today?	Did we think of how we could help others?
Do we owe an apology? And if so to whom?	Did we study literature today?
What could we have done better?	Did we go to a meeting today?
Did we blame our feelings on someone else?	Did we call our sponsor today?
Do we need to write 10th Step on something?	Did we do anything that is improved over our past?

Journal—Gratitude List—Tomorrows Action Plan

STEP 10

BALANCE SHEETS

Day _____ Month _____ Year _____

Food		Money	
Breakfast		Item	Amount
Lunch			
Dinner			
Snack			
Exercise			
		Total Spent Today	
Litres Water Hours Sleep		Quality of Life Today	%

When we retire at night we constructively review our day. We remember we have ceased fighting anything and anyone—love and tolerance of others is our code.

We Draw Up a Balance Sheet

The "Negative Side" (-)	The "Positive Side" (+)
Were we resentful?	Have we stayed clean of our addiction today?
Were we selfish?	Were we kind?
Were we dishonest?	Were we loving toward all?
Were we afraid?	What did we pack into life?
Have we kept something to ourselves?	Did we pray and meditate?
Were we thinking of ourselves most of the time?	Did we call someone we could help today?
Were we "disturbed" today?	Did we think of how we could help others?
Do we owe an apology? And if so to whom?	Did we study literature today?
What could we have done better?	Did we go to a meeting today?
Did we blame our feelings on someone else?	Did we call our sponsor today?
Do we need to write 10th Step on something?	Did we do anything that is improved over our past?

Journal—Gratitude List—Tomorrows Action Plan

MAINTAINING THE PROMISES...DAILY

BALANCE SHEETS

Day _____ Month _____ Year_____

Food		Money	
Breakfast		Item	Amount
Lunch			
Dinner			
Snack			
Exercise			
		Total Spent Today	
Litres Water	Hours Sleep	Quality of Life Today	%

When we retire at night we constructively review our day. We remember we have ceased fighting anything and anyone—love and tolerance of others is our code.

We Draw Up a Balance Sheet

The "Negative Side" (-)	The "Positive Side" (+)
Were we resentful?	Have we stayed clean of our addiction today?
Were we selfish?	Were we kind?
Were we dishonest?	Were we loving toward all?
Were we afraid?	What did we pack into life?
Have we kept something to ourselves?	Did we pray and meditate?
Were we thinking of ourselves most of the time?	Did we call someone we could help today?
Were we "disturbed" today?	Did we think of how we could help others?
Do we owe an apology? And if so to whom?	Did we study literature today?
What could we have done better?	Did we go to a meeting today?
Did we blame our feelings on someone else?	Did we call our sponsor today?
Do we need to write 10th Step on something?	Did we do anything that is improved over our past?

Journal—Gratitude List—Tomorrows Action Plan

STEP 10

BALANCE SHEETS

Day _____ Month _____ Year _____

Food		Money	
Breakfast		Item	Amount
Lunch			
Dinner			
Snack			
Exercise			
		Total Spent Today	
Litres Water	Hours Sleep	Quality of Life Today	%

When we retire at night we constructively review our day. We remember we have ceased fighting anything and anyone—love and tolerance of others is our code.

We Draw Up a Balance Sheet

The "Negative Side" (-)	The "Positive Side" (+)
Were we resentful?	Have we stayed clean of our addiction today?
Were we selfish?	Were we kind?
Were we dishonest?	Were we loving toward all?
Were we afraid?	What did we pack into life?
Have we kept something to ourselves?	Did we pray and meditate?
Were we thinking of ourselves most of the time?	Did we call someone we could help today?
Were we "disturbed" today?	Did we think of how we could help others?
Do we owe an apology? And if so to whom?	Did we study literature today?
What could we have done better?	Did we go to a meeting today?
Did we blame our feelings on someone else?	Did we call our sponsor today?
Do we need to write 10th Step on something?	Did we do anything that is improved over our past?

Journal—Gratitude List—Tomorrows Action Plan

BALANCE SHEETS

Day _____ Month _____ Year _____

Food		Money	
Breakfast		Item	Amount
Lunch			
Dinner			
Snack			
Exercise			
		Total Spent Today	
Litres Water	Hours Sleep	Quality of Life Today	%

When we retire at night we constructively review our day. We remember we have ceased fighting anything and anyone—love and tolerance of others is our code.

We Draw Up a Balance Sheet

The "Negative Side" (-)	The "Positive Side" (+)
Were we resentful?	Have we stayed clean of our addiction today?
Were we selfish?	Were we kind?
Were we dishonest?	Were we loving toward all?
Were we afraid?	What did we pack into life?
Have we kept something to ourselves?	Did we pray and meditate?
Were we thinking of ourselves most of the time?	Did we call someone we could help today?
Were we "disturbed" today?	Did we think of how we could help others?
Do we owe an apology? And if so to whom?	Did we study literature today?
What could we have done better?	Did we go to a meeting today?
Did we blame our feelings on someone else?	Did we call our sponsor today?
Do we need to write 10th Step on something?	Did we do anything that is improved over our past?

Journal—Gratitude List—Tomorrows Action Plan

STEP 10

BALANCE SHEETS

Day _____ Month _____ Year _____

Food		Money	
Breakfast		Item	Amount
Lunch			
Dinner			
Snack			
Exercise			
		Total Spent Today	
Litres Water	Hours Sleep	Quality of Life Today	%

When we retire at night we constructively review our day. We remember we have ceased fighting anything and anyone—love and tolerance of others is our code.

We Draw Up a Balance Sheet

The "Negative Side" (-)	The "Positive Side" (+)
Were we resentful?	Have we stayed clean of our addiction today?
Were we selfish?	Were we kind?
Were we dishonest?	Were we loving toward all?
Were we afraid?	What did we pack into life?
Have we kept something to ourselves?	Did we pray and meditate?
Were we thinking of ourselves most of the time?	Did we call someone we could help today?
Were we "disturbed" today?	Did we think of how we could help others?
Do we owe an apology? And if so to whom?	Did we study literature today?
What could we have done better?	Did we go to a meeting today?
Did we blame our feelings on someone else?	Did we call our sponsor today?
Do we need to write 10th Step on something?	Did we do anything that is improved over our past?

Journal—Gratitude List—Tomorrows Action Plan

BALANCE SHEETS

Day _____ Month _____ Year _____

Food

Breakfast		
Lunch		
Dinner		
Snack		
Exercise		
Litres Water Hours Sleep		

Money

Item	Amount
Total Spent Today	
Quality of Life Today	%

When we retire at night we constructively review our day. We remember we have ceased fighting anything and anyone—love and tolerance of others is our code.

We Draw Up a Balance Sheet

The "Negative Side" (-)	The "Positive Side" (+)
Were we resentful?	Have we stayed clean of our addiction today?
Were we selfish?	Were we kind?
Were we dishonest?	Were we loving toward all?
Were we afraid?	What did we pack into life?
Have we kept something to ourselves?	Did we pray and meditate?
Were we thinking of ourselves most of the time?	Did we call someone we could help today?
Were we "disturbed" today?	Did we think of how we could help others?
Do we owe an apology? And if so to whom?	Did we study literature today?
What could we have done better?	Did we go to a meeting today?
Did we blame our feelings on someone else?	Did we call our sponsor today?
Do we need to write 10th Step on something?	Did we do anything that is improved over our past?

Journal—Gratitude List—Tomorrows Action Plan

STEP 10

BALANCE SHEETS

Day _____ Month _____ Year _____

Food		Money	
Breakfast		Item	Amount
Lunch			
Dinner			
Snack			
Exercise			
		Total Spent Today	
Litres Water	Hours Sleep	Quality of Life Today	%

When we retire at night we constructively review our day. We remember we have ceased fighting anything and anyone—love and tolerance of others is our code.

We Draw Up a Balance Sheet

The "Negative Side" (-)	The "Positive Side" (+)
Were we resentful?	Have we stayed clean of our addiction today?
Were we selfish?	Were we kind?
Were we dishonest?	Were we loving toward all?
Were we afraid?	What did we pack into life?
Have we kept something to ourselves?	Did we pray and meditate?
Were we thinking of ourselves most of the time?	Did we call someone we could help today?
Were we "disturbed" today?	Did we think of how we could help others?
Do we owe an apology? And if so to whom?	Did we study literature today?
What could we have done better?	Did we go to a meeting today?
Did we blame our feelings on someone else?	Did we call our sponsor today?
Do we need to write 10th Step on something?	Did we do anything that is improved over our past?

Journal—Gratitude List—Tomorrows Action Plan

BALANCE SHEETS

Day _____ Month _____ Year _____

Food

Breakfast	
Lunch	
Dinner	
Snack	
Exercise	
Litres Water	Hours Sleep

Money

Item	Amount
Total Spent Today	
Quality of Life Today	%

When we retire at night we constructively review our day. We remember we have ceased fighting anything and anyone—love and tolerance of others is our code.

We Draw Up a Balance Sheet

The "Negative Side" (-)	The "Positive Side" (+)
Were we resentful?	Have we stayed clean of our addiction today?
Were we selfish?	Were we kind?
Were we dishonest?	Were we loving toward all?
Were we afraid?	What did we pack into life?
Have we kept something to ourselves?	Did we pray and meditate?
Were we thinking of ourselves most of the time?	Did we call someone we could help today?
Were we "disturbed" today?	Did we think of how we could help others?
Do we owe an apology? And if so to whom?	Did we study literature today?
What could we have done better?	Did we go to a meeting today?
Did we blame our feelings on someone else?	Did we call our sponsor today?
Do we need to write 10th Step on something?	Did we do anything that is improved over our past?

Journal—Gratitude List—Tomorrows Action Plan

STEP 10

BALANCE SHEETS

Day _____ Month _____ Year _____

Food

Breakfast		Money	
		Item	Amount
Lunch			
Dinner			
Snack			
Exercise			
		Total Spent Today	
Litres Water	Hours Sleep	Quality of Life Today	%

When we retire at night we constructively review our day. We remember we have ceased fighting anything and anyone—love and tolerance of others is our code.

We Draw Up a Balance Sheet

The "Negative Side" (−)	The "Positive Side" (+)
Were we resentful?	Have we stayed clean of our addiction today?
Were we selfish?	Were we kind?
Were we dishonest?	Were we loving toward all?
Were we afraid?	What did we pack into life?
Have we kept something to ourselves?	Did we pray and meditate?
Were we thinking of ourselves most of the time?	Did we call someone we could help today?
Were we "disturbed" today?	Did we think of how we could help others?
Do we owe an apology? And if so to whom?	Did we study literature today?
What could we have done better?	Did we go to a meeting today?
Did we blame our feelings on someone else?	Did we call our sponsor today?
Do we need to write 10th Step on something?	Did we do anything that is improved over our past?

Journal—Gratitude List—Tomorrows Action Plan

BALANCE SHEETS

Day _____ Month _____ Year _____

Food		Money	
Breakfast		Item	Amount
Lunch			
Dinner			
Snack			
Exercise			
		Total Spent Today	
Litres Water Hours Sleep		Quality of Life Today	%

When we retire at night we constructively review our day. We remember we have ceased fighting anything and anyone—love and tolerance of others is our code.

We Draw Up a Balance Sheet

The "Negative Side" (-)	The "Positive Side" (+)
Were we resentful?	Have we stayed clean of our addiction today?
Were we selfish?	Were we kind?
Were we dishonest?	Were we loving toward all?
Were we afraid?	What did we pack into life?
Have we kept something to ourselves?	Did we pray and meditate?
Were we thinking of ourselves most of the time?	Did we call someone we could help today?
Were we "disturbed" today?	Did we think of how we could help others?
Do we owe an apology? And if so to whom?	Did we study literature today?
What could we have done better?	Did we go to a meeting today?
Did we blame our feelings on someone else?	Did we call our sponsor today?
Do we need to write 10th Step on something?	Did we do anything that is improved over our past?

Journal—Gratitude List—Tomorrows Action Plan

STEP 10

BALANCE SHEETS

Day _____ Month _____ Year _____

Food		Money	
Breakfast		Item	Amount
Lunch			
Dinner			
Snack			
Exercise			
		Total Spent Today	
Litres Water	Hours Sleep	Quality of Life Today	%

When we retire at night we constructively review our day. We remember we have ceased fighting anything and anyone—love and tolerance of others is our code.

We Draw Up a Balance Sheet

The "Negative Side" (-)	The "Positive Side" (+)
Were we resentful?	Have we stayed clean of our addiction today?
Were we selfish?	Were we kind?
Were we dishonest?	Were we loving toward all?
Were we afraid?	What did we pack into life?
Have we kept something to ourselves?	Did we pray and meditate?
Were we thinking of ourselves most of the time?	Did we call someone we could help today?
Were we "disturbed" today?	Did we think of how we could help others?
Do we owe an apology? And if so to whom?	Did we study literature today?
What could we have done better?	Did we go to a meeting today?
Did we blame our feelings on someone else?	Did we call our sponsor today?
Do we need to write 10th Step on something?	Did we do anything that is improved over our past?

Journal—Gratitude List—Tomorrows Action Plan

BALANCE SHEETS

Day _____ Month _____ Year _____

Food

Breakfast		
Lunch		
Dinner		
Snack		
Exercise		
Litres Water	Hours Sleep	

Money

Item	Amount
Total Spent Today	
Quality of Life Today	%

When we retire at night we constructively review our day. We remember we have ceased fighting anything and anyone—love and tolerance of others is our code.

We Draw Up a Balance Sheet

The "Negative Side" (-)	The "Positive Side" (+)
Were we resentful?	Have we stayed clean of our addiction today?
Were we selfish?	Were we kind?
Were we dishonest?	Were we loving toward all?
Were we afraid?	What did we pack into life?
Have we kept something to ourselves?	Did we pray and meditate?
Were we thinking of ourselves most of the time?	Did we call someone we could help today?
Were we "disturbed" today?	Did we think of how we could help others?
Do we owe an apology? And if so to whom?	Did we study literature today?
What could we have done better?	Did we go to a meeting today?
Did we blame our feelings on someone else?	Did we call our sponsor today?
Do we need to write 10th Step on something?	Did we do anything that is improved over our past?

Journal—Gratitude List—Tomorrows Action Plan

STEP 10

BALANCE SHEETS

Day _____ Month _____ Year _____

Food		Money	
Breakfast		Item	Amount
Lunch			
Dinner			
Snack			
Exercise			
		Total Spent Today	
Litres Water	Hours Sleep	Quality of Life Today	%

When we retire at night we constructively review our day. We remember we have ceased fighting anything and anyone—love and tolerance of others is our code.

We Draw Up a Balance Sheet

The "Negative Side" (-)	The "Positive Side" (+)
Were we resentful?	Have we stayed clean of our addiction today?
Were we selfish?	Were we kind?
Were we dishonest?	Were we loving toward all?
Were we afraid?	What did we pack into life?
Have we kept something to ourselves?	Did we pray and meditate?
Were we thinking of ourselves most of the time?	Did we call someone we could help today?
Were we "disturbed" today?	Did we think of how we could help others?
Do we owe an apology? And if so to whom?	Did we study literature today?
What could we have done better?	Did we go to a meeting today?
Did we blame our feelings on someone else?	Did we call our sponsor today?
Do we need to write 10th Step on something?	Did we do anything that is improved over our past?

Journal—Gratitude List—Tomorrows Action Plan

BALANCE SHEETS

Day _____ Month _____ Year _____

Food

Breakfast	
Lunch	
Dinner	
Snack	
Exercise	
Litres Water _____ Hours Sleep _____	

Money

Item	Amount
Total Spent Today	
Quality of Life Today	%

When we retire at night we constructively review our day. We remember we have ceased fighting anything and anyone—love and tolerance of others is our code.

We Draw Up a Balance Sheet

The "Negative Side" (-)	The "Positive Side" (+)
Were we resentful?	Have we stayed clean of our addiction today?
Were we selfish?	Were we kind?
Were we dishonest?	Were we loving toward all?
Were we afraid?	What did we pack into life?
Have we kept something to ourselves?	Did we pray and meditate?
Were we thinking of ourselves most of the time?	Did we call someone we could help today?
Were we "disturbed" today?	Did we think of how we could help others?
Do we owe an apology? And if so to whom?	Did we study literature today?
What could we have done better?	Did we go to a meeting today?
Did we blame our feelings on someone else?	Did we call our sponsor today?
Do we need to write 10th Step on something?	Did we do anything that is improved over our past?

Journal—Gratitude List—Tomorrows Action Plan

STEP 10

BALANCE SHEETS

Day _____ Month _____ Year _____

Food		Money	
Breakfast		Item	Amount
Lunch			
Dinner			
Snack			
Exercise			
		Total Spent Today	
Litres Water	Hours Sleep	Quality of Life Today	%

When we retire at night we constructively review our day. We remember we have ceased fighting anything and anyone—love and tolerance of others is our code.

We Draw Up a Balance Sheet

The "Negative Side" (-)	The "Positive Side" (+)
Were we resentful?	Have we stayed clean of our addiction today?
Were we selfish?	Were we kind?
Were we dishonest?	Were we loving toward all?
Were we afraid?	What did we pack into life?
Have we kept something to ourselves?	Did we pray and meditate?
Were we thinking of ourselves most of the time?	Did we call someone we could help today?
Were we "disturbed" today?	Did we think of how we could help others?
Do we owe an apology? And if so to whom?	Did we study literature today?
What could we have done better?	Did we go to a meeting today?
Did we blame our feelings on someone else?	Did we call our sponsor today?
Do we need to write 10th Step on something?	Did we do anything that is improved over our past?

Journal—Gratitude List—Tomorrows Action Plan

BALANCE SHEETS

Day _____ Month _____ Year _____

Food		Money	
Breakfast		Item	Amount
Lunch			
Dinner			
Snack			
Exercise			
		Total Spent Today	
Litres Water Hours Sleep		Quality of Life Today	%

When we retire at night we constructively review our day. We remember we have ceased fighting anything and anyone—love and tolerance of others is our code.

We Draw Up a Balance Sheet

The "Negative Side" (-)	The "Positive Side" (+)
Were we resentful?	Have we stayed clean of our addiction today?
Were we selfish?	Were we kind?
Were we dishonest?	Were we loving toward all?
Were we afraid?	What did we pack into life?
Have we kept something to ourselves?	Did we pray and meditate?
Were we thinking of ourselves most of the time?	Did we call someone we could help today?
Were we "disturbed" today?	Did we think of how we could help others?
Do we owe an apology? And if so to whom?	Did we study literature today?
What could we have done better?	Did we go to a meeting today?
Did we blame our feelings on someone else?	Did we call our sponsor today?
Do we need to write 10th Step on something?	Did we do anything that is improved over our past?

Journal—Gratitude List—Tomorrows Action Plan

STEP 10

BALANCE SHEETS

Day _____ Month _____ Year _____

Food		Money	
Breakfast		Item	Amount
Lunch			
Dinner			
Snack			
Exercise			
		Total Spent Today	
Litres Water	Hours Sleep	Quality of Life Today	%

When we retire at night we constructively review our day. We remember we have ceased fighting anything and anyone—love and tolerance of others is our code.

We Draw Up a Balance Sheet

The "Negative Side" (-)	The "Positive Side" (+)
Were we resentful?	Have we stayed clean of our addiction today?
Were we selfish?	Were we kind?
Were we dishonest?	Were we loving toward all?
Were we afraid?	What did we pack into life?
Have we kept something to ourselves?	Did we pray and meditate?
Were we thinking of ourselves most of the time?	Did we call someone we could help today?
Were we "disturbed" today?	Did we think of how we could help others?
Do we owe an apology? And if so to whom?	Did we study literature today?
What could we have done better?	Did we go to a meeting today?
Did we blame our feelings on someone else?	Did we call our sponsor today?
Do we need to write 10th Step on something?	Did we do anything that is improved over our past?

Journal—Gratitude List—Tomorrows Action Plan

BALANCE SHEETS

Day _____ Month _____ Year _____

Food		Money	
Breakfast		Item	Amount
Lunch			
Dinner			
Snack			
Exercise			
		Total Spent Today	
Litres Water	Hours Sleep	Quality of Life Today	%

When we retire at night we constructively review our day. We remember we have ceased fighting anything and anyone—love and tolerance of others is our code.

We Draw Up a Balance Sheet

The "Negative Side" (-)	The "Positive Side" (+)
Were we resentful?	Have we stayed clean of our addiction today?
Were we selfish?	Were we kind?
Were we dishonest?	Were we loving toward all?
Were we afraid?	What did we pack into life?
Have we kept something to ourselves?	Did we pray and meditate?
Were we thinking of ourselves most of the time?	Did we call someone we could help today?
Were we "disturbed" today?	Did we think of how we could help others?
Do we owe an apology? And if so to whom?	Did we study literature today?
What could we have done better?	Did we go to a meeting today?
Did we blame our feelings on someone else?	Did we call our sponsor today?
Do we need to write 10th Step on something?	Did we do anything that is improved over our past?

Journal—Gratitude List—Tomorrows Action Plan

STEP 10

BALANCE SHEETS

Day _____ Month _____ Year _____

Food		Money	
Breakfast		Item	Amount
Lunch			
Dinner			
Snack			
Exercise			
		Total Spent Today	
Litres Water _____ Hours Sleep _____		Quality of Life Today	%

When we retire at night we constructively review our day. We remember we have ceased fighting anything and anyone—love and tolerance of others is our code.

We Draw Up a Balance Sheet

The "Negative Side" (−)	The "Positive Side" (+)
Were we resentful?	Have we stayed clean of our addiction today?
Were we selfish?	Were we kind?
Were we dishonest?	Were we loving toward all?
Were we afraid?	What did we pack into life?
Have we kept something to ourselves?	Did we pray and meditate?
Were we thinking of ourselves most of the time?	Did we call someone we could help today?
Were we "disturbed" today?	Did we think of how we could help others?
Do we owe an apology? And if so to whom?	Did we study literature today?
What could we have done better?	Did we go to a meeting today?
Did we blame our feelings on someone else?	Did we call our sponsor today?
Do we need to write 10th Step on something?	Did we do anything that is improved over our past?

Journal—Gratitude List—Tomorrows Action Plan

MAINTAINING THE PROMISES...DAILY

BALANCE SHEETS

Day _____ Month _____ Year _____

Food

Breakfast		Money	
		Item	Amount
Lunch			
Dinner			
Snack			
Exercise			
		Total Spent Today	
Litres Water	Hours Sleep	Quality of Life Today	%

When we retire at night we constructively review our day. We remember we have ceased fighting anything and anyone—love and tolerance of others is our code.

We Draw Up a Balance Sheet

The "Negative Side" (-)	The "Positive Side" (+)
Were we resentful?	Have we stayed clean of our addiction today?
Were we selfish?	Were we kind?
Were we dishonest?	Were we loving toward all?
Were we afraid?	What did we pack into life?
Have we kept something to ourselves?	Did we pray and meditate?
Were we thinking of ourselves most of the time?	Did we call someone we could help today?
Were we "disturbed" today?	Did we think of how we could help others?
Do we owe an apology? And if so to whom?	Did we study literature today?
What could we have done better?	Did we go to a meeting today?
Did we blame our feelings on someone else?	Did we call our sponsor today?
Do we need to write 10th Step on something?	Did we do anything that is improved over our past?

Journal—Gratitude List—Tomorrows Action Plan

STEP 10

BALANCE SHEETS

Day _____ Month _____ Year _____

Food

Breakfast		Money	
		Item	Amount
Lunch			
Dinner			
Snack			
Exercise			
		Total Spent Today	
Litres Water	Hours Sleep	Quality of Life Today	%

When we retire at night we constructively review our day. We remember we have ceased fighting anything and anyone—love and tolerance of others is our code.

We Draw Up a Balance Sheet

The "Negative Side" (-)	The "Positive Side" (+)
Were we resentful?	Have we stayed clean of our addiction today?
Were we selfish?	Were we kind?
Were we dishonest?	Were we loving toward all?
Were we afraid?	What did we pack into life?
Have we kept something to ourselves?	Did we pray and meditate?
Were we thinking of ourselves most of the time?	Did we call someone we could help today?
Were we "disturbed" today?	Did we think of how we could help others?
Do we owe an apology? And if so to whom?	Did we study literature today?
What could we have done better?	Did we go to a meeting today?
Did we blame our feelings on someone else?	Did we call our sponsor today?
Do we need to write 10th Step on something?	Did we do anything that is improved over our past?

Journal—Gratitude List—Tomorrows Action Plan

BALANCE SHEETS

Day _____ Month _____ Year _____

Food		Money	
Breakfast		Item	Amount
Lunch			
Dinner			
Snack			
Exercise			
		Total Spent Today	
Litres Water Hours Sleep		Quality of Life Today	%

When we retire at night we constructively review our day. We remember we have ceased fighting anything and anyone—love and tolerance of others is our code.

We Draw Up a Balance Sheet

The "Negative Side" (-)	The "Positive Side" (+)
Were we resentful?	Have we stayed clean of our addiction today?
Were we selfish?	Were we kind?
Were we dishonest?	Were we loving toward all?
Were we afraid?	What did we pack into life?
Have we kept something to ourselves?	Did we pray and meditate?
Were we thinking of ourselves most of the time?	Did we call someone we could help today?
Were we "disturbed" today?	Did we think of how we could help others?
Do we owe an apology? And if so to whom?	Did we study literature today?
What could we have done better?	Did we go to a meeting today?
Did we blame our feelings on someone else?	Did we call our sponsor today?
Do we need to write 10th Step on something?	Did we do anything that is improved over our past?

Journal—Gratitude List—Tomorrows Action Plan

STEP 10

BALANCE SHEETS

Day _____ Month _____ Year _____

Food

Breakfast		
Lunch		
Dinner		
Snack		
Exercise		
Litres Water	Hours Sleep	

Money

Item		Amount
Total Spent Today		
Quality of Life Today		%

When we retire at night we constructively review our day. We remember we have ceased fighting anything and anyone—love and tolerance of others is our code.

We Draw Up a Balance Sheet

The "Negative Side" (-)	The "Positive Side" (+)
Were we resentful?	Have we stayed clean of our addiction today?
Were we selfish?	Were we kind?
Were we dishonest?	Were we loving toward all?
Were we afraid?	What did we pack into life?
Have we kept something to ourselves?	Did we pray and meditate?
Were we thinking of ourselves most of the time?	Did we call someone we could help today?
Were we "disturbed" today?	Did we think of how we could help others?
Do we owe an apology? And if so to whom?	Did we study literature today?
What could we have done better?	Did we go to a meeting today?
Did we blame our feelings on someone else?	Did we call our sponsor today?
Do we need to write 10th Step on something?	Did we do anything that is improved over our past?

Journal—Gratitude List—Tomorrows Action Plan

BALANCE SHEETS

Day _____ Month _____ Year_____

Food		Money	
Breakfast		Item	Amount
Lunch			
Dinner			
Snack			
Exercise			
		Total Spent Today	
Litres Water	Hours Sleep	Quality of Life Today	%

When we retire at night we constructively review our day. We remember we have ceased fighting anything and anyone—love and tolerance of others is our code.

We Draw Up a Balance Sheet

The "Negative Side" (-)	The "Positive Side" (+)
Were we resentful?	Have we stayed clean of our addiction today?
Were we selfish?	Were we kind?
Were we dishonest?	Were we loving toward all?
Were we afraid?	What did we pack into life?
Have we kept something to ourselves?	Did we pray and meditate?
Were we thinking of ourselves most of the time?	Did we call someone we could help today?
Were we "disturbed" today?	Did we think of how we could help others?
Do we owe an apology? And if so to whom?	Did we study literature today?
What could we have done better?	Did we go to a meeting today?
Did we blame our feelings on someone else?	Did we call our sponsor today?
Do we need to write 10th Step on something?	Did we do anything that is improved over our past?

Journal—Gratitude List—Tomorrows Action Plan

STEP 10

BALANCE SHEETS

Day _____ Month _____ Year _____

Food

Breakfast		Money	
		Item	Amount
Lunch			
Dinner			
Snack			
Exercise			
		Total Spent Today	
Litres Water	Hours Sleep	Quality of Life Today	%

When we retire at night we constructively review our day. We remember we have ceased fighting anything and anyone—love and tolerance of others is our code.

We Draw Up a Balance Sheet

The "Negative Side" (-)	The "Positive Side" (+)
Were we resentful?	Have we stayed clean of our addiction today?
Were we selfish?	Were we kind?
Were we dishonest?	Were we loving toward all?
Were we afraid?	What did we pack into life?
Have we kept something to ourselves?	Did we pray and meditate?
Were we thinking of ourselves most of the time?	Did we call someone we could help today?
Were we "disturbed" today?	Did we think of how we could help others?
Do we owe an apology? And if so to whom?	Did we study literature today?
What could we have done better?	Did we go to a meeting today?
Did we blame our feelings on someone else?	Did we call our sponsor today?
Do we need to write 10th Step on something?	Did we do anything that is improved over our past?

Journal—Gratitude List—Tomorrows Action Plan

BALANCE SHEETS

Day _____ Month _____ Year _____

Food		Money	
Breakfast		Item	Amount
Lunch			
Dinner			
Snack			
Exercise			
		Total Spent Today	
Litres Water Hours Sleep		Quality of Life Today	%

When we retire at night we constructively review our day. We remember we have ceased fighting anything and anyone—love and tolerance of others is our code.

We Draw Up a Balance Sheet

The "Negative Side" (-)	The "Positive Side" (+)
Were we resentful?	Have we stayed clean of our addiction today?
Were we selfish?	Were we kind?
Were we dishonest?	Were we loving toward all?
Were we afraid?	What did we pack into life?
Have we kept something to ourselves?	Did we pray and meditate?
Were we thinking of ourselves most of the time?	Did we call someone we could help today?
Were we "disturbed" today?	Did we think of how we could help others?
Do we owe an apology? And if so to whom?	Did we study literature today?
What could we have done better?	Did we go to a meeting today?
Did we blame our feelings on someone else?	Did we call our sponsor today?
Do we need to write 10th Step on something?	Did we do anything that is improved over our past?

Journal—Gratitude List—Tomorrows Action Plan

STEP 10

BALANCE SHEETS

Day _____ Month _____ Year _____

Food		Money	
Breakfast		Item	Amount
Lunch			
Dinner			
Snack			
Exercise			
		Total Spent Today	
Litres Water	Hours Sleep	Quality of Life Today	%

When we retire at night we constructively review our day. We remember we have ceased fighting anything and anyone—love and tolerance of others is our code.

We Draw Up a Balance Sheet

The "Negative Side" (-)	The "Positive Side" (+)
Were we resentful?	Have we stayed clean of our addiction today?
Were we selfish?	Were we kind?
Were we dishonest?	Were we loving toward all?
Were we afraid?	What did we pack into life?
Have we kept something to ourselves?	Did we pray and meditate?
Were we thinking of ourselves most of the time?	Did we call someone we could help today?
Were we "disturbed" today?	Did we think of how we could help others?
Do we owe an apology? And if so to whom?	Did we study literature today?
What could we have done better?	Did we go to a meeting today?
Did we blame our feelings on someone else?	Did we call our sponsor today?
Do we need to write 10th Step on something?	Did we do anything that is improved over our past?

Journal—Gratitude List—Tomorrows Action Plan

BALANCE SHEETS

Day _____ Month _____ Year _____

Food		Money	
Breakfast		Item	Amount
Lunch			
Dinner			
Snack			
Exercise			
		Total Spent Today	
Litres Water	Hours Sleep	Quality of Life Today	%

When we retire at night we constructively review our day. We remember we have ceased fighting anything and anyone—love and tolerance of others is our code.

We Draw Up a Balance Sheet

The "Negative Side" (-)	The "Positive Side" (+)
Were we resentful?	Have we stayed clean of our addiction today?
Were we selfish?	Were we kind?
Were we dishonest?	Were we loving toward all?
Were we afraid?	What did we pack into life?
Have we kept something to ourselves?	Did we pray and meditate?
Were we thinking of ourselves most of the time?	Did we call someone we could help today?
Were we "disturbed" today?	Did we think of how we could help others?
Do we owe an apology? And if so to whom?	Did we study literature today?
What could we have done better?	Did we go to a meeting today?
Did we blame our feelings on someone else?	Did we call our sponsor today?
Do we need to write 10th Step on something?	Did we do anything that is improved over our past?

Journal—Gratitude List—Tomorrows Action Plan

STEP 10

BALANCE SHEETS

Day _____ Month _____ Year _____

Food		Money	
Breakfast		Item	Amount
Lunch			
Dinner			
Snack			
Exercise			
		Total Spent Today	
Litres Water	Hours Sleep	Quality of Life Today	%

When we retire at night we constructively review our day. We remember we have ceased fighting anything and anyone—love and tolerance of others is our code.

We Draw Up a Balance Sheet

The "Negative Side" (-)	The "Positive Side" (+)
Were we resentful?	Have we stayed clean of our addiction today?
Were we selfish?	Were we kind?
Were we dishonest?	Were we loving toward all?
Were we afraid?	What did we pack into life?
Have we kept something to ourselves?	Did we pray and meditate?
Were we thinking of ourselves most of the time?	Did we call someone we could help today?
Were we "disturbed" today?	Did we think of how we could help others?
Do we owe an apology? And if so to whom?	Did we study literature today?
What could we have done better?	Did we go to a meeting today?
Did we blame our feelings on someone else?	Did we call our sponsor today?
Do we need to write 10th Step on something?	Did we do anything that is improved over our past?

Journal—Gratitude List—Tomorrows Action Plan

BALANCE SHEETS

Day _____ Month _____ Year _____

Food		Money	
Breakfast		Item	Amount
Lunch			
Dinner			
Snack			
Exercise			
		Total Spent Today	
Litres Water Hours Sleep		Quality of Life Today	%

When we retire at night we constructively review our day. We remember we have ceased fighting anything and anyone—love and tolerance of others is our code.

We Draw Up a Balance Sheet

The "Negative Side" (-)	The "Positive Side" (+)
Were we resentful?	Have we stayed clean of our addiction today?
Were we selfish?	Were we kind?
Were we dishonest?	Were we loving toward all?
Were we afraid?	What did we pack into life?
Have we kept something to ourselves?	Did we pray and meditate?
Were we thinking of ourselves most of the time?	Did we call someone we could help today?
Were we "disturbed" today?	Did we think of how we could help others?
Do we owe an apology? And if so to whom?	Did we study literature today?
What could we have done better?	Did we go to a meeting today?
Did we blame our feelings on someone else?	Did we call our sponsor today?
Do we need to write 10th Step on something?	Did we do anything that is improved over our past?

Journal—Gratitude List—Tomorrows Action Plan

STEP 10

BALANCE SHEETS

Day _____ Month _____ Year _____

Food		Money	
Breakfast		Item	Amount
Lunch			
Dinner			
Snack			
Exercise			
		Total Spent Today	
Litres Water _____ Hours Sleep _____		Quality of Life Today	%

When we retire at night we constructively review our day. We remember we have ceased fighting anything and anyone—love and tolerance of others is our code.

We Draw Up a Balance Sheet

The "Negative Side" (−)	The "Positive Side" (+)
Were we resentful?	Have we stayed clean of our addiction today?
Were we selfish?	Were we kind?
Were we dishonest?	Were we loving toward all?
Were we afraid?	What did we pack into life?
Have we kept something to ourselves?	Did we pray and meditate?
Were we thinking of ourselves most of the time?	Did we call someone we could help today?
Were we "disturbed" today?	Did we think of how we could help others?
Do we owe an apology? And if so to whom?	Did we study literature today?
What could we have done better?	Did we go to a meeting today?
Did we blame our feelings on someone else?	Did we call our sponsor today?
Do we need to write 10th Step on something?	Did we do anything that is improved over our past?

Journal—Gratitude List—Tomorrows Action Plan

BALANCE SHEETS

Day _____ Month _____ Year_____

Food		Money	
Breakfast		Item	Amount
Lunch			
Dinner			
Snack			
Exercise			
		Total Spent Today	
Litres Water	Hours Sleep	Quality of Life Today	%

When we retire at night we constructively review our day. We remember we have ceased fighting anything and anyone—love and tolerance of others is our code.

We Draw Up a Balance Sheet

The "Negative Side" (-)	The "Positive Side" (+)
Were we resentful?	Have we stayed clean of our addiction today?
Were we selfish?	Were we kind?
Were we dishonest?	Were we loving toward all?
Were we afraid?	What did we pack into life?
Have we kept something to ourselves?	Did we pray and meditate?
Were we thinking of ourselves most of the time?	Did we call someone we could help today?
Were we "disturbed" today?	Did we think of how we could help others?
Do we owe an apology? And if so to whom?	Did we study literature today?
What could we have done better?	Did we go to a meeting today?
Did we blame our feelings on someone else?	Did we call our sponsor today?
Do we need to write 10th Step on something?	Did we do anything that is improved over our past?

Journal—Gratitude List—Tomorrows Action Plan

STEP 10

BALANCE SHEETS

Day _____ Month _____ Year_____

Food

Breakfast		
Lunch		
Dinner		
Snack		
Exercise		
Litres Water	Hours Sleep	

Money

Item	Amount
Total Spent Today	
Quality of Life Today	%

When we retire at night we constructively review our day. We remember we have ceased fighting anything and anyone—love and tolerance of others is our code.

We Draw Up a Balance Sheet

The "Negative Side" (-)	The "Positive Side" (+)
Were we resentful?	Have we stayed clean of our addiction today?
Were we selfish?	Were we kind?
Were we dishonest?	Were we loving toward all?
Were we afraid?	What did we pack into life?
Have we kept something to ourselves?	Did we pray and meditate?
Were we thinking of ourselves most of the time?	Did we call someone we could help today?
Were we "disturbed" today?	Did we think of how we could help others?
Do we owe an apology? And if so to whom?	Did we study literature today?
What could we have done better?	Did we go to a meeting today?
Did we blame our feelings on someone else?	Did we call our sponsor today?
Do we need to write 10th Step on something?	Did we do anything that is improved over our past?

Journal—Gratitude List—Tomorrows Action Plan

BALANCE SHEETS

Day _____ Month _____ Year _____

Food		Money	
Breakfast		Item	Amount
Lunch			
Dinner			
Snack			
Exercise			
		Total Spent Today	
Litres Water _____ Hours Sleep _____		Quality of Life Today	%

When we retire at night we constructively review our day. We remember we have ceased fighting anything and anyone—love and tolerance of others is our code.

We Draw Up a Balance Sheet

The "Negative Side" (−)	The "Positive Side" (+)
Were we resentful?	Have we stayed clean of our addiction today?
Were we selfish?	Were we kind?
Were we dishonest?	Were we loving toward all?
Were we afraid?	What did we pack into life?
Have we kept something to ourselves?	Did we pray and meditate?
Were we thinking of ourselves most of the time?	Did we call someone we could help today?
Were we "disturbed" today?	Did we think of how we could help others?
Do we owe an apology? And if so to whom?	Did we study literature today?
What could we have done better?	Did we go to a meeting today?
Did we blame our feelings on someone else?	Did we call our sponsor today?
Do we need to write 10th Step on something?	Did we do anything that is improved over our past?

Journal—Gratitude List—Tomorrows Action Plan

STEP 10

BALANCE SHEETS

Day _____ Month _____ Year _____

Food		Money	
Breakfast		Item	Amount
Lunch			
Dinner			
Snack			
Exercise			
		Total Spent Today	
Litres Water	Hours Sleep	Quality of Life Today	%

When we retire at night we constructively review our day. We remember we have ceased fighting anything and anyone—love and tolerance of others is our code.

We Draw Up a Balance Sheet

The "Negative Side" (-)	The "Positive Side" (+)
Were we resentful?	Have we stayed clean of our addiction today?
Were we selfish?	Were we kind?
Were we dishonest?	Were we loving toward all?
Were we afraid?	What did we pack into life?
Have we kept something to ourselves?	Did we pray and meditate?
Were we thinking of ourselves most of the time?	Did we call someone we could help today?
Were we "disturbed" today?	Did we think of how we could help others?
Do we owe an apology? And if so to whom?	Did we study literature today?
What could we have done better?	Did we go to a meeting today?
Did we blame our feelings on someone else?	Did we call our sponsor today?
Do we need to write 10th Step on something?	Did we do anything that is improved over our past?

Journal—Gratitude List—Tomorrows Action Plan

BALANCE SHEETS

Day _____ Month _____ Year _____

Food		Money	
Breakfast		Item	Amount
Lunch			
Dinner			
Snack			
Exercise			
		Total Spent Today	
Litres Water	Hours Sleep	Quality of Life Today	%

When we retire at night we constructively review our day. We remember we have ceased fighting anything and anyone—love and tolerance of others is our code.

We Draw Up a Balance Sheet

The "Negative Side" (-)	The "Positive Side" (+)
Were we resentful?	Have we stayed clean of our addiction today?
Were we selfish?	Were we kind?
Were we dishonest?	Were we loving toward all?
Were we afraid?	What did we pack into life?
Have we kept something to ourselves?	Did we pray and meditate?
Were we thinking of ourselves most of the time?	Did we call someone we could help today?
Were we "disturbed" today?	Did we think of how we could help others?
Do we owe an apology? And if so to whom?	Did we study literature today?
What could we have done better?	Did we go to a meeting today?
Did we blame our feelings on someone else?	Did we call our sponsor today?
Do we need to write 10th Step on something?	Did we do anything that is improved over our past?

Journal—Gratitude List—Tomorrows Action Plan

STEP 10

BALANCE SHEETS

Day _____ Month _____ Year _____

Food

Breakfast		Money	
		Item	Amount
Lunch			
Dinner			
Snack			
Exercise			
		Total Spent Today	
Litres Water ____ Hours Sleep ____		Quality of Life Today	%

When we retire at night we constructively review our day. We remember we have ceased fighting anything and anyone—love and tolerance of others is our code.

We Draw Up a Balance Sheet

The "Negative Side" (-)	The "Positive Side" (+)
Were we resentful?	Have we stayed clean of our addiction today?
Were we selfish?	Were we kind?
Were we dishonest?	Were we loving toward all?
Were we afraid?	What did we pack into life?
Have we kept something to ourselves?	Did we pray and meditate?
Were we thinking of ourselves most of the time?	Did we call someone we could help today?
Were we "disturbed" today?	Did we think of how we could help others?
Do we owe an apology? And if so to whom?	Did we study literature today?
What could we have done better?	Did we go to a meeting today?
Did we blame our feelings on someone else?	Did we call our sponsor today?
Do we need to write 10th Step on something?	Did we do anything that is improved over our past?

Journal—Gratitude List—Tomorrows Action Plan

BALANCE SHEETS

Day _____ Month _____ Year _____

Food		Money	
Breakfast		Item	Amount
Lunch			
Dinner			
Snack			
Exercise			
		Total Spent Today	
Litres Water ____ Hours Sleep ____		Quality of Life Today	%

When we retire at night we constructively review our day. We remember we have ceased fighting anything and anyone—love and tolerance of others is our code.

We Draw Up a Balance Sheet

The "Negative Side" (-)	The "Positive Side" (+)
Were we resentful?	Have we stayed clean of our addiction today?
Were we selfish?	Were we kind?
Were we dishonest?	Were we loving toward all?
Were we afraid?	What did we pack into life?
Have we kept something to ourselves?	Did we pray and meditate?
Were we thinking of ourselves most of the time?	Did we call someone we could help today?
Were we "disturbed" today?	Did we think of how we could help others?
Do we owe an apology? And if so to whom?	Did we study literature today?
What could we have done better?	Did we go to a meeting today?
Did we blame our feelings on someone else?	Did we call our sponsor today?
Do we need to write 10th Step on something?	Did we do anything that is improved over our past?

Journal—Gratitude List—Tomorrows Action Plan

STEP 10

BALANCE SHEETS

Day _____ Month _____ Year _____

Food		Money	
Breakfast		Item	Amount
Lunch			
Dinner			
Snack			
Exercise			
		Total Spent Today	
Litres Water	Hours Sleep	Quality of Life Today	%

When we retire at night we constructively review our day. We remember we have ceased fighting anything and anyone—love and tolerance of others is our code.

We Draw Up a Balance Sheet

The "Negative Side" (-)	The "Positive Side" (+)
Were we resentful?	Have we stayed clean of our addiction today?
Were we selfish?	Were we kind?
Were we dishonest?	Were we loving toward all?
Were we afraid?	What did we pack into life?
Have we kept something to ourselves?	Did we pray and meditate?
Were we thinking of ourselves most of the time?	Did we call someone we could help today?
Were we "disturbed" today?	Did we think of how we could help others?
Do we owe an apology? And if so to whom?	Did we study literature today?
What could we have done better?	Did we go to a meeting today?
Did we blame our feelings on someone else?	Did we call our sponsor today?
Do we need to write 10th Step on something?	Did we do anything that is improved over our past?

Journal—Gratitude List—Tomorrows Action Plan

BALANCE SHEETS

Day _____ Month _____ Year _____

Food		Money	
Breakfast		Item	Amount
Lunch			
Dinner			
Snack			
Exercise			
		Total Spent Today	
Litres Water ____ Hours Sleep ____		Quality of Life Today	%

When we retire at night we constructively review our day. We remember we have ceased fighting anything and anyone—love and tolerance of others is our code.

We Draw Up a Balance Sheet

The "Negative Side" (-)	The "Positive Side" (+)
Were we resentful?	Have we stayed clean of our addiction today?
Were we selfish?	Were we kind?
Were we dishonest?	Were we loving toward all?
Were we afraid?	What did we pack into life?
Have we kept something to ourselves?	Did we pray and meditate?
Were we thinking of ourselves most of the time?	Did we call someone we could help today?
Were we "disturbed" today?	Did we think of how we could help others?
Do we owe an apology? And if so to whom?	Did we study literature today?
What could we have done better?	Did we go to a meeting today?
Did we blame our feelings on someone else?	Did we call our sponsor today?
Do we need to write 10th Step on something?	Did we do anything that is improved over our past?

Journal—Gratitude List—Tomorrows Action Plan

STEP 10

BALANCE SHEETS

Day _____ Month _____ Year _____

Food		Money	
Breakfast		Item	Amount
Lunch			
Dinner			
Snack			
Exercise			
		Total Spent Today	
Litres Water	Hours Sleep	Quality of Life Today	%

When we retire at night we constructively review our day. We remember we have ceased fighting anything and anyone—love and tolerance of others is our code.

We Draw Up a Balance Sheet

The "Negative Side" (-)	The "Positive Side" (+)
Were we resentful?	Have we stayed clean of our addiction today?
Were we selfish?	Were we kind?
Were we dishonest?	Were we loving toward all?
Were we afraid?	What did we pack into life?
Have we kept something to ourselves?	Did we pray and meditate?
Were we thinking of ourselves most of the time?	Did we call someone we could help today?
Were we "disturbed" today?	Did we think of how we could help others?
Do we owe an apology? And if so to whom?	Did we study literature today?
What could we have done better?	Did we go to a meeting today?
Did we blame our feelings on someone else?	Did we call our sponsor today?
Do we need to write 10th Step on something?	Did we do anything that is improved over our past?

Journal—Gratitude List—Tomorrows Action Plan

MAINTAINING THE PROMISES...DAILY

BALANCE SHEETS

Day _____ Month _____ Year _____

Food		Money	
Breakfast		Item	Amount
Lunch			
Dinner			
Snack			
Exercise			
		Total Spent Today	
Litres Water ____ Hours Sleep ____		Quality of Life Today	%

When we retire at night we constructively review our day. We remember we have ceased fighting anything and anyone—love and tolerance of others is our code.

We Draw Up a Balance Sheet

The "Negative Side" (-)	The "Positive Side" (+)
Were we resentful?	Have we stayed clean of our addiction today?
Were we selfish?	Were we kind?
Were we dishonest?	Were we loving toward all?
Were we afraid?	What did we pack into life?
Have we kept something to ourselves?	Did we pray and meditate?
Were we thinking of ourselves most of the time?	Did we call someone we could help today?
Were we "disturbed" today?	Did we think of how we could help others?
Do we owe an apology? And if so to whom?	Did we study literature today?
What could we have done better?	Did we go to a meeting today?
Did we blame our feelings on someone else?	Did we call our sponsor today?
Do we need to write 10th Step on something?	Did we do anything that is improved over our past?

Journal—Gratitude List—Tomorrows Action Plan

STEP 10

BALANCE SHEETS

Day _____ Month _____ Year _____

Food		Money	
Breakfast		Item	Amount
Lunch			
Dinner			
Snack			
Exercise			
		Total Spent Today	
Litres Water	Hours Sleep	Quality of Life Today	%

When we retire at night we constructively review our day. We remember we have ceased fighting anything and anyone—love and tolerance of others is our code.

We Draw Up a Balance Sheet

The "Negative Side" (-)	The "Positive Side" (+)
Were we resentful?	Have we stayed clean of our addiction today?
Were we selfish?	Were we kind?
Were we dishonest?	Were we loving toward all?
Were we afraid?	What did we pack into life?
Have we kept something to ourselves?	Did we pray and meditate?
Were we thinking of ourselves most of the time?	Did we call someone we could help today?
Were we "disturbed" today?	Did we think of how we could help others?
Do we owe an apology? And if so to whom?	Did we study literature today?
What could we have done better?	Did we go to a meeting today?
Did we blame our feelings on someone else?	Did we call our sponsor today?
Do we need to write 10th Step on something?	Did we do anything that is improved over our past?

Journal—Gratitude List—Tomorrows Action Plan

BALANCE SHEETS

Day _____ Month _____ Year _____

Food		Money	
Breakfast		Item	Amount
Lunch			
Dinner			
Snack			
Exercise			
		Total Spent Today	
Litres Water _____ Hours Sleep _____		Quality of Life Today	%

When we retire at night we constructively review our day. We remember we have ceased fighting anything and anyone—love and tolerance of others is our code.

We Draw Up a Balance Sheet

The "Negative Side" (-)	The "Positive Side" (+)
Were we resentful?	Have we stayed clean of our addiction today?
Were we selfish?	Were we kind?
Were we dishonest?	Were we loving toward all?
Were we afraid?	What did we pack into life?
Have we kept something to ourselves?	Did we pray and meditate?
Were we thinking of ourselves most of the time?	Did we call someone we could help today?
Were we "disturbed" today?	Did we think of how we could help others?
Do we owe an apology? And if so to whom?	Did we study literature today?
What could we have done better?	Did we go to a meeting today?
Did we blame our feelings on someone else?	Did we call our sponsor today?
Do we need to write 10th Step on something?	Did we do anything that is improved over our past?

Journal—Gratitude List—Tomorrows Action Plan

STEP 10

BALANCE SHEETS

Day _____ Month _____ Year _____

Food

Breakfast	
Lunch	
Dinner	
Snack	
Exercise	

Litres Water	Hours Sleep

Money

Item	Amount
Total Spent Today	
Quality of Life Today	%

When we retire at night we constructively review our day. We remember we have ceased fighting anything and anyone—love and tolerance of others is our code.

We Draw Up a Balance Sheet

The "Negative Side" (-)	The "Positive Side" (+)
Were we resentful?	Have we stayed clean of our addiction today?
Were we selfish?	Were we kind?
Were we dishonest?	Were we loving toward all?
Were we afraid?	What did we pack into life?
Have we kept something to ourselves?	Did we pray and meditate?
Were we thinking of ourselves most of the time?	Did we call someone we could help today?
Were we "disturbed" today?	Did we think of how we could help others?
Do we owe an apology? And if so to whom?	Did we study literature today?
What could we have done better?	Did we go to a meeting today?
Did we blame our feelings on someone else?	Did we call our sponsor today?
Do we need to write 10th Step on something?	Did we do anything that is improved over our past?

Journal—Gratitude List—Tomorrows Action Plan

BALANCE SHEETS

Day _____ Month _____ Year_____

Food		Money	
Breakfast		Item	Amount
Lunch			
Dinner			
Snack			
Exercise			
		Total Spent Today	
Litres Water _____ Hours Sleep _____		Quality of Life Today	%

When we retire at night we constructively review our day. We remember we have ceased fighting anything and anyone—love and tolerance of others is our code.

We Draw Up a Balance Sheet

The "Negative Side"　　(-)	The "Positive Side"　　(+)
Were we resentful?	Have we stayed clean of our addiction today?
Were we selfish?	Were we kind?
Were we dishonest?	Were we loving toward all?
Were we afraid?	What did we pack into life?
Have we kept something to ourselves?	Did we pray and meditate?
Were we thinking of ourselves most of the time?	Did we call someone we could help today?
Were we "disturbed" today?	Did we think of how we could help others?
Do we owe an apology? And if so to whom?	Did we study literature today?
What could we have done better?	Did we go to a meeting today?
Did we blame our feelings on someone else?	Did we call our sponsor today?
Do we need to write 10th Step on something?	Did we do anything that is improved over our past?

Journal—Gratitude List—Tomorrows Action Plan

STEP 10

BALANCE SHEETS

Day _____ Month _____ Year _____

Food		Money	
Breakfast		Item	Amount
Lunch			
Dinner			
Snack			
Exercise			
		Total Spent Today	
Litres Water	Hours Sleep	Quality of Life Today	%

When we retire at night we constructively review our day. We remember we have ceased fighting anything and anyone—love and tolerance of others is our code.

We Draw Up a Balance Sheet

The "Negative Side" (−)	The "Positive Side" (+)
Were we resentful?	Have we stayed clean of our addiction today?
Were we selfish?	Were we kind?
Were we dishonest?	Were we loving toward all?
Were we afraid?	What did we pack into life?
Have we kept something to ourselves?	Did we pray and meditate?
Were we thinking of ourselves most of the time?	Did we call someone we could help today?
Were we "disturbed" today?	Did we think of how we could help others?
Do we owe an apology? And if so to whom?	Did we study literature today?
What could we have done better?	Did we go to a meeting today?
Did we blame our feelings on someone else?	Did we call our sponsor today?
Do we need to write 10th Step on something?	Did we do anything that is improved over our past?

Journal—Gratitude List—Tomorrows Action Plan

BALANCE SHEETS

Day _____ Month _____ Year _____

Food		Money	
Breakfast		Item	Amount
Lunch			
Dinner			
Snack			
Exercise			
		Total Spent Today	
Litres Water Hours Sleep		Quality of Life Today	%

When we retire at night we constructively review our day. We remember we have ceased fighting anything and anyone—love and tolerance of others is our code.

We Draw Up a Balance Sheet

The "Negative Side" (-)	The "Positive Side" (+)
Were we resentful?	Have we stayed clean of our addiction today?
Were we selfish?	Were we kind?
Were we dishonest?	Were we loving toward all?
Were we afraid?	What did we pack into life?
Have we kept something to ourselves?	Did we pray and meditate?
Were we thinking of ourselves most of the time?	Did we call someone we could help today?
Were we "disturbed" today?	Did we think of how we could help others?
Do we owe an apology? And if so to whom?	Did we study literature today?
What could we have done better?	Did we go to a meeting today?
Did we blame our feelings on someone else?	Did we call our sponsor today?
Do we need to write 10th Step on something?	Did we do anything that is improved over our past?

Journal—Gratitude List—Tomorrows Action Plan

STEP 10

BALANCE SHEETS

Day _____ Month _____ Year _____

Food		Money	
Breakfast		Item	Amount
Lunch			
Dinner			
Snack			
Exercise			
		Total Spent Today	
Litres Water Hours Sleep		Quality of Life Today	%

When we retire at night we constructively review our day. We remember we have ceased fighting anything and anyone—love and tolerance of others is our code.

We Draw Up a Balance Sheet

The "Negative Side" (-)	The "Positive Side" (+)
Were we resentful?	Have we stayed clean of our addiction today?
Were we selfish?	Were we kind?
Were we dishonest?	Were we loving toward all?
Were we afraid?	What did we pack into life?
Have we kept something to ourselves?	Did we pray and meditate?
Were we thinking of ourselves most of the time?	Did we call someone we could help today?
Were we "disturbed" today?	Did we think of how we could help others?
Do we owe an apology? And if so to whom?	Did we study literature today?
What could we have done better?	Did we go to a meeting today?
Did we blame our feelings on someone else?	Did we call our sponsor today?
Do we need to write 10th Step on something?	Did we do anything that is improved over our past?

Journal—Gratitude List—Tomorrows Action Plan

BALANCE SHEETS

Day _____ Month _____ Year _____

Food		Money		
Breakfast		Item		Amount
Lunch				
Dinner				
Snack				
Exercise				
		Total Spent Today		
Litres Water	Hours Sleep	Quality of Life Today		%

When we retire at night we constructively review our day. We remember we have ceased fighting anything and anyone—love and tolerance of others is our code.

We Draw Up a Balance Sheet

The "Negative Side" (-)	The "Positive Side" (+)
Were we resentful?	Have we stayed clean of our addiction today?
Were we selfish?	Were we kind?
Were we dishonest?	Were we loving toward all?
Were we afraid?	What did we pack into life?
Have we kept something to ourselves?	Did we pray and meditate?
Were we thinking of ourselves most of the time?	Did we call someone we could help today?
Were we "disturbed" today?	Did we think of how we could help others?
Do we owe an apology? And if so to whom?	Did we study literature today?
What could we have done better?	Did we go to a meeting today?
Did we blame our feelings on someone else?	Did we call our sponsor today?
Do we need to write 10th Step on something?	Did we do anything that is improved over our past?

Journal—Gratitude List—Tomorrows Action Plan

STEP 10

BALANCE SHEETS

Day _____ Month _____ Year _____

Food

Breakfast	
Lunch	
Dinner	
Snack	
Exercise	
Litres Water	Hours Sleep

Money

Item	Amount
Total Spent Today	
Quality of Life Today	%

When we retire at night we constructively review our day. We remember we have ceased fighting anything and anyone—love and tolerance of others is our code.

We Draw Up a Balance Sheet

The "Negative Side" (-)	The "Positive Side" (+)
Were we resentful?	Have we stayed clean of our addiction today?
Were we selfish?	Were we kind?
Were we dishonest?	Were we loving toward all?
Were we afraid?	What did we pack into life?
Have we kept something to ourselves?	Did we pray and meditate?
Were we thinking of ourselves most of the time?	Did we call someone we could help today?
Were we "disturbed" today?	Did we think of how we could help others?
Do we owe an apology? And if so to whom?	Did we study literature today?
What could we have done better?	Did we go to a meeting today?
Did we blame our feelings on someone else?	Did we call our sponsor today?
Do we need to write 10th Step on something?	Did we do anything that is improved over our past?

Journal—Gratitude List—Tomorrows Action Plan

BALANCE SHEETS

Day _____ Month _____ Year _____

Food

Breakfast

Lunch

Dinner

Snack

Exercise

Litres Water	Hours Sleep

Money

Item	Amount
Total Spent Today	
Quality of Life Today	%

When we retire at night we constructively review our day. We remember we have ceased fighting anything and anyone—love and tolerance of others is our code.

We Draw Up a Balance Sheet

The "Negative Side" (-)	The "Positive Side" (+)
Were we resentful?	Have we stayed clean of our addiction today?
Were we selfish?	Were we kind?
Were we dishonest?	Were we loving toward all?
Were we afraid?	What did we pack into life?
Have we kept something to ourselves?	Did we pray and meditate?
Were we thinking of ourselves most of the time?	Did we call someone we could help today?
Were we "disturbed" today?	Did we think of how we could help others?
Do we owe an apology? And if so to whom?	Did we study literature today?
What could we have done better?	Did we go to a meeting today?
Did we blame our feelings on someone else?	Did we call our sponsor today?
Do we need to write 10th Step on something?	Did we do anything that is improved over our past?

Journal—Gratitude List—Tomorrows Action Plan

STEP 10

BALANCE SHEETS

Day _____ Month _____ Year _____

Food		Money	
Breakfast		Item	Amount
Lunch			
Dinner			
Snack			
Exercise			
		Total Spent Today	
Litres Water	Hours Sleep	Quality of Life Today	%

When we retire at night we constructively review our day. We remember we have ceased fighting anything and anyone—love and tolerance of others is our code.

We Draw Up a Balance Sheet

The "Negative Side" (-)	The "Positive Side" (+)
Were we resentful?	Have we stayed clean of our addiction today?
Were we selfish?	Were we kind?
Were we dishonest?	Were we loving toward all?
Were we afraid?	What did we pack into life?
Have we kept something to ourselves?	Did we pray and meditate?
Were we thinking of ourselves most of the time?	Did we call someone we could help today?
Were we "disturbed" today?	Did we think of how we could help others?
Do we owe an apology? And if so to whom?	Did we study literature today?
What could we have done better?	Did we go to a meeting today?
Did we blame our feelings on someone else?	Did we call our sponsor today?
Do we need to write 10th Step on something?	Did we do anything that is improved over our past?

Journal—Gratitude List—Tomorrows Action Plan

BALANCE SHEETS

Day _____ Month _____ Year _____

Food		Money	
Breakfast		Item	Amount
Lunch			
Dinner			
Snack			
Exercise			
		Total Spent Today	
Litres Water Hours Sleep		Quality of Life Today	%

When we retire at night we constructively review our day. We remember we have ceased fighting anything and anyone—love and tolerance of others is our code.

We Draw Up a Balance Sheet

The "Negative Side" (-)	The "Positive Side" (+)
Were we resentful?	Have we stayed clean of our addiction today?
Were we selfish?	Were we kind?
Were we dishonest?	Were we loving toward all?
Were we afraid?	What did we pack into life?
Have we kept something to ourselves?	Did we pray and meditate?
Were we thinking of ourselves most of the time?	Did we call someone we could help today?
Were we "disturbed" today?	Did we think of how we could help others?
Do we owe an apology? And if so to whom?	Did we study literature today?
What could we have done better?	Did we go to a meeting today?
Did we blame our feelings on someone else?	Did we call our sponsor today?
Do we need to write 10th Step on something?	Did we do anything that is improved over our past?

Journal—Gratitude List—Tomorrows Action Plan

STEP 10

BALANCE SHEETS

Day _____ Month _____ Year _____

Food		Money	
Breakfast		Item	Amount
Lunch			
Dinner			
Snack			
Exercise			
		Total Spent Today	
Litres Water Hours Sleep		Quality of Life Today	%

When we retire at night we constructively review our day. We remember we have ceased fighting anything and anyone—love and tolerance of others is our code.

We Draw Up a Balance Sheet

The "Negative Side" (-)	The "Positive Side" (+)
Were we resentful?	Have we stayed clean of our addiction today?
Were we selfish?	Were we kind?
Were we dishonest?	Were we loving toward all?
Were we afraid?	What did we pack into life?
Have we kept something to ourselves?	Did we pray and meditate?
Were we thinking of ourselves most of the time?	Did we call someone we could help today?
Were we "disturbed" today?	Did we think of how we could help others?
Do we owe an apology? And if so to whom?	Did we study literature today?
What could we have done better?	Did we go to a meeting today?
Did we blame our feelings on someone else?	Did we call our sponsor today?
Do we need to write 10th Step on something?	Did we do anything that is improved over our past?

Journal—Gratitude List—Tomorrows Action Plan

MAINTAINING THE PROMISES...DAILY

BALANCE SHEETS

Day _____ Month _____ Year_____

Food		Money	
Breakfast		Item	Amount
Lunch			
Dinner			
Snack			
Exercise			
		Total Spent Today	
Litres Water Hours Sleep		Quality of Life Today	%

When we retire at night we constructively review our day. We remember we have ceased fighting anything and anyone—love and tolerance of others is our code.

We Draw Up a Balance Sheet

The "Negative Side" (-)	The "Positive Side" (+)
Were we resentful?	Have we stayed clean of our addiction today?
Were we selfish?	Were we kind?
Were we dishonest?	Were we loving toward all?
Were we afraid?	What did we pack into life?
Have we kept something to ourselves?	Did we pray and meditate?
Were we thinking of ourselves most of the time?	Did we call someone we could help today?
Were we "disturbed" today?	Did we think of how we could help others?
Do we owe an apology? And if so to whom?	Did we study literature today?
What could we have done better?	Did we go to a meeting today?
Did we blame our feelings on someone else?	Did we call our sponsor today?
Do we need to write 10th Step on something?	Did we do anything that is improved over our past?

Journal—Gratitude List—Tomorrows Action Plan

STEP 10

BALANCE SHEETS

Day _____ Month _____ Year_____

Food		Money	
Breakfast		Item	Amount
Lunch			
Dinner			
Snack			
Exercise			
		Total Spent Today	
Litres Water	Hours Sleep	Quality of Life Today	%

When we retire at night we constructively review our day. We remember we have ceased fighting anything and anyone—love and tolerance of others is our code.

We Draw Up a Balance Sheet

The "Negative Side" (-)	The "Positive Side" (+)
Were we resentful?	Have we stayed clean of our addiction today?
Were we selfish?	Were we kind?
Were we dishonest?	Were we loving toward all?
Were we afraid?	What did we pack into life?
Have we kept something to ourselves?	Did we pray and meditate?
Were we thinking of ourselves most of the time?	Did we call someone we could help today?
Were we "disturbed" today?	Did we think of how we could help others?
Do we owe an apology? And if so to whom?	Did we study literature today?
What could we have done better?	Did we go to a meeting today?
Did we blame our feelings on someone else?	Did we call our sponsor today?
Do we need to write 10th Step on something?	Did we do anything that is improved over our past?

Journal—Gratitude List—Tomorrows Action Plan

220   MAINTAINING THE PROMISES...DAILY

BALANCE SHEETS

Day _____ Month _____ Year _____

Food		Money	
Breakfast		Item	Amount
Lunch			
Dinner			
Snack			
Exercise			
		Total Spent Today	
Litres Water	Hours Sleep	Quality of Life Today	%

When we retire at night we constructively review our day. We remember we have ceased fighting anything and anyone—love and tolerance of others is our code.

We Draw Up a Balance Sheet

The "Negative Side" (-)	The "Positive Side" (+)
Were we resentful?	Have we stayed clean of our addiction today?
Were we selfish?	Were we kind?
Were we dishonest?	Were we loving toward all?
Were we afraid?	What did we pack into life?
Have we kept something to ourselves?	Did we pray and meditate?
Were we thinking of ourselves most of the time?	Did we call someone we could help today?
Were we "disturbed" today?	Did we think of how we could help others?
Do we owe an apology? And if so to whom?	Did we study literature today?
What could we have done better?	Did we go to a meeting today?
Did we blame our feelings on someone else?	Did we call our sponsor today?
Do we need to write 10th Step on something?	Did we do anything that is improved over our past?

Journal—Gratitude List—Tomorrows Action Plan

STEP 10

BALANCE SHEETS

Day _____ Month _____ Year _____

Food		Money	
Breakfast		Item	Amount
Lunch			
Dinner			
Snack			
Exercise			
		Total Spent Today	
Litres Water	Hours Sleep	Quality of Life Today	%

When we retire at night we constructively review our day. We remember we have ceased fighting anything and anyone—love and tolerance of others is our code.

We Draw Up a Balance Sheet

The "Negative Side" (−)	The "Positive Side" (+)
Were we resentful?	Have we stayed clean of our addiction today?
Were we selfish?	Were we kind?
Were we dishonest?	Were we loving toward all?
Were we afraid?	What did we pack into life?
Have we kept something to ourselves?	Did we pray and meditate?
Were we thinking of ourselves most of the time?	Did we call someone we could help today?
Were we "disturbed" today?	Did we think of how we could help others?
Do we owe an apology? And if so to whom?	Did we study literature today?
What could we have done better?	Did we go to a meeting today?
Did we blame our feelings on someone else?	Did we call our sponsor today?
Do we need to write 10th Step on something?	Did we do anything that is improved over our past?

Journal—Gratitude List—Tomorrows Action Plan

BALANCE SHEETS

Day _____ Month _____ Year _____

Food

Breakfast		
Lunch		
Dinner		
Snack		
Exercise		
Litres Water	Hours Sleep	

Money

Item		Amount
Total Spent Today		
Quality of Life Today		%

When we retire at night we constructively review our day. We remember we have ceased fighting anything and anyone—love and tolerance of others is our code.

We Draw Up a Balance Sheet

The "Negative Side" (-)	The "Positive Side" (+)
Were we resentful?	Have we stayed clean of our addiction today?
Were we selfish?	Were we kind?
Were we dishonest?	Were we loving toward all?
Were we afraid?	What did we pack into life?
Have we kept something to ourselves?	Did we pray and meditate?
Were we thinking of ourselves most of the time?	Did we call someone we could help today?
Were we "disturbed" today?	Did we think of how we could help others?
Do we owe an apology? And if so to whom?	Did we study literature today?
What could we have done better?	Did we go to a meeting today?
Did we blame our feelings on someone else?	Did we call our sponsor today?
Do we need to write 10th Step on something?	Did we do anything that is improved over our past?

Journal—Gratitude List—Tomorrows Action Plan

STEP 10

BALANCE SHEETS

Day _____ Month _____ Year _____

Food		Money	
Breakfast		Item	Amount
Lunch			
Dinner			
Snack			
Exercise			
		Total Spent Today	
Litres Water	Hours Sleep	Quality of Life Today	%

When we retire at night we constructively review our day. We remember we have ceased fighting anything and anyone—love and tolerance of others is our code.

We Draw Up a Balance Sheet

The "Negative Side" (-)	The "Positive Side" (+)
Were we resentful?	Have we stayed clean of our addiction today?
Were we selfish?	Were we kind?
Were we dishonest?	Were we loving toward all?
Were we afraid?	What did we pack into life?
Have we kept something to ourselves?	Did we pray and meditate?
Were we thinking of ourselves most of the time?	Did we call someone we could help today?
Were we "disturbed" today?	Did we think of how we could help others?
Do we owe an apology? And if so to whom?	Did we study literature today?
What could we have done better?	Did we go to a meeting today?
Did we blame our feelings on someone else?	Did we call our sponsor today?
Do we need to write 10th Step on something?	Did we do anything that is improved over our past?

Journal—Gratitude List—Tomorrows Action Plan

BALANCE SHEETS

Day _____ Month _____ Year _____

Food

Breakfast		
Lunch		
Dinner		
Snack		
Exercise		
Litres Water	Hours Sleep	

Money

Item	Amount
Total Spent Today	
Quality of Life Today	**%**

When we retire at night we constructively review our day. We remember we have ceased fighting anything and anyone—love and tolerance of others is our code.

We Draw Up a Balance Sheet

The "Negative Side" (-)	The "Positive Side" (+)
Were we resentful?	Have we stayed clean of our addiction today?
Were we selfish?	Were we kind?
Were we dishonest?	Were we loving toward all?
Were we afraid?	What did we pack into life?
Have we kept something to ourselves?	Did we pray and meditate?
Were we thinking of ourselves most of the time?	Did we call someone we could help today?
Were we "disturbed" today?	Did we think of how we could help others?
Do we owe an apology? And if so to whom?	Did we study literature today?
What could we have done better?	Did we go to a meeting today?
Did we blame our feelings on someone else?	Did we call our sponsor today?
Do we need to write 10th Step on something?	Did we do anything that is improved over our past?

Journal—Gratitude List—Tomorrows Action Plan

STEP 10

BALANCE SHEETS

Day _____ Month _____ Year_____

Food		Money	
Breakfast		Item	Amount
Lunch			
Dinner			
Snack			
Exercise			
		Total Spent Today	
Litres Water	Hours Sleep	Quality of Life Today	%

When we retire at night we constructively review our day. We remember we have ceased fighting anything and anyone—love and tolerance of others is our code.

We Draw Up a Balance Sheet

The "Negative Side" (-)	The "Positive Side" (+)
Were we resentful?	Have we stayed clean of our addiction today?
Were we selfish?	Were we kind?
Were we dishonest?	Were we loving toward all?
Were we afraid?	What did we pack into life?
Have we kept something to ourselves?	Did we pray and meditate?
Were we thinking of ourselves most of the time?	Did we call someone we could help today?
Were we "disturbed" today?	Did we think of how we could help others?
Do we owe an apology? And if so to whom?	Did we study literature today?
What could we have done better?	Did we go to a meeting today?
Did we blame our feelings on someone else?	Did we call our sponsor today?
Do we need to write 10th Step on something?	Did we do anything that is improved over our past?

Journal—Gratitude List—Tomorrows Action Plan

MAINTAINING THE PROMISES...DAILY

BALANCE SHEETS

Day _____ Month _____ Year_____

Food

Breakfast		
Lunch		
Dinner		
Snack		
Exercise		
Litres Water Hours Sleep		

Money

Item	Amount
Total Spent Today	
Quality of Life Today	%

When we retire at night we constructively review our day. We remember we have ceased fighting anything and anyone—love and tolerance of others is our code.

We Draw Up a Balance Sheet

The "Negative Side" (-)	The "Positive Side" (+)
Were we resentful?	Have we stayed clean of our addiction today?
Were we selfish?	Were we kind?
Were we dishonest?	Were we loving toward all?
Were we afraid?	What did we pack into life?
Have we kept something to ourselves?	Did we pray and meditate?
Were we thinking of ourselves most of the time?	Did we call someone we could help today?
Were we "disturbed" today?	Did we think of how we could help others?
Do we owe an apology? And if so to whom?	Did we study literature today?
What could we have done better?	Did we go to a meeting today?
Did we blame our feelings on someone else?	Did we call our sponsor today?
Do we need to write 10th Step on something?	Did we do anything that is improved over our past?

Journal—Gratitude List—Tomorrows Action Plan

STEP 10

BALANCE SHEETS

Day _____ Month _____ Year _____

Food		Money		
Breakfast		Item		Amount
Lunch				
Dinner				
Snack				
Exercise				
		Total Spent Today		
Litres Water	Hours Sleep	Quality of Life Today		%

When we retire at night we constructively review our day. We remember we have ceased fighting anything and anyone—love and tolerance of others is our code.

We Draw Up a Balance Sheet

The "Negative Side" (-)	The "Positive Side" (+)
Were we resentful?	Have we stayed clean of our addiction today?
Were we selfish?	Were we kind?
Were we dishonest?	Were we loving toward all?
Were we afraid?	What did we pack into life?
Have we kept something to ourselves?	Did we pray and meditate?
Were we thinking of ourselves most of the time?	Did we call someone we could help today?
Were we "disturbed" today?	Did we think of how we could help others?
Do we owe an apology? And if so to whom?	Did we study literature today?
What could we have done better?	Did we go to a meeting today?
Did we blame our feelings on someone else?	Did we call our sponsor today?
Do we need to write 10th Step on something?	Did we do anything that is improved over our past?

Journal—Gratitude List—Tomorrows Action Plan

BALANCE SHEETS

Day _____ Month _____ Year _____

Food

Breakfast		Money	
		Item	Amount
Lunch			
Dinner			
Snack			
Exercise			
		Total Spent Today	
Litres Water	Hours Sleep	Quality of Life Today	%

When we retire at night we constructively review our day. We remember we have ceased fighting anything and anyone—love and tolerance of others is our code.

We Draw Up a Balance Sheet

The "Negative Side" (-)	The "Positive Side" (+)
Were we resentful?	Have we stayed clean of our addiction today?
Were we selfish?	Were we kind?
Were we dishonest?	Were we loving toward all?
Were we afraid?	What did we pack into life?
Have we kept something to ourselves?	Did we pray and meditate?
Were we thinking of ourselves most of the time?	Did we call someone we could help today?
Were we "disturbed" today?	Did we think of how we could help others?
Do we owe an apology? And if so to whom?	Did we study literature today?
What could we have done better?	Did we go to a meeting today?
Did we blame our feelings on someone else?	Did we call our sponsor today?
Do we need to write 10th Step on something?	Did we do anything that is improved over our past?

Journal—Gratitude List—Tomorrows Action Plan

STEP 10

BALANCE SHEETS

Day _____ Month _____ Year _____

Food		Money	
Breakfast		Item	Amount
Lunch			
Dinner			
Snack			
Exercise			
		Total Spent Today	
Litres Water	Hours Sleep	Quality of Life Today	%

When we retire at night we constructively review our day. We remember we have ceased fighting anything and anyone—love and tolerance of others is our code.

We Draw Up a Balance Sheet

The "Negative Side" (-)	The "Positive Side" (+)
Were we resentful?	Have we stayed clean of our addiction today?
Were we selfish?	Were we kind?
Were we dishonest?	Were we loving toward all?
Were we afraid?	What did we pack into life?
Have we kept something to ourselves?	Did we pray and meditate?
Were we thinking of ourselves most of the time?	Did we call someone we could help today?
Were we "disturbed" today?	Did we think of how we could help others?
Do we owe an apology? And if so to whom?	Did we study literature today?
What could we have done better?	Did we go to a meeting today?
Did we blame our feelings on someone else?	Did we call our sponsor today?
Do we need to write 10th Step on something?	Did we do anything that is improved over our past?

Journal—Gratitude List—Tomorrows Action Plan

BALANCE SHEETS

Day _____ Month _____ Year _____

Food		Money	
Breakfast		Item	Amount
Lunch			
Dinner			
Snack			
Exercise			
		Total Spent Today	
Litres Water ___ Hours Sleep ___		Quality of Life Today	%

When we retire at night we constructively review our day. We remember we have ceased fighting anything and anyone—love and tolerance of others is our code.

We Draw Up a Balance Sheet

The "Negative Side" (-)	The "Positive Side" (+)
Were we resentful?	Have we stayed clean of our addiction today?
Were we selfish?	Were we kind?
Were we dishonest?	Were we loving toward all?
Were we afraid?	What did we pack into life?
Have we kept something to ourselves?	Did we pray and meditate?
Were we thinking of ourselves most of the time?	Did we call someone we could help today?
Were we "disturbed" today?	Did we think of how we could help others?
Do we owe an apology? And if so to whom?	Did we study literature today?
What could we have done better?	Did we go to a meeting today?
Did we blame our feelings on someone else?	Did we call our sponsor today?
Do we need to write 10th Step on something?	Did we do anything that is improved over our past?

Journal—Gratitude List—Tomorrows Action Plan

STEP 10

BALANCE SHEETS

Day _____ Month _____ Year _____

Food

Breakfast		
Lunch		
Dinner		
Snack		
Exercise		
Litres Water	Hours Sleep	

Money

Item	Amount
Total Spent Today	
Quality of Life Today	%

When we retire at night we constructively review our day. We remember we have ceased fighting anything and anyone—love and tolerance of others is our code.

We Draw Up a Balance Sheet

The "Negative Side" (-)	The "Positive Side" (+)
Were we resentful?	Have we stayed clean of our addiction today?
Were we selfish?	Were we kind?
Were we dishonest?	Were we loving toward all?
Were we afraid?	What did we pack into life?
Have we kept something to ourselves?	Did we pray and meditate?
Were we thinking of ourselves most of the time?	Did we call someone we could help today?
Were we "disturbed" today?	Did we think of how we could help others?
Do we owe an apology? And if so to whom?	Did we study literature today?
What could we have done better?	Did we go to a meeting today?
Did we blame our feelings on someone else?	Did we call our sponsor today?
Do we need to write 10th Step on something?	Did we do anything that is improved over our past?

Journal—Gratitude List—Tomorrows Action Plan

BALANCE SHEETS

Day _____ Month _____ Year _____

Food		Money	
Breakfast		Item	Amount
Lunch			
Dinner			
Snack			
Exercise			
		Total Spent Today	
Litres Water	Hours Sleep	Quality of Life Today	%

When we retire at night we constructively review our day. We remember we have ceased fighting anything and anyone—love and tolerance of others is our code.

We Draw Up a Balance Sheet

The "Negative Side" (-)	The "Positive Side" (+)
Were we resentful?	Have we stayed clean of our addiction today?
Were we selfish?	Were we kind?
Were we dishonest?	Were we loving toward all?
Were we afraid?	What did we pack into life?
Have we kept something to ourselves?	Did we pray and meditate?
Were we thinking of ourselves most of the time?	Did we call someone we could help today?
Were we "disturbed" today?	Did we think of how we could help others?
Do we owe an apology? And if so to whom?	Did we study literature today?
What could we have done better?	Did we go to a meeting today?
Did we blame our feelings on someone else?	Did we call our sponsor today?
Do we need to write 10th Step on something?	Did we do anything that is improved over our past?

Journal—Gratitude List—Tomorrows Action Plan

STEP 10

BALANCE SHEETS

Day _____ Month _____ Year _____

Food

Breakfast		
Lunch		
Dinner		
Snack		
Exercise		
Litres Water	Hours Sleep	

Money

Item		Amount
Total Spent Today		
Quality of Life Today		%

When we retire at night we constructively review our day. We remember we have ceased fighting anything and anyone—love and tolerance of others is our code.

We Draw Up a Balance Sheet

The "Negative Side" (−)	The "Positive Side" (+)
Were we resentful?	Have we stayed clean of our addiction today?
Were we selfish?	Were we kind?
Were we dishonest?	Were we loving toward all?
Were we afraid?	What did we pack into life?
Have we kept something to ourselves?	Did we pray and meditate?
Were we thinking of ourselves most of the time?	Did we call someone we could help today?
Were we "disturbed" today?	Did we think of how we could help others?
Do we owe an apology? And if so to whom?	Did we study literature today?
What could we have done better?	Did we go to a meeting today?
Did we blame our feelings on someone else?	Did we call our sponsor today?
Do we need to write 10th Step on something?	Did we do anything that is improved over our past?

Journal—Gratitude List—Tomorrows Action Plan

BALANCE SHEETS

Day _____ Month _____ Year _____

Food		Money	
Breakfast		Item	Amount
Lunch			
Dinner			
Snack			
Exercise			
		Total Spent Today	
Litres Water	Hours Sleep	Quality of Life Today	%

When we retire at night we constructively review our day. We remember we have ceased fighting anything and anyone—love and tolerance of others is our code.

We Draw Up a Balance Sheet

The "Negative Side" (-)	The "Positive Side" (+)
Were we resentful?	Have we stayed clean of our addiction today?
Were we selfish?	Were we kind?
Were we dishonest?	Were we loving toward all?
Were we afraid?	What did we pack into life?
Have we kept something to ourselves?	Did we pray and meditate?
Were we thinking of ourselves most of the time?	Did we call someone we could help today?
Were we "disturbed" today?	Did we think of how we could help others?
Do we owe an apology? And if so to whom?	Did we study literature today?
What could we have done better?	Did we go to a meeting today?
Did we blame our feelings on someone else?	Did we call our sponsor today?
Do we need to write 10th Step on something?	Did we do anything that is improved over our past?

Journal—Gratitude List—Tomorrows Action Plan

STEP 10

BALANCE SHEETS

Day _____ Month _____ Year _____

Food		Money	
Breakfast		Item	Amount
Lunch			
Dinner			
Snack			
Exercise			
		Total Spent Today	
Litres Water	Hours Sleep	Quality of Life Today	%

When we retire at night we constructively review our day. We remember we have ceased fighting anything and anyone—love and tolerance of others is our code.

We Draw Up a Balance Sheet

The "Negative Side" (-)	The "Positive Side" (+)
Were we resentful?	Have we stayed clean of our addiction today?
Were we selfish?	Were we kind?
Were we dishonest?	Were we loving toward all?
Were we afraid?	What did we pack into life?
Have we kept something to ourselves?	Did we pray and meditate?
Were we thinking of ourselves most of the time?	Did we call someone we could help today?
Were we "disturbed" today?	Did we think of how we could help others?
Do we owe an apology? And if so to whom?	Did we study literature today?
What could we have done better?	Did we go to a meeting today?
Did we blame our feelings on someone else?	Did we call our sponsor today?
Do we need to write 10th Step on something?	Did we do anything that is improved over our past?

Journal—Gratitude List—Tomorrows Action Plan

BALANCE SHEETS

Day _____ Month _____ Year_____

Food		Money	
Breakfast		Item	Amount
Lunch			
Dinner			
Snack			
Exercise			
		Total Spent Today	
Litres Water	Hours Sleep	Quality of Life Today	%

When we retire at night we constructively review our day. We remember we have ceased fighting anything and anyone—love and tolerance of others is our code.

We Draw Up a Balance Sheet

The "Negative Side" (-)	The "Positive Side" (+)
Were we resentful?	Have we stayed clean of our addiction today?
Were we selfish?	Were we kind?
Were we dishonest?	Were we loving toward all?
Were we afraid?	What did we pack into life?
Have we kept something to ourselves?	Did we pray and meditate?
Were we thinking of ourselves most of the time?	Did we call someone we could help today?
Were we "disturbed" today?	Did we think of how we could help others?
Do we owe an apology? And if so to whom?	Did we study literature today?
What could we have done better?	Did we go to a meeting today?
Did we blame our feelings on someone else?	Did we call our sponsor today?
Do we need to write 10th Step on something?	Did we do anything that is improved over our past?

Journal—Gratitude List—Tomorrows Action Plan

STEP 10

BALANCE SHEETS

Day _____ Month _____ Year_____

Food

Breakfast		Money	
		Item	Amount
Lunch			
Dinner			
Snack			
Exercise			
		Total Spent Today	
Litres Water	Hours Sleep	Quality of Life Today	%

When we retire at night we constructively review our day. We remember we have ceased fighting anything and anyone—love and tolerance of others is our code.

We Draw Up a Balance Sheet

The "Negative Side" (-)	The "Positive Side" (+)
Were we resentful?	Have we stayed clean of our addiction today?
Were we selfish?	Were we kind?
Were we dishonest?	Were we loving toward all?
Were we afraid?	What did we pack into life?
Have we kept something to ourselves?	Did we pray and meditate?
Were we thinking of ourselves most of the time?	Did we call someone we could help today?
Were we "disturbed" today?	Did we think of how we could help others?
Do we owe an apology? And if so to whom?	Did we study literature today?
What could we have done better?	Did we go to a meeting today?
Did we blame our feelings on someone else?	Did we call our sponsor today?
Do we need to write 10th Step on something?	Did we do anything that is improved over our past?

Journal—Gratitude List—Tomorrows Action Plan

MAINTAINING THE PROMISES...DAILY

BALANCE SHEETS

Day _____ Month _____ Year _____

Food		Money	
Breakfast		Item	Amount
Lunch			
Dinner			
Snack			
Exercise			
		Total Spent Today	
Litres Water ____ Hours Sleep ____		Quality of Life Today	%

When we retire at night we constructively review our day. We remember we have ceased fighting anything and anyone—love and tolerance of others is our code.

We Draw Up a Balance Sheet

The "Negative Side" (-)	The "Positive Side" (+)
Were we resentful?	Have we stayed clean of our addiction today?
Were we selfish?	Were we kind?
Were we dishonest?	Were we loving toward all?
Were we afraid?	What did we pack into life?
Have we kept something to ourselves?	Did we pray and meditate?
Were we thinking of ourselves most of the time?	Did we call someone we could help today?
Were we "disturbed" today?	Did we think of how we could help others?
Do we owe an apology? And if so to whom?	Did we study literature today?
What could we have done better?	Did we go to a meeting today?
Did we blame our feelings on someone else?	Did we call our sponsor today?
Do we need to write 10th Step on something?	Did we do anything that is improved over our past?

Journal—Gratitude List—Tomorrows Action Plan

STEP 10

BALANCE SHEETS

Day _____ Month _____ Year _____

Food		Money	
Breakfast		Item	Amount
Lunch			
Dinner			
Snack			
Exercise			
		Total Spent Today	
Litres Water	Hours Sleep	Quality of Life Today	%

When we retire at night we constructively review our day. We remember we have ceased fighting anything and anyone—love and tolerance of others is our code.

We Draw Up a Balance Sheet

The "Negative Side" (−)	The "Positive Side" (+)
Were we resentful?	Have we stayed clean of our addiction today?
Were we selfish?	Were we kind?
Were we dishonest?	Were we loving toward all?
Were we afraid?	What did we pack into life?
Have we kept something to ourselves?	Did we pray and meditate?
Were we thinking of ourselves most of the time?	Did we call someone we could help today?
Were we "disturbed" today?	Did we think of how we could help others?
Do we owe an apology? And if so to whom?	Did we study literature today?
What could we have done better?	Did we go to a meeting today?
Did we blame our feelings on someone else?	Did we call our sponsor today?
Do we need to write 10th Step on something?	Did we do anything that is improved over our past?

Journal—Gratitude List—Tomorrows Action Plan

240   MAINTAINING THE PROMISES...DAILY

BALANCE SHEETS

Day _____ Month _____ Year _____

Food		Money	
Breakfast		Item	Amount
Lunch			
Dinner			
Snack			
Exercise			
		Total Spent Today	
Litres Water Hours Sleep		Quality of Life Today	%

When we retire at night we constructively review our day. We remember we have ceased fighting anything and anyone—love and tolerance of others is our code.

We Draw Up a Balance Sheet

The "Negative Side" (-)	The "Positive Side" (+)
Were we resentful?	Have we stayed clean of our addiction today?
Were we selfish?	Were we kind?
Were we dishonest?	Were we loving toward all?
Were we afraid?	What did we pack into life?
Have we kept something to ourselves?	Did we pray and meditate?
Were we thinking of ourselves most of the time?	Did we call someone we could help today?
Were we "disturbed" today?	Did we think of how we could help others?
Do we owe an apology? And if so to whom?	Did we study literature today?
What could we have done better?	Did we go to a meeting today?
Did we blame our feelings on someone else?	Did we call our sponsor today?
Do we need to write 10th Step on something?	Did we do anything that is improved over our past?

Journal—Gratitude List—Tomorrows Action Plan

STEP 10

BALANCE SHEETS

Day _____ Month _____ Year _____

Food		Money	
Breakfast		Item	Amount
Lunch			
Dinner			
Snack			
Exercise			
		Total Spent Today	
Litres Water Hours Sleep		Quality of Life Today	%

When we retire at night we constructively review our day. We remember we have ceased fighting anything and anyone—love and tolerance of others is our code.

We Draw Up a Balance Sheet

The "Negative Side" (-)	The "Positive Side" (+)
Were we resentful?	Have we stayed clean of our addiction today?
Were we selfish?	Were we kind?
Were we dishonest?	Were we loving toward all?
Were we afraid?	What did we pack into life?
Have we kept something to ourselves?	Did we pray and meditate?
Were we thinking of ourselves most of the time?	Did we call someone we could help today?
Were we "disturbed" today?	Did we think of how we could help others?
Do we owe an apology? And if so to whom?	Did we study literature today?
What could we have done better?	Did we go to a meeting today?
Did we blame our feelings on someone else?	Did we call our sponsor today?
Do we need to write 10th Step on something?	Did we do anything that is improved over our past?

Journal—Gratitude List—Tomorrows Action Plan

BALANCE SHEETS

Day _____ Month _____ Year _____

Food		Money	
Breakfast		Item	Amount
Lunch			
Dinner			
Snack			
Exercise			
		Total Spent Today	
Litres Water	Hours Sleep	Quality of Life Today	%

When we retire at night we constructively review our day. We remember we have ceased fighting anything and anyone—love and tolerance of others is our code.

We Draw Up a Balance Sheet

The "Negative Side" (-)	The "Positive Side" (+)
Were we resentful?	Have we stayed clean of our addiction today?
Were we selfish?	Were we kind?
Were we dishonest?	Were we loving toward all?
Were we afraid?	What did we pack into life?
Have we kept something to ourselves?	Did we pray and meditate?
Were we thinking of ourselves most of the time?	Did we call someone we could help today?
Were we "disturbed" today?	Did we think of how we could help others?
Do we owe an apology? And if so to whom?	Did we study literature today?
What could we have done better?	Did we go to a meeting today?
Did we blame our feelings on someone else?	Did we call our sponsor today?
Do we need to write 10th Step on something?	Did we do anything that is improved over our past?

Journal—Gratitude List—Tomorrows Action Plan

STEP 10

BALANCE SHEETS

Day _____ Month _____ Year _____

Food		Money	
Breakfast		Item	Amount
Lunch			
Dinner			
Snack			
Exercise			
		Total Spent Today	
Litres Water Hours Sleep		Quality of Life Today	%

When we retire at night we constructively review our day. We remember we have ceased fighting anything and anyone—love and tolerance of others is our code.

We Draw Up a Balance Sheet

The "Negative Side" (-)	The "Positive Side" (+)
Were we resentful?	Have we stayed clean of our addiction today?
Were we selfish?	Were we kind?
Were we dishonest?	Were we loving toward all?
Were we afraid?	What did we pack into life?
Have we kept something to ourselves?	Did we pray and meditate?
Were we thinking of ourselves most of the time?	Did we call someone we could help today?
Were we "disturbed" today?	Did we think of how we could help others?
Do we owe an apology? And if so to whom?	Did we study literature today?
What could we have done better?	Did we go to a meeting today?
Did we blame our feelings on someone else?	Did we call our sponsor today?
Do we need to write 10th Step on something?	Did we do anything that is improved over our past?

Journal—Gratitude List—Tomorrows Action Plan

BALANCE SHEETS

Day _____ Month _____ Year_____

Food		Money	
Breakfast		Item	Amount
Lunch			
Dinner			
Snack			
Exercise			
		Total Spent Today	
Litres Water ____ Hours Sleep ____		Quality of Life Today	%

When we retire at night we constructively review our day. We remember we have ceased fighting anything and anyone—love and tolerance of others is our code.

We Draw Up a Balance Sheet

The "Negative Side" (-)	The "Positive Side" (+)
Were we resentful?	Have we stayed clean of our addiction today?
Were we selfish?	Were we kind?
Were we dishonest?	Were we loving toward all?
Were we afraid?	What did we pack into life?
Have we kept something to ourselves?	Did we pray and meditate?
Were we thinking of ourselves most of the time?	Did we call someone we could help today?
Were we "disturbed" today?	Did we think of how we could help others?
Do we owe an apology? And if so to whom?	Did we study literature today?
What could we have done better?	Did we go to a meeting today?
Did we blame our feelings on someone else?	Did we call our sponsor today?
Do we need to write 10th Step on something?	Did we do anything that is improved over our past?

Journal—Gratitude List—Tomorrows Action Plan

STEP 10

BALANCE SHEETS

Day _____ Month _____ Year _____

Food		Money	
Breakfast		Item	Amount
Lunch			
Dinner			
Snack			
Exercise			
		Total Spent Today	
Litres Water	Hours Sleep	Quality of Life Today	%

When we retire at night we constructively review our day. We remember we have ceased fighting anything and anyone—love and tolerance of others is our code.

We Draw Up a Balance Sheet

The "Negative Side" (-)	The "Positive Side" (+)
Were we resentful?	Have we stayed clean of our addiction today?
Were we selfish?	Were we kind?
Were we dishonest?	Were we loving toward all?
Were we afraid?	What did we pack into life?
Have we kept something to ourselves?	Did we pray and meditate?
Were we thinking of ourselves most of the time?	Did we call someone we could help today?
Were we "disturbed" today?	Did we think of how we could help others?
Do we owe an apology? And if so to whom?	Did we study literature today?
What could we have done better?	Did we go to a meeting today?
Did we blame our feelings on someone else?	Did we call our sponsor today?
Do we need to write 10th Step on something?	Did we do anything that is improved over our past?

Journal—Gratitude List—Tomorrows Action Plan

BALANCE SHEETS

Day _____ Month _____ Year _____

Food

Breakfast		
Lunch		
Dinner		
Snack		
Exercise		
Litres Water	Hours Sleep	

Money

Item	Amount
Total Spent Today	
Quality of Life Today	%

When we retire at night we constructively review our day. We remember we have ceased fighting anything and anyone—love and tolerance of others is our code.

We Draw Up a Balance Sheet

The "Negative Side" (-)	The "Positive Side" (+)
Were we resentful?	Have we stayed clean of our addiction today?
Were we selfish?	Were we kind?
Were we dishonest?	Were we loving toward all?
Were we afraid?	What did we pack into life?
Have we kept something to ourselves?	Did we pray and meditate?
Were we thinking of ourselves most of the time?	Did we call someone we could help today?
Were we "disturbed" today?	Did we think of how we could help others?
Do we owe an apology? And if so to whom?	Did we study literature today?
What could we have done better?	Did we go to a meeting today?
Did we blame our feelings on someone else?	Did we call our sponsor today?
Do we need to write 10th Step on something?	Did we do anything that is improved over our past?

Journal—Gratitude List—Tomorrows Action Plan

STEP 10

BALANCE SHEETS

Day _____ Month _____ Year _____

Food		Money	
Breakfast		Item	Amount
Lunch			
Dinner			
Snack			
Exercise			
		Total Spent Today	
Litres Water	Hours Sleep	Quality of Life Today	%

When we retire at night we constructively review our day. We remember we have ceased fighting anything and anyone—love and tolerance of others is our code.

We Draw Up a Balance Sheet

The "Negative Side" (-)	The "Positive Side" (+)
Were we resentful?	Have we stayed clean of our addiction today?
Were we selfish?	Were we kind?
Were we dishonest?	Were we loving toward all?
Were we afraid?	What did we pack into life?
Have we kept something to ourselves?	Did we pray and meditate?
Were we thinking of ourselves most of the time?	Did we call someone we could help today?
Were we "disturbed" today?	Did we think of how we could help others?
Do we owe an apology? And if so to whom?	Did we study literature today?
What could we have done better?	Did we go to a meeting today?
Did we blame our feelings on someone else?	Did we call our sponsor today?
Do we need to write 10th Step on something?	Did we do anything that is improved over our past?

Journal—Gratitude List—Tomorrows Action Plan

MAINTAINING THE PROMISES...DAILY

BALANCE SHEETS

Day _____ Month _____ Year _____

Food

Breakfast		
Lunch		
Dinner		
Snack		
Exercise		
Litres Water	Hours Sleep	

Money

Item	Amount
Total Spent Today	
Quality of Life Today	%

When we retire at night we constructively review our day. We remember we have ceased fighting anything and anyone—love and tolerance of others is our code.

We Draw Up a Balance Sheet

The "Negative Side" (-)	The "Positive Side" (+)
Were we resentful?	Have we stayed clean of our addiction today?
Were we selfish?	Were we kind?
Were we dishonest?	Were we loving toward all?
Were we afraid?	What did we pack into life?
Have we kept something to ourselves?	Did we pray and meditate?
Were we thinking of ourselves most of the time?	Did we call someone we could help today?
Were we "disturbed" today?	Did we think of how we could help others?
Do we owe an apology? And if so to whom?	Did we study literature today?
What could we have done better?	Did we go to a meeting today?
Did we blame our feelings on someone else?	Did we call our sponsor today?
Do we need to write 10th Step on something?	Did we do anything that is improved over our past?

Journal—Gratitude List—Tomorrows Action Plan

STEP 10

BALANCE SHEETS

Day _____ Month _____ Year _____

Food

Breakfast	
Lunch	
Dinner	
Snack	
Exercise	
Litres Water	Hours Sleep

Money

Item	Amount
Total Spent Today	
Quality of Life Today	%

When we retire at night we constructively review our day. We remember we have ceased fighting anything and anyone—love and tolerance of others is our code.

We Draw Up a Balance Sheet

The "Negative Side" (-)	The "Positive Side" (+)
Were we resentful?	Have we stayed clean of our addiction today?
Were we selfish?	Were we kind?
Were we dishonest?	Were we loving toward all?
Were we afraid?	What did we pack into life?
Have we kept something to ourselves?	Did we pray and meditate?
Were we thinking of ourselves most of the time?	Did we call someone we could help today?
Were we "disturbed" today?	Did we think of how we could help others?
Do we owe an apology? And if so to whom?	Did we study literature today?
What could we have done better?	Did we go to a meeting today?
Did we blame our feelings on someone else?	Did we call our sponsor today?
Do we need to write 10th Step on something?	Did we do anything that is improved over our past?

Journal—Gratitude List—Tomorrows Action Plan

BALANCE SHEETS

Day _____ Month _____ Year _____

Food		Money	
Breakfast		Item	Amount
Lunch			
Dinner			
Snack			
Exercise			
		Total Spent Today	
Litres Water ___ Hours Sleep ___		Quality of Life Today	%

When we retire at night we constructively review our day. We remember we have ceased fighting anything and anyone—love and tolerance of others is our code.

We Draw Up a Balance Sheet

The "Negative Side" (-)	The "Positive Side" (+)
Were we resentful?	Have we stayed clean of our addiction today?
Were we selfish?	Were we kind?
Were we dishonest?	Were we loving toward all?
Were we afraid?	What did we pack into life?
Have we kept something to ourselves?	Did we pray and meditate?
Were we thinking of ourselves most of the time?	Did we call someone we could help today?
Were we "disturbed" today?	Did we think of how we could help others?
Do we owe an apology? And if so to whom?	Did we study literature today?
What could we have done better?	Did we go to a meeting today?
Did we blame our feelings on someone else?	Did we call our sponsor today?
Do we need to write 10th Step on something?	Did we do anything that is improved over our past?

Journal—Gratitude List—Tomorrows Action Plan

STEP 10

BALANCE SHEETS

Day _____ Month _____ Year _____

Food		Money	
Breakfast		Item	Amount
Lunch			
Dinner			
Snack			
Exercise			
		Total Spent Today	
Litres Water	Hours Sleep	Quality of Life Today	%

When we retire at night we constructively review our day. We remember we have ceased fighting anything and anyone—love and tolerance of others is our code.

We Draw Up a Balance Sheet

The "Negative Side" (-)	The "Positive Side" (+)
Were we resentful?	Have we stayed clean of our addiction today?
Were we selfish?	Were we kind?
Were we dishonest?	Were we loving toward all?
Were we afraid?	What did we pack into life?
Have we kept something to ourselves?	Did we pray and meditate?
Were we thinking of ourselves most of the time?	Did we call someone we could help today?
Were we "disturbed" today?	Did we think of how we could help others?
Do we owe an apology? And if so to whom?	Did we study literature today?
What could we have done better?	Did we go to a meeting today?
Did we blame our feelings on someone else?	Did we call our sponsor today?
Do we need to write 10th Step on something?	Did we do anything that is improved over our past?

Journal—Gratitude List—Tomorrows Action Plan

BALANCE SHEETS

Day _____ Month _____ Year _____

Food		Money		
Breakfast		Item		Amount
Lunch				
Dinner				
Snack				
Exercise				
		Total Spent Today		
Litres Water	Hours Sleep	Quality of Life Today		%

When we retire at night we constructively review our day. We remember we have ceased fighting anything and anyone—love and tolerance of others is our code.

We Draw Up a Balance Sheet

The "Negative Side" (-)	The "Positive Side" (+)
Were we resentful?	Have we stayed clean of our addiction today?
Were we selfish?	Were we kind?
Were we dishonest?	Were we loving toward all?
Were we afraid?	What did we pack into life?
Have we kept something to ourselves?	Did we pray and meditate?
Were we thinking of ourselves most of the time?	Did we call someone we could help today?
Were we "disturbed" today?	Did we think of how we could help others?
Do we owe an apology? And if so to whom?	Did we study literature today?
What could we have done better?	Did we go to a meeting today?
Did we blame our feelings on someone else?	Did we call our sponsor today?
Do we need to write 10th Step on something?	Did we do anything that is improved over our past?

Journal—Gratitude List—Tomorrows Action Plan

STEP 10

BALANCE SHEETS

Day _____ Month _____ Year_____

Food		Money	
Breakfast		Item	Amount
Lunch			
Dinner			
Snack			
Exercise			
		Total Spent Today	
Litres Water	Hours Sleep	Quality of Life Today	%

When we retire at night we constructively review our day. We remember we have ceased fighting anything and anyone—love and tolerance of others is our code.

We Draw Up a Balance Sheet

The "Negative Side" (-)	The "Positive Side" (+)
Were we resentful?	Have we stayed clean of our addiction today?
Were we selfish?	Were we kind?
Were we dishonest?	Were we loving toward all?
Were we afraid?	What did we pack into life?
Have we kept something to ourselves?	Did we pray and meditate?
Were we thinking of ourselves most of the time?	Did we call someone we could help today?
Were we "disturbed" today?	Did we think of how we could help others?
Do we owe an apology? And if so to whom?	Did we study literature today?
What could we have done better?	Did we go to a meeting today?
Did we blame our feelings on someone else?	Did we call our sponsor today?
Do we need to write 10th Step on something?	Did we do anything that is improved over our past?

Journal—Gratitude List—Tomorrows Action Plan

BALANCE SHEETS

Day _____ Month _____ Year _____

Food		Money	
Breakfast		Item	Amount
Lunch			
Dinner			
Snack			
Exercise			
		Total Spent Today	
Litres Water	Hours Sleep	Quality of Life Today	%

When we retire at night we constructively review our day. We remember we have ceased fighting anything and anyone—love and tolerance of others is our code.

We Draw Up a Balance Sheet

The "Negative Side" (-)	The "Positive Side" (+)
Were we resentful?	Have we stayed clean of our addiction today?
Were we selfish?	Were we kind?
Were we dishonest?	Were we loving toward all?
Were we afraid?	What did we pack into life?
Have we kept something to ourselves?	Did we pray and meditate?
Were we thinking of ourselves most of the time?	Did we call someone we could help today?
Were we "disturbed" today?	Did we think of how we could help others?
Do we owe an apology? And if so to whom?	Did we study literature today?
What could we have done better?	Did we go to a meeting today?
Did we blame our feelings on someone else?	Did we call our sponsor today?
Do we need to write 10th Step on something?	Did we do anything that is improved over our past?

Journal—Gratitude List—Tomorrows Action Plan

STEP 10

BALANCE SHEETS

Day _____ Month _____ Year _____

Food		Money	
Breakfast		Item	Amount
Lunch			
Dinner			
Snack			
Exercise			
		Total Spent Today	
Litres Water	Hours Sleep	Quality of Life Today	%

When we retire at night we constructively review our day. We remember we have ceased fighting anything and anyone—love and tolerance of others is our code.

We Draw Up a Balance Sheet

The "Negative Side" (-)	The "Positive Side" (+)
Were we resentful?	Have we stayed clean of our addiction today?
Were we selfish?	Were we kind?
Were we dishonest?	Were we loving toward all?
Were we afraid?	What did we pack into life?
Have we kept something to ourselves?	Did we pray and meditate?
Were we thinking of ourselves most of the time?	Did we call someone we could help today?
Were we "disturbed" today?	Did we think of how we could help others?
Do we owe an apology? And if so to whom?	Did we study literature today?
What could we have done better?	Did we go to a meeting today?
Did we blame our feelings on someone else?	Did we call our sponsor today?
Do we need to write 10th Step on something?	Did we do anything that is improved over our past?

Journal—Gratitude List—Tomorrows Action Plan

MAINTAINING THE PROMISES...DAILY

BALANCE SHEETS

Day _____ Month _____ Year _____

Food		Money	
Breakfast		Item	Amount
Lunch			
Dinner			
Snack			
Exercise			
		Total Spent Today	
Litres Water	Hours Sleep	Quality of Life Today	%

When we retire at night we constructively review our day. We remember we have ceased fighting anything and anyone—love and tolerance of others is our code.

We Draw Up a Balance Sheet

The "Negative Side" (−)	The "Positive Side" (+)
Were we resentful?	Have we stayed clean of our addiction today?
Were we selfish?	Were we kind?
Were we dishonest?	Were we loving toward all?
Were we afraid?	What did we pack into life?
Have we kept something to ourselves?	Did we pray and meditate?
Were we thinking of ourselves most of the time?	Did we call someone we could help today?
Were we "disturbed" today?	Did we think of how we could help others?
Do we owe an apology? And if so to whom?	Did we study literature today?
What could we have done better?	Did we go to a meeting today?
Did we blame our feelings on someone else?	Did we call our sponsor today?
Do we need to write 10th Step on something?	Did we do anything that is improved over our past?

Journal—Gratitude List—Tomorrows Action Plan

STEP 10

BALANCE SHEETS

Day _____ Month _____ Year _____

Food

Breakfast	
Lunch	
Dinner	
Snack	
Exercise	
Litres Water	Hours Sleep

Money

Item	Amount
Total Spent Today	
Quality of Life Today	%

When we retire at night we constructively review our day. We remember we have ceased fighting anything and anyone—love and tolerance of others is our code.

We Draw Up a Balance Sheet

The "Negative Side" (-)	The "Positive Side" (+)
Were we resentful?	Have we stayed clean of our addiction today?
Were we selfish?	Were we kind?
Were we dishonest?	Were we loving toward all?
Were we afraid?	What did we pack into life?
Have we kept something to ourselves?	Did we pray and meditate?
Were we thinking of ourselves most of the time?	Did we call someone we could help today?
Were we "disturbed" today?	Did we think of how we could help others?
Do we owe an apology? And if so to whom?	Did we study literature today?
What could we have done better?	Did we go to a meeting today?
Did we blame our feelings on someone else?	Did we call our sponsor today?
Do we need to write 10th Step on something?	Did we do anything that is improved over our past?

Journal—Gratitude List—Tomorrows Action Plan

BALANCE SHEETS

Day _____ Month _____ Year _____

Food

Breakfast		
Lunch		
Dinner		
Snack		
Exercise		
Litres Water _____ Hours Sleep _____		

Money

Item	Amount
Total Spent Today	
Quality of Life Today	%

When we retire at night we constructively review our day. We remember we have ceased fighting anything and anyone—love and tolerance of others is our code.

We Draw Up a Balance Sheet

The "Negative Side" (-)	The "Positive Side" (+)
Were we resentful?	Have we stayed clean of our addiction today?
Were we selfish?	Were we kind?
Were we dishonest?	Were we loving toward all?
Were we afraid?	What did we pack into life?
Have we kept something to ourselves?	Did we pray and meditate?
Were we thinking of ourselves most of the time?	Did we call someone we could help today?
Were we "disturbed" today?	Did we think of how we could help others?
Do we owe an apology? And if so to whom?	Did we study literature today?
What could we have done better?	Did we go to a meeting today?
Did we blame our feelings on someone else?	Did we call our sponsor today?
Do we need to write 10th Step on something?	Did we do anything that is improved over our past?

Journal—Gratitude List—Tomorrows Action Plan

STEP 10

BALANCE SHEETS

Day _____ Month _____ Year _____

Food

Breakfast		Money	
		Item	Amount
Lunch			
Dinner			
Snack			
Exercise			
		Total Spent Today	
Litres Water	Hours Sleep	Quality of Life Today	%

When we retire at night we constructively review our day. We remember we have ceased fighting anything and anyone—love and tolerance of others is our code.

We Draw Up a Balance Sheet

The "Negative Side" (-)	The "Positive Side" (+)
Were we resentful?	Have we stayed clean of our addiction today?
Were we selfish?	Were we kind?
Were we dishonest?	Were we loving toward all?
Were we afraid?	What did we pack into life?
Have we kept something to ourselves?	Did we pray and meditate?
Were we thinking of ourselves most of the time?	Did we call someone we could help today?
Were we "disturbed" today?	Did we think of how we could help others?
Do we owe an apology? And if so to whom?	Did we study literature today?
What could we have done better?	Did we go to a meeting today?
Did we blame our feelings on someone else?	Did we call our sponsor today?
Do we need to write 10th Step on something?	Did we do anything that is improved over our past?

Journal—Gratitude List—Tomorrows Action Plan

BALANCE SHEETS

Day _____ Month _____ Year _____

Food

Breakfast		
Lunch		
Dinner		
Snack		
Exercise		
Litres Water	Hours Sleep	

Money

Item	Amount
Total Spent Today	
Quality of Life Today	%

When we retire at night we constructively review our day. We remember we have ceased fighting anything and anyone—love and tolerance of others is our code.

We Draw Up a Balance Sheet

The "Negative Side" (-)	The "Positive Side" (+)
Were we resentful?	Have we stayed clean of our addiction today?
Were we selfish?	Were we kind?
Were we dishonest?	Were we loving toward all?
Were we afraid?	What did we pack into life?
Have we kept something to ourselves?	Did we pray and meditate?
Were we thinking of ourselves most of the time?	Did we call someone we could help today?
Were we "disturbed" today?	Did we think of how we could help others?
Do we owe an apology? And if so to whom?	Did we study literature today?
What could we have done better?	Did we go to a meeting today?
Did we blame our feelings on someone else?	Did we call our sponsor today?
Do we need to write 10th Step on something?	Did we do anything that is improved over our past?

Journal—Gratitude List—Tomorrows Action Plan

STEP 10

BALANCE SHEETS

Day _____ Month _____ Year _____

Food		Money	
Breakfast		Item	Amount
Lunch			
Dinner			
Snack			
Exercise			
		Total Spent Today	
Litres Water	Hours Sleep	Quality of Life Today	%

When we retire at night we constructively review our day. We remember we have ceased fighting anything and anyone—love and tolerance of others is our code.

We Draw Up a Balance Sheet

The "Negative Side" (-)	The "Positive Side" (+)
Were we resentful?	Have we stayed clean of our addiction today?
Were we selfish?	Were we kind?
Were we dishonest?	Were we loving toward all?
Were we afraid?	What did we pack into life?
Have we kept something to ourselves?	Did we pray and meditate?
Were we thinking of ourselves most of the time?	Did we call someone we could help today?
Were we "disturbed" today?	Did we think of how we could help others?
Do we owe an apology? And if so to whom?	Did we study literature today?
What could we have done better?	Did we go to a meeting today?
Did we blame our feelings on someone else?	Did we call our sponsor today?
Do we need to write 10th Step on something?	Did we do anything that is improved over our past?

Journal—Gratitude List—Tomorrows Action Plan

BALANCE SHEETS

Day _____ Month _____ Year _____

Food		Money	
Breakfast		Item	Amount
Lunch			
Dinner			
Snack			
Exercise			
		Total Spent Today	
Litres Water	Hours Sleep	Quality of Life Today	%

When we retire at night we constructively review our day. We remember we have ceased fighting anything and anyone—love and tolerance of others is our code.

We Draw Up a Balance Sheet

The "Negative Side" (−)	The "Positive Side" (+)
Were we resentful?	Have we stayed clean of our addiction today?
Were we selfish?	Were we kind?
Were we dishonest?	Were we loving toward all?
Were we afraid?	What did we pack into life?
Have we kept something to ourselves?	Did we pray and meditate?
Were we thinking of ourselves most of the time?	Did we call someone we could help today?
Were we "disturbed" today?	Did we think of how we could help others?
Do we owe an apology? And if so to whom?	Did we study literature today?
What could we have done better?	Did we go to a meeting today?
Did we blame our feelings on someone else?	Did we call our sponsor today?
Do we need to write 10th Step on something?	Did we do anything that is improved over our past?

Journal—Gratitude List—Tomorrows Action Plan

STEP 10

BALANCE SHEETS

Day _____ Month _____ Year _____

Food

Breakfast	
Lunch	
Dinner	
Snack	
Exercise	
Litres Water _____ Hours Sleep _____	

Money

Item	Amount
Total Spent Today	
Quality of Life Today	%

When we retire at night we constructively review our day. We remember we have ceased fighting anything and anyone—love and tolerance of others is our code.

We Draw Up a Balance Sheet

The "Negative Side" (-)	The "Positive Side" (+)
Were we resentful?	Have we stayed clean of our addiction today?
Were we selfish?	Were we kind?
Were we dishonest?	Were we loving toward all?
Were we afraid?	What did we pack into life?
Have we kept something to ourselves?	Did we pray and meditate?
Were we thinking of ourselves most of the time?	Did we call someone we could help today?
Were we "disturbed" today?	Did we think of how we could help others?
Do we owe an apology? And if so to whom?	Did we study literature today?
What could we have done better?	Did we go to a meeting today?
Did we blame our feelings on someone else?	Did we call our sponsor today?
Do we need to write 10th Step on something?	Did we do anything that is improved over our past?

Journal—Gratitude List—Tomorrows Action Plan

BALANCE SHEETS

Day _____ Month _____ Year _____

Food		Money	
Breakfast		Item	Amount
Lunch			
Dinner			
Snack			
Exercise			
		Total Spent Today	
Litres Water	Hours Sleep	Quality of Life Today	%

When we retire at night we constructively review our day. We remember we have ceased fighting anything and anyone—love and tolerance of others is our code.

We Draw Up a Balance Sheet

The "Negative Side" (-)	The "Positive Side" (+)
Were we resentful?	Have we stayed clean of our addiction today?
Were we selfish?	Were we kind?
Were we dishonest?	Were we loving toward all?
Were we afraid?	What did we pack into life?
Have we kept something to ourselves?	Did we pray and meditate?
Were we thinking of ourselves most of the time?	Did we call someone we could help today?
Were we "disturbed" today?	Did we think of how we could help others?
Do we owe an apology? And if so to whom?	Did we study literature today?
What could we have done better?	Did we go to a meeting today?
Did we blame our feelings on someone else?	Did we call our sponsor today?
Do we need to write 10th Step on something?	Did we do anything that is improved over our past?

Journal—Gratitude List—Tomorrows Action Plan

STEP 10

BALANCE SHEETS

Day _____ Month _____ Year _____

Food

Breakfast		Money	
		Item	Amount
Lunch			
Dinner			
Snack			
Exercise			
		Total Spent Today	
Litres Water	Hours Sleep	Quality of Life Today	%

When we retire at night we constructively review our day. We remember we have ceased fighting anything and anyone—love and tolerance of others is our code.

We Draw Up a Balance Sheet

The "Negative Side" (-)	The "Positive Side" (+)
Were we resentful?	Have we stayed clean of our addiction today?
Were we selfish?	Were we kind?
Were we dishonest?	Were we loving toward all?
Were we afraid?	What did we pack into life?
Have we kept something to ourselves?	Did we pray and meditate?
Were we thinking of ourselves most of the time?	Did we call someone we could help today?
Were we "disturbed" today?	Did we think of how we could help others?
Do we owe an apology? And if so to whom?	Did we study literature today?
What could we have done better?	Did we go to a meeting today?
Did we blame our feelings on someone else?	Did we call our sponsor today?
Do we need to write 10th Step on something?	Did we do anything that is improved over our past?

Journal—Gratitude List—Tomorrows Action Plan

BALANCE SHEETS

Day _____ Month _____ Year _____

Food

Breakfast		
Lunch		
Dinner		
Snack		
Exercise		
Litres Water	Hours Sleep	

Money

Item	Amount
Total Spent Today	
Quality of Life Today	%

When we retire at night we constructively review our day. We remember we have ceased fighting anything and anyone—love and tolerance of others is our code.

We Draw Up a Balance Sheet

The "Negative Side" (-)	The "Positive Side" (+)
Were we resentful?	Have we stayed clean of our addiction today?
Were we selfish?	Were we kind?
Were we dishonest?	Were we loving toward all?
Were we afraid?	What did we pack into life?
Have we kept something to ourselves?	Did we pray and meditate?
Were we thinking of ourselves most of the time?	Did we call someone we could help today?
Were we "disturbed" today?	Did we think of how we could help others?
Do we owe an apology? And if so to whom?	Did we study literature today?
What could we have done better?	Did we go to a meeting today?
Did we blame our feelings on someone else?	Did we call our sponsor today?
Do we need to write 10th Step on something?	Did we do anything that is improved over our past?

Journal—Gratitude List—Tomorrows Action Plan

STEP 10

BALANCE SHEETS

Day _____ Month _____ Year _____

Food

Breakfast		
Lunch		
Dinner		
Snack		
Exercise		
Litres Water	Hours Sleep	

Money

Item	Amount
Total Spent Today	
Quality of Life Today	%

When we retire at night we constructively review our day. We remember we have ceased fighting anything and anyone—love and tolerance of others is our code.

We Draw Up a Balance Sheet

The "Negative Side" (-)	The "Positive Side" (+)
Were we resentful?	Have we stayed clean of our addiction today?
Were we selfish?	Were we kind?
Were we dishonest?	Were we loving toward all?
Were we afraid?	What did we pack into life?
Have we kept something to ourselves?	Did we pray and meditate?
Were we thinking of ourselves most of the time?	Did we call someone we could help today?
Were we "disturbed" today?	Did we think of how we could help others?
Do we owe an apology? And if so to whom?	Did we study literature today?
What could we have done better?	Did we go to a meeting today?
Did we blame our feelings on someone else?	Did we call our sponsor today?
Do we need to write 10th Step on something?	Did we do anything that is improved over our past?

Journal—Gratitude List—Tomorrows Action Plan

MAINTAINING THE PROMISES...DAILY

BALANCE SHEETS

Day _____ Month _____ Year _____

Food		Money	
Breakfast		Item	Amount
Lunch			
Dinner			
Snack			
Exercise			
		Total Spent Today	
Litres Water Hours Sleep		Quality of Life Today	%

When we retire at night we constructively review our day. We remember we have ceased fighting anything and anyone—love and tolerance of others is our code.

We Draw Up a Balance Sheet

The "Negative Side" (−)	The "Positive Side" (+)
Were we resentful?	Have we stayed clean of our addiction today?
Were we selfish?	Were we kind?
Were we dishonest?	Were we loving toward all?
Were we afraid?	What did we pack into life?
Have we kept something to ourselves?	Did we pray and meditate?
Were we thinking of ourselves most of the time?	Did we call someone we could help today?
Were we "disturbed" today?	Did we think of how we could help others?
Do we owe an apology? And if so to whom?	Did we study literature today?
What could we have done better?	Did we go to a meeting today?
Did we blame our feelings on someone else?	Did we call our sponsor today?
Do we need to write 10th Step on something?	Did we do anything that is improved over our past?

Journal—Gratitude List—Tomorrows Action Plan

STEP 10

BALANCE SHEETS

Day _____ Month _____ Year _____

Food		Money	
Breakfast		Item	Amount
Lunch			
Dinner			
Snack			
Exercise			
		Total Spent Today	
Litres Water	Hours Sleep	Quality of Life Today	%

When we retire at night we constructively review our day. We remember we have ceased fighting anything and anyone—love and tolerance of others is our code.

We Draw Up a Balance Sheet

The "Negative Side" (-)	The "Positive Side" (+)
Were we resentful?	Have we stayed clean of our addiction today?
Were we selfish?	Were we kind?
Were we dishonest?	Were we loving toward all?
Were we afraid?	What did we pack into life?
Have we kept something to ourselves?	Did we pray and meditate?
Were we thinking of ourselves most of the time?	Did we call someone we could help today?
Were we "disturbed" today?	Did we think of how we could help others?
Do we owe an apology? And if so to whom?	Did we study literature today?
What could we have done better?	Did we go to a meeting today?
Did we blame our feelings on someone else?	Did we call our sponsor today?
Do we need to write 10th Step on something?	Did we do anything that is improved over our past?

Journal—Gratitude List—Tomorrows Action Plan

BALANCE SHEETS

Day _____ Month _____ Year _____

Food		Money	
Breakfast		Item	Amount
Lunch			
Dinner			
Snack			
Exercise			
		Total Spent Today	
Litres Water Hours Sleep		Quality of Life Today	%

When we retire at night we constructively review our day. We remember we have ceased fighting anything and anyone—love and tolerance of others is our code.

We Draw Up a Balance Sheet

The "Negative Side" (-)	The "Positive Side" (+)
Were we resentful?	Have we stayed clean of our addiction today?
Were we selfish?	Were we kind?
Were we dishonest?	Were we loving toward all?
Were we afraid?	What did we pack into life?
Have we kept something to ourselves?	Did we pray and meditate?
Were we thinking of ourselves most of the time?	Did we call someone we could help today?
Were we "disturbed" today?	Did we think of how we could help others?
Do we owe an apology? And if so to whom?	Did we study literature today?
What could we have done better?	Did we go to a meeting today?
Did we blame our feelings on someone else?	Did we call our sponsor today?
Do we need to write 10th Step on something?	Did we do anything that is improved over our past?

Journal—Gratitude List—Tomorrows Action Plan

STEP 10

BALANCE SHEETS

Day _____ Month _____ Year _____

Food

Breakfast		Money	
		Item	Amount
Lunch			
Dinner			
Snack			
Exercise			
		Total Spent Today	
Litres Water	Hours Sleep	Quality of Life Today	%

When we retire at night we constructively review our day. We remember we have ceased fighting anything and anyone—love and tolerance of others is our code.

We Draw Up a Balance Sheet

The "Negative Side" (-)	The "Positive Side" (+)
Were we resentful?	Have we stayed clean of our addiction today?
Were we selfish?	Were we kind?
Were we dishonest?	Were we loving toward all?
Were we afraid?	What did we pack into life?
Have we kept something to ourselves?	Did we pray and meditate?
Were we thinking of ourselves most of the time?	Did we call someone we could help today?
Were we "disturbed" today?	Did we think of how we could help others?
Do we owe an apology? And if so to whom?	Did we study literature today?
What could we have done better?	Did we go to a meeting today?
Did we blame our feelings on someone else?	Did we call our sponsor today?
Do we need to write 10th Step on something?	Did we do anything that is improved over our past?

Journal—Gratitude List—Tomorrows Action Plan

BALANCE SHEETS

Day _____ Month _____ Year_____

Food		Money	
Breakfast		Item	Amount
Lunch			
Dinner			
Snack			
Exercise			
		Total Spent Today	
Litres Water _____ Hours Sleep _____		Quality of Life Today	%

When we retire at night we constructively review our day. We remember we have ceased fighting anything and anyone—love and tolerance of others is our code.

We Draw Up a Balance Sheet

The "Negative Side" (-)	The "Positive Side" (+)
Were we resentful?	Have we stayed clean of our addiction today?
Were we selfish?	Were we kind?
Were we dishonest?	Were we loving toward all?
Were we afraid?	What did we pack into life?
Have we kept something to ourselves?	Did we pray and meditate?
Were we thinking of ourselves most of the time?	Did we call someone we could help today?
Were we "disturbed" today?	Did we think of how we could help others?
Do we owe an apology? And if so to whom?	Did we study literature today?
What could we have done better?	Did we go to a meeting today?
Did we blame our feelings on someone else?	Did we call our sponsor today?
Do we need to write 10th Step on something?	Did we do anything that is improved over our past?

Journal—Gratitude List—Tomorrows Action Plan

STEP 10

BALANCE SHEETS

Day _____ Month _____ Year _____

Food		Money	
Breakfast		Item	Amount
Lunch			
Dinner			
Snack			
Exercise			
		Total Spent Today	
Litres Water	Hours Sleep	Quality of Life Today	%

When we retire at night we constructively review our day. We remember we have ceased fighting anything and anyone—love and tolerance of others is our code.

We Draw Up a Balance Sheet

The "Negative Side" (-)	The "Positive Side" (+)
Were we resentful?	Have we stayed clean of our addiction today?
Were we selfish?	Were we kind?
Were we dishonest?	Were we loving toward all?
Were we afraid?	What did we pack into life?
Have we kept something to ourselves?	Did we pray and meditate?
Were we thinking of ourselves most of the time?	Did we call someone we could help today?
Were we "disturbed" today?	Did we think of how we could help others?
Do we owe an apology? And if so to whom?	Did we study literature today?
What could we have done better?	Did we go to a meeting today?
Did we blame our feelings on someone else?	Did we call our sponsor today?
Do we need to write 10th Step on something?	Did we do anything that is improved over our past?

Journal—Gratitude List—Tomorrows Action Plan

BALANCE SHEETS

Day _____ Month _____ Year _____

Food		Money	
Breakfast		Item	Amount
Lunch			
Dinner			
Snack			
Exercise			
		Total Spent Today	
Litres Water ___ Hours Sleep ___		Quality of Life Today	%

When we retire at night we constructively review our day. We remember we have ceased fighting anything and anyone—love and tolerance of others is our code.

We Draw Up a Balance Sheet

The "Negative Side" (-)	The "Positive Side" (+)
Were we resentful?	Have we stayed clean of our addiction today?
Were we selfish?	Were we kind?
Were we dishonest?	Were we loving toward all?
Were we afraid?	What did we pack into life?
Have we kept something to ourselves?	Did we pray and meditate?
Were we thinking of ourselves most of the time?	Did we call someone we could help today?
Were we "disturbed" today?	Did we think of how we could help others?
Do we owe an apology? And if so to whom?	Did we study literature today?
What could we have done better?	Did we go to a meeting today?
Did we blame our feelings on someone else?	Did we call our sponsor today?
Do we need to write 10th Step on something?	Did we do anything that is improved over our past?

Journal—Gratitude List—Tomorrows Action Plan

STEP 10

BALANCE SHEETS

Day _____ Month _____ Year _____

Food		Money	
Breakfast		Item	Amount
Lunch			
Dinner			
Snack			
Exercise			
		Total Spent Today	
Litres Water	Hours Sleep	Quality of Life Today	%

When we retire at night we constructively review our day. We remember we have ceased fighting anything and anyone—love and tolerance of others is our code.

We Draw Up a Balance Sheet

The "Negative Side" (-)	The "Positive Side" (+)
Were we resentful?	Have we stayed clean of our addiction today?
Were we selfish?	Were we kind?
Were we dishonest?	Were we loving toward all?
Were we afraid?	What did we pack into life?
Have we kept something to ourselves?	Did we pray and meditate?
Were we thinking of ourselves most of the time?	Did we call someone we could help today?
Were we "disturbed" today?	Did we think of how we could help others?
Do we owe an apology? And if so to whom?	Did we study literature today?
What could we have done better?	Did we go to a meeting today?
Did we blame our feelings on someone else?	Did we call our sponsor today?
Do we need to write 10th Step on something?	Did we do anything that is improved over our past?

Journal—Gratitude List—Tomorrows Action Plan

BALANCE SHEETS

Day _____ Month _____ Year _____

Food

Breakfast	
Lunch	
Dinner	
Snack	
Exercise	
Litres Water _____ Hours Sleep _____	

Money

Item	Amount
Total Spent Today	
Quality of Life Today	%

When we retire at night we constructively review our day. We remember we have ceased fighting anything and anyone—love and tolerance of others is our code.

We Draw Up a Balance Sheet

The "Negative Side" (-)	The "Positive Side" (+)
Were we resentful?	Have we stayed clean of our addiction today?
Were we selfish?	Were we kind?
Were we dishonest?	Were we loving toward all?
Were we afraid?	What did we pack into life?
Have we kept something to ourselves?	Did we pray and meditate?
Were we thinking of ourselves most of the time?	Did we call someone we could help today?
Were we "disturbed" today?	Did we think of how we could help others?
Do we owe an apology? And if so to whom?	Did we study literature today?
What could we have done better?	Did we go to a meeting today?
Did we blame our feelings on someone else?	Did we call our sponsor today?
Do we need to write 10th Step on something?	Did we do anything that is improved over our past?

Journal—Gratitude List—Tomorrows Action Plan

STEP 10

BALANCE SHEETS

Day _____ Month _____ Year _____

Food		Money	
Breakfast		Item	Amount
Lunch			
Dinner			
Snack			
Exercise			
		Total Spent Today	
Litres Water Hours Sleep		Quality of Life Today	%

When we retire at night we constructively review our day. We remember we have ceased fighting anything and anyone—love and tolerance of others is our code.

We Draw Up a Balance Sheet

The "Negative Side" (-)	The "Positive Side" (+)
Were we resentful?	Have we stayed clean of our addiction today?
Were we selfish?	Were we kind?
Were we dishonest?	Were we loving toward all?
Were we afraid?	What did we pack into life?
Have we kept something to ourselves?	Did we pray and meditate?
Were we thinking of ourselves most of the time?	Did we call someone we could help today?
Were we "disturbed" today?	Did we think of how we could help others?
Do we owe an apology? And if so to whom?	Did we study literature today?
What could we have done better?	Did we go to a meeting today?
Did we blame our feelings on someone else?	Did we call our sponsor today?
Do we need to write 10th Step on something?	Did we do anything that is improved over our past?

Journal—Gratitude List—Tomorrows Action Plan

MAINTAINING THE PROMISES...DAILY

BALANCE SHEETS

Day _____ Month _____ Year _____

Food		Money	
Breakfast		Item	Amount
Lunch			
Dinner			
Snack			
Exercise			
		Total Spent Today	
Litres Water ____ Hours Sleep ____		Quality of Life Today	%

When we retire at night we constructively review our day. We remember we have ceased fighting anything and anyone—love and tolerance of others is our code.

We Draw Up a Balance Sheet

The "Negative Side" (-)	The "Positive Side" (+)
Were we resentful?	Have we stayed clean of our addiction today?
Were we selfish?	Were we kind?
Were we dishonest?	Were we loving toward all?
Were we afraid?	What did we pack into life?
Have we kept something to ourselves?	Did we pray and meditate?
Were we thinking of ourselves most of the time?	Did we call someone we could help today?
Were we "disturbed" today?	Did we think of how we could help others?
Do we owe an apology? And if so to whom?	Did we study literature today?
What could we have done better?	Did we go to a meeting today?
Did we blame our feelings on someone else?	Did we call our sponsor today?
Do we need to write 10th Step on something?	Did we do anything that is improved over our past?

Journal—Gratitude List—Tomorrows Action Plan

BALANCE SHEETS

Day _____ Month _____ Year _____

Food		Money	
Breakfast		Item	Amount
Lunch			
Dinner			
Snack			
Exercise			
		Total Spent Today	
Litres Water	Hours Sleep	Quality of Life Today	%

When we retire at night we constructively review our day. We remember we have ceased fighting anything and anyone—love and tolerance of others is our code.

We Draw Up a Balance Sheet

The "Negative Side" (-)	The "Positive Side" (+)
Were we resentful?	Have we stayed clean of our addiction today?
Were we selfish?	Were we kind?
Were we dishonest?	Were we loving toward all?
Were we afraid?	What did we pack into life?
Have we kept something to ourselves?	Did we pray and meditate?
Were we thinking of ourselves most of the time?	Did we call someone we could help today?
Were we "disturbed" today?	Did we think of how we could help others?
Do we owe an apology? And if so to whom?	Did we study literature today?
What could we have done better?	Did we go to a meeting today?
Did we blame our feelings on someone else?	Did we call our sponsor today?
Do we need to write 10th Step on something?	Did we do anything that is improved over our past?

Journal—Gratitude List—Tomorrows Action Plan

BALANCE SHEETS

Day _____ Month _____ Year ____

Food

Breakfast		
Lunch		
Dinner		
Snack		
Exercise		

Litres Water	Hours Sleep

Money

Item	Amount
Total Spent Today	
Quality of Life Today	%

When we retire at night we constructively review our day. We remember we have ceased fighting anything and anyone—love and tolerance of others is our code.

We Draw Up a Balance Sheet

The "Negative Side" (-)	The "Positive Side" (+)
Were we resentful?	Have we stayed clean of our addiction today?
Were we selfish?	Were we kind?
Were we dishonest?	Were we loving toward all?
Were we afraid?	What did we pack into life?
Have we kept something to ourselves?	Did we pray and meditate?
Were we thinking of ourselves most of the time?	Did we call someone we could help today?
Were we "disturbed" today?	Did we think of how we could help others?
Do we owe an apology? And if so to whom?	Did we study literature today?
What could we have done better?	Did we go to a meeting today?
Did we blame our feelings on someone else?	Did we call our sponsor today?
Do we need to write 10th Step on something?	Did we do anything that is improved over our past?

Journal—Gratitude List—Tomorrows Action Plan

STEP 10

BALANCE SHEETS

Day _____ Month _____ Year _____

Food		Money	
Breakfast		Item	Amount
Lunch			
Dinner			
Snack			
Exercise			
		Total Spent Today	
Litres Water	Hours Sleep	Quality of Life Today	%

When we retire at night we constructively review our day. We remember we have ceased fighting anything and anyone—love and tolerance of others is our code.

We Draw Up a Balance Sheet

The "Negative Side" (-)	The "Positive Side" (+)
Were we resentful?	Have we stayed clean of our addiction today?
Were we selfish?	Were we kind?
Were we dishonest?	Were we loving toward all?
Were we afraid?	What did we pack into life?
Have we kept something to ourselves?	Did we pray and meditate?
Were we thinking of ourselves most of the time?	Did we call someone we could help today?
Were we "disturbed" today?	Did we think of how we could help others?
Do we owe an apology? And if so to whom?	Did we study literature today?
What could we have done better?	Did we go to a meeting today?
Did we blame our feelings on someone else?	Did we call our sponsor today?
Do we need to write 10th Step on something?	Did we do anything that is improved over our past?

Journal—Gratitude List—Tomorrows Action Plan

_____
_____
_____
_____
_____
_____
_____

BALANCE SHEETS

Day _____ Month _____ Year _____

Food

Breakfast		
Lunch		
Dinner		
Snack		
Exercise		

Money

Item	Amount
Total Spent Today	

Litres Water	Hours Sleep	Quality of Life Today	%

When we retire at night we constructively review our day. We remember we have ceased fighting anything and anyone—love and tolerance of others is our code.

We Draw Up a Balance Sheet

The "Negative Side" (-)	The "Positive Side" (+)
Were we resentful?	Have we stayed clean of our addiction today?
Were we selfish?	Were we kind?
Were we dishonest?	Were we loving toward all?
Were we afraid?	What did we pack into life?
Have we kept something to ourselves?	Did we pray and meditate?
Were we thinking of ourselves most of the time?	Did we call someone we could help today?
Were we "disturbed" today?	Did we think of how we could help others?
Do we owe an apology? And if so to whom?	Did we study literature today?
What could we have done better?	Did we go to a meeting today?
Did we blame our feelings on someone else?	Did we call our sponsor today?
Do we need to write 10th Step on something?	Did we do anything that is improved over our past?

Journal—Gratitude List—Tomorrows Action Plan

STEP 10

BALANCE SHEETS

Day _____ Month _____ Year _____

Food		Money	
Breakfast		Item	Amount
Lunch			
Dinner			
Snack			
Exercise			
		Total Spent Today	
Litres Water _____ Hours Sleep _____		Quality of Life Today	%

When we retire at night we constructively review our day. We remember we have ceased fighting anything and anyone—love and tolerance of others is our code.

We Draw Up a Balance Sheet

The "Negative Side" (-)	The "Positive Side" (+)
Were we resentful?	Have we stayed clean of our addiction today?
Were we selfish?	Were we kind?
Were we dishonest?	Were we loving toward all?
Were we afraid?	What did we pack into life?
Have we kept something to ourselves?	Did we pray and meditate?
Were we thinking of ourselves most of the time?	Did we call someone we could help today?
Were we "disturbed" today?	Did we think of how we could help others?
Do we owe an apology? And if so to whom?	Did we study literature today?
What could we have done better?	Did we go to a meeting today?
Did we blame our feelings on someone else?	Did we call our sponsor today?
Do we need to write 10th Step on something?	Did we do anything that is improved over our past?

Journal—Gratitude List—Tomorrows Action Plan

BALANCE SHEETS

Day _____ Month _____ Year _____

Food

Breakfast		
Lunch		
Dinner		
Snack		
Exercise		

Money

Item		Amount
Total Spent Today		

Litres Water	Hours Sleep	Quality of Life Today	%

When we retire at night we constructively review our day. We remember we have ceased fighting anything and anyone—love and tolerance of others is our code.

We Draw Up a Balance Sheet

The "Negative Side" (-)	The "Positive Side" (+)
Were we resentful?	Have we stayed clean of our addiction today?
Were we selfish?	Were we kind?
Were we dishonest?	Were we loving toward all?
Were we afraid?	What did we pack into life?
Have we kept something to ourselves?	Did we pray and meditate?
Were we thinking of ourselves most of the time?	Did we call someone we could help today?
Were we "disturbed" today?	Did we think of how we could help others?
Do we owe an apology? And if so to whom?	Did we study literature today?
What could we have done better?	Did we go to a meeting today?
Did we blame our feelings on someone else?	Did we call our sponsor today?
Do we need to write 10th Step on something?	Did we do anything that is improved over our past?

Journal—Gratitude List—Tomorrows Action Plan

STEP 10

BALANCE SHEETS

Day _____ Month _____ Year _____

Food		Money	
Breakfast		Item	Amount
Lunch			
Dinner			
Snack			
Exercise			
		Total Spent Today	
Litres Water _____ Hours Sleep _____		Quality of Life Today	%

When we retire at night we constructively review our day. We remember we have ceased fighting anything and anyone—love and tolerance of others is our code.

We Draw Up a Balance Sheet

The "Negative Side" (−)	The "Positive Side" (+)
Were we resentful?	Have we stayed clean of our addiction today?
Were we selfish?	Were we kind?
Were we dishonest?	Were we loving toward all?
Were we afraid?	What did we pack into life?
Have we kept something to ourselves?	Did we pray and meditate?
Were we thinking of ourselves most of the time?	Did we call someone we could help today?
Were we "disturbed" today?	Did we think of how we could help others?
Do we owe an apology? And if so to whom?	Did we study literature today?
What could we have done better?	Did we go to a meeting today?
Did we blame our feelings on someone else?	Did we call our sponsor today?
Do we need to write 10th Step on something?	Did we do anything that is improved over our past?

Journal—Gratitude List—Tomorrows Action Plan

BALANCE SHEETS

Day _____ Month _____ Year _____

Food		Money	
Breakfast		Item	Amount
Lunch			
Dinner			
Snack			
Exercise			
		Total Spent Today	
Litres Water ____ Hours Sleep ____		Quality of Life Today	%

When we retire at night we constructively review our day. We remember we have ceased fighting anything and anyone—love and tolerance of others is our code.

We Draw Up a Balance Sheet

The "Negative Side" (−)	The "Positive Side" (+)
Were we resentful?	Have we stayed clean of our addiction today?
Were we selfish?	Were we kind?
Were we dishonest?	Were we loving toward all?
Were we afraid?	What did we pack into life?
Have we kept something to ourselves?	Did we pray and meditate?
Were we thinking of ourselves most of the time?	Did we call someone we could help today?
Were we "disturbed" today?	Did we think of how we could help others?
Do we owe an apology? And if so to whom?	Did we study literature today?
What could we have done better?	Did we go to a meeting today?
Did we blame our feelings on someone else?	Did we call our sponsor today?
Do we need to write 10th Step on something?	Did we do anything that is improved over our past?

Journal—Gratitude List—Tomorrows Action Plan

STEP 10

BALANCE SHEETS

Day _____ Month _____ Year _____

Food

Breakfast		
Lunch		
Dinner		
Snack		
Exercise		
Litres Water	Hours Sleep	

Money

Item		Amount
Total Spent Today		
Quality of Life Today		%

When we retire at night we constructively review our day. We remember we have ceased fighting anything and anyone—love and tolerance of others is our code.

We Draw Up a Balance Sheet

The "Negative Side" (-)	The "Positive Side" (+)
Were we resentful?	Have we stayed clean of our addiction today?
Were we selfish?	Were we kind?
Were we dishonest?	Were we loving toward all?
Were we afraid?	What did we pack into life?
Have we kept something to ourselves?	Did we pray and meditate?
Were we thinking of ourselves most of the time?	Did we call someone we could help today?
Were we "disturbed" today?	Did we think of how we could help others?
Do we owe an apology? And if so to whom?	Did we study literature today?
What could we have done better?	Did we go to a meeting today?
Did we blame our feelings on someone else?	Did we call our sponsor today?
Do we need to write 10th Step on something?	Did we do anything that is improved over our past?

Journal—Gratitude List—Tomorrows Action Plan

BALANCE SHEETS

Day _____ Month _____ Year _____

Food		Money		
Breakfast		Item		Amount
Lunch				
Dinner				
Snack				
Exercise				
		Total Spent Today		
Litres Water	Hours Sleep	Quality of Life Today		%

When we retire at night we constructively review our day. We remember we have ceased fighting anything and anyone—love and tolerance of others is our code.

We Draw Up a Balance Sheet

The "Negative Side" (-)	The "Positive Side" (+)
Were we resentful?	Have we stayed clean of our addiction today?
Were we selfish?	Were we kind?
Were we dishonest?	Were we loving toward all?
Were we afraid?	What did we pack into life?
Have we kept something to ourselves?	Did we pray and meditate?
Were we thinking of ourselves most of the time?	Did we call someone we could help today?
Were we "disturbed" today?	Did we think of how we could help others?
Do we owe an apology? And if so to whom?	Did we study literature today?
What could we have done better?	Did we go to a meeting today?
Did we blame our feelings on someone else?	Did we call our sponsor today?
Do we need to write 10th Step on something?	Did we do anything that is improved over our past?

Journal—Gratitude List—Tomorrows Action Plan

STEP 10

BALANCE SHEETS

Day _____ Month _____ Year_____

Food

Breakfast	
Lunch	
Dinner	
Snack	
Exercise	
Litres Water	Hours Sleep

Money

Item	Amount
Total Spent Today	
Quality of Life Today	%

When we retire at night we constructively review our day. We remember we have ceased fighting anything and anyone—love and tolerance of others is our code.

We Draw Up a Balance Sheet

The "Negative Side" (-)	The "Positive Side" (+)
Were we resentful?	Have we stayed clean of our addiction today?
Were we selfish?	Were we kind?
Were we dishonest?	Were we loving toward all?
Were we afraid?	What did we pack into life?
Have we kept something to ourselves?	Did we pray and meditate?
Were we thinking of ourselves most of the time?	Did we call someone we could help today?
Were we "disturbed" today?	Did we think of how we could help others?
Do we owe an apology? And if so to whom?	Did we study literature today?
What could we have done better?	Did we go to a meeting today?
Did we blame our feelings on someone else?	Did we call our sponsor today?
Do we need to write 10th Step on something?	Did we do anything that is improved over our past?

Journal—Gratitude List—Tomorrows Action Plan

BALANCE SHEETS

Day _____ Month _____ Year _____

Food		Money	
Breakfast		Item	Amount
Lunch			
Dinner			
Snack			
Exercise			
		Total Spent Today	
Litres Water	Hours Sleep	Quality of Life Today	%

When we retire at night we constructively review our day. We remember we have ceased fighting anything and anyone—love and tolerance of others is our code.

We Draw Up a Balance Sheet

The "Negative Side" (-)	The "Positive Side" (+)
Were we resentful?	Have we stayed clean of our addiction today?
Were we selfish?	Were we kind?
Were we dishonest?	Were we loving toward all?
Were we afraid?	What did we pack into life?
Have we kept something to ourselves?	Did we pray and meditate?
Were we thinking of ourselves most of the time?	Did we call someone we could help today?
Were we "disturbed" today?	Did we think of how we could help others?
Do we owe an apology? And if so to whom?	Did we study literature today?
What could we have done better?	Did we go to a meeting today?
Did we blame our feelings on someone else?	Did we call our sponsor today?
Do we need to write 10th Step on something?	Did we do anything that is improved over our past?

Journal—Gratitude List—Tomorrows Action Plan

STEP 10

BALANCE SHEETS

Day _____ Month _____ Year _____

Food		Money	
Breakfast		Item	Amount
Lunch			
Dinner			
Snack			
Exercise			
		Total Spent Today	
Litres Water	Hours Sleep	Quality of Life Today	%

When we retire at night we constructively review our day. We remember we have ceased fighting anything and anyone—love and tolerance of others is our code.

We Draw Up a Balance Sheet

The "Negative Side" (-)	The "Positive Side" (+)
Were we resentful?	Have we stayed clean of our addiction today?
Were we selfish?	Were we kind?
Were we dishonest?	Were we loving toward all?
Were we afraid?	What did we pack into life?
Have we kept something to ourselves?	Did we pray and meditate?
Were we thinking of ourselves most of the time?	Did we call someone we could help today?
Were we "disturbed" today?	Did we think of how we could help others?
Do we owe an apology? And if so to whom?	Did we study literature today?
What could we have done better?	Did we go to a meeting today?
Did we blame our feelings on someone else?	Did we call our sponsor today?
Do we need to write 10th Step on something?	Did we do anything that is improved over our past?

Journal—Gratitude List—Tomorrows Action Plan

MAINTAINING THE PROMISES...DAILY

BALANCE SHEETS

Day _____ Month _____ Year _____

Food		Money	
Breakfast		Item	Amount
Lunch			
Dinner			
Snack			
Exercise			
		Total Spent Today	
Litres Water	Hours Sleep	Quality of Life Today	%

When we retire at night we constructively review our day. We remember we have ceased fighting anything and anyone—love and tolerance of others is our code.

We Draw Up a Balance Sheet

The "Negative Side" (−)	The "Positive Side" (+)
Were we resentful?	Have we stayed clean of our addiction today?
Were we selfish?	Were we kind?
Were we dishonest?	Were we loving toward all?
Were we afraid?	What did we pack into life?
Have we kept something to ourselves?	Did we pray and meditate?
Were we thinking of ourselves most of the time?	Did we call someone we could help today?
Were we "disturbed" today?	Did we think of how we could help others?
Do we owe an apology? And if so to whom?	Did we study literature today?
What could we have done better?	Did we go to a meeting today?
Did we blame our feelings on someone else?	Did we call our sponsor today?
Do we need to write 10th Step on something?	Did we do anything that is improved over our past?

Journal—Gratitude List—Tomorrows Action Plan

STEP 10

BALANCE SHEETS

Day _____ Month _____ Year _____

Food		Money	
Breakfast		Item	Amount
Lunch			
Dinner			
Snack			
Exercise			
		Total Spent Today	
Litres Water	Hours Sleep	Quality of Life Today	%

When we retire at night we constructively review our day. We remember we have ceased fighting anything and anyone—love and tolerance of others is our code.

We Draw Up a Balance Sheet

The "Negative Side" (-)	The "Positive Side" (+)
Were we resentful?	Have we stayed clean of our addiction today?
Were we selfish?	Were we kind?
Were we dishonest?	Were we loving toward all?
Were we afraid?	What did we pack into life?
Have we kept something to ourselves?	Did we pray and meditate?
Were we thinking of ourselves most of the time?	Did we call someone we could help today?
Were we "disturbed" today?	Did we think of how we could help others?
Do we owe an apology? And if so to whom?	Did we study literature today?
What could we have done better?	Did we go to a meeting today?
Did we blame our feelings on someone else?	Did we call our sponsor today?
Do we need to write 10th Step on something?	Did we do anything that is improved over our past?

Journal—Gratitude List—Tomorrows Action Plan

MAINTAINING THE PROMISES...DAILY

BALANCE SHEETS

Day _____ Month _____ Year _____

Food		Money	
Breakfast		Item	Amount
Lunch			
Dinner			
Snack			
Exercise			
		Total Spent Today	
Litres Water ____ Hours Sleep ____		Quality of Life Today	%

When we retire at night we constructively review our day. We remember we have ceased fighting anything and anyone—love and tolerance of others is our code.

We Draw Up a Balance Sheet

The "Negative Side" (-)	The "Positive Side" (+)
Were we resentful?	Have we stayed clean of our addiction today?
Were we selfish?	Were we kind?
Were we dishonest?	Were we loving toward all?
Were we afraid?	What did we pack into life?
Have we kept something to ourselves?	Did we pray and meditate?
Were we thinking of ourselves most of the time?	Did we call someone we could help today?
Were we "disturbed" today?	Did we think of how we could help others?
Do we owe an apology? And if so to whom?	Did we study literature today?
What could we have done better?	Did we go to a meeting today?
Did we blame our feelings on someone else?	Did we call our sponsor today?
Do we need to write 10th Step on something?	Did we do anything that is improved over our past?

Journal—Gratitude List—Tomorrows Action Plan

STEP 10

BALANCE SHEETS

Day _____ Month _____ Year _____

Food		Money	
Breakfast		Item	Amount
Lunch			
Dinner			
Snack			
Exercise			
		Total Spent Today	
Litres Water Hours Sleep		Quality of Life Today	%

When we retire at night we constructively review our day. We remember we have ceased fighting anything and anyone—love and tolerance of others is our code.

We Draw Up a Balance Sheet

The "Negative Side" (-)	The "Positive Side" (+)
Were we resentful?	Have we stayed clean of our addiction today?
Were we selfish?	Were we kind?
Were we dishonest?	Were we loving toward all?
Were we afraid?	What did we pack into life?
Have we kept something to ourselves?	Did we pray and meditate?
Were we thinking of ourselves most of the time?	Did we call someone we could help today?
Were we "disturbed" today?	Did we think of how we could help others?
Do we owe an apology? And if so to whom?	Did we study literature today?
What could we have done better?	Did we go to a meeting today?
Did we blame our feelings on someone else?	Did we call our sponsor today?
Do we need to write 10th Step on something?	Did we do anything that is improved over our past?

Journal—Gratitude List—Tomorrows Action Plan

BALANCE SHEETS

Day _____ Month _____ Year _____

Food

Breakfast		
Lunch		
Dinner		
Snack		
Exercise		
Litres Water	Hours Sleep	

Money

Item	Amount
Total Spent Today	
Quality of Life Today	%

When we retire at night we constructively review our day. We remember we have ceased fighting anything and anyone—love and tolerance of others is our code.

We Draw Up a Balance Sheet

The "Negative Side" (-)	The "Positive Side" (+)
Were we resentful?	Have we stayed clean of our addiction today?
Were we selfish?	Were we kind?
Were we dishonest?	Were we loving toward all?
Were we afraid?	What did we pack into life?
Have we kept something to ourselves?	Did we pray and meditate?
Were we thinking of ourselves most of the time?	Did we call someone we could help today?
Were we "disturbed" today?	Did we think of how we could help others?
Do we owe an apology? And if so to whom?	Did we study literature today?
What could we have done better?	Did we go to a meeting today?
Did we blame our feelings on someone else?	Did we call our sponsor today?
Do we need to write 10th Step on something?	Did we do anything that is improved over our past?

Journal—Gratitude List—Tomorrows Action Plan

STEP 10

BALANCE SHEETS

Day _____ Month _____ Year _____

Food

Breakfast		
Lunch		
Dinner		
Snack		
Exercise		
Litres Water	Hours Sleep	

Money

Item	Amount
Total Spent Today	
Quality of Life Today	%

When we retire at night we constructively review our day. We remember we have ceased fighting anything and anyone—love and tolerance of others is our code.

We Draw Up a Balance Sheet

The "Negative Side" (-)	The "Positive Side" (+)
Were we resentful?	Have we stayed clean of our addiction today?
Were we selfish?	Were we kind?
Were we dishonest?	Were we loving toward all?
Were we afraid?	What did we pack into life?
Have we kept something to ourselves?	Did we pray and meditate?
Were we thinking of ourselves most of the time?	Did we call someone we could help today?
Were we "disturbed" today?	Did we think of how we could help others?
Do we owe an apology? And if so to whom?	Did we study literature today?
What could we have done better?	Did we go to a meeting today?
Did we blame our feelings on someone else?	Did we call our sponsor today?
Do we need to write 10th Step on something?	Did we do anything that is improved over our past?

Journal—Gratitude List—Tomorrows Action Plan

BALANCE SHEETS

Day _____ Month _____ Year _____

Food		Money	
Breakfast		Item	Amount
Lunch			
Dinner			
Snack			
Exercise			
		Total Spent Today	
Litres Water Hours Sleep		Quality of Life Today	%

When we retire at night we constructively review our day. We remember we have ceased fighting anything and anyone—love and tolerance of others is our code.

We Draw Up a Balance Sheet

The "Negative Side" (-)	The "Positive Side" (+)
Were we resentful?	Have we stayed clean of our addiction today?
Were we selfish?	Were we kind?
Were we dishonest?	Were we loving toward all?
Were we afraid?	What did we pack into life?
Have we kept something to ourselves?	Did we pray and meditate?
Were we thinking of ourselves most of the time?	Did we call someone we could help today?
Were we "disturbed" today?	Did we think of how we could help others?
Do we owe an apology? And if so to whom?	Did we study literature today?
What could we have done better?	Did we go to a meeting today?
Did we blame our feelings on someone else?	Did we call our sponsor today?
Do we need to write 10th Step on something?	Did we do anything that is improved over our past?

Journal—Gratitude List—Tomorrows Action Plan

STEP 10

BALANCE SHEETS

Day _____ Month _____ Year _____

Food		Money	
Breakfast		Item	Amount
Lunch			
Dinner			
Snack			
Exercise			
		Total Spent Today	
Litres Water	Hours Sleep	Quality of Life Today	%

When we retire at night we constructively review our day. We remember we have ceased fighting anything and anyone—love and tolerance of others is our code.

We Draw Up a Balance Sheet

The "Negative Side" (-)	The "Positive Side" (+)
Were we resentful?	Have we stayed clean of our addiction today?
Were we selfish?	Were we kind?
Were we dishonest?	Were we loving toward all?
Were we afraid?	What did we pack into life?
Have we kept something to ourselves?	Did we pray and meditate?
Were we thinking of ourselves most of the time?	Did we call someone we could help today?
Were we "disturbed" today?	Did we think of how we could help others?
Do we owe an apology? And if so to whom?	Did we study literature today?
What could we have done better?	Did we go to a meeting today?
Did we blame our feelings on someone else?	Did we call our sponsor today?
Do we need to write 10th Step on something?	Did we do anything that is improved over our past?

Journal—Gratitude List—Tomorrows Action Plan

BALANCE SHEETS

Day _____ Month _____ Year _____

Food

Breakfast	

Lunch	

Dinner	

Snack	

Exercise	

Litres Water	Hours Sleep

Money

Item	Amount
Total Spent Today	
Quality of Life Today	%

When we retire at night we constructively review our day. We remember we have ceased fighting anything and anyone—love and tolerance of others is our code.

We Draw Up a Balance Sheet

The "Negative Side" (-)	The "Positive Side" (+)
Were we resentful?	Have we stayed clean of our addiction today?
Were we selfish?	Were we kind?
Were we dishonest?	Were we loving toward all?
Were we afraid?	What did we pack into life?
Have we kept something to ourselves?	Did we pray and meditate?
Were we thinking of ourselves most of the time?	Did we call someone we could help today?
Were we "disturbed" today?	Did we think of how we could help others?
Do we owe an apology? And if so to whom?	Did we study literature today?
What could we have done better?	Did we go to a meeting today?
Did we blame our feelings on someone else?	Did we call our sponsor today?
Do we need to write 10th Step on something?	Did we do anything that is improved over our past?

Journal—Gratitude List—Tomorrows Action Plan

STEP 10

BALANCE SHEETS

Day _____ Month _____ Year _____

Food		Money		
Breakfast		Item		Amount
Lunch				
Dinner				
Snack				
Exercise				
		Total Spent Today		
Litres Water Hours Sleep		Quality of Life Today		%

When we retire at night we constructively review our day. We remember we have ceased fighting anything and anyone—love and tolerance of others is our code.

We Draw Up a Balance Sheet

The "Negative Side" (-)	The "Positive Side" (+)
Were we resentful?	Have we stayed clean of our addiction today?
Were we selfish?	Were we kind?
Were we dishonest?	Were we loving toward all?
Were we afraid?	What did we pack into life?
Have we kept something to ourselves?	Did we pray and meditate?
Were we thinking of ourselves most of the time?	Did we call someone we could help today?
Were we "disturbed" today?	Did we think of how we could help others?
Do we owe an apology? And if so to whom?	Did we study literature today?
What could we have done better?	Did we go to a meeting today?
Did we blame our feelings on someone else?	Did we call our sponsor today?
Do we need to write 10th Step on something?	Did we do anything that is improved over our past?

Journal—Gratitude List—Tomorrows Action Plan

BALANCE SHEETS

Day _____ Month _____ Year _____

Food

Breakfast	
Lunch	
Dinner	
Snack	
Exercise	

Litres Water	Hours Sleep

Money

Item	Amount
Total Spent Today	
Quality of Life Today	%

When we retire at night we constructively review our day. We remember we have ceased fighting anything and anyone—love and tolerance of others is our code.

We Draw Up a Balance Sheet

The "Negative Side" (-)	The "Positive Side" (+)
Were we resentful?	Have we stayed clean of our addiction today?
Were we selfish?	Were we kind?
Were we dishonest?	Were we loving toward all?
Were we afraid?	What did we pack into life?
Have we kept something to ourselves?	Did we pray and meditate?
Were we thinking of ourselves most of the time?	Did we call someone we could help today?
Were we "disturbed" today?	Did we think of how we could help others?
Do we owe an apology? And if so to whom?	Did we study literature today?
What could we have done better?	Did we go to a meeting today?
Did we blame our feelings on someone else?	Did we call our sponsor today?
Do we need to write 10th Step on something?	Did we do anything that is improved over our past?

Journal—Gratitude List—Tomorrows Action Plan

STEP 10

BALANCE SHEETS

Day _____ Month _____ Year _____

Food

Breakfast		Money	
		Item	Amount
Lunch			
Dinner			
Snack			
Exercise			
		Total Spent Today	
Litres Water	Hours Sleep	Quality of Life Today	%

When we retire at night we constructively review our day. We remember we have ceased fighting anything and anyone—love and tolerance of others is our code.

We Draw Up a Balance Sheet

The "Negative Side" (-)	The "Positive Side" (+)
Were we resentful?	Have we stayed clean of our addiction today?
Were we selfish?	Were we kind?
Were we dishonest?	Were we loving toward all?
Were we afraid?	What did we pack into life?
Have we kept something to ourselves?	Did we pray and meditate?
Were we thinking of ourselves most of the time?	Did we call someone we could help today?
Were we "disturbed" today?	Did we think of how we could help others?
Do we owe an apology? And if so to whom?	Did we study literature today?
What could we have done better?	Did we go to a meeting today?
Did we blame our feelings on someone else?	Did we call our sponsor today?
Do we need to write 10th Step on something?	Did we do anything that is improved over our past?

Journal—Gratitude List—Tomorrows Action Plan

MAINTAINING THE PROMISES...DAILY

BALANCE SHEETS

Day _____ Month _____ Year _____

Food		Money	
Breakfast		Item	Amount
Lunch			
Dinner			
Snack			
Exercise			
		Total Spent Today	
Litres Water Hours Sleep		Quality of Life Today	%

When we retire at night we constructively review our day. We remember we have ceased fighting anything and anyone—love and tolerance of others is our code.

We Draw Up a Balance Sheet

The "Negative Side" (-)	The "Positive Side" (+)
Were we resentful?	Have we stayed clean of our addiction today?
Were we selfish?	Were we kind?
Were we dishonest?	Were we loving toward all?
Were we afraid?	What did we pack into life?
Have we kept something to ourselves?	Did we pray and meditate?
Were we thinking of ourselves most of the time?	Did we call someone we could help today?
Were we "disturbed" today?	Did we think of how we could help others?
Do we owe an apology? And if so to whom?	Did we study literature today?
What could we have done better?	Did we go to a meeting today?
Did we blame our feelings on someone else?	Did we call our sponsor today?
Do we need to write 10th Step on something?	Did we do anything that is improved over our past?

Journal—Gratitude List—Tomorrows Action Plan

STEP 10

BALANCE SHEETS

Day _____ Month _____ Year_____

Food		Money	
Breakfast		Item	Amount
Lunch			
Dinner			
Snack			
Exercise			
		Total Spent Today	
Litres Water	Hours Sleep	Quality of Life Today	%

When we retire at night we constructively review our day. We remember we have ceased fighting anything and anyone—love and tolerance of others is our code.

We Draw Up a Balance Sheet

The "Negative Side" (-)	The "Positive Side" (+)
Were we resentful?	Have we stayed clean of our addiction today?
Were we selfish?	Were we kind?
Were we dishonest?	Were we loving toward all?
Were we afraid?	What did we pack into life?
Have we kept something to ourselves?	Did we pray and meditate?
Were we thinking of ourselves most of the time?	Did we call someone we could help today?
Were we "disturbed" today?	Did we think of how we could help others?
Do we owe an apology? And if so to whom?	Did we study literature today?
What could we have done better?	Did we go to a meeting today?
Did we blame our feelings on someone else?	Did we call our sponsor today?
Do we need to write 10th Step on something?	Did we do anything that is improved over our past?

Journal—Gratitude List—Tomorrows Action Plan

BALANCE SHEETS

Day _____ Month _____ Year _____

Food

Breakfast		
Lunch		
Dinner		
Snack		
Exercise		
Litres Water	Hours Sleep	

Money

Item	Amount
Total Spent Today	
Quality of Life Today	%

When we retire at night we constructively review our day. We remember we have ceased fighting anything and anyone—love and tolerance of others is our code.

We Draw Up a Balance Sheet

The "Negative Side" (-)	The "Positive Side" (+)
Were we resentful?	Have we stayed clean of our addiction today?
Were we selfish?	Were we kind?
Were we dishonest?	Were we loving toward all?
Were we afraid?	What did we pack into life?
Have we kept something to ourselves?	Did we pray and meditate?
Were we thinking of ourselves most of the time?	Did we call someone we could help today?
Were we "disturbed" today?	Did we think of how we could help others?
Do we owe an apology? And if so to whom?	Did we study literature today?
What could we have done better?	Did we go to a meeting today?
Did we blame our feelings on someone else?	Did we call our sponsor today?
Do we need to write 10th Step on something?	Did we do anything that is improved over our past?

Journal—Gratitude List—Tomorrows Action Plan

STEP 10

BALANCE SHEETS

Day _____ Month _____ Year _____

Food		Money		
Breakfast		Item		Amount
Lunch				
Dinner				
Snack				
Exercise				
		Total Spent Today		
Litres Water Hours Sleep		Quality of Life Today		%

When we retire at night we constructively review our day. We remember we have ceased fighting anything and anyone—love and tolerance of others is our code.

We Draw Up a Balance Sheet

The "Negative Side" (-)	The "Positive Side" (+)
Were we resentful?	Have we stayed clean of our addiction today?
Were we selfish?	Were we kind?
Were we dishonest?	Were we loving toward all?
Were we afraid?	What did we pack into life?
Have we kept something to ourselves?	Did we pray and meditate?
Were we thinking of ourselves most of the time?	Did we call someone we could help today?
Were we "disturbed" today?	Did we think of how we could help others?
Do we owe an apology? And if so to whom?	Did we study literature today?
What could we have done better?	Did we go to a meeting today?
Did we blame our feelings on someone else?	Did we call our sponsor today?
Do we need to write 10th Step on something?	Did we do anything that is improved over our past?

Journal—Gratitude List—Tomorrows Action Plan

MAINTAINING THE PROMISES...DAILY

BALANCE SHEETS

Day _____ Month _____ Year _____

Food

Breakfast

Lunch

Dinner

Snack

Exercise

Litres Water	Hours Sleep

Money

Item	Amount
Total Spent Today	
Quality of Life Today	%

When we retire at night we constructively review our day. We remember we have ceased fighting anything and anyone—love and tolerance of others is our code.

We Draw Up a Balance Sheet

The "Negative Side" (-)	The "Positive Side" (+)
Were we resentful?	Have we stayed clean of our addiction today?
Were we selfish?	Were we kind?
Were we dishonest?	Were we loving toward all?
Were we afraid?	What did we pack into life?
Have we kept something to ourselves?	Did we pray and meditate?
Were we thinking of ourselves most of the time?	Did we call someone we could help today?
Were we "disturbed" today?	Did we think of how we could help others?
Do we owe an apology? And if so to whom?	Did we study literature today?
What could we have done better?	Did we go to a meeting today?
Did we blame our feelings on someone else?	Did we call our sponsor today?
Do we need to write 10th Step on something?	Did we do anything that is improved over our past?

Journal—Gratitude List—Tomorrows Action Plan

STEP 10

BALANCE SHEETS

Day _____ Month _____ Year _____

Food		Money	
Breakfast		Item	Amount
Lunch			
Dinner			
Snack			
Exercise			
		Total Spent Today	
Litres Water Hours Sleep		Quality of Life Today	%

When we retire at night we constructively review our day. We remember we have ceased fighting anything and anyone—love and tolerance of others is our code.

We Draw Up a Balance Sheet

The "Negative Side" (-)	The "Positive Side" (+)
Were we resentful?	Have we stayed clean of our addiction today?
Were we selfish?	Were we kind?
Were we dishonest?	Were we loving toward all?
Were we afraid?	What did we pack into life?
Have we kept something to ourselves?	Did we pray and meditate?
Were we thinking of ourselves most of the time?	Did we call someone we could help today?
Were we "disturbed" today?	Did we think of how we could help others?
Do we owe an apology? And if so to whom?	Did we study literature today?
What could we have done better?	Did we go to a meeting today?
Did we blame our feelings on someone else?	Did we call our sponsor today?
Do we need to write 10th Step on something?	Did we do anything that is improved over our past?

Journal—Gratitude List—Tomorrows Action Plan

BALANCE SHEETS

Day _____ Month _____ Year _____

Food		Money	
Breakfast		Item	Amount
Lunch			
Dinner			
Snack			
Exercise			
		Total Spent Today	
Litres Water Hours Sleep		Quality of Life Today	%

When we retire at night we constructively review our day. We remember we have ceased fighting anything and anyone—love and tolerance of others is our code.

We Draw Up a Balance Sheet

The "Negative Side" (-)	The "Positive Side" (+)
Were we resentful?	Have we stayed clean of our addiction today?
Were we selfish?	Were we kind?
Were we dishonest?	Were we loving toward all?
Were we afraid?	What did we pack into life?
Have we kept something to ourselves?	Did we pray and meditate?
Were we thinking of ourselves most of the time?	Did we call someone we could help today?
Were we "disturbed" today?	Did we think of how we could help others?
Do we owe an apology? And if so to whom?	Did we study literature today?
What could we have done better?	Did we go to a meeting today?
Did we blame our feelings on someone else?	Did we call our sponsor today?
Do we need to write 10th Step on something?	Did we do anything that is improved over our past?

Journal—Gratitude List—Tomorrows Action Plan

STEP 10

BALANCE SHEETS

Day _____ Month _____ Year _____

Food		Money	
Breakfast		Item	Amount
Lunch			
Dinner			
Snack			
Exercise			
		Total Spent Today	
Litres Water	Hours Sleep	Quality of Life Today	%

When we retire at night we constructively review our day. We remember we have ceased fighting anything and anyone—love and tolerance of others is our code.

We Draw Up a Balance Sheet

The "Negative Side" (-)	The "Positive Side" (+)
Were we resentful?	Have we stayed clean of our addiction today?
Were we selfish?	Were we kind?
Were we dishonest?	Were we loving toward all?
Were we afraid?	What did we pack into life?
Have we kept something to ourselves?	Did we pray and meditate?
Were we thinking of ourselves most of the time?	Did we call someone we could help today?
Were we "disturbed" today?	Did we think of how we could help others?
Do we owe an apology? And if so to whom?	Did we study literature today?
What could we have done better?	Did we go to a meeting today?
Did we blame our feelings on someone else?	Did we call our sponsor today?
Do we need to write 10th Step on something?	Did we do anything that is improved over our past?

Journal—Gratitude List—Tomorrows Action Plan

BALANCE SHEETS

Day _____ Month _____ Year _____

Food

Breakfast	

Lunch	

Dinner	

Snack	

Exercise	

Money

Item	Amount
Total Spent Today	
Quality of Life Today	%

Litres Water	Hours Sleep

When we retire at night we constructively review our day. We remember we have ceased fighting anything and anyone—love and tolerance of others is our code.

We Draw Up a Balance Sheet

The "Negative Side" (-)	The "Positive Side" (+)
Were we resentful?	Have we stayed clean of our addiction today?
Were we selfish?	Were we kind?
Were we dishonest?	Were we loving toward all?
Were we afraid?	What did we pack into life?
Have we kept something to ourselves?	Did we pray and meditate?
Were we thinking of ourselves most of the time?	Did we call someone we could help today?
Were we "disturbed" today?	Did we think of how we could help others?
Do we owe an apology? And if so to whom?	Did we study literature today?
What could we have done better?	Did we go to a meeting today?
Did we blame our feelings on someone else?	Did we call our sponsor today?
Do we need to write 10th Step on something?	Did we do anything that is improved over our past?

Journal—Gratitude List—Tomorrows Action Plan

STEP 10

BALANCE SHEETS

Day _____ Month _____ Year _____

Food		Money	
Breakfast		Item	Amount
Lunch			
Dinner			
Snack			
Exercise			
		Total Spent Today	
Litres Water _____ Hours Sleep _____		Quality of Life Today	%

When we retire at night we constructively review our day. We remember we have ceased fighting anything and anyone—love and tolerance of others is our code.

We Draw Up a Balance Sheet

The "Negative Side" (-)	The "Positive Side" (+)
Were we resentful?	Have we stayed clean of our addiction today?
Were we selfish?	Were we kind?
Were we dishonest?	Were we loving toward all?
Were we afraid?	What did we pack into life?
Have we kept something to ourselves?	Did we pray and meditate?
Were we thinking of ourselves most of the time?	Did we call someone we could help today?
Were we "disturbed" today?	Did we think of how we could help others?
Do we owe an apology? And if so to whom?	Did we study literature today?
What could we have done better?	Did we go to a meeting today?
Did we blame our feelings on someone else?	Did we call our sponsor today?
Do we need to write 10th Step on something?	Did we do anything that is improved over our past?

Journal—Gratitude List—Tomorrows Action Plan

MAINTAINING THE PROMISES...DAILY

BALANCE SHEETS

Day _____ Month _____ Year _____

Food		Money	
Breakfast		Item	Amount
Lunch			
Dinner			
Snack			
Exercise			
		Total Spent Today	
Litres Water ____ Hours Sleep ____		Quality of Life Today	%

When we retire at night we constructively review our day. We remember we have ceased fighting anything and anyone—love and tolerance of others is our code.

We Draw Up a Balance Sheet

The "Negative Side" (-)	The "Positive Side" (+)
Were we resentful?	Have we stayed clean of our addiction today?
Were we selfish?	Were we kind?
Were we dishonest?	Were we loving toward all?
Were we afraid?	What did we pack into life?
Have we kept something to ourselves?	Did we pray and meditate?
Were we thinking of ourselves most of the time?	Did we call someone we could help today?
Were we "disturbed" today?	Did we think of how we could help others?
Do we owe an apology? And if so to whom?	Did we study literature today?
What could we have done better?	Did we go to a meeting today?
Did we blame our feelings on someone else?	Did we call our sponsor today?
Do we need to write 10th Step on something?	Did we do anything that is improved over our past?

Journal—Gratitude List—Tomorrows Action Plan

STEP 10

BALANCE SHEETS

Day _____ Month _____ Year _____

Food		Money	
Breakfast		Item	Amount
Lunch			
Dinner			
Snack			
Exercise			
		Total Spent Today	
Litres Water	Hours Sleep	Quality of Life Today	%

When we retire at night we constructively review our day. We remember we have ceased fighting anything and anyone—love and tolerance of others is our code.

We Draw Up a Balance Sheet

The "Negative Side" (−)	The "Positive Side" (+)
Were we resentful?	Have we stayed clean of our addiction today?
Were we selfish?	Were we kind?
Were we dishonest?	Were we loving toward all?
Were we afraid?	What did we pack into life?
Have we kept something to ourselves?	Did we pray and meditate?
Were we thinking of ourselves most of the time?	Did we call someone we could help today?
Were we "disturbed" today?	Did we think of how we could help others?
Do we owe an apology? And if so to whom?	Did we study literature today?
What could we have done better?	Did we go to a meeting today?
Did we blame our feelings on someone else?	Did we call our sponsor today?
Do we need to write 10th Step on something?	Did we do anything that is improved over our past?

Journal—Gratitude List—Tomorrows Action Plan

BALANCE SHEETS

Day _____ Month _____ Year _____

Food		Money	
Breakfast		Item	Amount
Lunch			
Dinner			
Snack			
Exercise			
		Total Spent Today	
Litres Water ____ Hours Sleep ____		Quality of Life Today	%

When we retire at night we constructively review our day. We remember we have ceased fighting anything and anyone—love and tolerance of others is our code.

We Draw Up a Balance Sheet

The "Negative Side" (-)	The "Positive Side" (+)
Were we resentful?	Have we stayed clean of our addiction today?
Were we selfish?	Were we kind?
Were we dishonest?	Were we loving toward all?
Were we afraid?	What did we pack into life?
Have we kept something to ourselves?	Did we pray and meditate?
Were we thinking of ourselves most of the time?	Did we call someone we could help today?
Were we "disturbed" today?	Did we think of how we could help others?
Do we owe an apology? And if so to whom?	Did we study literature today?
What could we have done better?	Did we go to a meeting today?
Did we blame our feelings on someone else?	Did we call our sponsor today?
Do we need to write 10th Step on something?	Did we do anything that is improved over our past?

Journal—Gratitude List—Tomorrows Action Plan

STEP 10

BALANCE SHEETS

Day _____ Month _____ Year_____

Food		Money	
Breakfast		Item	Amount
Lunch			
Dinner			
Snack			
Exercise			
		Total Spent Today	
Litres Water	Hours Sleep	Quality of Life Today	%

When we retire at night we constructively review our day. We remember we have ceased fighting anything and anyone—love and tolerance of others is our code.

We Draw Up a Balance Sheet

The "Negative Side" (-)	The "Positive Side" (+)
Were we resentful?	Have we stayed clean of our addiction today?
Were we selfish?	Were we kind?
Were we dishonest?	Were we loving toward all?
Were we afraid?	What did we pack into life?
Have we kept something to ourselves?	Did we pray and meditate?
Were we thinking of ourselves most of the time?	Did we call someone we could help today?
Were we "disturbed" today?	Did we think of how we could help others?
Do we owe an apology? And if so to whom?	Did we study literature today?
What could we have done better?	Did we go to a meeting today?
Did we blame our feelings on someone else?	Did we call our sponsor today?
Do we need to write 10th Step on something?	Did we do anything that is improved over our past?

Journal—Gratitude List—Tomorrows Action Plan

BALANCE SHEETS

Day _____ Month _____ Year _____

Food

Breakfast		
Lunch		
Dinner		
Snack		
Exercise		
Litres Water	Hours Sleep	

Money

Item	Amount
Total Spent Today	
Quality of Life Today	%

When we retire at night we constructively review our day. We remember we have ceased fighting anything and anyone—love and tolerance of others is our code.

We Draw Up a Balance Sheet

The "Negative Side" (−)	The "Positive Side" (+)
Were we resentful?	Have we stayed clean of our addiction today?
Were we selfish?	Were we kind?
Were we dishonest?	Were we loving toward all?
Were we afraid?	What did we pack into life?
Have we kept something to ourselves?	Did we pray and meditate?
Were we thinking of ourselves most of the time?	Did we call someone we could help today?
Were we "disturbed" today?	Did we think of how we could help others?
Do we owe an apology? And if so to whom?	Did we study literature today?
What could we have done better?	Did we go to a meeting today?
Did we blame our feelings on someone else?	Did we call our sponsor today?
Do we need to write 10th Step on something?	Did we do anything that is improved over our past?

Journal—Gratitude List—Tomorrows Action Plan

STEP 10

BALANCE SHEETS

Day _____ Month _____ Year _____

Food		Money	
Breakfast		Item	Amount
Lunch			
Dinner			
Snack			
Exercise			
		Total Spent Today	
Litres Water Hours Sleep		Quality of Life Today	%

When we retire at night we constructively review our day. We remember we have ceased fighting anything and anyone—love and tolerance of others is our code.

We Draw Up a Balance Sheet

The "Negative Side" (-)	The "Positive Side" (+)
Were we resentful?	Have we stayed clean of our addiction today?
Were we selfish?	Were we kind?
Were we dishonest?	Were we loving toward all?
Were we afraid?	What did we pack into life?
Have we kept something to ourselves?	Did we pray and meditate?
Were we thinking of ourselves most of the time?	Did we call someone we could help today?
Were we "disturbed" today?	Did we think of how we could help others?
Do we owe an apology? And if so to whom?	Did we study literature today?
What could we have done better?	Did we go to a meeting today?
Did we blame our feelings on someone else?	Did we call our sponsor today?
Do we need to write 10th Step on something?	Did we do anything that is improved over our past?

Journal—Gratitude List—Tomorrows Action Plan

MAINTAINING THE PROMISES...DAILY

BALANCE SHEETS

Day _____ Month _____ Year _____

Food

Breakfast	
Lunch	
Dinner	
Snack	
Exercise	
Litres Water ____ Hours Sleep ____	

Money

Item	Amount
Total Spent Today	
Quality of Life Today	%

When we retire at night we constructively review our day. We remember we have ceased fighting anything and anyone—love and tolerance of others is our code.

We Draw Up a Balance Sheet

The "Negative Side" (-)	The "Positive Side" (+)
Were we resentful?	Have we stayed clean of our addiction today?
Were we selfish?	Were we kind?
Were we dishonest?	Were we loving toward all?
Were we afraid?	What did we pack into life?
Have we kept something to ourselves?	Did we pray and meditate?
Were we thinking of ourselves most of the time?	Did we call someone we could help today?
Were we "disturbed" today?	Did we think of how we could help others?
Do we owe an apology? And if so to whom?	Did we study literature today?
What could we have done better?	Did we go to a meeting today?
Did we blame our feelings on someone else?	Did we call our sponsor today?
Do we need to write 10th Step on something?	Did we do anything that is improved over our past?

Journal—Gratitude List—Tomorrows Action Plan

STEP 10

BALANCE SHEETS

Day _____ Month _____ Year _____

Food

Breakfast		
Lunch		
Dinner		
Snack		
Exercise		
Litres Water	Hours Sleep	

Money

Item		Amount
Total Spent Today		
Quality of Life Today		%

When we retire at night we constructively review our day. We remember we have ceased fighting anything and anyone—love and tolerance of others is our code.

We Draw Up a Balance Sheet

The "Negative Side" (-)	The "Positive Side" (+)
Were we resentful?	Have we stayed clean of our addiction today?
Were we selfish?	Were we kind?
Were we dishonest?	Were we loving toward all?
Were we afraid?	What did we pack into life?
Have we kept something to ourselves?	Did we pray and meditate?
Were we thinking of ourselves most of the time?	Did we call someone we could help today?
Were we "disturbed" today?	Did we think of how we could help others?
Do we owe an apology? And if so to whom?	Did we study literature today?
What could we have done better?	Did we go to a meeting today?
Did we blame our feelings on someone else?	Did we call our sponsor today?
Do we need to write 10th Step on something?	Did we do anything that is improved over our past?

Journal—Gratitude List—Tomorrows Action Plan

BALANCE SHEETS

Day _____ Month _____ Year _____

Food		Money	
Breakfast		Item	Amount
Lunch			
Dinner			
Snack			
Exercise			
		Total Spent Today	
Litres Water Hours Sleep		Quality of Life Today	%

When we retire at night we constructively review our day. We remember we have ceased fighting anything and anyone—love and tolerance of others is our code.

We Draw Up a Balance Sheet

The "Negative Side" (-)	The "Positive Side" (+)
Were we resentful?	Have we stayed clean of our addiction today?
Were we selfish?	Were we kind?
Were we dishonest?	Were we loving toward all?
Were we afraid?	What did we pack into life?
Have we kept something to ourselves?	Did we pray and meditate?
Were we thinking of ourselves most of the time?	Did we call someone we could help today?
Were we "disturbed" today?	Did we think of how we could help others?
Do we owe an apology? And if so to whom?	Did we study literature today?
What could we have done better?	Did we go to a meeting today?
Did we blame our feelings on someone else?	Did we call our sponsor today?
Do we need to write 10th Step on something?	Did we do anything that is improved over our past?

Journal—Gratitude List—Tomorrows Action Plan

STEP 10

BALANCE SHEETS

Day _____ Month _____ Year _____

Food		Money	
Breakfast		Item	Amount
Lunch			
Dinner			
Snack			
Exercise			
		Total Spent Today	
Litres Water	Hours Sleep	Quality of Life Today	%

When we retire at night we constructively review our day. We remember we have ceased fighting anything and anyone—love and tolerance of others is our code.

We Draw Up a Balance Sheet

The "Negative Side" (-)	The "Positive Side" (+)
Were we resentful?	Have we stayed clean of our addiction today?
Were we selfish?	Were we kind?
Were we dishonest?	Were we loving toward all?
Were we afraid?	What did we pack into life?
Have we kept something to ourselves?	Did we pray and meditate?
Were we thinking of ourselves most of the time?	Did we call someone we could help today?
Were we "disturbed" today?	Did we think of how we could help others?
Do we owe an apology? And if so to whom?	Did we study literature today?
What could we have done better?	Did we go to a meeting today?
Did we blame our feelings on someone else?	Did we call our sponsor today?
Do we need to write 10th Step on something?	Did we do anything that is improved over our past?

Journal—Gratitude List—Tomorrows Action Plan

_____
_____
_____
_____
_____
_____

BALANCE SHEETS

Day _____ Month _____ Year _____

Food

Breakfast		
Lunch		
Dinner		
Snack		
Exercise		
Litres Water	Hours Sleep	

Money

Item		Amount
Total Spent Today		
Quality of Life Today		%

When we retire at night we constructively review our day. We remember we have ceased fighting anything and anyone—love and tolerance of others is our code.

We Draw Up a Balance Sheet

The "Negative Side" (-)	The "Positive Side" (+)
Were we resentful?	Have we stayed clean of our addiction today?
Were we selfish?	Were we kind?
Were we dishonest?	Were we loving toward all?
Were we afraid?	What did we pack into life?
Have we kept something to ourselves?	Did we pray and meditate?
Were we thinking of ourselves most of the time?	Did we call someone we could help today?
Were we "disturbed" today?	Did we think of how we could help others?
Do we owe an apology? And if so to whom?	Did we study literature today?
What could we have done better?	Did we go to a meeting today?
Did we blame our feelings on someone else?	Did we call our sponsor today?
Do we need to write 10th Step on something?	Did we do anything that is improved over our past?

Journal—Gratitude List—Tomorrows Action Plan

STEP 10

BALANCE SHEETS

Day _____ Month _____ Year_____

Food		Money	
Breakfast		Item	Amount
Lunch			
Dinner			
Snack			
Exercise			
		Total Spent Today	
Litres Water Hours Sleep		Quality of Life Today	%

When we retire at night we constructively review our day. We remember we have ceased fighting anything and anyone—love and tolerance of others is our code.

We Draw Up a Balance Sheet

The "Negative Side" (-)	The "Positive Side" (+)
Were we resentful?	Have we stayed clean of our addiction today?
Were we selfish?	Were we kind?
Were we dishonest?	Were we loving toward all?
Were we afraid?	What did we pack into life?
Have we kept something to ourselves?	Did we pray and meditate?
Were we thinking of ourselves most of the time?	Did we call someone we could help today?
Were we "disturbed" today?	Did we think of how we could help others?
Do we owe an apology? And if so to whom?	Did we study literature today?
What could we have done better?	Did we go to a meeting today?
Did we blame our feelings on someone else?	Did we call our sponsor today?
Do we need to write 10th Step on something?	Did we do anything that is improved over our past?

Journal—Gratitude List—Tomorrows Action Plan

MAINTAINING THE PROMISES...DAILY

BALANCE SHEETS

Day _____ Month _____ Year _____

Food		Money	
Breakfast		Item	Amount
Lunch			
Dinner			
Snack			
Exercise			
		Total Spent Today	
Litres Water ___ Hours Sleep ___		Quality of Life Today	%

When we retire at night we constructively review our day. We remember we have ceased fighting anything and anyone—love and tolerance of others is our code.

We Draw Up a Balance Sheet

The "Negative Side" (-)	The "Positive Side" (+)
Were we resentful?	Have we stayed clean of our addiction today?
Were we selfish?	Were we kind?
Were we dishonest?	Were we loving toward all?
Were we afraid?	What did we pack into life?
Have we kept something to ourselves?	Did we pray and meditate?
Were we thinking of ourselves most of the time?	Did we call someone we could help today?
Were we "disturbed" today?	Did we think of how we could help others?
Do we owe an apology? And if so to whom?	Did we study literature today?
What could we have done better?	Did we go to a meeting today?
Did we blame our feelings on someone else?	Did we call our sponsor today?
Do we need to write 10th Step on something?	Did we do anything that is improved over our past?

Journal—Gratitude List—Tomorrows Action Plan

STEP 10

BALANCE SHEETS

Day _____ Month _____ Year _____

Food		Money	
Breakfast		Item	Amount
Lunch			
Dinner			
Snack			
Exercise			
		Total Spent Today	
Litres Water Hours Sleep		Quality of Life Today	%

When we retire at night we constructively review our day. We remember we have ceased fighting anything and anyone—love and tolerance of others is our code.

We Draw Up a Balance Sheet

The "Negative Side" (-)	The "Positive Side" (+)
Were we resentful?	Have we stayed clean of our addiction today?
Were we selfish?	Were we kind?
Were we dishonest?	Were we loving toward all?
Were we afraid?	What did we pack into life?
Have we kept something to ourselves?	Did we pray and meditate?
Were we thinking of ourselves most of the time?	Did we call someone we could help today?
Were we "disturbed" today?	Did we think of how we could help others?
Do we owe an apology? And if so to whom?	Did we study literature today?
What could we have done better?	Did we go to a meeting today?
Did we blame our feelings on someone else?	Did we call our sponsor today?
Do we need to write 10th Step on something?	Did we do anything that is improved over our past?

Journal—Gratitude List—Tomorrows Action Plan

BALANCE SHEETS

Day _____ Month _____ Year _____

Food		Money	
Breakfast		Item	Amount
Lunch			
Dinner			
Snack			
Exercise			
		Total Spent Today	
Litres Water Hours Sleep		Quality of Life Today	%

When we retire at night we constructively review our day. We remember we have ceased fighting anything and anyone—love and tolerance of others is our code.

We Draw Up a Balance Sheet

The "Negative Side" (-)	The "Positive Side" (+)
Were we resentful?	Have we stayed clean of our addiction today?
Were we selfish?	Were we kind?
Were we dishonest?	Were we loving toward all?
Were we afraid?	What did we pack into life?
Have we kept something to ourselves?	Did we pray and meditate?
Were we thinking of ourselves most of the time?	Did we call someone we could help today?
Were we "disturbed" today?	Did we think of how we could help others?
Do we owe an apology? And if so to whom?	Did we study literature today?
What could we have done better?	Did we go to a meeting today?
Did we blame our feelings on someone else?	Did we call our sponsor today?
Do we need to write 10th Step on something?	Did we do anything that is improved over our past?

Journal—Gratitude List—Tomorrows Action Plan

STEP 10

BALANCE SHEETS

Day _____ Month _____ Year _____

Food

Breakfast	
Lunch	
Dinner	
Snack	
Exercise	
Litres Water	Hours Sleep

Money

Item	Amount
Total Spent Today	
Quality of Life Today	%

When we retire at night we constructively review our day. We remember we have ceased fighting anything and anyone—love and tolerance of others is our code.

We Draw Up a Balance Sheet

The "Negative Side" (-)	The "Positive Side" (+)
Were we resentful?	Have we stayed clean of our addiction today?
Were we selfish?	Were we kind?
Were we dishonest?	Were we loving toward all?
Were we afraid?	What did we pack into life?
Have we kept something to ourselves?	Did we pray and meditate?
Were we thinking of ourselves most of the time?	Did we call someone we could help today?
Were we "disturbed" today?	Did we think of how we could help others?
Do we owe an apology? And if so to whom?	Did we study literature today?
What could we have done better?	Did we go to a meeting today?
Did we blame our feelings on someone else?	Did we call our sponsor today?
Do we need to write 10th Step on something?	Did we do anything that is improved over our past?

Journal—Gratitude List—Tomorrows Action Plan

MAINTAINING THE PROMISES...DAILY

BALANCE SHEETS

Day _____ Month _____ Year _____

Food

Breakfast		
Lunch		
Dinner		
Snack		
Exercise		
Litres Water	Hours Sleep	

Money

Item	Amount
Total Spent Today	
Quality of Life Today	%

When we retire at night we constructively review our day. We remember we have ceased fighting anything and anyone—love and tolerance of others is our code.

We Draw Up a Balance Sheet

The "Negative Side" (-)	The "Positive Side" (+)
Were we resentful?	Have we stayed clean of our addiction today?
Were we selfish?	Were we kind?
Were we dishonest?	Were we loving toward all?
Were we afraid?	What did we pack into life?
Have we kept something to ourselves?	Did we pray and meditate?
Were we thinking of ourselves most of the time?	Did we call someone we could help today?
Were we "disturbed" today?	Did we think of how we could help others?
Do we owe an apology? And if so to whom?	Did we study literature today?
What could we have done better?	Did we go to a meeting today?
Did we blame our feelings on someone else?	Did we call our sponsor today?
Do we need to write 10th Step on something?	Did we do anything that is improved over our past?

Journal—Gratitude List—Tomorrows Action Plan

STEP 10

BALANCE SHEETS

Day _____ Month _____ Year _____

Food		Money	
Breakfast		Item	Amount
Lunch			
Dinner			
Snack			
Exercise			
		Total Spent Today	
Litres Water	Hours Sleep	Quality of Life Today	%

When we retire at night we constructively review our day. We remember we have ceased fighting anything and anyone—love and tolerance of others is our code.

We Draw Up a Balance Sheet

The "Negative Side" (-)	The "Positive Side" (+)
Were we resentful?	Have we stayed clean of our addiction today?
Were we selfish?	Were we kind?
Were we dishonest?	Were we loving toward all?
Were we afraid?	What did we pack into life?
Have we kept something to ourselves?	Did we pray and meditate?
Were we thinking of ourselves most of the time?	Did we call someone we could help today?
Were we "disturbed" today?	Did we think of how we could help others?
Do we owe an apology? And if so to whom?	Did we study literature today?
What could we have done better?	Did we go to a meeting today?
Did we blame our feelings on someone else?	Did we call our sponsor today?
Do we need to write 10th Step on something?	Did we do anything that is improved over our past?

Journal—Gratitude List—Tomorrows Action Plan

BALANCE SHEETS

Day _____ Month _____ Year _____

Food		Money	
Breakfast		Item	Amount
Lunch			
Dinner			
Snack			
Exercise			
		Total Spent Today	
Litres Water Hours Sleep		Quality of Life Today	%

When we retire at night we constructively review our day. We remember we have ceased fighting anything and anyone—love and tolerance of others is our code.

We Draw Up a Balance Sheet

The "Negative Side" (-)	The "Positive Side" (+)
Were we resentful?	Have we stayed clean of our addiction today?
Were we selfish?	Were we kind?
Were we dishonest?	Were we loving toward all?
Were we afraid?	What did we pack into life?
Have we kept something to ourselves?	Did we pray and meditate?
Were we thinking of ourselves most of the time?	Did we call someone we could help today?
Were we "disturbed" today?	Did we think of how we could help others?
Do we owe an apology? And if so to whom?	Did we study literature today?
What could we have done better?	Did we go to a meeting today?
Did we blame our feelings on someone else?	Did we call our sponsor today?
Do we need to write 10th Step on something?	Did we do anything that is improved over our past?

Journal—Gratitude List—Tomorrows Action Plan

STEP 10

BALANCE SHEETS

Day _____ Month _____ Year _____

Food		Money	
Breakfast		Item	Amount
Lunch			
Dinner			
Snack			
Exercise			
		Total Spent Today	
Litres Water	Hours Sleep	Quality of Life Today	%

When we retire at night we constructively review our day. We remember we have ceased fighting anything and anyone—love and tolerance of others is our code.

We Draw Up a Balance Sheet

The "Negative Side" (-)	The "Positive Side" (+)
Were we resentful?	Have we stayed clean of our addiction today?
Were we selfish?	Were we kind?
Were we dishonest?	Were we loving toward all?
Were we afraid?	What did we pack into life?
Have we kept something to ourselves?	Did we pray and meditate?
Were we thinking of ourselves most of the time?	Did we call someone we could help today?
Were we "disturbed" today?	Did we think of how we could help others?
Do we owe an apology? And if so to whom?	Did we study literature today?
What could we have done better?	Did we go to a meeting today?
Did we blame our feelings on someone else?	Did we call our sponsor today?
Do we need to write 10th Step on something?	Did we do anything that is improved over our past?

Journal—Gratitude List—Tomorrows Action Plan

BALANCE SHEETS

Day _____ Month _____ Year _____

Food		Money		
Breakfast		Item		Amount
Lunch				
Dinner				
Snack				
Exercise				
		Total Spent Today		
Litres Water Hours Sleep		Quality of Life Today		%

When we retire at night we constructively review our day. We remember we have ceased fighting anything and anyone—love and tolerance of others is our code.

We Draw Up a Balance Sheet

The "Negative Side" (-)	The "Positive Side" (+)
Were we resentful?	Have we stayed clean of our addiction today?
Were we selfish?	Were we kind?
Were we dishonest?	Were we loving toward all?
Were we afraid?	What did we pack into life?
Have we kept something to ourselves?	Did we pray and meditate?
Were we thinking of ourselves most of the time?	Did we call someone we could help today?
Were we "disturbed" today?	Did we think of how we could help others?
Do we owe an apology? And if so to whom?	Did we study literature today?
What could we have done better?	Did we go to a meeting today?
Did we blame our feelings on someone else?	Did we call our sponsor today?
Do we need to write 10th Step on something?	Did we do anything that is improved over our past?

Journal—Gratitude List—Tomorrows Action Plan

STEP 10

BALANCE SHEETS

Day _____ Month _____ Year _____

Food		Money	
Breakfast		Item	Amount
Lunch			
Dinner			
Snack			
Exercise			
		Total Spent Today	
Litres Water	Hours Sleep	Quality of Life Today	%

When we retire at night we constructively review our day. We remember we have ceased fighting anything and anyone—love and tolerance of others is our code.

We Draw Up a Balance Sheet

The "Negative Side" (-)	The "Positive Side" (+)
Were we resentful?	Have we stayed clean of our addiction today?
Were we selfish?	Were we kind?
Were we dishonest?	Were we loving toward all?
Were we afraid?	What did we pack into life?
Have we kept something to ourselves?	Did we pray and meditate?
Were we thinking of ourselves most of the time?	Did we call someone we could help today?
Were we "disturbed" today?	Did we think of how we could help others?
Do we owe an apology? And if so to whom?	Did we study literature today?
What could we have done better?	Did we go to a meeting today?
Did we blame our feelings on someone else?	Did we call our sponsor today?
Do we need to write 10th Step on something?	Did we do anything that is improved over our past?

Journal—Gratitude List—Tomorrows Action Plan

MAINTAINING THE PROMISES...DAILY

BALANCE SHEETS

Day _____ Month _____ Year _____

Food		Money	
Breakfast		Item	Amount
Lunch			
Dinner			
Snack			
Exercise			
		Total Spent Today	
Litres Water	Hours Sleep	Quality of Life Today	%

When we retire at night we constructively review our day. We remember we have ceased fighting anything and anyone—love and tolerance of others is our code.

We Draw Up a Balance Sheet

The "Negative Side" (-)	The "Positive Side" (+)
Were we resentful?	Have we stayed clean of our addiction today?
Were we selfish?	Were we kind?
Were we dishonest?	Were we loving toward all?
Were we afraid?	What did we pack into life?
Have we kept something to ourselves?	Did we pray and meditate?
Were we thinking of ourselves most of the time?	Did we call someone we could help today?
Were we "disturbed" today?	Did we think of how we could help others?
Do we owe an apology? And if so to whom?	Did we study literature today?
What could we have done better?	Did we go to a meeting today?
Did we blame our feelings on someone else?	Did we call our sponsor today?
Do we need to write 10th Step on something?	Did we do anything that is improved over our past?

Journal—Gratitude List—Tomorrows Action Plan

STEP 10

BALANCE SHEETS

Day _____ Month _____ Year _____

Food		Money	
Breakfast		Item	Amount
Lunch			
Dinner			
Snack			
Exercise			
		Total Spent Today	
Litres Water Hours Sleep		Quality of Life Today	%

When we retire at night we constructively review our day. We remember we have ceased fighting anything and anyone—love and tolerance of others is our code.

We Draw Up a Balance Sheet

The "Negative Side" (-)	The "Positive Side" (+)
Were we resentful?	Have we stayed clean of our addiction today?
Were we selfish?	Were we kind?
Were we dishonest?	Were we loving toward all?
Were we afraid?	What did we pack into life?
Have we kept something to ourselves?	Did we pray and meditate?
Were we thinking of ourselves most of the time?	Did we call someone we could help today?
Were we "disturbed" today?	Did we think of how we could help others?
Do we owe an apology? And if so to whom?	Did we study literature today?
What could we have done better?	Did we go to a meeting today?
Did we blame our feelings on someone else?	Did we call our sponsor today?
Do we need to write 10th Step on something?	Did we do anything that is improved over our past?

Journal—Gratitude List—Tomorrows Action Plan

MAINTAINING THE PROMISES...DAILY

BALANCE SHEETS

Day _____ Month _____ Year _____

Food		Money	
Breakfast		Item	Amount
Lunch			
Dinner			
Snack			
Exercise			
		Total Spent Today	
Litres Water Hours Sleep		Quality of Life Today	%

When we retire at night we constructively review our day. We remember we have ceased fighting anything and anyone—love and tolerance of others is our code.

We Draw Up a Balance Sheet

The "Negative Side" (-)	The "Positive Side" (+)
Were we resentful?	Have we stayed clean of our addiction today?
Were we selfish?	Were we kind?
Were we dishonest?	Were we loving toward all?
Were we afraid?	What did we pack into life?
Have we kept something to ourselves?	Did we pray and meditate?
Were we thinking of ourselves most of the time?	Did we call someone we could help today?
Were we "disturbed" today?	Did we think of how we could help others?
Do we owe an apology? And if so to whom?	Did we study literature today?
What could we have done better?	Did we go to a meeting today?
Did we blame our feelings on someone else?	Did we call our sponsor today?
Do we need to write 10th Step on something?	Did we do anything that is improved over our past?

Journal—Gratitude List—Tomorrows Action Plan

STEP 10

BALANCE SHEETS

Day _____ Month _____ Year _____

Food		Money		
Breakfast		Item		Amount
Lunch				
Dinner				
Snack				
Exercise				
		Total Spent Today		
Litres Water	Hours Sleep	Quality of Life Today		%

When we retire at night we constructively review our day. We remember we have ceased fighting anything and anyone—love and tolerance of others is our code.

We Draw Up a Balance Sheet

The "Negative Side" (-)	The "Positive Side" (+)
Were we resentful?	Have we stayed clean of our addiction today?
Were we selfish?	Were we kind?
Were we dishonest?	Were we loving toward all?
Were we afraid?	What did we pack into life?
Have we kept something to ourselves?	Did we pray and meditate?
Were we thinking of ourselves most of the time?	Did we call someone we could help today?
Were we "disturbed" today?	Did we think of how we could help others?
Do we owe an apology? And if so to whom?	Did we study literature today?
What could we have done better?	Did we go to a meeting today?
Did we blame our feelings on someone else?	Did we call our sponsor today?
Do we need to write 10th Step on something?	Did we do anything that is improved over our past?

Journal—Gratitude List—Tomorrows Action Plan

340   MAINTAINING THE PROMISES...DAILY

BALANCE SHEETS

Day _____ Month _____ Year _____

Food		Money	
Breakfast		Item	Amount
Lunch			
Dinner			
Snack			
Exercise			
		Total Spent Today	
Litres Water	Hours Sleep	Quality of Life Today	%

When we retire at night we constructively review our day. We remember we have ceased fighting anything and anyone—love and tolerance of others is our code.

We Draw Up a Balance Sheet

The "Negative Side" (-)	The "Positive Side" (+)
Were we resentful?	Have we stayed clean of our addiction today?
Were we selfish?	Were we kind?
Were we dishonest?	Were we loving toward all?
Were we afraid?	What did we pack into life?
Have we kept something to ourselves?	Did we pray and meditate?
Were we thinking of ourselves most of the time?	Did we call someone we could help today?
Were we "disturbed" today?	Did we think of how we could help others?
Do we owe an apology? And if so to whom?	Did we study literature today?
What could we have done better?	Did we go to a meeting today?
Did we blame our feelings on someone else?	Did we call our sponsor today?
Do we need to write 10th Step on something?	Did we do anything that is improved over our past?

Journal—Gratitude List—Tomorrows Action Plan

STEP 10

BALANCE SHEETS

Day _____ Month _____ Year _____

Food		Money	
Breakfast		Item	Amount
Lunch			
Dinner			
Snack			
Exercise			
		Total Spent Today	
Litres Water	Hours Sleep	Quality of Life Today	%

When we retire at night we constructively review our day. We remember we have ceased fighting anything and anyone—love and tolerance of others is our code.

We Draw Up a Balance Sheet

The "Negative Side" (-)	The "Positive Side" (+)
Were we resentful?	Have we stayed clean of our addiction today?
Were we selfish?	Were we kind?
Were we dishonest?	Were we loving toward all?
Were we afraid?	What did we pack into life?
Have we kept something to ourselves?	Did we pray and meditate?
Were we thinking of ourselves most of the time?	Did we call someone we could help today?
Were we "disturbed" today?	Did we think of how we could help others?
Do we owe an apology? And if so to whom?	Did we study literature today?
What could we have done better?	Did we go to a meeting today?
Did we blame our feelings on someone else?	Did we call our sponsor today?
Do we need to write 10th Step on something?	Did we do anything that is improved over our past?

Journal—Gratitude List—Tomorrows Action Plan

BALANCE SHEETS

Day _____ Month _____ Year _____

Food

Breakfast		
Lunch		
Dinner		
Snack		
Exercise		
Litres Water	Hours Sleep	

Money

Item	Amount
Total Spent Today	
Quality of Life Today	%

When we retire at night we constructively review our day. We remember we have ceased fighting anything and anyone—love and tolerance of others is our code.

We Draw Up a Balance Sheet

The "Negative Side" (-)	The "Positive Side" (+)
Were we resentful?	Have we stayed clean of our addiction today?
Were we selfish?	Were we kind?
Were we dishonest?	Were we loving toward all?
Were we afraid?	What did we pack into life?
Have we kept something to ourselves?	Did we pray and meditate?
Were we thinking of ourselves most of the time?	Did we call someone we could help today?
Were we "disturbed" today?	Did we think of how we could help others?
Do we owe an apology? And if so to whom?	Did we study literature today?
What could we have done better?	Did we go to a meeting today?
Did we blame our feelings on someone else?	Did we call our sponsor today?
Do we need to write 10th Step on something?	Did we do anything that is improved over our past?

Journal—Gratitude List—Tomorrows Action Plan

STEP 10

BALANCE SHEETS

Day _____ Month _____ Year _____

Food

Breakfast		Money	
		Item	Amount
Lunch			
Dinner			
Snack			
Exercise			
		Total Spent Today	
Litres Water	Hours Sleep	Quality of Life Today	%

When we retire at night we constructively review our day. We remember we have ceased fighting anything and anyone—love and tolerance of others is our code.

We Draw Up a Balance Sheet

The "Negative Side" (-)	The "Positive Side" (+)
Were we resentful?	Have we stayed clean of our addiction today?
Were we selfish?	Were we kind?
Were we dishonest?	Were we loving toward all?
Were we afraid?	What did we pack into life?
Have we kept something to ourselves?	Did we pray and meditate?
Were we thinking of ourselves most of the time?	Did we call someone we could help today?
Were we "disturbed" today?	Did we think of how we could help others?
Do we owe an apology? And if so to whom?	Did we study literature today?
What could we have done better?	Did we go to a meeting today?
Did we blame our feelings on someone else?	Did we call our sponsor today?
Do we need to write 10th Step on something?	Did we do anything that is improved over our past?

Journal—Gratitude List—Tomorrows Action Plan

MAINTAINING THE PROMISES...DAILY

BALANCE SHEETS

Day _____ Month _____ Year _____

Food		Money		
Breakfast		Item		Amount
Lunch				
Dinner				
Snack				
Exercise				
		Total Spent Today		
Litres Water	Hours Sleep	Quality of Life Today		%

When we retire at night we constructively review our day. We remember we have ceased fighting anything and anyone—love and tolerance of others is our code.

We Draw Up a Balance Sheet

The "Negative Side" (−)	The "Positive Side" (+)
Were we resentful?	Have we stayed clean of our addiction today?
Were we selfish?	Were we kind?
Were we dishonest?	Were we loving toward all?
Were we afraid?	What did we pack into life?
Have we kept something to ourselves?	Did we pray and meditate?
Were we thinking of ourselves most of the time?	Did we call someone we could help today?
Were we "disturbed" today?	Did we think of how we could help others?
Do we owe an apology? And if so to whom?	Did we study literature today?
What could we have done better?	Did we go to a meeting today?
Did we blame our feelings on someone else?	Did we call our sponsor today?
Do we need to write 10th Step on something?	Did we do anything that is improved over our past?

Journal—Gratitude List—Tomorrows Action Plan

STEP 10

BALANCE SHEETS

Day _____ Month _____ Year _____

Food		Money	
Breakfast		Item	Amount
Lunch			
Dinner			
Snack			
Exercise			
		Total Spent Today	
Litres Water Hours Sleep		Quality of Life Today	%

When we retire at night we constructively review our day. We remember we have ceased fighting anything and anyone—love and tolerance of others is our code.

We Draw Up a Balance Sheet

The "Negative Side" (-)	The "Positive Side" (+)
Were we resentful?	Have we stayed clean of our addiction today?
Were we selfish?	Were we kind?
Were we dishonest?	Were we loving toward all?
Were we afraid?	What did we pack into life?
Have we kept something to ourselves?	Did we pray and meditate?
Were we thinking of ourselves most of the time?	Did we call someone we could help today?
Were we "disturbed" today?	Did we think of how we could help others?
Do we owe an apology? And if so to whom?	Did we study literature today?
What could we have done better?	Did we go to a meeting today?
Did we blame our feelings on someone else?	Did we call our sponsor today?
Do we need to write 10th Step on something?	Did we do anything that is improved over our past?

Journal—Gratitude List—Tomorrows Action Plan

BALANCE SHEETS

Day _____ Month _____ Year _____

Food		Money	
Breakfast		Item	Amount
Lunch			
Dinner			
Snack			
Exercise			
		Total Spent Today	
Litres Water ___ Hours Sleep ___		Quality of Life Today	%

When we retire at night we constructively review our day. We remember we have ceased fighting anything and anyone—love and tolerance of others is our code.

We Draw Up a Balance Sheet

The "Negative Side" (−)	The "Positive Side" (+)
Were we resentful?	Have we stayed clean of our addiction today?
Were we selfish?	Were we kind?
Were we dishonest?	Were we loving toward all?
Were we afraid?	What did we pack into life?
Have we kept something to ourselves?	Did we pray and meditate?
Were we thinking of ourselves most of the time?	Did we call someone we could help today?
Were we "disturbed" today?	Did we think of how we could help others?
Do we owe an apology? And if so to whom?	Did we study literature today?
What could we have done better?	Did we go to a meeting today?
Did we blame our feelings on someone else?	Did we call our sponsor today?
Do we need to write 10th Step on something?	Did we do anything that is improved over our past?

Journal—Gratitude List—Tomorrows Action Plan

STEP 10

BALANCE SHEETS

Day _____ Month _____ Year _____

Food		Money	
Breakfast		Item	Amount
Lunch			
Dinner			
Snack			
Exercise			
		Total Spent Today	
Litres Water	Hours Sleep	Quality of Life Today	%

When we retire at night we constructively review our day. We remember we have ceased fighting anything and anyone—love and tolerance of others is our code.

We Draw Up a Balance Sheet

The "Negative Side" (-)	The "Positive Side" (+)
Were we resentful?	Have we stayed clean of our addiction today?
Were we selfish?	Were we kind?
Were we dishonest?	Were we loving toward all?
Were we afraid?	What did we pack into life?
Have we kept something to ourselves?	Did we pray and meditate?
Were we thinking of ourselves most of the time?	Did we call someone we could help today?
Were we "disturbed" today?	Did we think of how we could help others?
Do we owe an apology? And if so to whom?	Did we study literature today?
What could we have done better?	Did we go to a meeting today?
Did we blame our feelings on someone else?	Did we call our sponsor today?
Do we need to write 10th Step on something?	Did we do anything that is improved over our past?

Journal—Gratitude List—Tomorrows Action Plan

BALANCE SHEETS

Day _____ Month _____ Year _____

Food

Breakfast	
Lunch	
Dinner	
Snack	
Exercise	

Litres Water	Hours Sleep

Money

Item	Amount
Total Spent Today	
Quality of Life Today	%

When we retire at night we constructively review our day. We remember we have ceased fighting anything and anyone—love and tolerance of others is our code.

We Draw Up a Balance Sheet

The "Negative Side" (-)	The "Positive Side" (+)
Were we resentful?	Have we stayed clean of our addiction today?
Were we selfish?	Were we kind?
Were we dishonest?	Were we loving toward all?
Were we afraid?	What did we pack into life?
Have we kept something to ourselves?	Did we pray and meditate?
Were we thinking of ourselves most of the time?	Did we call someone we could help today?
Were we "disturbed" today?	Did we think of how we could help others?
Do we owe an apology? And if so to whom?	Did we study literature today?
What could we have done better?	Did we go to a meeting today?
Did we blame our feelings on someone else?	Did we call our sponsor today?
Do we need to write 10th Step on something?	Did we do anything that is improved over our past?

Journal—Gratitude List—Tomorrows Action Plan

STEP 10

BALANCE SHEETS

Day _____ Month _____ Year _____

Food		Money	
Breakfast		Item	Amount
Lunch			
Dinner			
Snack			
Exercise			
		Total Spent Today	
Litres Water	Hours Sleep	Quality of Life Today	%

When we retire at night we constructively review our day. We remember we have ceased fighting anything and anyone—love and tolerance of others is our code.

We Draw Up a Balance Sheet

The "Negative Side" (-)	The "Positive Side" (+)
Were we resentful?	Have we stayed clean of our addiction today?
Were we selfish?	Were we kind?
Were we dishonest?	Were we loving toward all?
Were we afraid?	What did we pack into life?
Have we kept something to ourselves?	Did we pray and meditate?
Were we thinking of ourselves most of the time?	Did we call someone we could help today?
Were we "disturbed" today?	Did we think of how we could help others?
Do we owe an apology? And if so to whom?	Did we study literature today?
What could we have done better?	Did we go to a meeting today?
Did we blame our feelings on someone else?	Did we call our sponsor today?
Do we need to write 10th Step on something?	Did we do anything that is improved over our past?

Journal—Gratitude List—Tomorrows Action Plan

BALANCE SHEETS

Day _____ Month _____ Year _____

Food

Breakfast	
Lunch	
Dinner	
Snack	
Exercise	
Litres Water _____ Hours Sleep _____	

Money

Item	Amount
Total Spent Today	
Quality of Life Today	%

When we retire at night we constructively review our day. We remember we have ceased fighting anything and anyone—love and tolerance of others is our code.

We Draw Up a Balance Sheet

The "Negative Side" (-)	The "Positive Side" (+)
Were we resentful?	Have we stayed clean of our addiction today?
Were we selfish?	Were we kind?
Were we dishonest?	Were we loving toward all?
Were we afraid?	What did we pack into life?
Have we kept something to ourselves?	Did we pray and meditate?
Were we thinking of ourselves most of the time?	Did we call someone we could help today?
Were we "disturbed" today?	Did we think of how we could help others?
Do we owe an apology? And if so to whom?	Did we study literature today?
What could we have done better?	Did we go to a meeting today?
Did we blame our feelings on someone else?	Did we call our sponsor today?
Do we need to write 10th Step on something?	Did we do anything that is improved over our past?

Journal—Gratitude List—Tomorrows Action Plan

STEP 10

BALANCE SHEETS

Day _____ Month _____ Year _____

Food		Money	
Breakfast		Item	Amount
Lunch			
Dinner			
Snack			
Exercise			
		Total Spent Today	
Litres Water Hours Sleep		Quality of Life Today	%

When we retire at night we constructively review our day. We remember we have ceased fighting anything and anyone—love and tolerance of others is our code.

We Draw Up a Balance Sheet

The "Negative Side" (-)	The "Positive Side" (+)
Were we resentful?	Have we stayed clean of our addiction today?
Were we selfish?	Were we kind?
Were we dishonest?	Were we loving toward all?
Were we afraid?	What did we pack into life?
Have we kept something to ourselves?	Did we pray and meditate?
Were we thinking of ourselves most of the time?	Did we call someone we could help today?
Were we "disturbed" today?	Did we think of how we could help others?
Do we owe an apology? And if so to whom?	Did we study literature today?
What could we have done better?	Did we go to a meeting today?
Did we blame our feelings on someone else?	Did we call our sponsor today?
Do we need to write 10th Step on something?	Did we do anything that is improved over our past?

Journal—Gratitude List—Tomorrows Action Plan

BALANCE SHEETS

Day _____ Month _____ Year _____

Food		Money	
Breakfast		Item	Amount
Lunch			
Dinner			
Snack			
Exercise			
		Total Spent Today	
Litres Water Hours Sleep		Quality of Life Today	%

When we retire at night we constructively review our day. We remember we have ceased fighting anything and anyone—love and tolerance of others is our code.

We Draw Up a Balance Sheet

The "Negative Side" (-)	The "Positive Side" (+)
Were we resentful?	Have we stayed clean of our addiction today?
Were we selfish?	Were we kind?
Were we dishonest?	Were we loving toward all?
Were we afraid?	What did we pack into life?
Have we kept something to ourselves?	Did we pray and meditate?
Were we thinking of ourselves most of the time?	Did we call someone we could help today?
Were we "disturbed" today?	Did we think of how we could help others?
Do we owe an apology? And if so to whom?	Did we study literature today?
What could we have done better?	Did we go to a meeting today?
Did we blame our feelings on someone else?	Did we call our sponsor today?
Do we need to write 10th Step on something?	Did we do anything that is improved over our past?

Journal—Gratitude List—Tomorrows Action Plan

STEP 10

BALANCE SHEETS

Day _____ Month _____ Year _____

Food		Money	
Breakfast		Item	Amount
Lunch			
Dinner			
Snack			
Exercise			
		Total Spent Today	
Litres Water	Hours Sleep	Quality of Life Today	%

When we retire at night we constructively review our day. We remember we have ceased fighting anything and anyone—love and tolerance of others is our code.

We Draw Up a Balance Sheet

The "Negative Side" (-)	The "Positive Side" (+)
Were we resentful?	Have we stayed clean of our addiction today?
Were we selfish?	Were we kind?
Were we dishonest?	Were we loving toward all?
Were we afraid?	What did we pack into life?
Have we kept something to ourselves?	Did we pray and meditate?
Were we thinking of ourselves most of the time?	Did we call someone we could help today?
Were we "disturbed" today?	Did we think of how we could help others?
Do we owe an apology? And if so to whom?	Did we study literature today?
What could we have done better?	Did we go to a meeting today?
Did we blame our feelings on someone else?	Did we call our sponsor today?
Do we need to write 10th Step on something?	Did we do anything that is improved over our past?

Journal—Gratitude List—Tomorrows Action Plan

BALANCE SHEETS

Day _____ Month _____ Year _____

Food

Breakfast		Money	
		Item	Amount
Lunch			
Dinner			
Snack			
Exercise			
		Total Spent Today	
Litres Water	Hours Sleep	Quality of Life Today	%

When we retire at night we constructively review our day. We remember we have ceased fighting anything and anyone—love and tolerance of others is our code.

We Draw Up a Balance Sheet

The "Negative Side" (-)	The "Positive Side" (+)
Were we resentful?	Have we stayed clean of our addiction today?
Were we selfish?	Were we kind?
Were we dishonest?	Were we loving toward all?
Were we afraid?	What did we pack into life?
Have we kept something to ourselves?	Did we pray and meditate?
Were we thinking of ourselves most of the time?	Did we call someone we could help today?
Were we "disturbed" today?	Did we think of how we could help others?
Do we owe an apology? And if so to whom?	Did we study literature today?
What could we have done better?	Did we go to a meeting today?
Did we blame our feelings on someone else?	Did we call our sponsor today?
Do we need to write 10th Step on something?	Did we do anything that is improved over our past?

Journal—Gratitude List—Tomorrows Action Plan

STEP 10

BALANCE SHEETS

Day _____ Month _____ Year _____

Food		Money	
Breakfast		Item	Amount
Lunch			
Dinner			
Snack			
Exercise			
		Total Spent Today	
Litres Water	Hours Sleep	Quality of Life Today	%

When we retire at night we constructively review our day. We remember we have ceased fighting anything and anyone—love and tolerance of others is our code.

We Draw Up a Balance Sheet

The "Negative Side" (−)	The "Positive Side" (+)
Were we resentful?	Have we stayed clean of our addiction today?
Were we selfish?	Were we kind?
Were we dishonest?	Were we loving toward all?
Were we afraid?	What did we pack into life?
Have we kept something to ourselves?	Did we pray and meditate?
Were we thinking of ourselves most of the time?	Did we call someone we could help today?
Were we "disturbed" today?	Did we think of how we could help others?
Do we owe an apology? And if so to whom?	Did we study literature today?
What could we have done better?	Did we go to a meeting today?
Did we blame our feelings on someone else?	Did we call our sponsor today?
Do we need to write 10th Step on something?	Did we do anything that is improved over our past?

Journal—Gratitude List—Tomorrows Action Plan

BALANCE SHEETS

Day _____ Month _____ Year _____

Food

Breakfast		

Money

Item	Amount

Lunch		

Dinner		

Snack		

Exercise		
	Total Spent Today	
Litres Water _____ Hours Sleep _____	Quality of Life Today	%

When we retire at night we constructively review our day. We remember we have ceased fighting anything and anyone—love and tolerance of others is our code.

We Draw Up a Balance Sheet

The "Negative Side" (-)	The "Positive Side" (+)
Were we resentful?	Have we stayed clean of our addiction today?
Were we selfish?	Were we kind?
Were we dishonest?	Were we loving toward all?
Were we afraid?	What did we pack into life?
Have we kept something to ourselves?	Did we pray and meditate?
Were we thinking of ourselves most of the time?	Did we call someone we could help today?
Were we "disturbed" today?	Did we think of how we could help others?
Do we owe an apology? And if so to whom?	Did we study literature today?
What could we have done better?	Did we go to a meeting today?
Did we blame our feelings on someone else?	Did we call our sponsor today?
Do we need to write 10th Step on something?	Did we do anything that is improved over our past?

Journal—Gratitude List—Tomorrows Action Plan

STEP 10

BALANCE SHEETS

Day _____ Month _____ Year _____

Food		Money	
Breakfast		Item	Amount
Lunch			
Dinner			
Snack			
Exercise			
		Total Spent Today	
Litres Water _____ Hours Sleep _____		Quality of Life Today	%

When we retire at night we constructively review our day. We remember we have ceased fighting anything and anyone—love and tolerance of others is our code.

We Draw Up a Balance Sheet

The "Negative Side" (−)	The "Positive Side" (+)
Were we resentful?	Have we stayed clean of our addiction today?
Were we selfish?	Were we kind?
Were we dishonest?	Were we loving toward all?
Were we afraid?	What did we pack into life?
Have we kept something to ourselves?	Did we pray and meditate?
Were we thinking of ourselves most of the time?	Did we call someone we could help today?
Were we "disturbed" today?	Did we think of how we could help others?
Do we owe an apology? And if so to whom?	Did we study literature today?
What could we have done better?	Did we go to a meeting today?
Did we blame our feelings on someone else?	Did we call our sponsor today?
Do we need to write 10th Step on something?	Did we do anything that is improved over our past?

Journal—Gratitude List—Tomorrows Action Plan

BALANCE SHEETS

Day _____ Month _____ Year _____

Food		Money	
Breakfast		Item	Amount
Lunch			
Dinner			
Snack			
Exercise			
		Total Spent Today	
Litres Water _____ Hours Sleep _____		Quality of Life Today	%

When we retire at night we constructively review our day. We remember we have ceased fighting anything and anyone—love and tolerance of others is our code.

We Draw Up a Balance Sheet

The "Negative Side" (-)	The "Positive Side" (+)
Were we resentful?	Have we stayed clean of our addiction today?
Were we selfish?	Were we kind?
Were we dishonest?	Were we loving toward all?
Were we afraid?	What did we pack into life?
Have we kept something to ourselves?	Did we pray and meditate?
Were we thinking of ourselves most of the time?	Did we call someone we could help today?
Were we "disturbed" today?	Did we think of how we could help others?
Do we owe an apology? And if so to whom?	Did we study literature today?
What could we have done better?	Did we go to a meeting today?
Did we blame our feelings on someone else?	Did we call our sponsor today?
Do we need to write 10th Step on something?	Did we do anything that is improved over our past?

Journal—Gratitude List—Tomorrows Action Plan

STEP 10

BALANCE SHEETS

Day _____ Month _____ Year _____

Food		Money	
Breakfast		Item	Amount
Lunch			
Dinner			
Snack			
Exercise			
		Total Spent Today	
Litres Water	Hours Sleep	Quality of Life Today	%

When we retire at night we constructively review our day. We remember we have ceased fighting anything and anyone—love and tolerance of others is our code.

We Draw Up a Balance Sheet

The "Negative Side" (-)	The "Positive Side" (+)
Were we resentful?	Have we stayed clean of our addiction today?
Were we selfish?	Were we kind?
Were we dishonest?	Were we loving toward all?
Were we afraid?	What did we pack into life?
Have we kept something to ourselves?	Did we pray and meditate?
Were we thinking of ourselves most of the time?	Did we call someone we could help today?
Were we "disturbed" today?	Did we think of how we could help others?
Do we owe an apology? And if so to whom?	Did we study literature today?
What could we have done better?	Did we go to a meeting today?
Did we blame our feelings on someone else?	Did we call our sponsor today?
Do we need to write 10th Step on something?	Did we do anything that is improved over our past?

Journal—Gratitude List—Tomorrows Action Plan

BALANCE SHEETS

Day _____ Month _____ Year _____

Food		Money	
Breakfast		Item	Amount
Lunch			
Dinner			
Snack			
Exercise			
		Total Spent Today	
Litres Water	Hours Sleep	Quality of Life Today	%

When we retire at night we constructively review our day. We remember we have ceased fighting anything and anyone—love and tolerance of others is our code.

We Draw Up a Balance Sheet

The "Negative Side" (-)	The "Positive Side" (+)
Were we resentful?	Have we stayed clean of our addiction today?
Were we selfish?	Were we kind?
Were we dishonest?	Were we loving toward all?
Were we afraid?	What did we pack into life?
Have we kept something to ourselves?	Did we pray and meditate?
Were we thinking of ourselves most of the time?	Did we call someone we could help today?
Were we "disturbed" today?	Did we think of how we could help others?
Do we owe an apology? And if so to whom?	Did we study literature today?
What could we have done better?	Did we go to a meeting today?
Did we blame our feelings on someone else?	Did we call our sponsor today?
Do we need to write 10th Step on something?	Did we do anything that is improved over our past?

Journal—Gratitude List—Tomorrows Action Plan

STEP 10

BALANCE SHEETS

Day _____ Month _____ Year _____

Food		Money	
Breakfast		Item	Amount
Lunch			
Dinner			
Snack			
Exercise			
		Total Spent Today	
Litres Water Hours Sleep		Quality of Life Today	%

When we retire at night we constructively review our day. We remember we have ceased fighting anything and anyone—love and tolerance of others is our code.

We Draw Up a Balance Sheet

The "Negative Side" (-)	The "Positive Side" (+)
Were we resentful?	Have we stayed clean of our addiction today?
Were we selfish?	Were we kind?
Were we dishonest?	Were we loving toward all?
Were we afraid?	What did we pack into life?
Have we kept something to ourselves?	Did we pray and meditate?
Were we thinking of ourselves most of the time?	Did we call someone we could help today?
Were we "disturbed" today?	Did we think of how we could help others?
Do we owe an apology? And if so to whom?	Did we study literature today?
What could we have done better?	Did we go to a meeting today?
Did we blame our feelings on someone else?	Did we call our sponsor today?
Do we need to write 10th Step on something?	Did we do anything that is improved over our past?

Journal—Gratitude List—Tomorrows Action Plan

BALANCE SHEETS

Day _____ Month _____ Year _____

Food

Breakfast		
Lunch		
Dinner		
Snack		
Exercise		

Money

Item		Amount
Total Spent Today		
Quality of Life Today		%

Litres Water _____ Hours Sleep _____

When we retire at night we constructively review our day. We remember we have ceased fighting anything and anyone—love and tolerance of others is our code.

We Draw Up a Balance Sheet

The "Negative Side" (-)	The "Positive Side" (+)
Were we resentful?	Have we stayed clean of our addiction today?
Were we selfish?	Were we kind?
Were we dishonest?	Were we loving toward all?
Were we afraid?	What did we pack into life?
Have we kept something to ourselves?	Did we pray and meditate?
Were we thinking of ourselves most of the time?	Did we call someone we could help today?
Were we "disturbed" today?	Did we think of how we could help others?
Do we owe an apology? And if so to whom?	Did we study literature today?
What could we have done better?	Did we go to a meeting today?
Did we blame our feelings on someone else?	Did we call our sponsor today?
Do we need to write 10th Step on something?	Did we do anything that is improved over our past?

Journal—Gratitude List—Tomorrows Action Plan

STEP 10

BALANCE SHEETS

Day _____ Month _____ Year _____

Food		Money	
Breakfast		Item	Amount
Lunch			
Dinner			
Snack			
Exercise			
		Total Spent Today	
Litres Water _____ Hours Sleep _____		Quality of Life Today	%

When we retire at night we constructively review our day. We remember we have ceased fighting anything and anyone—love and tolerance of others is our code.

We Draw Up a Balance Sheet

The "Negative Side" (-)	The "Positive Side" (+)
Were we resentful?	Have we stayed clean of our addiction today?
Were we selfish?	Were we kind?
Were we dishonest?	Were we loving toward all?
Were we afraid?	What did we pack into life?
Have we kept something to ourselves?	Did we pray and meditate?
Were we thinking of ourselves most of the time?	Did we call someone we could help today?
Were we "disturbed" today?	Did we think of how we could help others?
Do we owe an apology? And if so to whom?	Did we study literature today?
What could we have done better?	Did we go to a meeting today?
Did we blame our feelings on someone else?	Did we call our sponsor today?
Do we need to write 10th Step on something?	Did we do anything that is improved over our past?

Journal—Gratitude List—Tomorrows Action Plan

MAINTAINING THE PROMISES...DAILY

BALANCE SHEETS

Day _____ Month _____ Year _____

Food		Money	
Breakfast		Item	Amount
Lunch			
Dinner			
Snack			
Exercise			
		Total Spent Today	
Litres Water ___ Hours Sleep ___		Quality of Life Today	%

When we retire at night we constructively review our day. We remember we have ceased fighting anything and anyone—love and tolerance of others is our code.

We Draw Up a Balance Sheet

The "Negative Side" (-)	The "Positive Side" (+)
Were we resentful?	Have we stayed clean of our addiction today?
Were we selfish?	Were we kind?
Were we dishonest?	Were we loving toward all?
Were we afraid?	What did we pack into life?
Have we kept something to ourselves?	Did we pray and meditate?
Were we thinking of ourselves most of the time?	Did we call someone we could help today?
Were we "disturbed" today?	Did we think of how we could help others?
Do we owe an apology? And if so to whom?	Did we study literature today?
What could we have done better?	Did we go to a meeting today?
Did we blame our feelings on someone else?	Did we call our sponsor today?
Do we need to write 10th Step on something?	Did we do anything that is improved over our past?

Journal—Gratitude List—Tomorrows Action Plan

STEP 10

BALANCE SHEETS

Day _____ Month _____ Year _____

Food		Money	
Breakfast		Item	Amount
Lunch			
Dinner			
Snack			
Exercise			
		Total Spent Today	
Litres Water _____ Hours Sleep _____		Quality of Life Today	%

When we retire at night we constructively review our day. We remember we have ceased fighting anything and anyone—love and tolerance of others is our code.

We Draw Up a Balance Sheet

The "Negative Side" (-)	The "Positive Side" (+)
Were we resentful?	Have we stayed clean of our addiction today?
Were we selfish?	Were we kind?
Were we dishonest?	Were we loving toward all?
Were we afraid?	What did we pack into life?
Have we kept something to ourselves?	Did we pray and meditate?
Were we thinking of ourselves most of the time?	Did we call someone we could help today?
Were we "disturbed" today?	Did we think of how we could help others?
Do we owe an apology? And if so to whom?	Did we study literature today?
What could we have done better?	Did we go to a meeting today?
Did we blame our feelings on someone else?	Did we call our sponsor today?
Do we need to write 10th Step on something?	Did we do anything that is improved over our past?

Journal—Gratitude List—Tomorrows Action Plan

BALANCE SHEETS

Day _____ Month _____ Year _____

Food

Breakfast	
Lunch	
Dinner	
Snack	
Exercise	

Money

Item	Amount
Total Spent Today	
Quality of Life Today	%

Litres Water	Hours Sleep

When we retire at night we constructively review our day. We remember we have ceased fighting anything and anyone—love and tolerance of others is our code.

We Draw Up a Balance Sheet

The "Negative Side" (-)	The "Positive Side" (+)
Were we resentful?	Have we stayed clean of our addiction today?
Were we selfish?	Were we kind?
Were we dishonest?	Were we loving toward all?
Were we afraid?	What did we pack into life?
Have we kept something to ourselves?	Did we pray and meditate?
Were we thinking of ourselves most of the time?	Did we call someone we could help today?
Were we "disturbed" today?	Did we think of how we could help others?
Do we owe an apology? And if so to whom?	Did we study literature today?
What could we have done better?	Did we go to a meeting today?
Did we blame our feelings on someone else?	Did we call our sponsor today?
Do we need to write 10th Step on something?	Did we do anything that is improved over our past?

Journal—Gratitude List—Tomorrows Action Plan

STEP 10

BALANCE SHEETS

Day _____ Month _____ Year _____

Food		Money	
Breakfast		Item	Amount
Lunch			
Dinner			
Snack			
Exercise			
		Total Spent Today	
Litres Water _____ Hours Sleep _____		Quality of Life Today	%

When we retire at night we constructively review our day. We remember we have ceased fighting anything and anyone—love and tolerance of others is our code.

We Draw Up a Balance Sheet

The "Negative Side" (-)	The "Positive Side" (+)
Were we resentful?	Have we stayed clean of our addiction today?
Were we selfish?	Were we kind?
Were we dishonest?	Were we loving toward all?
Were we afraid?	What did we pack into life?
Have we kept something to ourselves?	Did we pray and meditate?
Were we thinking of ourselves most of the time?	Did we call someone we could help today?
Were we "disturbed" today?	Did we think of how we could help others?
Do we owe an apology? And if so to whom?	Did we study literature today?
What could we have done better?	Did we go to a meeting today?
Did we blame our feelings on someone else?	Did we call our sponsor today?
Do we need to write 10th Step on something?	Did we do anything that is improved over our past?

Journal—Gratitude List—Tomorrows Action Plan

368   MAINTAINING THE PROMISES...DAILY

BALANCE SHEETS

Day _____ Month _____ Year _____

Food

Breakfast		
Lunch		
Dinner		
Snack		
Exercise		

Money

Item	Amount
Total Spent Today	
Quality of Life Today	%

Litres Water	Hours Sleep

When we retire at night we constructively review our day. We remember we have ceased fighting anything and anyone—love and tolerance of others is our code.

We Draw Up a Balance Sheet

The "Negative Side" (-)	The "Positive Side" (+)
Were we resentful?	Have we stayed clean of our addiction today?
Were we selfish?	Were we kind?
Were we dishonest?	Were we loving toward all?
Were we afraid?	What did we pack into life?
Have we kept something to ourselves?	Did we pray and meditate?
Were we thinking of ourselves most of the time?	Did we call someone we could help today?
Were we "disturbed" today?	Did we think of how we could help others?
Do we owe an apology? And if so to whom?	Did we study literature today?
What could we have done better?	Did we go to a meeting today?
Did we blame our feelings on someone else?	Did we call our sponsor today?
Do we need to write 10th Step on something?	Did we do anything that is improved over our past?

Journal—Gratitude List—Tomorrows Action Plan

STEP 10

BALANCE SHEETS

Day _____ Month _____ Year _____

Food		Money	
Breakfast		Item	Amount
Lunch			
Dinner			
Snack			
Exercise			
		Total Spent Today	
Litres Water _____ Hours Sleep _____		Quality of Life Today	%

When we retire at night we constructively review our day. We remember we have ceased fighting anything and anyone—love and tolerance of others is our code.

We Draw Up a Balance Sheet

The "Negative Side" (-)	The "Positive Side" (+)
Were we resentful?	Have we stayed clean of our addiction today?
Were we selfish?	Were we kind?
Were we dishonest?	Were we loving toward all?
Were we afraid?	What did we pack into life?
Have we kept something to ourselves?	Did we pray and meditate?
Were we thinking of ourselves most of the time?	Did we call someone we could help today?
Were we "disturbed" today?	Did we think of how we could help others?
Do we owe an apology? And if so to whom?	Did we study literature today?
What could we have done better?	Did we go to a meeting today?
Did we blame our feelings on someone else?	Did we call our sponsor today?
Do we need to write 10th Step on something?	Did we do anything that is improved over our past?

Journal—Gratitude List—Tomorrows Action Plan

BALANCE SHEETS

Day _____ Month _____ Year _____

Food		Money	
Breakfast		Item	Amount
Lunch			
Dinner			
Snack			
Exercise			
		Total Spent Today	
Litres Water ___ Hours Sleep ___		Quality of Life Today	%

When we retire at night we constructively review our day. We remember we have ceased fighting anything and anyone—love and tolerance of others is our code.

We Draw Up a Balance Sheet

The "Negative Side" (-)	The "Positive Side" (+)
Were we resentful?	Have we stayed clean of our addiction today?
Were we selfish?	Were we kind?
Were we dishonest?	Were we loving toward all?
Were we afraid?	What did we pack into life?
Have we kept something to ourselves?	Did we pray and meditate?
Were we thinking of ourselves most of the time?	Did we call someone we could help today?
Were we "disturbed" today?	Did we think of how we could help others?
Do we owe an apology? And if so to whom?	Did we study literature today?
What could we have done better?	Did we go to a meeting today?
Did we blame our feelings on someone else?	Did we call our sponsor today?
Do we need to write 10th Step on something?	Did we do anything that is improved over our past?

Journal—Gratitude List—Tomorrows Action Plan

STEP 10

BALANCE SHEETS

Day _____ Month _____ Year _____

Food		Money	
Breakfast		Item	Amount
Lunch			
Dinner			
Snack			
Exercise			
		Total Spent Today	
Litres Water	Hours Sleep	Quality of Life Today	%

When we retire at night we constructively review our day. We remember we have ceased fighting anything and anyone—love and tolerance of others is our code.

We Draw Up a Balance Sheet

The "Negative Side" (-)	The "Positive Side" (+)
Were we resentful?	Have we stayed clean of our addiction today?
Were we selfish?	Were we kind?
Were we dishonest?	Were we loving toward all?
Were we afraid?	What did we pack into life?
Have we kept something to ourselves?	Did we pray and meditate?
Were we thinking of ourselves most of the time?	Did we call someone we could help today?
Were we "disturbed" today?	Did we think of how we could help others?
Do we owe an apology? And if so to whom?	Did we study literature today?
What could we have done better?	Did we go to a meeting today?
Did we blame our feelings on someone else?	Did we call our sponsor today?
Do we need to write 10th Step on something?	Did we do anything that is improved over our past?

Journal—Gratitude List—Tomorrows Action Plan

_____
_____
_____
_____
_____
_____

BALANCE SHEETS

Day _____ Month _____ Year _____

Food

Breakfast		
Lunch		
Dinner		
Snack		
Exercise		

Money

Item		Amount
Total Spent Today		

Litres Water	Hours Sleep	Quality of Life Today	%

When we retire at night we constructively review our day. We remember we have ceased fighting anything and anyone—love and tolerance of others is our code.

We Draw Up a Balance Sheet

The "Negative Side" (-)	The "Positive Side" (+)
Were we resentful?	Have we stayed clean of our addiction today?
Were we selfish?	Were we kind?
Were we dishonest?	Were we loving toward all?
Were we afraid?	What did we pack into life?
Have we kept something to ourselves?	Did we pray and meditate?
Were we thinking of ourselves most of the time?	Did we call someone we could help today?
Were we "disturbed" today?	Did we think of how we could help others?
Do we owe an apology? And if so to whom?	Did we study literature today?
What could we have done better?	Did we go to a meeting today?
Did we blame our feelings on someone else?	Did we call our sponsor today?
Do we need to write 10th Step on something?	Did we do anything that is improved over our past?

Journal—Gratitude List—Tomorrows Action Plan

STEP 10

BALANCE SHEETS

Day _____ Month _____ Year _____

Food		Money	
Breakfast		Item	Amount
Lunch			
Dinner			
Snack			
Exercise			
		Total Spent Today	
Litres Water	Hours Sleep	Quality of Life Today	%

When we retire at night we constructively review our day. We remember we have ceased fighting anything and anyone—love and tolerance of others is our code.

We Draw Up a Balance Sheet

The "Negative Side" (-)	The "Positive Side" (+)
Were we resentful?	Have we stayed clean of our addiction today?
Were we selfish?	Were we kind?
Were we dishonest?	Were we loving toward all?
Were we afraid?	What did we pack into life?
Have we kept something to ourselves?	Did we pray and meditate?
Were we thinking of ourselves most of the time?	Did we call someone we could help today?
Were we "disturbed" today?	Did we think of how we could help others?
Do we owe an apology? And if so to whom?	Did we study literature today?
What could we have done better?	Did we go to a meeting today?
Did we blame our feelings on someone else?	Did we call our sponsor today?
Do we need to write 10th Step on something?	Did we do anything that is improved over our past?

Journal—Gratitude List—Tomorrows Action Plan

_____
_____
_____
_____
_____
_____

BALANCE SHEETS

Day _____ Month _____ Year _____

Food

Breakfast		
Lunch		
Dinner		
Snack		
Exercise		
Litres Water	Hours Sleep	

Money

Item	Amount
Total Spent Today	
Quality of Life Today	%

When we retire at night we constructively review our day. We remember we have ceased fighting anything and anyone—love and tolerance of others is our code.

We Draw Up a Balance Sheet

The "Negative Side" (-)	The "Positive Side" (+)
Were we resentful?	Have we stayed clean of our addiction today?
Were we selfish?	Were we kind?
Were we dishonest?	Were we loving toward all?
Were we afraid?	What did we pack into life?
Have we kept something to ourselves?	Did we pray and meditate?
Were we thinking of ourselves most of the time?	Did we call someone we could help today?
Were we "disturbed" today?	Did we think of how we could help others?
Do we owe an apology? And if so to whom?	Did we study literature today?
What could we have done better?	Did we go to a meeting today?
Did we blame our feelings on someone else?	Did we call our sponsor today?
Do we need to write 10th Step on something?	Did we do anything that is improved over our past?

Journal—Gratitude List—Tomorrows Action Plan

STEP 10

BALANCE SHEETS

Day _____ Month _____ Year _____

Food		Money	
Breakfast		Item	Amount
Lunch			
Dinner			
Snack			
Exercise			
		Total Spent Today	
Litres Water Hours Sleep		Quality of Life Today	%

When we retire at night we constructively review our day. We remember we have ceased fighting anything and anyone—love and tolerance of others is our code.

We Draw Up a Balance Sheet

The "Negative Side" (-)	The "Positive Side" (+)
Were we resentful?	Have we stayed clean of our addiction today?
Were we selfish?	Were we kind?
Were we dishonest?	Were we loving toward all?
Were we afraid?	What did we pack into life?
Have we kept something to ourselves?	Did we pray and meditate?
Were we thinking of ourselves most of the time?	Did we call someone we could help today?
Were we "disturbed" today?	Did we think of how we could help others?
Do we owe an apology? And if so to whom?	Did we study literature today?
What could we have done better?	Did we go to a meeting today?
Did we blame our feelings on someone else?	Did we call our sponsor today?
Do we need to write 10th Step on something?	Did we do anything that is improved over our past?

Journal—Gratitude List—Tomorrows Action Plan

MAINTAINING THE PROMISES...DAILY

BALANCE SHEETS

Day _____ Month _____ Year _____

Food		Money	
Breakfast		Item	Amount
Lunch			
Dinner			
Snack			
Exercise			
		Total Spent Today	
Litres Water _____ Hours Sleep _____		Quality of Life Today	%

When we retire at night we constructively review our day. We remember we have ceased fighting anything and anyone—love and tolerance of others is our code.

We Draw Up a Balance Sheet

The "Negative Side" (-)	The "Positive Side" (+)
Were we resentful?	Have we stayed clean of our addiction today?
Were we selfish?	Were we kind?
Were we dishonest?	Were we loving toward all?
Were we afraid?	What did we pack into life?
Have we kept something to ourselves?	Did we pray and meditate?
Were we thinking of ourselves most of the time?	Did we call someone we could help today?
Were we "disturbed" today?	Did we think of how we could help others?
Do we owe an apology? And if so to whom?	Did we study literature today?
What could we have done better?	Did we go to a meeting today?
Did we blame our feelings on someone else?	Did we call our sponsor today?
Do we need to write 10th Step on something?	Did we do anything that is improved over our past?

Journal—Gratitude List—Tomorrows Action Plan

STEP 10

BALANCE SHEETS

Day _____ Month _____ Year _____

Food		Money	
Breakfast		Item	Amount
Lunch			
Dinner			
Snack			
Exercise			
		Total Spent Today	
Litres Water	Hours Sleep	Quality of Life Today	%

When we retire at night we constructively review our day. We remember we have ceased fighting anything and anyone—love and tolerance of others is our code.

We Draw Up a Balance Sheet

The "Negative Side" (−)	The "Positive Side" (+)
Were we resentful?	Have we stayed clean of our addiction today?
Were we selfish?	Were we kind?
Were we dishonest?	Were we loving toward all?
Were we afraid?	What did we pack into life?
Have we kept something to ourselves?	Did we pray and meditate?
Were we thinking of ourselves most of the time?	Did we call someone we could help today?
Were we "disturbed" today?	Did we think of how we could help others?
Do we owe an apology? And if so to whom?	Did we study literature today?
What could we have done better?	Did we go to a meeting today?
Did we blame our feelings on someone else?	Did we call our sponsor today?
Do we need to write 10th Step on something?	Did we do anything that is improved over our past?

Journal—Gratitude List—Tomorrows Action Plan

BALANCE SHEETS

Day _____ Month _____ Year_____

Food

Breakfast	
Lunch	
Dinner	
Snack	
Exercise	
Litres Water	Hours Sleep

Money

Item	Amount
Total Spent Today	
Quality of Life Today	%

When we retire at night we constructively review our day. We remember we have ceased fighting anything and anyone—love and tolerance of others is our code.

We Draw Up a Balance Sheet

The "Negative Side" (-)	The "Positive Side" (+)
Were we resentful?	Have we stayed clean of our addiction today?
Were we selfish?	Were we kind?
Were we dishonest?	Were we loving toward all?
Were we afraid?	What did we pack into life?
Have we kept something to ourselves?	Did we pray and meditate?
Were we thinking of ourselves most of the time?	Did we call someone we could help today?
Were we "disturbed" today?	Did we think of how we could help others?
Do we owe an apology? And if so to whom?	Did we study literature today?
What could we have done better?	Did we go to a meeting today?
Did we blame our feelings on someone else?	Did we call our sponsor today?
Do we need to write 10th Step on something?	Did we do anything that is improved over our past?

Journal—Gratitude List—Tomorrows Action Plan

STEP 10

BALANCE SHEETS

Day _____ Month _____ Year _____

Food		Money	
Breakfast		Item	Amount
Lunch			
Dinner			
Snack			
Exercise			
		Total Spent Today	
Litres Water _____ Hours Sleep _____		Quality of Life Today	%

When we retire at night we constructively review our day. We remember we have ceased fighting anything and anyone—love and tolerance of others is our code.

We Draw Up a Balance Sheet

The "Negative Side" (-)	The "Positive Side" (+)
Were we resentful?	Have we stayed clean of our addiction today?
Were we selfish?	Were we kind?
Were we dishonest?	Were we loving toward all?
Were we afraid?	What did we pack into life?
Have we kept something to ourselves?	Did we pray and meditate?
Were we thinking of ourselves most of the time?	Did we call someone we could help today?
Were we "disturbed" today?	Did we think of how we could help others?
Do we owe an apology? And if so to whom?	Did we study literature today?
What could we have done better?	Did we go to a meeting today?
Did we blame our feelings on someone else?	Did we call our sponsor today?
Do we need to write 10th Step on something?	Did we do anything that is improved over our past?

Journal—Gratitude List—Tomorrows Action Plan

BALANCE SHEETS

Day _____ Month _____ Year _____

Food

Breakfast		
Lunch		
Dinner		
Snack		
Exercise		
Litres Water ____ Hours Sleep ____		

Money

Item	Amount
Total Spent Today	
Quality of Life Today	%

When we retire at night we constructively review our day. We remember we have ceased fighting anything and anyone—love and tolerance of others is our code.

We Draw Up a Balance Sheet

The "Negative Side" (-)	The "Positive Side" (+)
Were we resentful?	Have we stayed clean of our addiction today?
Were we selfish?	Were we kind?
Were we dishonest?	Were we loving toward all?
Were we afraid?	What did we pack into life?
Have we kept something to ourselves?	Did we pray and meditate?
Were we thinking of ourselves most of the time?	Did we call someone we could help today?
Were we "disturbed" today?	Did we think of how we could help others?
Do we owe an apology? And if so to whom?	Did we study literature today?
What could we have done better?	Did we go to a meeting today?
Did we blame our feelings on someone else?	Did we call our sponsor today?
Do we need to write 10th Step on something?	Did we do anything that is improved over our past?

Journal—Gratitude List—Tomorrows Action Plan

STEP 10

BALANCE SHEETS

Day _____ Month _____ Year _____

Food		Money	
Breakfast		Item	Amount
Lunch			
Dinner			
Snack			
Exercise			
		Total Spent Today	
Litres Water	Hours Sleep	Quality of Life Today	%

When we retire at night we constructively review our day. We remember we have ceased fighting anything and anyone—love and tolerance of others is our code.

We Draw Up a Balance Sheet

The "Negative Side" (-)	The "Positive Side" (+)
Were we resentful?	Have we stayed clean of our addiction today?
Were we selfish?	Were we kind?
Were we dishonest?	Were we loving toward all?
Were we afraid?	What did we pack into life?
Have we kept something to ourselves?	Did we pray and meditate?
Were we thinking of ourselves most of the time?	Did we call someone we could help today?
Were we "disturbed" today?	Did we think of how we could help others?
Do we owe an apology? And if so to whom?	Did we study literature today?
What could we have done better?	Did we go to a meeting today?
Did we blame our feelings on someone else?	Did we call our sponsor today?
Do we need to write 10th Step on something?	Did we do anything that is improved over our past?

Journal—Gratitude List—Tomorrows Action Plan

BALANCE SHEETS

Day _____ Month _____ Year _____

Food		Money	
Breakfast		Item	Amount
Lunch			
Dinner			
Snack			
Exercise			
		Total Spent Today	
Litres Water Hours Sleep		Quality of Life Today	%

When we retire at night we constructively review our day. We remember we have ceased fighting anything and anyone—love and tolerance of others is our code.

We Draw Up a Balance Sheet

The "Negative Side" (-)	The "Positive Side" (+)
Were we resentful?	Have we stayed clean of our addiction today?
Were we selfish?	Were we kind?
Were we dishonest?	Were we loving toward all?
Were we afraid?	What did we pack into life?
Have we kept something to ourselves?	Did we pray and meditate?
Were we thinking of ourselves most of the time?	Did we call someone we could help today?
Were we "disturbed" today?	Did we think of how we could help others?
Do we owe an apology? And if so to whom?	Did we study literature today?
What could we have done better?	Did we go to a meeting today?
Did we blame our feelings on someone else?	Did we call our sponsor today?
Do we need to write 10th Step on something?	Did we do anything that is improved over our past?

Journal—Gratitude List—Tomorrows Action Plan

STEP 10

BALANCE SHEETS

Day _____ Month _____ Year _____

Food		Money	
Breakfast		Item	Amount
Lunch			
Dinner			
Snack			
Exercise			
		Total Spent Today	
Litres Water	Hours Sleep	Quality of Life Today	%

When we retire at night we constructively review our day. We remember we have ceased fighting anything and anyone—love and tolerance of others is our code.

We Draw Up a Balance Sheet

The "Negative Side" (-)	The "Positive Side" (+)
Were we resentful?	Have we stayed clean of our addiction today?
Were we selfish?	Were we kind?
Were we dishonest?	Were we loving toward all?
Were we afraid?	What did we pack into life?
Have we kept something to ourselves?	Did we pray and meditate?
Were we thinking of ourselves most of the time?	Did we call someone we could help today?
Were we "disturbed" today?	Did we think of how we could help others?
Do we owe an apology? And if so to whom?	Did we study literature today?
What could we have done better?	Did we go to a meeting today?
Did we blame our feelings on someone else?	Did we call our sponsor today?
Do we need to write 10th Step on something?	Did we do anything that is improved over our past?

Journal—Gratitude List—Tomorrows Action Plan

BALANCE SHEETS

Day _____ Month _____ Year _____

Food		Money	
Breakfast		Item	Amount
Lunch			
Dinner			
Snack			
Exercise			
		Total Spent Today	
Litres Water	Hours Sleep	Quality of Life Today	%

When we retire at night we constructively review our day. We remember we have ceased fighting anything and anyone—love and tolerance of others is our code.

We Draw Up a Balance Sheet

The "Negative Side" (-)	The "Positive Side" (+)
Were we resentful?	Have we stayed clean of our addiction today?
Were we selfish?	Were we kind?
Were we dishonest?	Were we loving toward all?
Were we afraid?	What did we pack into life?
Have we kept something to ourselves?	Did we pray and meditate?
Were we thinking of ourselves most of the time?	Did we call someone we could help today?
Were we "disturbed" today?	Did we think of how we could help others?
Do we owe an apology? And if so to whom?	Did we study literature today?
What could we have done better?	Did we go to a meeting today?
Did we blame our feelings on someone else?	Did we call our sponsor today?
Do we need to write 10th Step on something?	Did we do anything that is improved over our past?

Journal—Gratitude List—Tomorrows Action Plan

BALANCE SHEETS

Day _____ Month _____ Year _____

Food		Money	
Breakfast		Item	Amount
Lunch			
Dinner			
Snack			
Exercise			
		Total Spent Today	
Litres Water	Hours Sleep	Quality of Life Today	%

When we retire at night we constructively review our day. We remember we have ceased fighting anything and anyone—love and tolerance of others is our code.

We Draw Up a Balance Sheet

The "Negative Side" (-)	The "Positive Side" (+)
Were we resentful?	Have we stayed clean of our addiction today?
Were we selfish?	Were we kind?
Were we dishonest?	Were we loving toward all?
Were we afraid?	What did we pack into life?
Have we kept something to ourselves?	Did we pray and meditate?
Were we thinking of ourselves most of the time?	Did we call someone we could help today?
Were we "disturbed" today?	Did we think of how we could help others?
Do we owe an apology? And if so to whom?	Did we study literature today?
What could we have done better?	Did we go to a meeting today?
Did we blame our feelings on someone else?	Did we call our sponsor today?
Do we need to write 10th Step on something?	Did we do anything that is improved over our past?

Journal—Gratitude List—Tomorrows Action Plan

BALANCE SHEETS

Day _____ Month _____ Year _____

Food

Breakfast	
Lunch	
Dinner	
Snack	
Exercise	
Litres Water ____ Hours Sleep ____	

Money

Item	Amount
Total Spent Today	
Quality of Life Today	%

When we retire at night we constructively review our day. We remember we have ceased fighting anything and anyone—love and tolerance of others is our code.

We Draw Up a Balance Sheet

The "Negative Side" (-)	The "Positive Side" (+)
Were we resentful?	Have we stayed clean of our addiction today?
Were we selfish?	Were we kind?
Were we dishonest?	Were we loving toward all?
Were we afraid?	What did we pack into life?
Have we kept something to ourselves?	Did we pray and meditate?
Were we thinking of ourselves most of the time?	Did we call someone we could help today?
Were we "disturbed" today?	Did we think of how we could help others?
Do we owe an apology? And if so to whom?	Did we study literature today?
What could we have done better?	Did we go to a meeting today?
Did we blame our feelings on someone else?	Did we call our sponsor today?
Do we need to write 10th Step on something?	Did we do anything that is improved over our past?

Journal—Gratitude List—Tomorrows Action Plan

BALANCE SHEETS

Day _____ Month _____ Year _____

Food		Money		
Breakfast		Item		Amount
Lunch				
Dinner				
Snack				
Exercise				
		Total Spent Today		
Litres Water	Hours Sleep	Quality of Life Today		%

When we retire at night we constructively review our day. We remember we have ceased fighting anything and anyone—love and tolerance of others is our code.

We Draw Up a Balance Sheet

The "Negative Side" (-)	The "Positive Side" (+)
Were we resentful?	Have we stayed clean of our addiction today?
Were we selfish?	Were we kind?
Were we dishonest?	Were we loving toward all?
Were we afraid?	What did we pack into life?
Have we kept something to ourselves?	Did we pray and meditate?
Were we thinking of ourselves most of the time?	Did we call someone we could help today?
Were we "disturbed" today?	Did we think of how we could help others?
Do we owe an apology? And if so to whom?	Did we study literature today?
What could we have done better?	Did we go to a meeting today?
Did we blame our feelings on someone else?	Did we call our sponsor today?
Do we need to write 10th Step on something?	Did we do anything that is improved over our past?

Journal—Gratitude List—Tomorrows Action Plan

BALANCE SHEETS

Day _____ Month _____ Year_____

Food		Money	
Breakfast		Item	Amount
Lunch			
Dinner			
Snack			
Exercise			
		Total Spent Today	
Litres Water	Hours Sleep	Quality of Life Today	%

When we retire at night we constructively review our day. We remember we have ceased fighting anything and anyone—love and tolerance of others is our code.

We Draw Up a Balance Sheet

The "Negative Side" (-)	The "Positive Side" (+)
Were we resentful?	Have we stayed clean of our addiction today?
Were we selfish?	Were we kind?
Were we dishonest?	Were we loving toward all?
Were we afraid?	What did we pack into life?
Have we kept something to ourselves?	Did we pray and meditate?
Were we thinking of ourselves most of the time?	Did we call someone we could help today?
Were we "disturbed" today?	Did we think of how we could help others?
Do we owe an apology? And if so to whom?	Did we study literature today?
What could we have done better?	Did we go to a meeting today?
Did we blame our feelings on someone else?	Did we call our sponsor today?
Do we need to write 10th Step on something?	Did we do anything that is improved over our past?

Journal—Gratitude List—Tomorrows Action Plan

STEP 10

BALANCE SHEETS

Day _____ Month _____ Year _____

Food		Money	
Breakfast		Item	Amount
Lunch			
Dinner			
Snack			
Exercise			
		Total Spent Today	
Litres Water	Hours Sleep	Quality of Life Today	%

When we retire at night we constructively review our day. We remember we have ceased fighting anything and anyone—love and tolerance of others is our code.

We Draw Up a Balance Sheet

The "Negative Side" (-)	The "Positive Side" (+)
Were we resentful?	Have we stayed clean of our addiction today?
Were we selfish?	Were we kind?
Were we dishonest?	Were we loving toward all?
Were we afraid?	What did we pack into life?
Have we kept something to ourselves?	Did we pray and meditate?
Were we thinking of ourselves most of the time?	Did we call someone we could help today?
Were we "disturbed" today?	Did we think of how we could help others?
Do we owe an apology? And if so to whom?	Did we study literature today?
What could we have done better?	Did we go to a meeting today?
Did we blame our feelings on someone else?	Did we call our sponsor today?
Do we need to write 10th Step on something?	Did we do anything that is improved over our past?

Journal—Gratitude List—Tomorrows Action Plan

Chapter 4

How to Answer Fourth Column Questions

HOW DO WE ANSWER SUCH QUESTIONS; AS?

- *"Where had we been selfish, self-centred or self-seeking?"*
- *"Where had we been dishonest?"*
- *"Where had we been frightened?"*
- *"Where had we been* (responsible) **to blame?"**
- *"What decisions did we make based on self that later placed us in a position to be hurt?"*
- *"When in the past can we remember making this decision?"*
- *"Where were we wrong? What was our part?"*

The more we work with people in these various programs the more we realise how very difficult it is to begin to look at life's situations from a whole new angle. Many of our sponsees look at us with blank stares when asked questions such as those above.

These are difficult questions. Most of us think that we are anything but selfish, dishonest, and are really victims to life's deranged sense of humour. But taking them one at a time, let's see if we just might be the architects of our own life. And if we are; can we reconstruct our lives?

- *"Where had we been selfish, self-centred or self-seeking?"*

Below we find a list of attitudes that may just suggest ways in which we might possibly be "selfish, self-centred or self-seeking." The most important trait to become aware of is that consideration of others, or other opinions, is not usually our first reaction.

HOW TO ANSWER...

SELFISH/SELF CENTRED —	**SELF-SEEKING**
• Wanting things our way	• Being possessive
• Wanting special treatment	• Thinking we're better
• Wanting our "needs" met	• Thinking others are jealous
• Wanting what others have	• Reacting from self-loathing
• Wanting control	• Reacting self-righteously
• Wanting to be the best	• Too concerned about me
• Wanting others to be like me	• Manipulating others to our will
• Wanting more than my share	• Putting others down to build us up (internally or externally)
• Wanting to look good at another's expense	• Engaging in character assassination
• Wanting to be liked	• Acting superior
• Not seeing others' POV	• Acting out to fill a void
• Not seeing others' problems	• Engaging in gluttony
	• Lusting after another
• Not seeing others' "needs"	• Ignoring others' needs
• Not being a friend	• Trying to control others
• Being dependant	• Getting revenge when I don't get my way
• Being dominant	
• Being grandiose	• Acting out to feel good
• Being miserly	• Simply holding a resentment

"Where had we been dishonest?"

Dishonesty covers much more than just "cheque book" honesty. There are many ways in which we lie to ourselves and others, both overtly and covertly. *"Life is a totality, and...it can't be compartmentalised. Dishonesty in one area creates problems in another area. Healing in one segment provides better health in another. It is all connected. Each Step blends with another in an integrated, comprehensive programme designed to transform you and me into human beings capable of willingly and joyously doing God's will."* [97]

"Doc (Dr. Bob)...was pretty positive that God's law was the Law of Love and that all my resentful feelings which I had fed and cultivated...were the result of either conscious or unconscious, it didn't matter which, disobedience to that law...

"Taking love as the basic command I discovered that my faithful attempt to practice a law of love led me to clear myself of

FOURTH COLUMN QUESTIONS

certain dishonesties." [98] These dishonesties we find in ourselves as well as others. We cannot fool ourselves about honesty as this woman did during her inventory process. **"The questions he asked me that I didn't answer honestly, I thought were none of his business."**[99] We justify our lies mainly by fooling ourselves that it is the right thing to do.

DISHONEST

- Not seeing/admitting where we were at fault
- Having a superior attitude
- Thinking we're better
- Blaming others for our problems
- Not admitting we've done the same thing
- Not expressing feelings
- Not expressing ideas
- Not being clear
- Hiding our true motives
- Lying
- Cheating
- Stealing
- Not facing facts
- Hiding from reality
- Holding on to false beliefs
- Breaking rules or laws
- Lying to ourselves
- Exaggerating
- Minimising
- Setting ourselves up to be "wronged"
- Expecting others to be what they're not
- Being a perfectionist

"Where had we been frightened?"

As it says earlier, **"fear is an evil and corroding thread"** that distorts and harms our lives. Psychology has demonstrated that humans are only born with two fears; fear of loud noises and fear of loss of physical support. Therefore all other fears are not natural. Could these fears be where our defiance comes from? **"I was as defiant as anybody could be because I was scared."** [100] Let us look at just a few of those "unnatural" fears.

FEARS

- Of peoples' opinions
- Of rejection
- Of abandonment
- Of loneliness
- Of physical injury
- Of abuse
- Of not being able to change ourselves or others
- Of not being in control
- Of our inferiority
- Of our inadequacy
- Of criticism
- Of expressing our feelings
- Of expressing our ideas
- Of getting trapped
- Of exposure
- Of embarrassment

HOW TO ANSWER...
"WHERE HAD WE BEEN (RESPONSIBLE) TO BLAME?"

"All my life I had blamed everything that ever happened to me on someone else, and I usually could find someone." [101] As we outlined earlier in a footnote the word *responsible* could be broken down into two words: **response** and **able**. So the word can be interpreted to mean: *"What* **response** *are we* **able** *to give to any situation?"* and for that we are responsible.

In the following exercise we will look at our response to what has happened in our lives and the results of those responses. We are looking for the lost power in our lives. By realising that it is not what has happened to us but how we reacted to those events that has defined our lives, we recognise that we can change our reactions. The goal is to have the events of our past be just that, past events and not remain decisive factors in our present. Very often we felt compelled to make these decisions or choices at an early age, when our reason was under-developed.

Most of us wouldn't ask a child for advice on how to deal with a complex emotional or spiritual dilemma. But isn't that what we have done? This has determined the very lives that we live today. All based on a child's decisions and choices? As a result we find ourselves living with emotional insecurity. The **"Common symptoms of emotional insecurity are worry, anger, self-pity and depression."** [102] Who among us would not want to rid ourselves of this emotional baggage?

Uncovering our imperfections and flaws, discovering where **we** are responsible and discarding these errors is a lifetime process. If we work the programme each day, every tomorrow gets better and better. Becoming a better human being is wonderful but it is not our final destination. It is just a step toward the purpose for which we were born. We were not born to cry, to strive, to struggle. We have lost our way, like the prodigal son. We were born in the image and likeness of an Intelligent Universe. The purpose of our life is to return to our Creator in that intelligent image and likeness; to see this **"Great Reality"** as our presence, our soul, our very being, and let It live our life for us, as us.

Our character defects have been passed down from generation to generation. While we are not to blame for inheriting these shortcomings, we are *responsible* for their continued use. Every thought, action, word, and deed is recorded in Universal Consciousness and, like radio waves, connects with those who are receptive. From birth these defects cause us to make mistakes over and over again with every one we come in contact with. They are impersonal; logged in our

FOURTH COLUMN QUESTIONS

memory. When a situation arises we sort through past experiences, often unconsciously, to work out how to handle it. It's all we know. If in our past experiences we became angry, violent and yelled; or became passive and weak then that's how we react now. If it was to lie, we lie; if we were grovelling, we grovel. It is impersonal. We are not to blame.

The most important thing for us to get from this question is that we are responsible for:

1. **Our emotions**—our feelings
2. **Our actions** and reactions
3. **Our beliefs,** stemming from our thinking—decisions and choices

BLAME (RESPONSIBLE)

- For harsh judgement
- For ignoring the facts
- Being careless
- Bringing the past into the present
- Not dealing with our feelings
- Blaming others for our feelings
- Not working our programme
- For our own upset
- For our ignorance

"WHAT DECISIONS DID WE MAKE BASED ON SELF THAT LATER PLACED US IN A POSITION TO BE HURT?"

"When in the past can we remember making this decision?"

In order to understand the decisions we have made in these situations, we should understand how the human mind works. What follows is an over-simplified explanation of the mental process involved. The human mind makes a decision or choice based on what it perceives as necessary for its survival. Once this judgment has been made, our mind then gathers evidence to prove to itself that it has made the right decision. Our mind never gathers evidence to prove it's wrong or even take into account facts that may suggest it's not right. Unless of course by proving that we are wrong again, is evidence of us being right about always being wrong. This is where everything could get very complicated. For this work let's "Keep it Simple": **Our mind never thinks it's wrong.**

The ultimate aim of our continuing inventory is to recognise and transform these past choices and decisions and replace them with reasonable ones. These choices and decisions are what have created

HOW TO ANSWER...

our beliefs in life; not what actually happened to us but what we made what happened mean. Regaining "Power" in our lives is accomplished by this recognition and the changing of these old decisions and choices; and therefore our beliefs. Then we find those beliefs are supported by the Universe just as our past beliefs have always been. As she looked back on her life, this woman said, **"Slowly, my life seemed to unfold before me, shedding insights on childhood resentments, jealousies, and fears that had mushroomed in adulthood."** [103]

On this subject of decisions or choices let us look at a few other things that can assist us in our quest for freedom. In early childhood we tend to watch our parents very closely, it doesn't seem to matter much whether we like who they are or not. Our choices as to who we emulate are usually based on who seemed to get their way. Who appeared to get what they wanted? This is why those of us who have had a bullying parent, even though we hated the way they were, end up being bullies ourselves. Or, when we have had what seemed to be a weak and whiney victim as one of our parents who in the end seems to get their way, we adopt the role of victim in life. Often our personalities are parts of both personality traits.

When taking the kind of look at our lives that this programme requires, we see that when establishing the very foundation of our lives we were *given choice* over our response to everything. This is what mystics (men who have walked in enlightenment) have been trying to tell us for millennia. At this stage of the Steps we resemble the Prodigal Son in the biblical story, who returned home and was presented with a ring and a cloak, symbols of maturity and responsibility. Likewise, when we make conscious connection to the presence of a Higher Power and take full responsibility for our own lives and actions, we become responsible, and therefore really free, adults.

Whatever we trusted and believed in yesterday we have become today. Whatever we trust and believe in today becomes our tomorrow. This is the miracle of the programme. We are no longer shackled by our past unconscious beliefs and behaviour patterns. Through exercising free choice today, we reshape our tomorrows. One day at a time.

The beliefs that we have held onto that do not serve us well we can, through inventory, discard. If we do not inventory them, and therefore find that they have no value, we are doomed to repeat these past beliefs again and again. We are surely free to do so, we are not automatons. If we truly desire a new life we *must* see that the things that we thought were good for us are not always so. The reason is that we are using the same old information locked in the memory banks of our minds. A human mind, that is weighing and measuring what is

FOURTH COLUMN QUESTIONS

best for its destiny, is waging a losing proposition. We only have to look at our lives up till now to see that our unaided judgement is flawed. Uncovering our past mistakes, discovering where **we** made the decisions and choices that truly harmed us, and discarding these errors is a lifetime practice.

What about our "geographic cures" for our problems? When things got too bad **"I moved away. I never thought about changing myself, I always thought about changing people, or changing places."**[104]

We are all trying to win at this game of life. What we learn in the programme is that we can only truly win when we create positive, loving attitudes towards life itself. Napoleon Hill once wrote: **"what ever the mind... can conceive and believe it can achieve."**[105] We lay particular emphasis on this part of the process acknowledged recently by us, as part of the inventory process. Yet it has always been there: **"we invariably find that in the past we have made decisions based on self which later placed us in a position to be hurt."**[106] Finally, the decisions that most affect us are those generalised ones that colour our overall beliefs about people, places and things.

So, what is the underlying personality characteristic of those of us with addictive personalities? Well **"a number of eminent psychologists and doctors made an exhaustive study of a good-sized group... The doctors weren't trying to find out how different we were from one another; they sought to find whatever personality traits, if any, this group...had in common. These distinguished men had the nerve to say that most...under investigation were still childish, emotionally sensitive, and grandiose."**[107] This implies that up till now our most defining decisions were made by **"childish, emotionally sensitive, and grandiose"** sides of ourselves. What a kettle of fish that is, no wonder our lives are such a mess.

HOW TO ANSWER...

DECISIONS

- People are stupid
- Women are weak
- Women are dangerous
- Women are ...
- Men are better off
- Men are liars
- Men are ...
- We can't trust women
- We can't trust men
- I am stupid
- I am always right
- I am always wrong
- Nobody loves me
- I'm unlovable
- I'm ugly
- I have a bad temper
- My nose is too big
- Sex is dirty
- Marriage is ...
- Life is ...
- Heights are...
- Bugs are ...
- Pets are ...
- Whites are ...
- Blacks are ...
- Spanish are ...
- Germans are ...
- Americans are ...
- British are ...
- French are ...
- Etc. etc. etc.

"WHERE WERE WE WRONG—WHAT WAS OUR PART?"

Admitting that we are wrong is very difficult for many of us. But we have all made mistakes, a lot of them. Besides for our purposes wrong simple means mistaken. Our part is often found after reviewing the answers to the above questions. What we are looking for here is that part for which we are responsible. That part that if we had not perpetrated, the damage to our present lives could not have happened.

OUR PART

- Gathering evidence to prove ourselves right
- Making sweeping generalisations
- The rest of our part will be a distillation of the answers to the preceding questions

Some of us use what we have learned in the programme to look at what others aren't doing; this is **"known as 'taking someone else's inventory,' a practice at which...** (We) **can be expert."** [108] But we find this practice to be a fruitless one.

The way to reach God and freedom is through a thorough self-survey. This is done by taking every disturbing defect, resentment, fear, financial and sex problem of our memory, and seeing where the problem and disinformation started. Finding out what decisions or choices we made and where we deceived and deluded ourselves. This is our chosen path of freedom.

Chapter 5

140 Inventory Forms ...Column Work

COLUMN WORK

Resentment (1) and/or Fear:	The Cause (Column 2)	Affects Our: (Column 3)
Person, Place or Thing		☐ Self-Esteem ☐ Security ☐ Ambitions ☐ Personal Relations ☐ Sex Relations ☐ Pride/Shame ☐ Fear
Ask Ourselves: ** (AA 67.3) * (AA 62.2)	Putting out of our mind the wrong others had done, we resolutely looked for our own mistakes... We admitted our wrongs honestly...** **STEPS 4 and/or 10 - (Column 4)**	
Where had I been selfish, self-centred or self-seeking?**		
Where had I been dishonest?**		
Where had I been frightened?**		
For what had I been responsible?**		
What decisions did I make based on self that later placed me in a position to be hurt?*		
When in the past did I make this decision? * (Earliest memory)		
Where was I wrong,** what was my part?		

STEPS 6 & 7 – List of Character Defects			

STEP 9 - Amends		STEP 8
		☐ Now ☐ Later ☐ Never

INVENTORY FORMS

Resentment (1) and/or Fear:	The Cause (Column 2)	Affects Our: (Column 3)
Person, Place or Thing		☐ Self-Esteem ☐ Security ☐ Ambitions ☐ Personal Relations ☐ Sex Relations ☐ Pride/Shame ☐ Fear
Ask Ourselves: ** (AA 67.3) * (AA 62.2)	Putting out of our mind the wrong others had done, we resolutely looked for our own mistakes... We admitted our wrongs honestly...** **STEPS 4** and/or **10 - (Column 4)**	
Where had I been selfish, self-centred or self-seeking?**		
Where had I been dishonest?**		
Where had I been frightened?**		
For what had I been responsible?**		
What decisions did I make based on self that later placed me in a position to be hurt?*		
When in the past did I make this decision? * (Earliest memory)		
Where was I wrong,** what was my part?		

STEPS 6 & 7 – List of Character Defects

STEP 9 - Amends	STEP 8
	☐ Now ☐ Later ☐ Never

COLUMN WORK

Resentment (1) and/or Fear:	The Cause (Column 2)	Affects Our: (Column 3)
Person, Place or Thing		☐ Self-Esteem ☐ Security ☐ Ambitions ☐ Personal Relations ☐ Sex Relations ☐ Pride/Shame ☐ Fear
Ask Ourselves: ** (AA 67.3) * (AA 62.2)	Putting out of our mind the wrong others had done, we resolutely looked for our own mistakes... We admitted our wrongs honestly...** **STEPS 4 and/or 10 - (Column 4)**	
Where had I been selfish, self-centred or self-seeking?**		
Where had I been dishonest?**		
Where had I been frightened?**		
For what had I been responsible?**		
What decisions did I make based on self that later placed me in a position to be hurt?*		
When in the past did I make this decision? * (Earliest memory)		
Where was I wrong,** what was my part?		

STEPS 6 & 7 – List of Character Defects				

STEP 9 - Amends	STEP 8
	☐ Now ☐ Later ☐ Never

STEP 10

INVENTORY FORMS

Resentment (1) and/or Fear:	The Cause (Column 2)	Affects Our: (Column 3)
Person, Place or Thing		☐ Self-Esteem ☐ Security ☐ Ambitions ☐ Personal Relations ☐ Sex Relations ☐ Pride/Shame ☐ Fear
Ask Ourselves: ** (AA 67.3) * (AA 62.2)	Putting out of our mind the wrong others had done, we resolutely looked for our own mistakes... We admitted our wrongs honestly...** **STEPS 4** and/or **10** - **(Column 4)**	
Where had I been selfish, self-centred or self-seeking?**		
Where had I been dishonest?**		
Where had I been frightened?**		
For what had I been responsible?**		
What decisions did I make based on self that later placed me in a position to be hurt?*		
When in the past did I make this decision? * (Earliest memory)		
Where was I wrong,** what was my part?		

STEPS 6 & 7 – List of Character Defects			

STEP 9 - Amends	STEP 8
	☐ Now ☐ Later ☐ Never

MAINTAINING THE PROMISES...DAILY

COLUMN WORK

Resentment (1) and/or Fear:	The Cause (Column 2)	Affects Our: (Column 3)
Person, Place or Thing		☐ Self-Esteem ☐ Security ☐ Ambitions ☐ Personal Relations ☐ Sex Relations ☐ Pride/Shame ☐ Fear
Ask Ourselves: ** (AA 67.3) * (AA 62.2)	Putting out of our mind the wrong others had done, we resolutely looked for our own mistakes… We admitted our wrongs honestly…** **STEPS 4 and/or 10 - (Column 4)**	
Where had I been selfish, self-centred or self-seeking?**		
Where had I been dishonest?**		
Where had I been frightened?**		
For what had I been responsible?**		
What decisions did I make based on self that later placed me in a position to be hurt?*		
When in the past did I make this decision? * (Earliest memory)		
Where was I wrong,** what was my part?		

STEPS 6 & 7 – List of Character Defects

STEP 9 - Amends

	STEP 8
	☐ Now ☐ Later ☐ Never

STEP 10

INVENTORY FORMS

Resentment (1) and/or Fear:	The Cause (Column 2)	Affects Our: (Column 3)
Person, Place or Thing		☐ Self-Esteem ☐ Security ☐ Ambitions ☐ Personal Relations ☐ Sex Relations ☐ Pride/Shame ☐ Fear
Ask Ourselves: ** (AA 67.3) * (AA 62.2)	Putting out of our mind the wrong others had done, we resolutely looked for our own mistakes… We admitted our wrongs honestly…** **STEPS 4 and/or 10 - (Column 4)**	
Where had I been selfish, self-centred or self-seeking?**		
Where had I been dishonest?**		
Where had I been frightened?**		
For what had I been responsible?**		
What decisions did I make based on self that later placed me in a position to be hurt?*		
When in the past did I make this decision? * (Earliest memory)		
Where was I wrong,** what was my part?		
STEPS 6 & 7 – List of Character Defects		
STEP 9 - Amends		**STEP 8**
		☐ Now ☐ Later ☐ Never

COLUMN WORK

Resentment (1) and/or Fear:	The Cause (Column 2)	Affects Our: (Column 3)
Person, Place or Thing		☐ Self-Esteem ☐ Security ☐ Ambitions ☐ Personal Relations ☐ Sex Relations ☐ Pride/Shame ☐ Fear
Ask Ourselves: ** (AA 67.3) * (AA 62.2)	Putting out of our mind the wrong others had done, we resolutely looked for our own mistakes… We admitted our wrongs honestly… ** **STEPS 4 and/or 10 - (Column 4)**	
Where had I been selfish, self-centred or self-seeking?**		
Where had I been dishonest?**		
Where had I been frightened?**		
For what had I been responsible?**		
What decisions did I make based on self that later placed me in a position to be hurt?*		
When in the past did I make this decision? * (Earliest memory)		
Where was I wrong,** what was my part?		
STEPS 6 & 7 – List of Character Defects		

STEP 9 - Amends		STEP 8
		☐ Now ☐ Later ☐ Never

STEP 10

INVENTORY FORMS

Resentment (1) and/or Fear:	The Cause (Column 2)	Affects Our: (Column 3)
Person, Place or Thing		☐ Self-Esteem ☐ Security ☐ Ambitions ☐ Personal Relations ☐ Sex Relations ☐ Pride/Shame ☐ Fear
Ask Ourselves: ** (AA 67.3) * (AA 62.2)	Putting out of our mind the wrong others had done, we resolutely looked for our own mistakes... We admitted our wrongs honestly... ** **STEPS 4** and/or **10** - **(Column 4)**	
Where had I been selfish, self-centred or self-seeking?**		
Where had I been dishonest?**		
Where had I been frightened?**		
For what had I been responsible?**		
What decisions did I make based on self that later placed me in a position to be hurt?*		
When in the past did I make this decision? * (Earliest memory)		
Where was I wrong,** what was my part?		

STEPS 6 & 7 – List of Character Defects					

STEP 9 - Amends	STEP 8
	☐ Now ☐ Later ☐ Never

MAINTAINING THE PROMISES...DAILY

COLUMN WORK

Resentment (1) and/or Fear:	The Cause (Column 2)	Affects Our: (Column 3)
Person, Place or Thing		☐ Self-Esteem ☐ Security ☐ Ambitions ☐ Personal Relations ☐ Sex Relations ☐ Pride/Shame ☐ Fear
Ask Ourselves: ** (AA 67.3) * (AA 62.2)	Putting out of our mind the wrong others had done, we resolutely looked for our own mistakes... We admitted our wrongs honestly...** **STEPS 4** and/or **10 - (Column 4)**	
Where had I been selfish, self-centred or self-seeking?**		
Where had I been dishonest?**		
Where had I been frightened?**		
For what had I been responsible?**		
What decisions did I make based on self that later placed me in a position to be hurt?*		
When in the past did I make this decision? * (Earliest memory)		
Where was I wrong,** what was my part?		

STEPS 6 & 7 – List of Character Defects

STEP 9 - Amends	STEP 8
	☐ Now ☐ Later ☐ Never

STEP 10

INVENTORY FORMS

Resentment (1) and/or Fear:	The Cause (Column 2)	Affects Our: (Column 3)
Person, Place or Thing		☐ Self-Esteem ☐ Security ☐ Ambitions ☐ Personal Relations ☐ Sex Relations ☐ Pride/Shame ☐ Fear
Ask Ourselves: ** (AA 67.3) * (AA 62.2)	Putting out of our mind the wrong others had done, we resolutely looked for our own mistakes... We admitted our wrongs honestly...** **STEPS 4** and/or **10 - (Column 4)**	
Where had I been selfish, self-centred or self-seeking?**		
Where had I been dishonest?**		
Where had I been frightened?**		
For what had I been responsible?**		
What decisions did I make based on self that later placed me in a position to be hurt?*		
When in the past did I make this decision? * (Earliest memory)		
Where was I wrong,** what was my part?		

STEPS 6 & 7 – List of Character Defects

STEP 9 - Amends	STEP 8
	☐ Now ☐ Later ☐ Never

COLUMN WORK

Resentment (1) and/or Fear:	The Cause (Column 2)	Affects Our: (Column 3)
Person, Place or Thing		☐ Self-Esteem ☐ Security ☐ Ambitions ☐ Personal Relations ☐ Sex Relations ☐ Pride/Shame ☐ Fear
Ask Ourselves: ** (AA 67.3) * (AA 62.2)	Putting out of our mind the wrong others had done, we resolutely looked for our own mistakes... We admitted our wrongs honestly...** **STEPS 4 and/or 10 - (Column 4)**	
Where had I been selfish, self-centred or self-seeking?**		
Where had I been dishonest?**		
Where had I been frightened?**		
For what had I been responsible?**		
What decisions did I make based on self that later placed me in a position to be hurt?*		
When in the past did I make this decision? * (Earliest memory)		
Where was I wrong,** what was my part?		

STEPS 6 & 7 – List of Character Defects					

STEP 9 - Amends	STEP 8
	☐ Now ☐ Later ☐ Never

STEP 10

INVENTORY FORMS

Resentment (1) and/or Fear:	The Cause (Column 2)	Affects Our: (Column 3)
Person, Place or Thing		☐ Self-Esteem ☐ Security ☐ Ambitions ☐ Personal Relations ☐ Sex Relations ☐ Pride/Shame ☐ Fear
Ask Ourselves: ** (AA 67.3) * (AA 62.2)	Putting out of our mind the wrong others had done, we resolutely looked for our own mistakes... We admitted our wrongs honestly...** **STEPS 4 and/or 10 - (Column 4)**	
Where had I been selfish, self-centred or self-seeking?**		
Where had I been dishonest?**		
Where had I been frightened?**		
For what had I been responsible?**		
What decisions did I make based on self that later placed me in a position to be hurt?*		
When in the past did I make this decision? * (Earliest memory)		
Where was I wrong,** what was my part?		

STEPS 6 & 7 – List of Character Defects					

STEP 9 - Amends	STEP 8
	☐ Now ☐ Later ☐ Never

414 MAINTAINING THE PROMISES...DAILY

COLUMN WORK

Resentment (1) and/or Fear:	The Cause (Column 2)	Affects Our: (Column 3)
Person, Place or Thing		☐ Self-Esteem ☐ Security ☐ Ambitions ☐ Personal Relations ☐ Sex Relations ☐ Pride/Shame ☐ Fear
Ask Ourselves: ** (AA 67.3) * (AA 62.2)	Putting out of our mind the wrong others had done, we resolutely looked for our own mistakes... We admitted our wrongs honestly...** **STEPS 4 and/or 10 - (Column 4)**	
Where had I been selfish, self-centred or self-seeking?**		
Where had I been dishonest?**		
Where had I been frightened?**		
For what had I been responsible?**		
What decisions did I make based on self that later placed me in a position to be hurt?*		
When in the past did I make this decision? * (Earliest memory)		
Where was I wrong,** what was my part?		

STEPS 6 & 7 – List of Character Defects				

STEP 9 - Amends	STEP 8
	☐ Now ☐ Later ☐ Never

STEP 10

INVENTORY FORMS

Resentment (1) and/or Fear:	The Cause (Column 2)	Affects Our: (Column 3)
Person, Place or Thing		☐ Self-Esteem ☐ Security ☐ Ambitions ☐ Personal Relations ☐ Sex Relations ☐ Pride/Shame ☐ Fear
Ask Ourselves: ** (AA 67.3) * (AA 62.2)	Putting out of our mind the wrong others had done, we resolutely looked for our own mistakes... We admitted our wrongs honestly...** **STEPS 4** and/or **10 - (Column 4)**	
Where had I been selfish, self-centred or self-seeking?**		
Where had I been dishonest?**		
Where had I been frightened?**		
For what had I been responsible?**		
What decisions did I make based on self that later placed me in a position to be hurt?*		
When in the past did I make this decision? * (Earliest memory)		
Where was I wrong,** what was my part?		

STEPS 6 & 7 – List of Character Defects

STEP 9 - Amends	STEP 8
	☐ Now ☐ Later ☐ Never

COLUMN WORK

Resentment (1) and/or Fear:	The Cause (Column 2)	Affects Our: (Column 3)
Person, Place or Thing		☐ Self-Esteem ☐ Security ☐ Ambitions ☐ Personal Relations ☐ Sex Relations ☐ Pride/Shame ☐ Fear
Ask Ourselves: ** (AA 67.3) * (AA 62.2)	Putting out of our mind the wrong others had done, we resolutely looked for our own mistakes... We admitted our wrongs honestly... ** **STEPS 4 and/or 10 - (Column 4)**	
Where had I been selfish, self-centred or self-seeking?**		
Where had I been dishonest?**		
Where had I been frightened?**		
For what had I been responsible?**		
What decisions did I make based on self that later placed me in a position to be hurt?*		
When in the past did I make this decision? * (Earliest memory)		
Where was I wrong,** what was my part?		

STEPS 6 & 7 – List of Character Defects

STEP 9 - Amends	STEP 8
	☐ Now ☐ Later ☐ Never

STEP 10

INVENTORY FORMS

Resentment (1) and/or Fear:	The Cause (Column 2)	Affects Our: (Column 3)
Person, Place or Thing		☐ Self-Esteem ☐ Security ☐ Ambitions ☐ Personal Relations ☐ Sex Relations ☐ Pride/Shame ☐ Fear
Ask Ourselves: ** (AA 67.3) * (AA 62.2)	Putting out of our mind the wrong others had done, we resolutely looked for our own mistakes... We admitted our wrongs honestly...** **STEPS 4** and/or **10** - **(Column 4)**	
Where had I been selfish, self-centred or self-seeking?**		
Where had I been dishonest?**		
Where had I been frightened?**		
For what had I been responsible?**		
What decisions did I make based on self that later placed me in a position to be hurt?*		
When in the past did I make this decision? * (Earliest memory)		
Where was I wrong,** what was my part?		

STEPS 6 & 7 – List of Character Defects

STEP 9 - Amends	STEP 8
	☐ Now ☐ Later ☐ Never

COLUMN WORK

Resentment (1) and/or Fear:	The Cause (Column 2)	Affects Our: (Column 3)
Person, Place or Thing		☐ Self-Esteem ☐ Security ☐ Ambitions ☐ Personal Relations ☐ Sex Relations ☐ Pride/Shame ☐ Fear
Ask Ourselves: ** (AA 67.3) * (AA 62.2)	Putting out of our mind the wrong others had done, we resolutely looked for our own mistakes... We admitted our wrongs honestly...** **STEPS 4 and/or 10 - (Column 4)**	
Where had I been selfish, self-centred or self-seeking?**		
Where had I been dishonest?**		
Where had I been frightened?**		
For what had I been responsible?**		
What decisions did I make based on self that later placed me in a position to be hurt?*		
When in the past did I make this decision? * (Earliest memory)		
Where was I wrong,** what was my part?		

STEPS 6 & 7 – List of Character Defects			

STEP 9 - Amends	STEP 8
	☐ Now ☐ Later ☐ Never

STEP 10

INVENTORY FORMS

Resentment (1) and/or Fear:	The Cause (Column 2)	Affects Our: (Column 3)
Person, Place or Thing		☐ Self-Esteem ☐ Security ☐ Ambitions ☐ Personal Relations ☐ Sex Relations ☐ Pride/Shame ☐ Fear
Ask Ourselves: ** (AA 67.3) * (AA 62.2)	Putting out of our mind the wrong others had done, we resolutely looked for our own mistakes… We admitted our wrongs honestly…** **STEPS 4** and/or **10** - **(Column 4)**	
Where had I been selfish, self-centred or self-seeking?**		
Where had I been dishonest?**		
Where had I been frightened?**		
For what had I been responsible?**		
What decisions did I make based on self that later placed me in a position to be hurt?*		
When in the past did I make this decision? * (Earliest memory)		
Where was I wrong,** what was my part?		

STEPS 6 & 7 – List of Character Defects			

STEP 9 - Amends	STEP 8
	☐ Now ☐ Later ☐ Never

COLUMN WORK

Resentment (1) and/or Fear:	The Cause (Column 2)	Affects Our: (Column 3)
Person, Place or Thing		☐ Self-Esteem ☐ Security ☐ Ambitions ☐ Personal Relations ☐ Sex Relations ☐ Pride/Shame ☐ Fear
Ask Ourselves: ** (AA 67.3) * (AA 62.2)	Putting out of our mind the wrong others had done, we resolutely looked for our own mistakes... We admitted our wrongs honestly...** **STEPS 4 and/or 10 - (Column 4)**	
Where had I been selfish, self-centred or self-seeking?**		
Where had I been dishonest?**		
Where had I been frightened?**		
For what had I been responsible?**		
What decisions did I make based on self that later placed me in a position to be hurt?*		
When in the past did I make this decision? * (Earliest memory)		
Where was I wrong,** what was my part?		

STEPS 6 & 7 – List of Character Defects				

STEP 9 - Amends	STEP 8
	☐ Now ☐ Later ☐ Never

STEP 10

INVENTORY FORMS

Resentment (1) and/or Fear:	The Cause (Column 2)	Affects Our: (Column 3)
Person, Place or Thing		☐ Self-Esteem ☐ Security ☐ Ambitions ☐ Personal Relations ☐ Sex Relations ☐ Pride/Shame ☐ Fear
Ask Ourselves: ** (AA 67.3) * (AA 62.2)	Putting out of our mind the wrong others had done, we resolutely looked for our own mistakes... We admitted our wrongs honestly...** **STEPS 4 and/or 10 - (Column 4)**	
Where had I been selfish, self-centred or self-seeking?**		
Where had I been dishonest?**		
Where had I been frightened?**		
For what had I been responsible?**		
What decisions did I make based on self that later placed me in a position to be hurt?*		
When in the past did I make this decision? * (Earliest memory)		
Where was I wrong,** what was my part?		

STEPS 6 & 7 – List of Character Defects			

STEP 9 - Amends	STEP 8
	☐ Now ☐ Later ☐ Never

COLUMN WORK

Resentment (1) and/or Fear:	The Cause (Column 2)	Affects Our: (Column 3)
Person, Place or Thing		☐ Self-Esteem ☐ Security ☐ Ambitions ☐ Personal Relations ☐ Sex Relations ☐ Pride/Shame ☐ Fear
Ask Ourselves: ** (AA 67.3) * (AA 62.2)	Putting out of our mind the wrong others had done, we resolutely looked for our own mistakes… We admitted our wrongs honestly…** **STEPS 4** and/or **10 - (Column 4)**	
Where had I been selfish, self-centred or self-seeking?**		
Where had I been dishonest?**		
Where had I been frightened?**		
For what had I been responsible?**		
What decisions did I make based on self that later placed me in a position to be hurt?*		
When in the past did I make this decision? * (Earliest memory)		
Where was I wrong,** what was my part?		
STEPS 6 & 7 – List of Character Defects		

STEP 9 - Amends	STEP 8
	☐ Now ☐ Later ☐ Never

STEP 10

INVENTORY FORMS

Resentment (1) and/or Fear:	The Cause (Column 2)	Affects Our: (Column 3)
Person, Place or Thing		☐ Self-Esteem ☐ Security ☐ Ambitions ☐ Personal Relations ☐ Sex Relations ☐ Pride/Shame ☐ Fear
Ask Ourselves: ** (AA 67.3) * (AA 62.2)	Putting out of our mind the wrong others had done, we resolutely looked for our own mistakes... We admitted our wrongs honestly...** **STEPS 4** and/or **10 - (Column 4)**	
Where had I been selfish, self-centred or self-seeking?**		
Where had I been dishonest?**		
Where had I been frightened?**		
For what had I been responsible?**		
What decisions did I make based on self that later placed me in a position to be hurt?*		
When in the past did I make this decision? * (Earliest memory)		
Where was I wrong,** what was my part?		

STEPS 6 & 7 – List of Character Defects

STEP 9 - Amends	STEP 8
	☐ Now ☐ Later ☐ Never

424   MAINTAINING THE PROMISES...DAILY

COLUMN WORK

Resentment (1) and/or Fear:	The Cause (Column 2)	Affects Our: (Column 3)
Person, Place or Thing		☐ Self-Esteem ☐ Security ☐ Ambitions ☐ Personal Relations ☐ Sex Relations ☐ Pride/Shame ☐ Fear
Ask Ourselves: ** (AA 67.3) * (AA 62.2)	Putting out of our mind the wrong others had done, we resolutely looked for our own mistakes… We admitted our wrongs honestly…** **STEPS 4 and/or 10 - (Column 4)**	
Where had I been selfish, self-centred or self-seeking?**		
Where had I been dishonest?**		
Where had I been frightened?**		
For what had I been responsible?**		
What decisions did I make based on self that later placed me in a position to be hurt?*		
When in the past did I make this decision? * (Earliest memory)		
Where was I wrong,** what was my part?		

STEPS 6 & 7 – List of Character Defects			

STEP 9 - Amends	STEP 8
	☐ Now ☐ Later ☐ Never

INVENTORY FORMS

Resentment (1) and/or Fear:	The Cause (Column 2)	Affects Our: (Column 3)
Person, Place or Thing		☐ Self-Esteem ☐ Security ☐ Ambitions ☐ Personal Relations ☐ Sex Relations ☐ Pride/Shame ☐ Fear
Ask Ourselves: ** (AA 67.3) * (AA 62.2)	Putting out of our mind the wrong others had done, we resolutely looked for our own mistakes… We admitted our wrongs honestly…** **STEPS 4** and/or **10** - **(Column 4)**	
Where had I been selfish, self-centred or self-seeking?**		
Where had I been dishonest?**		
Where had I been frightened?**		
For what had I been responsible?**		
What decisions did I make based on self that later placed me in a position to be hurt?*		
When in the past did I make this decision? * (Earliest memory)		
Where was I wrong,** what was my part?		
STEPS 6 & 7 – List of Character Defects		
STEP 9 - Amends		**STEP 8**
		☐ Now ☐ Later ☐ Never

426 MAINTAINING THE PROMISES…DAILY

COLUMN WORK

Resentment (1) and/or Fear:	The Cause (Column 2)	Affects Our: (Column 3)
Person, Place or Thing		☐ Self-Esteem ☐ Security ☐ Ambitions ☐ Personal Relations ☐ Sex Relations ☐ Pride/Shame ☐ Fear
Ask Ourselves: ** (AA 67.3) * (AA 62.2)	Putting out of our mind the wrong others had done, we resolutely looked for our own mistakes… We admitted our wrongs honestly…** **STEPS 4 and/or 10 - (Column 4)**	
Where had I been selfish, self-centred or self-seeking?**		
Where had I been dishonest?**		
Where had I been frightened?**		
For what had I been responsible?**		
What decisions did I make based on self that later placed me in a position to be hurt?*		
When in the past did I make this decision? * (Earliest memory)		
Where was I wrong,** what was my part?		

STEPS 6 & 7 – List of Character Defects					

STEP 9 - Amends	STEP 8
	☐ Now ☐ Later ☐ Never

STEP 10

INVENTORY FORMS

Resentment (1) and/or Fear:	The Cause (Column 2)	Affects Our: (Column 3)
Person, Place or Thing		☐ Self-Esteem ☐ Security ☐ Ambitions ☐ Personal Relations ☐ Sex Relations ☐ Pride/Shame ☐ Fear
Ask Ourselves: ** (AA 67.3) * (AA 62.2)	Putting out of our mind the wrong others had done, we resolutely looked for our own mistakes... We admitted our wrongs honestly...** **STEPS 4** and/or **10** - **(Column 4)**	
Where had I been selfish, self-centred or self-seeking?**		
Where had I been dishonest?**		
Where had I been frightened?**		
For what had I been responsible?**		
What decisions did I make based on self that later placed me in a position to be hurt?*		
When in the past did I make this decision? * (Earliest memory)		
Where was I wrong,** what was my part?		

STEPS 6 & 7 – List of Character Defects				

STEP 9 - Amends	STEP 8
	☐ Now ☐ Later ☐ Never

428   MAINTAINING THE PROMISES...DAILY

COLUMN WORK

Resentment (1) and/or Fear:	The Cause (Column 2)	Affects Our: (Column 3)
Person, Place or Thing		☐ Self-Esteem ☐ Security ☐ Ambitions ☐ Personal Relations ☐ Sex Relations ☐ Pride/Shame ☐ Fear
Ask Ourselves: ** (AA 67.3) * (AA 62.2)	Putting out of our mind the wrong others had done, we resolutely looked for our own mistakes... We admitted our wrongs honestly...** **STEPS 4 and/or 10 - (Column 4)**	
Where had I been selfish, self-centred or self-seeking?**		
Where had I been dishonest?**		
Where had I been frightened?**		
For what had I been responsible?**		
What decisions did I make based on self that later placed me in a position to be hurt?*		
When in the past did I make this decision? * (Earliest memory)		
Where was I wrong,** what was my part?		
STEPS 6 & 7 – List of Character Defects		

STEP 9 - Amends	STEP 8
	☐ Now ☐ Later ☐ Never

STEP 10

INVENTORY FORMS

Resentment (1) and/or Fear:	The Cause (Column 2)	Affects Our: (Column 3)
Person, Place or Thing		☐ Self-Esteem ☐ Security ☐ Ambitions ☐ Personal Relations ☐ Sex Relations ☐ Pride/Shame ☐ Fear
Ask Ourselves: ** (AA 67.3) * (AA 62.2)	Putting out of our mind the wrong others had done, we resolutely looked for our own mistakes... We admitted our wrongs honestly...** **STEPS 4** and/or **10** - **(Column 4)**	
Where had I been selfish, self-centred or self-seeking?**		
Where had I been dishonest?**		
Where had I been frightened?**		
For what had I been responsible?**		
What decisions did I make based on self that later placed me in a position to be hurt?*		
When in the past did I make this decision? * (Earliest memory)		
Where was I wrong,** what was my part?		

STEPS 6 & 7 – List of Character Defects				

STEP 9 - Amends	STEP 8
	☐ Now ☐ Later ☐ Never

MAINTAINING THE PROMISES...DAILY

COLUMN WORK

Resentment (1) and/or Fear:	The Cause (Column 2)	Affects Our: (Column 3)
Person, Place or Thing		☐ Self-Esteem ☐ Security ☐ Ambitions ☐ Personal Relations ☐ Sex Relations ☐ Pride/Shame ☐ Fear
Ask Ourselves: ** (AA 67.3) * (AA 62.2)	Putting out of our mind the wrong others had done, we resolutely looked for our own mistakes... We admitted our wrongs honestly...** **STEPS 4 and/or 10 - (Column 4)**	
Where had I been selfish, self-centred or self-seeking?**		
Where had I been dishonest?**		
Where had I been frightened?**		
For what had I been responsible?**		
What decisions did I make based on self that later placed me in a position to be hurt?*		
When in the past did I make this decision? * (Earliest memory)		
Where was I wrong,** what was my part?		

STEPS 6 & 7 – List of Character Defects			

STEP 9 - Amends	STEP 8
	☐ Now ☐ Later ☐ Never

STEP 10

INVENTORY FORMS

Resentment (1) and/or Fear:	The Cause (Column 2)	Affects Our: (Column 3)
Person, Place or Thing		☐ Self-Esteem ☐ Security ☐ Ambitions ☐ Personal Relations ☐ Sex Relations ☐ Pride/Shame ☐ Fear
Ask Ourselves: ** (AA 67.3) * (AA 62.2)	Putting out of our mind the wrong others had done, we resolutely looked for our own mistakes... We admitted our wrongs honestly...** **STEPS 4** and/or **10** - **(Column 4)**	
Where had I been selfish, self-centred or self-seeking?**		
Where had I been dishonest?**		
Where had I been frightened?**		
For what had I been responsible?**		
What decisions did I make based on self that later placed me in a position to be hurt?*		
When in the past did I make this decision? * (Earliest memory)		
Where was I wrong,** what was my part?		

STEPS 6 & 7 – List of Character Defects

STEP 9 - Amends	STEP 8
	☐ Now ☐ Later ☐ Never

432   MAINTAINING THE PROMISES...DAILY

COLUMN WORK

Resentment (1) and/or Fear:	The Cause (Column 2)	Affects Our: (Column 3)
Person, Place or Thing		☐ Self-Esteem ☐ Security ☐ Ambitions ☐ Personal Relations ☐ Sex Relations ☐ Pride/Shame ☐ Fear
Ask Ourselves: ** (AA 67.3) * (AA 62.2)	Putting out of our mind the wrong others had done, we resolutely looked for our own mistakes... We admitted our wrongs honestly...** **STEPS 4 and/or 10 - (Column 4)**	
Where had I been selfish, self-centred or self-seeking?**		
Where had I been dishonest?**		
Where had I been frightened?**		
For what had I been responsible?**		
What decisions did I make based on self that later placed me in a position to be hurt?*		
When in the past did I make this decision? * (Earliest memory)		
Where was I wrong,** what was my part?		

STEPS 6 & 7 – List of Character Defects					

STEP 9 - Amends	STEP 8
	☐ Now ☐ Later ☐ Never

STEP 10

INVENTORY FORMS

Resentment (1) and/or Fear:	The Cause (Column 2)	Affects Our: (Column 3)
Person, Place or Thing		☐ Self-Esteem ☐ Security ☐ Ambitions ☐ Personal Relations ☐ Sex Relations ☐ Pride/Shame ☐ Fear
Ask Ourselves: ** (AA 67.3) * (AA 62.2)	Putting out of our mind the wrong others had done, we resolutely looked for our own mistakes... We admitted our wrongs honestly...** **STEPS 4 and/or 10 - (Column 4)**	
Where had I been selfish, self-centred or self-seeking?**		
Where had I been dishonest?**		
Where had I been frightened?**		
For what had I been responsible?**		
What decisions did I make based on self that later placed me in a position to be hurt?*		
When in the past did I make this decision? * (Earliest memory)		
Where was I wrong,** what was my part?		

STEPS 6 & 7 – List of Character Defects

STEP 9 - Amends	STEP 8
	☐ Now ☐ Later ☐ Never

MAINTAINING THE PROMISES...DAILY

COLUMN WORK

Resentment (1) and/or Fear:	The Cause (Column 2)	Affects Our: (Column 3)
Person, Place or Thing		☐ Self-Esteem ☐ Security ☐ Ambitions ☐ Personal Relations ☐ Sex Relations ☐ Pride/Shame ☐ Fear
Ask Ourselves: ** (AA 67.3) * (AA 62.2)	Putting out of our mind the wrong others had done, we resolutely looked for our own mistakes... We admitted our wrongs honestly...** **STEPS 4 and/or 10 - (Column 4)**	
Where had I been selfish, self-centred or self-seeking?**		
Where had I been dishonest?**		
Where had I been frightened?**		
For what had I been responsible?**		
What decisions did I make based on self that later placed me in a position to be hurt?*		
When in the past did I make this decision? * (Earliest memory)		
Where was I wrong,** what was my part?		

STEPS 6 & 7 – List of Character Defects			

STEP 9 - Amends	STEP 8
	☐ Now ☐ Later ☐ Never

STEP 10

INVENTORY FORMS

Resentment (1) and/or Fear:	The Cause (Column 2)	Affects Our: (Column 3)
Person, Place or Thing		☐ Self-Esteem ☐ Security ☐ Ambitions ☐ Personal Relations ☐ Sex Relations ☐ Pride/Shame ☐ Fear
Ask Ourselves: ** (AA 67.3) * (AA 62.2)	Putting out of our mind the wrong others had done, we resolutely looked for our own mistakes… We admitted our wrongs honestly…** **STEPS 4** and/or **10 - (Column 4)**	
Where had I been selfish, self-centred or self-seeking?**		
Where had I been dishonest?**		
Where had I been frightened?**		
For what had I been responsible?**		
What decisions did I make based on self that later placed me in a position to be hurt?*		
When in the past did I make this decision? * (Earliest memory)		
Where was I wrong,** what was my part?		

STEPS 6 & 7 – List of Character Defects			

STEP 9 - Amends	STEP 8
	☐ Now ☐ Later ☐ Never

436   MAINTAINING THE PROMISES…DAILY

COLUMN WORK

Resentment (1) and/or Fear:	The Cause (Column 2)	Affects Our: (Column 3)
Person, Place or Thing		☐ Self-Esteem ☐ Security ☐ Ambitions ☐ Personal Relations ☐ Sex Relations ☐ Pride/Shame ☐ Fear
Ask Ourselves: ** (AA 67.3) * (AA 62.2)	Putting out of our mind the wrong others had done, we resolutely looked for our own mistakes... We admitted our wrongs honestly...** **STEPS 4** and/or **10 - (Column 4)**	
Where had I been selfish, self-centred or self-seeking?**		
Where had I been dishonest?**		
Where had I been frightened?**		
For what had I been responsible?**		
What decisions did I make based on self that later placed me in a position to be hurt?*		
When in the past did I make this decision? * (Earliest memory)		
Where was I wrong,** what was my part?		

STEPS 6 & 7 – List of Character Defects

STEP 9 - Amends	STEP 8
	☐ Now ☐ Later ☐ Never

STEP 10

INVENTORY FORMS

Resentment (1) and/or Fear:	The Cause (Column 2)	Affects Our: (Column 3)
Person, Place or Thing		☐ Self-Esteem ☐ Security ☐ Ambitions ☐ Personal Relations ☐ Sex Relations ☐ Pride/Shame ☐ Fear
Ask Ourselves: ** (AA 67.3) * (AA 62.2)	Putting out of our mind the wrong others had done, we resolutely looked for our own mistakes… We admitted our wrongs honestly…** **STEPS 4 and/or 10 - (Column 4)**	
Where had I been selfish, self-centred or self-seeking?**		
Where had I been dishonest?**		
Where had I been frightened?**		
For what had I been responsible?**		
What decisions did I make based on self that later placed me in a position to be hurt?*		
When in the past did I make this decision? * (Earliest memory)		
Where was I wrong,** what was my part?		
STEPS 6 & 7 – List of Character Defects		
STEP 9 - Amends		**STEP 8**
		☐ Now ☐ Later ☐ Never

MAINTAINING THE PROMISES…DAILY

COLUMN WORK

Resentment (1) and/or Fear:	The Cause (Column 2)	Affects Our: (Column 3)
Person, Place or Thing		☐ Self-Esteem ☐ Security ☐ Ambitions ☐ Personal Relations ☐ Sex Relations ☐ Pride/Shame ☐ Fear
Ask Ourselves: ** (AA 67.3) * (AA 62.2)	Putting out of our mind the wrong others had done, we resolutely looked for our own mistakes... We admitted our wrongs honestly...** **STEPS 4 and/or 10 - (Column 4)**	
Where had I been selfish, self-centred or self-seeking?**		
Where had I been dishonest?**		
Where had I been frightened?**		
For what had I been responsible?**		
What decisions did I make based on self that later placed me in a position to be hurt?*		
When in the past did I make this decision? * (Earliest memory)		
Where was I wrong,** what was my part?		

STEPS 6 & 7 – List of Character Defects			

STEP 9 - Amends	STEP 8
	☐ Now ☐ Later ☐ Never

STEP 10

INVENTORY FORMS

Resentment (1) and/or Fear:	The Cause (Column 2)	Affects Our: (Column 3)
Person, Place or Thing		☐ Self-Esteem ☐ Security ☐ Ambitions ☐ Personal Relations ☐ Sex Relations ☐ Pride/Shame ☐ Fear
Ask Ourselves: ** (AA 67.3) * (AA 62.2)	Putting out of our mind the wrong others had done, we resolutely looked for our own mistakes... We admitted our wrongs honestly...** **STEPS 4 and/or 10 - (Column 4)**	
Where had I been selfish, self-centred or self-seeking?**		
Where had I been dishonest?**		
Where had I been frightened?**		
For what had I been responsible?**		
What decisions did I make based on self that later placed me in a position to be hurt?*		
When in the past did I make this decision? * (Earliest memory)		
Where was I wrong,** what was my part?		

STEPS 6 & 7 – List of Character Defects

STEP 9 - Amends	STEP 8
	☐ Now ☐ Later ☐ Never

COLUMN WORK

Resentment (1) and/or Fear:	The Cause (Column 2)	Affects Our: (Column 3)
Person, Place or Thing		☐ Self-Esteem ☐ Security ☐ Ambitions ☐ Personal Relations ☐ Sex Relations ☐ Pride/Shame ☐ Fear
Ask Ourselves: ** (AA 67.3) * (AA 62.2)	Putting out of our mind the wrong others had done, we resolutely looked for our own mistakes... We admitted our wrongs honestly...** **STEPS 4 and/or 10 - (Column 4)**	
Where had I been selfish, self-centred or self-seeking?**		
Where had I been dishonest?**		
Where had I been frightened?**		
For what had I been responsible?**		
What decisions did I make based on self that later placed me in a position to be hurt?*		
When in the past did I make this decision? * (Earliest memory)		
Where was I wrong,** what was my part?		

STEPS 6 & 7 – List of Character Defects			

STEP 9 - Amends	STEP 8
	☐ Now ☐ Later ☐ Never

STEP 10

INVENTORY FORMS

Resentment (1) and/or Fear:	The Cause (Column 2)	Affects Our: (Column 3)
Person, Place or Thing		☐ Self-Esteem ☐ Security ☐ Ambitions ☐ Personal Relations ☐ Sex Relations ☐ Pride/Shame ☐ Fear
Ask Ourselves: ** (AA 67.3) * (AA 62.2)	Putting out of our mind the wrong others had done, we resolutely looked for our own mistakes… We admitted our wrongs honestly…** **STEPS 4** and/or **10 - (Column 4)**	
Where had I been selfish, self-centred or self-seeking?**		
Where had I been dishonest?**		
Where had I been frightened?**		
For what had I been responsible?**		
What decisions did I make based on self that later placed me in a position to be hurt?*		
When in the past did I make this decision? * (Earliest memory)		
Where was I wrong,** what was my part?		

STEPS 6 & 7 – List of Character Defects			

STEP 9 - Amends	STEP 8
	☐ Now ☐ Later ☐ Never

COLUMN WORK

Resentment (1) and/or Fear:	The Cause (Column 2)	Affects Our: (Column 3)
Person, Place or Thing		☐ Self-Esteem ☐ Security ☐ Ambitions ☐ Personal Relations ☐ Sex Relations ☐ Pride/Shame ☐ Fear
Ask Ourselves: ** (AA 67.3) * (AA 62.2)	Putting out of our mind the wrong others had done, we resolutely looked for our own mistakes… We admitted our wrongs honestly…** **STEPS 4 and/or 10 - (Column 4)**	
Where had I been selfish, self-centred or self-seeking?**		
Where had I been dishonest?**		
Where had I been frightened?**		
For what had I been responsible?**		
What decisions did I make based on self that later placed me in a position to be hurt?*		
When in the past did I make this decision? * (Earliest memory)		
Where was I wrong,** what was my part?		
STEPS 6 & 7 – List of Character Defects		

STEP 9 - Amends	STEP 8
	☐ Now ☐ Later ☐ Never

STEP 10

INVENTORY FORMS

Resentment (1) and/or Fear:	The Cause (Column 2)	Affects Our: (Column 3)
Person, Place or Thing		☐ Self-Esteem ☐ Security ☐ Ambitions ☐ Personal Relations ☐ Sex Relations ☐ Pride/Shame ☐ Fear
Ask Ourselves: ** (AA 67.3) * (AA 62.2)	Putting out of our mind the wrong others had done, we resolutely looked for our own mistakes... We admitted our wrongs honestly...** **STEPS 4 and/or 10 - (Column 4)**	
Where had I been selfish, self-centred or self-seeking?**		
Where had I been dishonest?**		
Where had I been frightened?**		
For what had I been responsible?**		
What decisions did I make based on self that later placed me in a position to be hurt?*		
When in the past did I make this decision? * (Earliest memory)		
Where was I wrong,** what was my part?		

STEPS 6 & 7 – List of Character Defects

STEP 9 - Amends	STEP 8
	☐ Now ☐ Later ☐ Never

MAINTAINING THE PROMISES...DAILY

COLUMN WORK

Resentment (1) and/or Fear:	The Cause (Column 2)	Affects Our: (Column 3)
Person, Place or Thing		☐ Self-Esteem ☐ Security ☐ Ambitions ☐ Personal Relations ☐ Sex Relations ☐ Pride/Shame ☐ Fear
Ask Ourselves: ** (AA 67.3) * (AA 62.2)	Putting out of our mind the wrong others had done, we resolutely looked for our own mistakes... We admitted our wrongs honestly...** **STEPS 4** and/or **10 - (Column 4)**	
Where had I been selfish, self-centred or self-seeking?**		
Where had I been dishonest?**		
Where had I been frightened?**		
For what had I been responsible?**		
What decisions did I make based on self that later placed me in a position to be hurt?*		
When in the past did I make this decision? * (Earliest memory)		
Where was I wrong,** what was my part?		

STEPS 6 & 7 – List of Character Defects

STEP 9 - Amends | **STEP 8**

☐ Now
☐ Later
☐ Never

STEP 10

INVENTORY FORMS

Resentment (1) and/or Fear:	The Cause (Column 2)	Affects Our: (Column 3)
Person, Place or Thing		☐ Self-Esteem ☐ Security ☐ Ambitions ☐ Personal Relations ☐ Sex Relations ☐ Pride/Shame ☐ Fear
Ask Ourselves: ** (AA 67.3) * (AA 62.2)	Putting out of our mind the wrong others had done, we resolutely looked for our own mistakes... We admitted our wrongs honestly...** **STEPS 4 and/or 10 - (Column 4)**	
Where had I been selfish, self-centred or self-seeking?**		
Where had I been dishonest?**		
Where had I been frightened?**		
For what had I been responsible?**		
What decisions did I make based on self that later placed me in a position to be hurt?*		
When in the past did I make this decision? * (Earliest memory)		
Where was I wrong,** what was my part?		

STEPS 6 & 7 – List of Character Defects			

STEP 9 - Amends	STEP 8
	☐ Now ☐ Later ☐ Never

COLUMN WORK

Resentment (1) and/or Fear:	The Cause (Column 2)	Affects Our: (Column 3)
Person, Place or Thing		☐ Self-Esteem ☐ Security ☐ Ambitions ☐ Personal Relations ☐ Sex Relations ☐ Pride/Shame ☐ Fear
Ask Ourselves: ** (AA 67.3) * (AA 62.2)	Putting out of our mind the wrong others had done, we resolutely looked for our own mistakes... We admitted our wrongs honestly...** **STEPS 4 and/or 10 - (Column 4)**	
Where had I been selfish, self-centred or self-seeking?**		
Where had I been dishonest?**		
Where had I been frightened?**		
For what had I been responsible?**		
What decisions did I make based on self that later placed me in a position to be hurt?*		
When in the past did I make this decision? * (Earliest memory)		
Where was I wrong,** what was my part?		

STEPS 6 & 7 – List of Character Defects

STEP 9 - Amends	STEP 8
	☐ Now ☐ Later ☐ Never

STEP 10

INVENTORY FORMS

Resentment (1) and/or Fear:	The Cause (Column 2)	Affects Our: (Column 3)
Person, Place or Thing		☐ Self-Esteem ☐ Security ☐ Ambitions ☐ Personal Relations ☐ Sex Relations ☐ Pride/Shame ☐ Fear
Ask Ourselves: ** (AA 67.3) * (AA 62.2)	Putting out of our mind the wrong others had done, we resolutely looked for our own mistakes... We admitted our wrongs honestly...** **STEPS 4** and/or **10 - (Column 4)**	
Where had I been selfish, self-centred or self-seeking?**		
Where had I been dishonest?**		
Where had I been frightened?**		
For what had I been responsible?**		
What decisions did I make based on self that later placed me in a position to be hurt?*		
When in the past did I make this decision? * (Earliest memory)		
Where was I wrong,** what was my part?		

STEPS 6 & 7 – List of Character Defects		

STEP 9 - Amends		STEP 8
		☐ Now ☐ Later ☐ Never

COLUMN WORK

Resentment (1) and/or Fear:	The Cause (Column 2)	Affects Our: (Column 3)
Person, Place or Thing		☐ Self-Esteem ☐ Security ☐ Ambitions ☐ Personal Relations ☐ Sex Relations ☐ Pride/Shame ☐ Fear
Ask Ourselves: ** (AA 67.3) * (AA 62.2)	Putting out of our mind the wrong others had done, we resolutely looked for our own mistakes... We admitted our wrongs honestly...** STEPS 4 and/or 10 - (Column 4)	
Where had I been selfish, self-centred or self-seeking?**		
Where had I been dishonest?**		
Where had I been frightened?**		
For what had I been responsible?**		
What decisions did I make based on self that later placed me in a position to be hurt?*		
When in the past did I make this decision? * (Earliest memory)		
Where was I wrong,** what was my part?		

STEPS 6 & 7 – List of Character Defects			

STEP 9 - Amends	STEP 8
	☐ Now ☐ Later ☐ Never

STEP 10

INVENTORY FORMS

Resentment (1) and/or Fear:	The Cause (Column 2)	Affects Our: (Column 3)
Person, Place or Thing		☐ Self-Esteem ☐ Security ☐ Ambitions ☐ Personal Relations ☐ Sex Relations ☐ Pride/Shame ☐ Fear
Ask Ourselves: ** (AA 67.3) * (AA 62.2)	Putting out of our mind the wrong others had done, we resolutely looked for our own mistakes... We admitted our wrongs honestly...** **STEPS 4** and/or **10 - (Column 4)**	
Where had I been selfish, self-centred or self-seeking?**		
Where had I been dishonest?**		
Where had I been frightened?**		
For what had I been responsible?**		
What decisions did I make based on self that later placed me in a position to be hurt?*		
When in the past did I make this decision? * (Earliest memory)		
Where was I wrong,** what was my part?		

STEPS 6 & 7 – List of Character Defects

STEP 9 - Amends	STEP 8
	☐ Now ☐ Later ☐ Never

COLUMN WORK

Resentment (1) and/or Fear:	The Cause (Column 2)	Affects Our: (Column 3)
Person, Place or Thing		☐ Self-Esteem ☐ Security ☐ Ambitions ☐ Personal Relations ☐ Sex Relations ☐ Pride/Shame ☐ Fear
Ask Ourselves: ** (AA 67.3) * (AA 62.2)	Putting out of our mind the wrong others had done, we resolutely looked for our own mistakes... We admitted our wrongs honestly...** **STEPS 4 and/or 10 - (Column 4)**	
Where had I been selfish, self-centred or self-seeking?**		
Where had I been dishonest?**		
Where had I been frightened?**		
For what had I been responsible?**		
What decisions did I make based on self that later placed me in a position to be hurt?*		
When in the past did I make this decision? * (Earliest memory)		
Where was I wrong,** what was my part?		

STEPS 6 & 7 – List of Character Defects

STEP 9 - Amends	STEP 8
	☐ Now ☐ Later ☐ Never

STEP 10

INVENTORY FORMS

Resentment (1) and/or Fear:	The Cause (Column 2)	Affects Our: (Column 3)
Person, Place or Thing		☐ Self-Esteem ☐ Security ☐ Ambitions ☐ Personal Relations ☐ Sex Relations ☐ Pride/Shame ☐ Fear
Ask Ourselves: ** (AA 67.3) * (AA 62.2)	Putting out of our mind the wrong others had done, we resolutely looked for our own mistakes... We admitted our wrongs honestly...** **STEPS 4 and/or 10 - (Column 4)**	
Where had I been selfish, self-centred or self-seeking?**		
Where had I been dishonest?**		
Where had I been frightened?**		
For what had I been responsible?**		
What decisions did I make based on self that later placed me in a position to be hurt?*		
When in the past did I make this decision? * (Earliest memory)		
Where was I wrong,** what was my part?		

STEPS 6 & 7 – List of Character Defects

STEP 9 - Amends		STEP 8
		☐ Now ☐ Later ☐ Never

COLUMN WORK

Resentment (1) and/or Fear:	The Cause (Column 2)	Affects Our: (Column 3)
Person, Place or Thing		☐ Self-Esteem ☐ Security ☐ Ambitions ☐ Personal Relations ☐ Sex Relations ☐ Pride/Shame ☐ Fear
Ask Ourselves: ** (AA 67.3) * (AA 62.2)	Putting out of our mind the wrong others had done, we resolutely looked for our own mistakes... We admitted our wrongs honestly...** **STEPS 4 and/or 10 - (Column 4)**	
Where had I been selfish, self-centred or self-seeking?**		
Where had I been dishonest?**		
Where had I been frightened?**		
For what had I been responsible?**		
What decisions did I make based on self that later placed me in a position to be hurt?*		
When in the past did I make this decision? * (Earliest memory)		
Where was I wrong,** what was my part?		

STEPS 6 & 7 – List of Character Defects				

STEP 9 - Amends	STEP 8
	☐ Now ☐ Later ☐ Never

STEP 10

INVENTORY FORMS

Resentment (1) and/or Fear:	The Cause (Column 2)	Affects Our: (Column 3)
Person, Place or Thing		☐ Self-Esteem ☐ Security ☐ Ambitions ☐ Personal Relations ☐ Sex Relations ☐ Pride/Shame ☐ Fear
Ask Ourselves: ** (AA 67.3) * (AA 62.2)	Putting out of our mind the wrong others had done, we resolutely looked for our own mistakes… We admitted our wrongs honestly…** **STEPS 4 and/or 10 - (Column 4)**	
Where had I been selfish, self-centred or self-seeking?**		
Where had I been dishonest?**		
Where had I been frightened?**		
For what had I been responsible?**		
What decisions did I make based on self that later placed me in a position to be hurt?*		
When in the past did I make this decision? * (Earliest memory)		
Where was I wrong,** what was my part?		

STEPS 6 & 7 – List of Character Defects				

STEP 9 - Amends	STEP 8
	☐ Now ☐ Later ☐ Never

COLUMN WORK

Resentment (1) and/or Fear:	The Cause (Column 2)	Affects Our: (Column 3)
Person, Place or Thing		☐ Self-Esteem ☐ Security ☐ Ambitions ☐ Personal Relations ☐ Sex Relations ☐ Pride/Shame ☐ Fear
Ask Ourselves: ** (AA 67.3) * (AA 62.2)	Putting out of our mind the wrong others had done, we resolutely looked for our own mistakes… We admitted our wrongs honestly…** **STEPS 4 and/or 10 - (Column 4)**	
Where had I been selfish, self-centred or self-seeking?**		
Where had I been dishonest?**		
Where had I been frightened?**		
For what had I been responsible?**		
What decisions did I make based on self that later placed me in a position to be hurt?*		
When in the past did I make this decision? * (Earliest memory)		
Where was I wrong,** what was my part?		

STEPS 6 & 7 – List of Character Defects				

STEP 9 - Amends	STEP 8
	☐ Now ☐ Later ☐ Never

STEP 10

INVENTORY FORMS

Resentment (1) and/or Fear:	The Cause (Column 2)	Affects Our: (Column 3)
Person, Place or Thing		☐ Self-Esteem ☐ Security ☐ Ambitions ☐ Personal Relations ☐ Sex Relations ☐ Pride/Shame ☐ Fear
Ask Ourselves: ** (AA 67.3) * (AA 62.2)	Putting out of our mind the wrong others had done, we resolutely looked for our own mistakes... We admitted our wrongs honestly... ** **STEPS 4 and/or 10 - (Column 4)**	
Where had I been selfish, self-centred or self-seeking?**		
Where had I been dishonest?**		
Where had I been frightened?**		
For what had I been responsible?**		
What decisions did I make based on self that later placed me in a position to be hurt?*		
When in the past did I make this decision? * (Earliest memory)		
Where was I wrong,** what was my part?		

STEPS 6 & 7 – List of Character Defects

STEP 9 - Amends	STEP 8
	☐ Now ☐ Later ☐ Never

COLUMN WORK

Resentment (1) and/or Fear:	The Cause (Column 2)	Affects Our: (Column 3)
Person, Place or Thing		☐ Self-Esteem ☐ Security ☐ Ambitions ☐ Personal Relations ☐ Sex Relations ☐ Pride/Shame ☐ Fear
Ask Ourselves: ** (AA 67.3) * (AA 62.2)	Putting out of our mind the wrong others had done, we resolutely looked for our own mistakes… We admitted our wrongs honestly…** **STEPS 4 and/or 10 - (Column 4)**	
Where had I been selfish, self-centred or self-seeking?**		
Where had I been dishonest?**		
Where had I been frightened?**		
For what had I been responsible?**		
What decisions did I make based on self that later placed me in a position to be hurt?*		
When in the past did I make this decision? * (Earliest memory)		
Where was I wrong,** what was my part?		

STEPS 6 & 7 – List of Character Defects

STEP 9 - Amends	STEP 8
	☐ Now ☐ Later ☐ Never

STEP 10

INVENTORY FORMS

Resentment (1) and/or Fear:	The Cause (Column 2)	Affects Our: (Column 3)
Person, Place or Thing		☐ Self-Esteem ☐ Security ☐ Ambitions ☐ Personal Relations ☐ Sex Relations ☐ Pride/Shame ☐ Fear
Ask Ourselves: ** (AA 67.3) * (AA 62.2)	Putting out of our mind the wrong others had done, we resolutely looked for our own mistakes… We admitted our wrongs honestly…** STEPS 4 and/or 10 - (Column 4)	
Where had I been selfish, self-centred or self-seeking?**		
Where had I been dishonest?**		
Where had I been frightened?**		
For what had I been responsible?**		
What decisions did I make based on self that later placed me in a position to be hurt?*		
When in the past did I make this decision? * (Earliest memory)		
Where was I wrong,** what was my part?		

STEPS 6 & 7 – List of Character Defects

STEP 9 - Amends	STEP 8
	☐ Now ☐ Later ☐ Never

COLUMN WORK

Resentment and/or Fear: (1)	The Cause (Column 2)	Affects Our: (Column 3)
Person, Place or Thing		☐ Self-Esteem ☐ Security ☐ Ambitions ☐ Personal Relations ☐ Sex Relations ☐ Pride/Shame ☐ Fear
Ask Ourselves: ** (AA 67.3) * (AA 62.2)	Putting out of our mind the wrong others had done, we resolutely looked for our own mistakes... We admitted our wrongs honestly...** **STEPS 4 and/or 10 - (Column 4)**	
Where had I been selfish, self-centred or self-seeking?**		
Where had I been dishonest?**		
Where had I been frightened?**		
For what had I been responsible?**		
What decisions did I make based on self that later placed me in a position to be hurt?*		
When in the past did I make this decision? * (Earliest memory)		
Where was I wrong,** what was my part?		

STEPS 6 & 7 – List of Character Defects

STEP 9 – Amends	STEP 8
	☐ Now ☐ Later ☐ Never

STEP 10

INVENTORY FORMS

Resentment (1) and/or Fear:	The Cause (Column 2)	Affects Our: (Column 3)
Person, Place or Thing		☐ Self-Esteem ☐ Security ☐ Ambitions ☐ Personal Relations ☐ Sex Relations ☐ Pride/Shame ☐ Fear
Ask Ourselves: ** (AA 67.3) * (AA 62.2)	Putting out of our mind the wrong others had done, we resolutely looked for our own mistakes… We admitted our wrongs honestly…** STEPS 4 and/or 10 - (Column 4)	
Where had I been selfish, self-centred or self-seeking?**		
Where had I been dishonest?**		
Where had I been frightened?**		
For what had I been responsible?**		
What decisions did I make based on self that later placed me in a position to be hurt?*		
When in the past did I make this decision? * (Earliest memory)		
Where was I wrong,** what was my part?		

STEPS 6 & 7 – List of Character Defects					

STEP 9 - Amends	STEP 8
	☐ Now ☐ Later ☐ Never

MAINTAINING THE PROMISES…DAILY

COLUMN WORK

Resentment (1) and/or Fear:	The Cause (Column 2)	Affects Our: (Column 3)
Person, Place or Thing		☐ Self-Esteem ☐ Security ☐ Ambitions ☐ Personal Relations ☐ Sex Relations ☐ Pride/Shame ☐ Fear
Ask Ourselves: ** (AA 67.3) * (AA 62.2)	Putting out of our mind the wrong others had done, we resolutely looked for our own mistakes… We admitted our wrongs honestly…** **STEPS 4 and/or 10 - (Column 4)**	
Where had I been selfish, self-centred or self-seeking?**		
Where had I been dishonest?**		
Where had I been frightened?**		
For what had I been responsible?**		
What decisions did I make based on self that later placed me in a position to be hurt?*		
When in the past did I make this decision? * (Earliest memory)		
Where was I wrong,** what was my part?		

STEPS 6 & 7 – List of Character Defects				

STEP 9 - Amends	STEP 8
	☐ Now ☐ Later ☐ Never

STEP 10

INVENTORY FORMS

Resentment (1) and/or Fear:	The Cause (Column 2)	Affects Our: (Column 3)
Person, Place or Thing		☐ Self-Esteem ☐ Security ☐ Ambitions ☐ Personal Relations ☐ Sex Relations ☐ Pride/Shame ☐ Fear
Ask Ourselves: ** (AA 67.3) * (AA 62.2)	Putting out of our mind the wrong others had done, we resolutely looked for our own mistakes... We admitted our wrongs honestly... ** **STEPS 4 and/or 10 - (Column 4)**	
Where had I been selfish, self-centred or self-seeking?**		
Where had I been dishonest?**		
Where had I been frightened?**		
For what had I been responsible?**		
What decisions did I make based on self that later placed me in a position to be hurt?*		
When in the past did I make this decision? * (Earliest memory)		
Where was I wrong,** what was my part?		

STEPS 6 & 7 – List of Character Defects

STEP 9 - Amends	STEP 8
	☐ Now ☐ Later ☐ Never

COLUMN WORK

Resentment (1) and/or Fear:	The Cause (Column 2)	Affects Our: (Column 3)
Person, Place or Thing		☐ Self-Esteem ☐ Security ☐ Ambitions ☐ Personal Relations ☐ Sex Relations ☐ Pride/Shame ☐ Fear
Ask Ourselves: ** (AA 67.3) * (AA 62.2)	Putting out of our mind the wrong others had done, we resolutely looked for our own mistakes… We admitted our wrongs honestly…** STEPS 4 and/or 10 - (Column 4)	
Where had I been selfish, self-centred or self-seeking?**		
Where had I been dishonest?**		
Where had I been frightened?**		
For what had I been responsible?**		
What decisions did I make based on self that later placed me in a position to be hurt?*		
When in the past did I make this decision? * (Earliest memory)		
Where was I wrong,** what was my part?		

STEPS 6 & 7 – List of Character Defects				

STEP 9 - Amends	STEP 8
	☐ Now ☐ Later ☐ Never

STEP 10

INVENTORY FORMS

Resentment (1) and/or Fear:	The Cause (Column 2)	Affects Our: (Column 3)
Person, Place or Thing		☐ Self-Esteem ☐ Security ☐ Ambitions ☐ Personal Relations ☐ Sex Relations ☐ Pride/Shame ☐ Fear
Ask Ourselves: ** (AA 67.3) * (AA 62.2)	Putting out of our mind the wrong others had done, we resolutely looked for our own mistakes... We admitted our wrongs honestly... ** **STEPS 4** and/or **10** - **(Column 4)**	
Where had I been selfish, self-centred or self-seeking?**		
Where had I been dishonest?**		
Where had I been frightened?**		
For what had I been responsible?**		
What decisions did I make based on self that later placed me in a position to be hurt?*		
When in the past did I make this decision? * (Earliest memory)		
Where was I wrong,** what was my part?		

STEPS 6 & 7 – List of Character Defects				

STEP 9 - Amends	STEP 8
	☐ Now ☐ Later ☐ Never

MAINTAINING THE PROMISES...DAILY

COLUMN WORK

Resentment (1) and/or Fear:	The Cause (Column 2)	Affects Our: (Column 3)
Person, Place or Thing		☐ Self-Esteem ☐ Security ☐ Ambitions ☐ Personal Relations ☐ Sex Relations ☐ Pride/Shame ☐ Fear
Ask Ourselves: ** (AA 67.3) * (AA 62.2)	Putting out of our mind the wrong others had done, we resolutely looked for our own mistakes... We admitted our wrongs honestly...** STEPS 4 and/or 10 - (Column 4)	
Where had I been selfish, self-centred or self-seeking?**		
Where had I been dishonest?**		
Where had I been frightened?**		
For what had I been responsible?**		
What decisions did I make based on self that later placed me in a position to be hurt?*		
When in the past did I make this decision? * (Earliest memory)		
Where was I wrong,** what was my part?		

STEPS 6 & 7 – List of Character Defects				

STEP 9 - Amends	STEP 8
	☐ Now ☐ Later ☐ Never

STEP 10

INVENTORY FORMS

Resentment (1) and/or Fear:	The Cause (Column 2)	Affects Our: (Column 3)
Person, Place or Thing		☐ Self-Esteem ☐ Security ☐ Ambitions ☐ Personal Relations ☐ Sex Relations ☐ Pride/Shame ☐ Fear
Ask Ourselves: ** (AA 67.3) * (AA 62.2)	Putting out of our mind the wrong others had done, we resolutely looked for our own mistakes… We admitted our wrongs honestly…** **STEPS 4** and/or **10 - (Column 4)**	
Where had I been selfish, self-centred or self-seeking?**		
Where had I been dishonest?**		
Where had I been frightened?**		
For what had I been responsible?**		
What decisions did I make based on self that later placed me in a position to be hurt?*		
When in the past did I make this decision? * (Earliest memory)		
Where was I wrong,** what was my part?		

STEPS 6 & 7 – List of Character Defects

STEP 9 - Amends	STEP 8
	☐ Now ☐ Later ☐ Never

COLUMN WORK

Resentment (1) and/or Fear:	The Cause (Column 2)	Affects Our: (Column 3)
Person, Place or Thing		☐ Self-Esteem ☐ Security ☐ Ambitions ☐ Personal Relations ☐ Sex Relations ☐ Pride/Shame ☐ Fear
Ask Ourselves: ** (AA 67.3) * (AA 62.2)	Putting out of our mind the wrong others had done, we resolutely looked for our own mistakes... We admitted our wrongs honestly...** **STEPS 4 and/or 10 - (Column 4)**	
Where had I been selfish, self-centred or self-seeking?**		
Where had I been dishonest?**		
Where had I been frightened?**		
For what had I been responsible?**		
What decisions did I make based on self that later placed me in a position to be hurt?*		
When in the past did I make this decision? * (Earliest memory)		
Where was I wrong,** what was my part?		

STEPS 6 & 7 – List of Character Defects

STEP 9 - Amends	**STEP 8**
	☐ Now ☐ Later ☐ Never

STEP 10

INVENTORY FORMS

Resentment (1) and/or Fear:	The Cause (Column 2)	Affects Our: (Column 3)
Person, Place or Thing		☐ Self-Esteem ☐ Security ☐ Ambitions ☐ Personal Relations ☐ Sex Relations ☐ Pride/Shame ☐ Fear
Ask Ourselves: ** (AA 67.3) * (AA 62.2)	Putting out of our mind the wrong others had done, we resolutely looked for our own mistakes… We admitted our wrongs honestly…** **STEPS 4 and/or 10 - (Column 4)**	
Where had I been selfish, self-centred or self-seeking?**		
Where had I been dishonest?**		
Where had I been frightened?**		
For what had I been responsible?**		
What decisions did I make based on self that later placed me in a position to be hurt?*		
When in the past did I make this decision? * (Earliest memory)		
Where was I wrong,** what was my part?		
STEPS 6 & 7 – List of Character Defects					
STEP 9 - Amends		**STEP 8**
		☐ Now ☐ Later ☐ Never

COLUMN WORK

Resentment (1) and/or Fear:	The Cause (Column 2)	Affects Our: (Column 3)
Person, Place or Thing		☐ Self-Esteem ☐ Security ☐ Ambitions ☐ Personal Relations ☐ Sex Relations ☐ Pride/Shame ☐ Fear
Ask Ourselves: ** (AA 67.3) * (AA 62.2)	Putting out of our mind the wrong others had done, we resolutely looked for our own mistakes... We admitted our wrongs honestly...** **STEPS 4 and/or 10 - (Column 4)**	
Where had I been selfish, self-centred or self-seeking?**		
Where had I been dishonest?**		
Where had I been frightened?**		
For what had I been responsible?**		
What decisions did I make based on self that later placed me in a position to be hurt?*		
When in the past did I make this decision? * (Earliest memory)		
Where was I wrong,** what was my part?		

STEPS 6 & 7 – List of Character Defects

STEP 9 - Amends	STEP 8
	☐ Now ☐ Later ☐ Never

STEP 10

INVENTORY FORMS

Resentment (1) and/or Fear:	The Cause (Column 2)	Affects Our: (Column 3)
Person, Place or Thing		☐ Self-Esteem ☐ Security ☐ Ambitions ☐ Personal Relations ☐ Sex Relations ☐ Pride/Shame ☐ Fear
Ask Ourselves: ** (AA 67.3) * (AA 62.2)	Putting out of our mind the wrong others had done, we resolutely looked for our own mistakes... We admitted our wrongs honestly...** **STEPS 4 and/or 10 - (Column 4)**	
Where had I been selfish, self-centred or self-seeking?**		
Where had I been dishonest?**		
Where had I been frightened?**		
For what had I been responsible?**		
What decisions did I make based on self that later placed me in a position to be hurt?*		
When in the past did I make this decision? * (Earliest memory)		
Where was I wrong,** what was my part?		

STEPS 6 & 7 – List of Character Defects				

STEP 9 - Amends	STEP 8
	☐ Now ☐ Later ☐ Never

470 MAINTAINING THE PROMISES...DAILY

COLUMN WORK

Resentment (1) and/or Fear:	The Cause (Column 2)	Affects Our: (Column 3)
Person, Place or Thing		☐ Self-Esteem ☐ Security ☐ Ambitions ☐ Personal Relations ☐ Sex Relations ☐ Pride/Shame ☐ Fear
Ask Ourselves: ** (AA 67.3) * (AA 62.2)	Putting out of our mind the wrong others had done, we resolutely looked for our own mistakes... We admitted our wrongs honestly...** STEPS 4 and/or 10 - (Column 4)	
Where had I been selfish, self-centred or self-seeking?**		
Where had I been dishonest?**		
Where had I been frightened?**		
For what had I been responsible?**		
What decisions did I make based on self that later placed me in a position to be hurt?*		
When in the past did I make this decision? * (Earliest memory)		
Where was I wrong,** what was my part?		

STEPS 6 & 7 – List of Character Defects				

STEP 9 - Amends	STEP 8
	☐ Now ☐ Later ☐ Never

INVENTORY FORMS

Resentment (1) and/or Fear:	The Cause (Column 2)	Affects Our: (Column 3)
Person, Place or Thing		☐ Self-Esteem ☐ Security ☐ Ambitions ☐ Personal Relations ☐ Sex Relations ☐ Pride/Shame ☐ Fear
Ask Ourselves: ** (AA 67.3) * (AA 62.2)	Putting out of our mind the wrong others had done, we resolutely looked for our own mistakes… We admitted our wrongs honestly…** **STEPS 4** and/or **10 - (Column 4)**	
Where had I been selfish, self-centred or self-seeking?**		
Where had I been dishonest?**		
Where had I been frightened?**		
For what had I been responsible?**		
What decisions did I make based on self that later placed me in a position to be hurt?*		
When in the past did I make this decision? * (Earliest memory)		
Where was I wrong,** what was my part?		

STEPS 6 & 7 – List of Character Defects				

STEP 9 - Amends	STEP 8
	☐ Now ☐ Later ☐ Never

MAINTAINING THE PROMISES…DAILY

COLUMN WORK

Resentment (1) and/or Fear:	The Cause (Column 2)	Affects Our: (Column 3)
Person, Place or Thing		☐ Self-Esteem ☐ Security ☐ Ambitions ☐ Personal Relations ☐ Sex Relations ☐ Pride/Shame ☐ Fear
Ask Ourselves: ** (AA 67.3) * (AA 62.2)	Putting out of our mind the wrong others had done, we resolutely looked for our own mistakes… We admitted our wrongs honestly…** **STEPS 4 and/or 10 - (Column 4)**	
Where had I been selfish, self-centred or self-seeking?**		
Where had I been dishonest?**		
Where had I been frightened?**		
For what had I been responsible?**		
What decisions did I make based on self that later placed me in a position to be hurt?*		
When in the past did I make this decision? * (Earliest memory)		
Where was I wrong,** what was my part?		

STEPS 6 & 7 – List of Character Defects

STEP 9 - Amends	STEP 8
	☐ Now ☐ Later ☐ Never

STEP 10

INVENTORY FORMS

Resentment (1) and/or Fear:	The Cause (Column 2)	Affects Our: (Column 3)
Person, Place or Thing		☐ Self-Esteem ☐ Security ☐ Ambitions ☐ Personal Relations ☐ Sex Relations ☐ Pride/Shame ☐ Fear
Ask Ourselves: ** (AA 67.3) * (AA 62.2)	Putting out of our mind the wrong others had done, we resolutely looked for our own mistakes... We admitted our wrongs honestly...** **STEPS 4 and/or 10 - (Column 4)**	
Where had I been selfish, self-centred or self-seeking?**		
Where had I been dishonest?**		
Where had I been frightened?**		
For what had I been responsible?**		
What decisions did I make based on self that later placed me in a position to be hurt?*		
When in the past did I make this decision? * (Earliest memory)		
Where was I wrong,** what was my part?		
STEPS 6 & 7 – List of Character Defects				

STEP 9 - Amends	STEP 8
	☐ Now ☐ Later ☐ Never

COLUMN WORK

Resentment (1) and/or Fear:	The Cause (Column 2)	Affects Our: (Column 3)
Person, Place or Thing		☐ Self-Esteem ☐ Security ☐ Ambitions ☐ Personal Relations ☐ Sex Relations ☐ Pride/Shame ☐ Fear
Ask Ourselves: ** (AA 67.3) * (AA 62.2)	Putting out of our mind the wrong others had done, we resolutely looked for our own mistakes… We admitted our wrongs honestly…** **STEPS 4 and/or 10 - (Column 4)**	
Where had I been selfish, self-centred or self-seeking?**		
Where had I been dishonest?**		
Where had I been frightened?**		
For what had I been responsible?**		
What decisions did I make based on self that later placed me in a position to be hurt?*		
When in the past did I make this decision? * (Earliest memory)		
Where was I wrong,** what was my part?		

STEPS 6 & 7 – List of Character Defects

STEP 9 - Amends		STEP 8
		☐ **Now** ☐ **Later** ☐ **Never**

INVENTORY FORMS

Resentment (1) and/or Fear:	The Cause (Column 2)	Affects Our: (Column 3)
Person, Place or Thing		☐ Self-Esteem ☐ Security ☐ Ambitions ☐ Personal Relations ☐ Sex Relations ☐ Pride/Shame ☐ Fear
Ask Ourselves: ** (AA 67.3) * (AA 62.2)	Putting out of our mind the wrong others had done, we resolutely looked for our own mistakes... We admitted our wrongs honestly...** STEPS 4 and/or 10 - (Column 4)	
Where had I been selfish, self-centred or self-seeking?**		
Where had I been dishonest?**		
Where had I been frightened?**		
For what had I been responsible?**		
What decisions did I make based on self that later placed me in a position to be hurt?*		
When in the past did I make this decision? * (Earliest memory)		
Where was I wrong,** what was my part?		

STEPS 6 & 7 – List of Character Defects

STEP 9 - Amends	STEP 8
	☐ Now ☐ Later ☐ Never

COLUMN WORK

Resentment (1) and/or Fear:	The Cause (Column 2)	Affects Our: (Column 3)
Person, Place or Thing		☐ Self-Esteem ☐ Security ☐ Ambitions ☐ Personal Relations ☐ Sex Relations ☐ Pride/Shame ☐ Fear
Ask Ourselves: ** (AA 67.3) * (AA 62.2)	Putting out of our mind the wrong others had done, we resolutely looked for our own mistakes... We admitted our wrongs honestly...** **STEPS 4 and/or 10 - (Column 4)**	
Where had I been selfish, self-centred or self-seeking?**		
Where had I been dishonest?**		
Where had I been frightened?**		
For what had I been responsible?**		
What decisions did I make based on self that later placed me in a position to be hurt?*		
When in the past did I make this decision? * (Earliest memory)		
Where was I wrong,** what was my part?		

STEPS 6 & 7 – List of Character Defects			

STEP 9 - Amends	STEP 8
	☐ Now ☐ Later ☐ Never

STEP 10

INVENTORY FORMS

Resentment (1) and/or Fear:	The Cause (Column 2)	Affects Our: (Column 3)
Person, Place or Thing		☐ Self-Esteem ☐ Security ☐ Ambitions ☐ Personal Relations ☐ Sex Relations ☐ Pride/Shame ☐ Fear
Ask Ourselves: ** (AA 67.3) * (AA 62.2)	Putting out of our mind the wrong others had done, we resolutely looked for our own mistakes... We admitted our wrongs honestly...** **STEPS 4** and/or **10 - (Column 4)**	
Where had I been selfish, self-centred or self-seeking?**		
Where had I been dishonest?**		
Where had I been frightened?**		
For what had I been responsible?**		
What decisions did I make based on self that later placed me in a position to be hurt?*		
When in the past did I make this decision? * (Earliest memory)		
Where was I wrong,** what was my part?		

STEPS 6 & 7 – List of Character Defects

STEP 9 - Amends	STEP 8
	☐ Now ☐ Later ☐ Never

COLUMN WORK

Resentment (1) and/or Fear:	The Cause (Column 2)	Affects Our: (Column 3)
Person, Place or Thing		☐ Self-Esteem ☐ Security ☐ Ambitions ☐ Personal Relations ☐ Sex Relations ☐ Pride/Shame ☐ Fear
Ask Ourselves: ** (AA 67.3) * (AA 62.2)	Putting out of our mind the wrong others had done, we resolutely looked for our own mistakes... We admitted our wrongs honestly...** **STEPS 4 and/or 10 - (Column 4)**	
Where had I been selfish, self-centred or self-seeking?**		
Where had I been dishonest?**		
Where had I been frightened?**		
For what had I been responsible?**		
What decisions did I make based on self that later placed me in a position to be hurt?*		
When in the past did I make this decision? * (Earliest memory)		
Where was I wrong,** what was my part?		

STEPS 6 & 7 – List of Character Defects

STEP 9 - Amends	STEP 8
	☐ Now ☐ Later ☐ Never

STEP 10

INVENTORY FORMS

Resentment (1) and/or Fear:	The Cause (Column 2)	Affects Our: (Column 3)
Person, Place or Thing		☐ Self-Esteem ☐ Security ☐ Ambitions ☐ Personal Relations ☐ Sex Relations ☐ Pride/Shame ☐ Fear
Ask Ourselves: ** (AA 67.3) * (AA 62.2)	Putting out of our mind the wrong others had done, we resolutely looked for our own mistakes… We admitted our wrongs honestly… ** **STEPS 4** and/or **10 - (Column 4)**	
Where had I been selfish, self-centred or self-seeking?**		
Where had I been dishonest?**		
Where had I been frightened?**		
For what had I been responsible?**		
What decisions did I make based on self that later placed me in a position to be hurt?*		
When in the past did I make this decision? * (Earliest memory)		
Where was I wrong,** what was my part?		

STEPS 6 & 7 – List of Character Defects			

STEP 9 - Amends	STEP 8
	☐ Now ☐ Later ☐ Never

MAINTAINING THE PROMISES…DAILY

COLUMN WORK

Resentment (1) and/or Fear:	The Cause (Column 2)	Affects Our: (Column 3)
Person, Place or Thing		☐ Self-Esteem ☐ Security ☐ Ambitions ☐ Personal Relations ☐ Sex Relations ☐ Pride/Shame ☐ Fear
Ask Ourselves: ** (AA 67.3) * (AA 62.2)	Putting out of our mind the wrong others had done, we resolutely looked for our own mistakes… We admitted our wrongs honestly…** **STEPS 4 and/or 10 - (Column 4)**	
Where had I been selfish, self-centred or self-seeking?**		
Where had I been dishonest?**		
Where had I been frightened?**		
For what had I been responsible?**		
What decisions did I make based on self that later placed me in a position to be hurt?*		
When in the past did I make this decision? * (Earliest memory)		
Where was I wrong,** what was my part?		

STEPS 6 & 7 – List of Character Defects				

STEP 9 - Amends		STEP 8
		☐ Now ☐ Later ☐ Never

STEP 10

INVENTORY FORMS

Resentment (1) and/or Fear:	The Cause (Column 2)	Affects Our: (Column 3)
Person, Place or Thing		☐ Self-Esteem ☐ Security ☐ Ambitions ☐ Personal Relations ☐ Sex Relations ☐ Pride/Shame ☐ Fear
Ask Ourselves: ** (AA 67.3) * (AA 62.2)	Putting out of our mind the wrong others had done, we resolutely looked for our own mistakes... We admitted our wrongs honestly...** **STEPS 4** and/or **10** - **(Column 4)**	
Where had I been selfish, self-centred or self-seeking?**		
Where had I been dishonest?**		
Where had I been frightened?**		
For what had I been responsible?**		
What decisions did I make based on self that later placed me in a position to be hurt?*		
When in the past did I make this decision? * (Earliest memory)		
Where was I wrong,** what was my part?		

STEPS 6 & 7 – List of Character Defects			

STEP 9 - Amends	STEP 8
	☐ Now ☐ Later ☐ Never

COLUMN WORK

Resentment (1) and/or Fear:	The Cause (Column 2)	Affects Our: (Column 3)
Person, Place or Thing		☐ Self-Esteem ☐ Security ☐ Ambitions ☐ Personal Relations ☐ Sex Relations ☐ Pride/Shame ☐ Fear
Ask Ourselves: ** (AA 67.3) * (AA 62.2)	Putting out of our mind the wrong others had done, we resolutely looked for our own mistakes... We admitted our wrongs honestly...** **STEPS 4 and/or 10 - (Column 4)**	
Where had I been selfish, self-centred or self-seeking?**		
Where had I been dishonest?**		
Where had I been frightened?**		
For what had I been responsible?**		
What decisions did I make based on self that later placed me in a position to be hurt?*		
When in the past did I make this decision? * (Earliest memory)		
Where was I wrong,** what was my part?		

STEPS 6 & 7 – List of Character Defects			

STEP 9 - Amends	STEP 8
	☐ Now ☐ Later ☐ Never

STEP 10

INVENTORY FORMS

Resentment (1) and/or Fear:	The Cause (Column 2)	Affects Our: (Column 3)
Person, Place or Thing		☐ Self-Esteem ☐ Security ☐ Ambitions ☐ Personal Relations ☐ Sex Relations ☐ Pride/Shame ☐ Fear
Ask Ourselves: ** (AA 67.3) * (AA 62.2)	Putting out of our mind the wrong others had done, we resolutely looked for our own mistakes… We admitted our wrongs honestly…** **STEPS 4** and/or **10 - (Column 4)**	
Where had I been selfish, self-centred or self-seeking?**		
Where had I been dishonest?**		
Where had I been frightened?**		
For what had I been responsible?**		
What decisions did I make based on self that later placed me in a position to be hurt?*		
When in the past did I make this decision? * (Earliest memory)		
Where was I wrong,** what was my part?		

STEPS 6 & 7 – List of Character Defects				

STEP 9 - Amends	STEP 8
	☐ Now ☐ Later ☐ Never

MAINTAINING THE PROMISES…DAILY

COLUMN WORK

Resentment (1) and/or Fear:	The Cause (Column 2)	Affects Our: (Column 3)
Person, Place or Thing		☐ Self-Esteem ☐ Security ☐ Ambitions ☐ Personal Relations ☐ Sex Relations ☐ Pride/Shame ☐ Fear
Ask Ourselves: ** (AA 67.3) * (AA 62.2)	Putting out of our mind the wrong others had done, we resolutely looked for our own mistakes... We admitted our wrongs honestly...** STEPS 4 and/or 10 - (Column 4)	
Where had I been selfish, self-centred or self-seeking?**		
Where had I been dishonest?**		
Where had I been frightened?**		
For what had I been responsible?**		
What decisions did I make based on self that later placed me in a position to be hurt?*		
When in the past did I make this decision? * (Earliest memory)		
Where was I wrong,** what was my part?		

STEPS 6 & 7 – List of Character Defects					

STEP 9 - Amends	STEP 8
	☐ Now ☐ Later ☐ Never

STEP 10

INVENTORY FORMS

Resentment (1) and/or Fear:	The Cause (Column 2)	Affects Our: (Column 3)
Person, Place or Thing		☐ Self-Esteem ☐ Security ☐ Ambitions ☐ Personal Relations ☐ Sex Relations ☐ Pride/Shame ☐ Fear
Ask Ourselves: ** (AA 67.3) * (AA 62.2)	Putting out of our mind the wrong others had done, we resolutely looked for our own mistakes... We admitted our wrongs honestly...** **STEPS 4** and/or **10 - (Column 4)**	
Where had I been selfish, self-centred or self-seeking?**		
Where had I been dishonest?**		
Where had I been frightened?**		
For what had I been responsible?**		
What decisions did I make based on self that later placed me in a position to be hurt?*		
When in the past did I make this decision? * (Earliest memory)		
Where was I wrong,** what was my part?		

STEPS 6 & 7 – List of Character Defects

STEP 9 - Amends		STEP 8
		☐ Now ☐ Later ☐ Never

COLUMN WORK

Resentment (1) and/or Fear:	The Cause (Column 2)	Affects Our: (Column 3)
Person, Place or Thing		☐ Self-Esteem ☐ Security ☐ Ambitions ☐ Personal Relations ☐ Sex Relations ☐ Pride/Shame ☐ Fear
Ask Ourselves: ** (AA 67.3) * (AA 62.2)	Putting out of our mind the wrong others had done, we resolutely looked for our own mistakes… We admitted our wrongs honestly…** **STEPS 4 and/or 10 - (Column 4)**	
Where had I been selfish, self-centred or self-seeking?**		
Where had I been dishonest?**		
Where had I been frightened?**		
For what had I been responsible?**		
What decisions did I make based on self that later placed me in a position to be hurt?*		
When in the past did I make this decision? * (Earliest memory)		
Where was I wrong,** what was my part?		
STEPS 6 & 7 – List of Character Defects		
---	---	---	---	---

STEP 9 - Amends	STEP 8
	☐ Now ☐ Later ☐ Never

STEP 10

INVENTORY FORMS

Resentment (1) and/or Fear:	The Cause (Column 2)	Affects Our: (Column 3)
Person, Place or Thing		☐ Self-Esteem ☐ Security ☐ Ambitions ☐ Personal Relations ☐ Sex Relations ☐ Pride/Shame ☐ Fear
Ask Ourselves: ** (AA 67.3) * (AA 62.2)	Putting out of our mind the wrong others had done, we resolutely looked for our own mistakes… We admitted our wrongs honestly… ** **STEPS 4 and/or 10 - (Column 4)**	
Where had I been selfish, self-centred or self-seeking?**		
Where had I been dishonest?**		
Where had I been frightened?**		
For what had I been responsible?**		
What decisions did I make based on self that later placed me in a position to be hurt?*		
When in the past did I make this decision? * (Earliest memory)		
Where was I wrong,** what was my part?		

STEPS 6 & 7 – List of Character Defects

STEP 9 - Amends		STEP 8
		☐ Now ☐ Later ☐ Never

COLUMN WORK

Resentment and/or Fear: (1)	The Cause (Column 2)	Affects Our: (Column 3)
Person, Place or Thing		☐ Self-Esteem ☐ Security ☐ Ambitions ☐ Personal Relations ☐ Sex Relations ☐ Pride/Shame ☐ Fear
Ask Ourselves: ** (AA 67.3) * (AA 62.2)	Putting out of our mind the wrong others had done, we resolutely looked for our own mistakes... We admitted our wrongs honestly...** STEPS 4 and/or 10 - (Column 4)	
Where had I been selfish, self-centred or self-seeking?**		
Where had I been dishonest?**		
Where had I been frightened?**		
For what had I been responsible?**		
What decisions did I make based on self that later placed me in a position to be hurt?*		
When in the past did I make this decision? * (Earliest memory)		
Where was I wrong,** what was my part?		
STEPS 6 & 7 – List of Character Defects		

STEP 9 - Amends	STEP 8
	☐ Now ☐ Later ☐ Never

STEP 10

INVENTORY FORMS

Resentment (1) and/or Fear:	The Cause (Column 2)	Affects Our: (Column 3)
Person, Place or Thing		☐ Self-Esteem ☐ Security ☐ Ambitions ☐ Personal Relations ☐ Sex Relations ☐ Pride/Shame ☐ Fear
Ask Ourselves: ** (AA 67.3) * (AA 62.2)	Putting out of our mind the wrong others had done, we resolutely looked for our own mistakes… We admitted our wrongs honestly…** **STEPS 4** and/or **10** - **(Column 4)**	
Where had I been selfish, self-centred or self-seeking?**		
Where had I been dishonest?**		
Where had I been frightened?**		
For what had I been responsible?**		
What decisions did I make based on self that later placed me in a position to be hurt?*		
When in the past did I make this decision? * (Earliest memory)		
Where was I wrong,** what was my part?		

STEPS 6 & 7 – List of Character Defects				

STEP 9 - Amends	STEP 8
	☐ Now ☐ Later ☐ Never

COLUMN WORK

Resentment (1) and/or Fear:	The Cause (Column 2)	Affects Our: (Column 3)
Person, Place or Thing		☐ Self-Esteem ☐ Security ☐ Ambitions ☐ Personal Relations ☐ Sex Relations ☐ Pride/Shame ☐ Fear
Ask Ourselves: ** (AA 67.3) * (AA 62.2)	Putting out of our mind the wrong others had done, we resolutely looked for our own mistakes... We admitted our wrongs honestly...** **STEPS 4 and/or 10 - (Column 4)**	
Where had I been selfish, self-centred or self-seeking?**		
Where had I been dishonest?**		
Where had I been frightened?**		
For what had I been responsible?**		
What decisions did I make based on self that later placed me in a position to be hurt?*		
When in the past did I make this decision? * (Earliest memory)		
Where was I wrong,** what was my part?		

STEPS 6 & 7 – List of Character Defects

STEP 9 - Amends	STEP 8
	☐ Now ☐ Later ☐ Never

STEP 10

INVENTORY FORMS

Resentment (1) and/or Fear:	The Cause (Column 2)	Affects Our: (Column 3)
Person, Place or Thing		☐ Self-Esteem ☐ Security ☐ Ambitions ☐ Personal Relations ☐ Sex Relations ☐ Pride/Shame ☐ Fear
Ask Ourselves: ** (AA 67.3) * (AA 62.2)	Putting out of our mind the wrong others had done, we resolutely looked for our own mistakes... We admitted our wrongs honestly...** **STEPS 4 and/or 10 - (Column 4)**	
Where had I been selfish, self-centred or self-seeking?**		
Where had I been dishonest?**		
Where had I been frightened?**		
For what had I been responsible?**		
What decisions did I make based on self that later placed me in a position to be hurt?*		
When in the past did I make this decision? * (Earliest memory)		
Where was I wrong,** what was my part?		
STEPS 6 & 7 – List of Character Defects		
STEP 9 - Amends		**STEP 8**
		☐ Now ☐ Later ☐ Never

COLUMN WORK

Resentment (1) and/or Fear:	The Cause (Column 2)	Affects Our: (Column 3)
Person, Place or Thing		☐ Self-Esteem ☐ Security ☐ Ambitions ☐ Personal Relations ☐ Sex Relations ☐ Pride/Shame ☐ Fear

Ask Ourselves: ** (AA 67.3) * (AA 62.2)	Putting out of our mind the wrong others had done, we resolutely looked for our own mistakes... We admitted our wrongs honestly...** STEPS 4 and/or 10 - (Column 4)
Where had I been selfish, self-centred or self-seeking?**	
Where had I been dishonest?**	
Where had I been frightened?**	
For what had I been responsible?**	
What decisions did I make based on self that later placed me in a position to be hurt?*	
When in the past did I make this decision? * (Earliest memory)	
Where was I wrong,** what was my part?	

STEPS 6 & 7 – List of Character Defects

STEP 9 - Amends	STEP 8
	☐ Now ☐ Later ☐ Never

INVENTORY FORMS

Resentment (1) and/or Fear:	The Cause (Column 2)	Affects Our: (Column 3)
Person, Place or Thing		☐ Self-Esteem ☐ Security ☐ Ambitions ☐ Personal Relations ☐ Sex Relations ☐ Pride/Shame ☐ Fear
Ask Ourselves: ** (AA 67.3) * (AA 62.2)	Putting out of our mind the wrong others had done, we resolutely looked for our own mistakes... We admitted our wrongs honestly... ** **STEPS 4 and/or 10 - (Column 4)**	
Where had I been selfish, self-centred or self-seeking?**		
Where had I been dishonest?**		
Where had I been frightened?**		
For what had I been responsible?**		
What decisions did I make based on self that later placed me in a position to be hurt?*		
When in the past did I make this decision? * (Earliest memory)		
Where was I wrong,** what was my part?		

STEPS 6 & 7 – List of Character Defects			

STEP 9 - Amends	STEP 8
	☐ Now ☐ Later ☐ Never

COLUMN WORK

Resentment (1) and/or Fear:	The Cause (Column 2)	Affects Our: (Column 3)
Person, Place or Thing		☐ Self-Esteem ☐ Security ☐ Ambitions ☐ Personal Relations ☐ Sex Relations ☐ Pride/Shame ☐ Fear
Ask Ourselves: ** (AA 67.3) * (AA 62.2)	Putting out of our mind the wrong others had done, we resolutely looked for our own mistakes… We admitted our wrongs honestly…** **STEPS 4 and/or 10 - (Column 4)**	
Where had I been selfish, self-centred or self-seeking?**		
Where had I been dishonest?**		
Where had I been frightened?**		
For what had I been responsible?**		
What decisions did I make based on self that later placed me in a position to be hurt?*		
When in the past did I make this decision? * (Earliest memory)		
Where was I wrong,** what was my part?		

STEPS 6 & 7 – List of Character Defects

STEP 9 - Amends | **STEP 8**

	☐ Now
	☐ Later
	☐ Never

STEP 10

INVENTORY FORMS

Resentment (1) and/or Fear:	The Cause (Column 2)	Affects Our: (Column 3)
Person, Place or Thing		☐ Self-Esteem ☐ Security ☐ Ambitions ☐ Personal Relations ☐ Sex Relations ☐ Pride/Shame ☐ Fear
Ask Ourselves: ** (AA 67.3) * (AA 62.2)	Putting out of our mind the wrong others had done, we resolutely looked for our own mistakes... We admitted our wrongs honestly...** **STEPS 4** and/or **10** - **(Column 4)**	
Where had I been selfish, self-centred or self-seeking?**		
Where had I been dishonest?**		
Where had I been frightened?**		
For what had I been responsible?**		
What decisions did I make based on self that later placed me in a position to be hurt?*		
When in the past did I make this decision? * (Earliest memory)		
Where was I wrong,** what was my part?		

STEPS 6 & 7 – List of Character Defects

STEP 9 - Amends	STEP 8
	☐ Now ☐ Later ☐ Never

496 MAINTAINING THE PROMISES...DAILY

COLUMN WORK

Resentment (1) and/or Fear:	The Cause (Column 2)	Affects Our: (Column 3)
Person, Place or Thing		☐ Self-Esteem ☐ Security ☐ Ambitions ☐ Personal Relations ☐ Sex Relations ☐ Pride/Shame ☐ Fear
Ask Ourselves: ** (AA 67.3) * (AA 62.2)	Putting out of our mind the wrong others had done, we resolutely looked for our own mistakes... We admitted our wrongs honestly... ** **STEPS 4 and/or 10 - (Column 4)**	
Where had I been selfish, self-centred or self-seeking?**		
Where had I been dishonest?**		
Where had I been frightened?**		
For what had I been responsible?**		
What decisions did I make based on self that later placed me in a position to be hurt?*		
When in the past did I make this decision? * (Earliest memory)		
Where was I wrong,** what was my part?		

STEPS 6 & 7 – List of Character Defects				

STEP 9 - Amends	STEP 8
	☐ Now ☐ Later ☐ Never

STEP 10

INVENTORY FORMS

Resentment (1) and/or Fear:	The Cause (Column 2)	Affects Our: (Column 3)
Person, Place or Thing		☐ Self-Esteem ☐ Security ☐ Ambitions ☐ Personal Relations ☐ Sex Relations ☐ Pride/Shame ☐ Fear
Ask Ourselves: ** (AA 67.3) * (AA 62.2)	Putting out of our mind the wrong others had done, we resolutely looked for our own mistakes... We admitted our wrongs honestly...** **STEPS 4 and/or 10 - (Column 4)**	
Where had I been selfish, self-centred or self-seeking?**		
Where had I been dishonest?**		
Where had I been frightened?**		
For what had I been responsible?**		
What decisions did I make based on self that later placed me in a position to be hurt?*		
When in the past did I make this decision? * (Earliest memory)		
Where was I wrong,** what was my part?		

STEPS 6 & 7 – List of Character Defects

STEP 9 - Amends	STEP 8
	☐ Now ☐ Later ☐ Never

COLUMN WORK

Resentment and/or Fear: (1)	The Cause (Column 2)	Affects Our: (Column 3)
Person, Place or Thing		☐ Self-Esteem ☐ Security ☐ Ambitions ☐ Personal Relations ☐ Sex Relations ☐ Pride/Shame ☐ Fear
Ask Ourselves: ** (AA 67:3) * (AA 62:2)	Putting out of our mind the wrong others had done, we resolutely looked for our own mistakes... We admitted our wrongs honestly...** **STEPS 4 and/or 10 - (Column 4)**	
Where had I been selfish, self-centred or self-seeking?**		
Where had I been dishonest?**		
Where had I been frightened?**		
For what had I been responsible?**		
What decisions did I make based on self that later placed me in a position to be hurt?*		
When in the past did I make this decision? * (Earliest memory)		
Where was I wrong,** what was my part?		

STEPS 6 & 7 – List of Character Defects

STEP 9 - Amends	STEP 8
	☐ Now ☐ Later ☐ Never

STEP 10

INVENTORY FORMS

Resentment (1) and/or Fear:	The Cause (Column 2)	Affects Our: (Column 3)
Person, Place or Thing		☐ Self-Esteem ☐ Security ☐ Ambitions ☐ Personal Relations ☐ Sex Relations ☐ Pride/Shame ☐ Fear
Ask Ourselves: ** (AA 67.3) * (AA 62.2)	Putting out of our mind the wrong others had done, we resolutely looked for our own mistakes... We admitted our wrongs honestly...** STEPS 4 and/or 10 - (Column 4)	
Where had I been selfish, self-centred or self-seeking?**		
Where had I been dishonest?**		
Where had I been frightened?**		
For what had I been responsible?**		
What decisions did I make based on self that later placed me in a position to be hurt?*		
When in the past did I make this decision? * (Earliest memory)		
Where was I wrong,** what was my part?		

STEPS 6 & 7 – List of Character Defects

STEP 9 - Amends	STEP 8
	☐ Now ☐ Later ☐ Never

COLUMN WORK

Resentment and/or Fear: (1)	The Cause (Column 2)	Affects Our: (Column 3)
Person, Place or Thing		☐ Self-Esteem ☐ Security ☐ Ambitions ☐ Personal Relations ☐ Sex Relations ☐ Pride/Shame ☐ Fear
Ask Ourselves: ** (AA 67.3) * (AA 62.2)	Putting out of our mind the wrong others had done, we resolutely looked for our own mistakes... We admitted our wrongs honestly...** **STEPS 4 and/or 10 - (Column 4)**	
Where had I been selfish, self-centred or self-seeking?**		
Where had I been dishonest?**		
Where had I been frightened?**		
For what had I been responsible?**		
What decisions did I make based on self that later placed me in a position to be hurt?*		
When in the past did I make this decision? * (Earliest memory)		
Where was I wrong,** what was my part?		

STEPS 6 & 7 – List of Character Defects

STEP 9 - Amends	STEP 8
	☐ Now ☐ Later ☐ Never

INVENTORY FORMS

Resentment (1) and/or Fear:	The Cause (Column 2)	Affects Our: (Column 3)
Person, Place or Thing		☐ Self-Esteem ☐ Security ☐ Ambitions ☐ Personal Relations ☐ Sex Relations ☐ Pride/Shame ☐ Fear
Ask Ourselves: ** (AA 67.3) * (AA 62.2)	Putting out of our mind the wrong others had done, we resolutely looked for our own mistakes… We admitted our wrongs honestly…** **STEPS 4** and/or **10** - **(Column 4)**	
Where had I been selfish, self-centred or self-seeking?**		
Where had I been dishonest?**		
Where had I been frightened?**		
For what had I been responsible?**		
What decisions did I make based on self that later placed me in a position to be hurt?*		
When in the past did I make this decision? * (Earliest memory)		
Where was I wrong,** what was my part?		

STEPS 6 & 7 – List of Character Defects

STEP 9 - Amends	STEP 8
	☐ Now ☐ Later ☐ Never

COLUMN WORK

Resentment (1) and/or Fear:	The Cause (Column 2)	Affects Our: (Column 3)
Person, Place or Thing		☐ Self-Esteem ☐ Security ☐ Ambitions ☐ Personal Relations ☐ Sex Relations ☐ Pride/Shame ☐ Fear
Ask Ourselves: ** (AA 67.3) * (AA 62.2)	Putting out of our mind the wrong others had done, we resolutely looked for our own mistakes... We admitted our wrongs honestly...** **STEPS 4 and/or 10 - (Column 4)**	
Where had I been selfish, self-centred or self-seeking?**		
Where had I been dishonest?**		
Where had I been frightened?**		
For what had I been responsible?**		
What decisions did I make based on self that later placed me in a position to be hurt?*		
When in the past did I make this decision? * (Earliest memory)		
Where was I wrong,** what was my part?		

STEPS 6 & 7 – List of Character Defects				

STEP 9 - Amends	STEP 8
	☐ Now ☐ Later ☐ Never

STEP 10

INVENTORY FORMS

Resentment (1) and/or Fear:	The Cause (Column 2)	Affects Our: (Column 3)
Person, Place or Thing		☐ Self-Esteem ☐ Security ☐ Ambitions ☐ Personal Relations ☐ Sex Relations ☐ Pride/Shame ☐ Fear
Ask Ourselves: ** (AA 67.3) * (AA 62.2)	Putting out of our mind the wrong others had done, we resolutely looked for our own mistakes... We admitted our wrongs honestly...** **STEPS 4 and/or 10 - (Column 4)**	
Where had I been selfish, self-centred or self-seeking?**		
Where had I been dishonest?**		
Where had I been frightened?**		
For what had I been responsible?**		
What decisions did I make based on self that later placed me in a position to be hurt?*		
When in the past did I make this decision? * (Earliest memory)		
Where was I wrong,** what was my part?		
STEPS 6 & 7 – List of Character Defects		
---	---	---	---	---

STEP 9 - Amends	STEP 8
	☐ Now ☐ Later ☐ Never

MAINTAINING THE PROMISES...DAILY

COLUMN WORK

Resentment (1) and/or Fear:	The Cause (Column 2)	Affects Our: (Column 3)
Person, Place or Thing		☐ Self-Esteem ☐ Security ☐ Ambitions ☐ Personal Relations ☐ Sex Relations ☐ Pride/Shame ☐ Fear
Ask Ourselves: ** (AA 67.3) * (AA 62.2)	Putting out of our mind the wrong others had done, we resolutely looked for our own mistakes… We admitted our wrongs honestly…** **STEPS 4 and/or 10 - (Column 4)**	
Where had I been selfish, self-centred or self-seeking?**		
Where had I been dishonest?**		
Where had I been frightened?**		
For what had I been responsible?**		
What decisions did I make based on self that later placed me in a position to be hurt?*		
When in the past did I make this decision? * (Earliest memory)		
Where was I wrong,** what was my part?		

STEPS 6 & 7 – List of Character Defects				

STEP 9 - Amends	STEP 8
	☐ Now ☐ Later ☐ Never

STEP 10

INVENTORY FORMS

Resentment (1) and/or Fear:	The Cause (Column 2)	Affects Our: (Column 3)
Person, Place or Thing		☐ Self-Esteem ☐ Security ☐ Ambitions ☐ Personal Relations ☐ Sex Relations ☐ Pride/Shame ☐ Fear
Ask Ourselves: ** (AA 67.3) * (AA 62.2)	Putting out of our mind the wrong others had done, we resolutely looked for our own mistakes... We admitted our wrongs honestly...** **STEPS 4** and/or **10** - **(Column 4)**	
Where had I been selfish, self-centred or self-seeking?**		
Where had I been dishonest?**		
Where had I been frightened?**		
For what had I been responsible?**		
What decisions did I make based on self that later placed me in a position to be hurt?*		
When in the past did I make this decision? * (Earliest memory)		
Where was I wrong,** what was my part?		
STEPS 6 & 7 – List of Character Defects		
STEP 9 - Amends		**STEP 8** ☐ Now ☐ Later ☐ Never

MAINTAINING THE PROMISES...DAILY

COLUMN WORK

Resentment (1) and/or Fear:	The Cause (Column 2)	Affects Our: (Column 3)
Person, Place or Thing		☐ Self-Esteem ☐ Security ☐ Ambitions ☐ Personal Relations ☐ Sex Relations ☐ Pride/Shame ☐ Fear
Ask Ourselves: ** (AA 67.3) * (AA 62.2)	Putting out of our mind the wrong others had done, we resolutely looked for our own mistakes… We admitted our wrongs honestly…** **STEPS 4 and/or 10 - (Column 4)**	
Where had I been selfish, self-centred or self-seeking?**		
Where had I been dishonest?**		
Where had I been frightened?**		
For what had I been responsible?**		
What decisions did I make based on self that later placed me in a position to be hurt?*		
When in the past did I make this decision? * (Earliest memory)		
Where was I wrong,** what was my part?		

STEPS 6 & 7 – List of Character Defects				

STEP 9 - Amends	STEP 8
	☐ Now ☐ Later ☐ Never

STEP 10

INVENTORY FORMS

Resentment (1) and/or Fear:	The Cause (Column 2)	Affects Our: (Column 3)
Person, Place or Thing		☐ Self-Esteem ☐ Security ☐ Ambitions ☐ Personal Relations ☐ Sex Relations ☐ Pride/Shame ☐ Fear
Ask Ourselves: ** (AA 67.3) * (AA 62.2)	Putting out of our mind the wrong others had done, we resolutely looked for our own mistakes... We admitted our wrongs honestly...** **STEPS 4 and/or 10 - (Column 4)**	
Where had I been selfish, self-centred or self-seeking?**		
Where had I been dishonest?**		
Where had I been frightened?**		
For what had I been responsible?**		
What decisions did I make based on self that later placed me in a position to be hurt?*		
When in the past did I make this decision? * (Earliest memory)		
Where was I wrong,** what was my part?		

STEPS 6 & 7 – List of Character Defects

STEP 9 - Amends	STEP 8
	☐ Now ☐ Later ☐ Never

MAINTAINING THE PROMISES...DAILY

COLUMN WORK

Resentment (1) and/or Fear:	The Cause (Column 2)	Affects Our: (Column 3)
Person, Place or Thing		☐ Self-Esteem ☐ Security ☐ Ambitions ☐ Personal Relations ☐ Sex Relations ☐ Pride/Shame ☐ Fear
Ask Ourselves: ** (AA 67.3) * (AA 62.2)	Putting out of our mind the wrong others had done, we resolutely looked for our own mistakes… We admitted our wrongs honestly…** STEPS 4 and/or 10 - (Column 4)	
Where had I been selfish, self-centred or self-seeking?**		
Where had I been dishonest?**		
Where had I been frightened?**		
For what had I been responsible?**		
What decisions did I make based on self that later placed me in a position to be hurt?*		
When in the past did I make this decision? * (Earliest memory)		
Where was I wrong,** what was my part?		

STEPS 6 & 7 – List of Character Defects				

STEP 9 - Amends	STEP 8
	☐ Now ☐ Later ☐ Never

STEP 10

INVENTORY FORMS

Resentment (1) and/or Fear:	The Cause (Column 2)	Affects Our: (Column 3)
Person, Place or Thing		☐ Self-Esteem ☐ Security ☐ Ambitions ☐ Personal Relations ☐ Sex Relations ☐ Pride/Shame ☐ Fear
Ask Ourselves: ** (AA 67.3) * (AA 62.2)	Putting out of our mind the wrong others had done, we resolutely looked for our own mistakes... We admitted our wrongs honestly...** **STEPS 4** and/or **10** - **(Column 4)**	
Where had I been selfish, self-centred or self-seeking?**		
Where had I been dishonest?**		
Where had I been frightened?**		
For what had I been responsible?**		
What decisions did I make based on self that later placed me in a position to be hurt?*		
When in the past did I make this decision? * (Earliest memory)		
Where was I wrong,** what was my part?		
STEPS 6 & 7 – List of Character Defects		
STEP 9 - Amends		**STEP 8**
		☐ Now ☐ Later ☐ Never

COLUMN WORK

Resentment (1) and/or Fear:	The Cause (Column 2)	Affects Our: (Column 3)
Person, Place or Thing		☐ Self-Esteem ☐ Security ☐ Ambitions ☐ Personal Relations ☐ Sex Relations ☐ Pride/Shame ☐ Fear
Ask Ourselves: ** (AA 67.3) * (AA 62.2)	Putting out of our mind the wrong others had done, we resolutely looked for our own mistakes… We admitted our wrongs honestly…** **STEPS 4 and/or 10 - (Column 4)**	
Where had I been selfish, self-centred or self-seeking?**		
Where had I been dishonest?**		
Where had I been frightened?**		
For what had I been responsible?**		
What decisions did I make based on self that later placed me in a position to be hurt?*		
When in the past did I make this decision? * (Earliest memory)		
Where was I wrong,** what was my part?		

STEPS 6 & 7 – List of Character Defects			

STEP 9 - Amends	STEP 8
	☐ Now ☐ Later ☐ Never

STEP 10

INVENTORY FORMS

Resentment (1) and/or Fear:	The Cause (Column 2)	Affects Our: (Column 3)
Person, Place or Thing		☐ Self-Esteem ☐ Security ☐ Ambitions ☐ Personal Relations ☐ Sex Relations ☐ Pride/Shame ☐ Fear
Ask Ourselves: ** (AA 67.3) * (AA 62.2)	Putting out of our mind the wrong others had done, we resolutely looked for our own mistakes… We admitted our wrongs honestly…** **STEPS 4** and/or **10** - **(Column 4)**	
Where had I been selfish, self-centred or self-seeking?**		
Where had I been dishonest?**		
Where had I been frightened?**		
For what had I been responsible?**		
What decisions did I make based on self that later placed me in a position to be hurt?*		
When in the past did I make this decision? * (Earliest memory)		
Where was I wrong,** what was my part?		

STEPS 6 & 7 – List of Character Defects			

STEP 9 - Amends	STEP 8
	☐ Now ☐ Later ☐ Never

COLUMN WORK

Resentment (1) and/or Fear:	The Cause (Column 2)	Affects Our: (Column 3)
Person, Place or Thing		☐ Self-Esteem ☐ Security ☐ Ambitions ☐ Personal Relations ☐ Sex Relations ☐ Pride/Shame ☐ Fear
Ask Ourselves: ** (AA 67.3) * (AA 62.2)	Putting out of our mind the wrong others had done, we resolutely looked for our own mistakes… We admitted our wrongs honestly…** **STEPS 4 and/or 10 - (Column 4)**	
Where had I been selfish, self-centred or self-seeking?**		
Where had I been dishonest?**		
Where had I been frightened?**		
For what had I been responsible?**		
What decisions did I make based on self that later placed me in a position to be hurt?*		
When in the past did I make this decision? * (Earliest memory)		
Where was I wrong,** what was my part?		

STEPS 6 & 7 – List of Character Defects				

STEP 9 - Amends	STEP 8
	☐ Now ☐ Later ☐ Never

STEP 10

INVENTORY FORMS

Resentment (1) and/or Fear:	The Cause (Column 2)	Affects Our: (Column 3)
Person, Place or Thing		☐ Self-Esteem ☐ Security ☐ Ambitions ☐ Personal Relations ☐ Sex Relations ☐ Pride/Shame ☐ Fear
Ask Ourselves: ** (AA 67.3) * (AA 62.2)	Putting out of our mind the wrong others had done, we resolutely looked for our own mistakes... We admitted our wrongs honestly...** STEPS 4 and/or 10 - (Column 4)	
Where had I been selfish, self-centred or self-seeking?**		
Where had I been dishonest?**		
Where had I been frightened?**		
For what had I been responsible?**		
What decisions did I make based on self that later placed me in a position to be hurt?*		
When in the past did I make this decision? * (Earliest memory)		
Where was I wrong,** what was my part?		

STEPS 6 & 7 – List of Character Defects				

STEP 9 - Amends	STEP 8
	☐ Now ☐ Later ☐ Never

COLUMN WORK

Resentment (1) and/or Fear:	The Cause (Column 2)	Affects Our: (Column 3)
Person, Place or Thing		☐ Self-Esteem ☐ Security ☐ Ambitions ☐ Personal Relations ☐ Sex Relations ☐ Pride/Shame ☐ Fear
Ask Ourselves: ** (AA 67.3) * (AA 62.2)	Putting out of our mind the wrong others had done, we resolutely looked for our own mistakes... We admitted our wrongs honestly...** **STEPS 4 and/or 10 - (Column 4)**	
Where had I been selfish, self-centred or self-seeking?**		
Where had I been dishonest?**		
Where had I been frightened?**		
For what had I been responsible?**		
What decisions did I make based on self that later placed me in a position to be hurt?*		
When in the past did I make this decision? * (Earliest memory)		
Where was I wrong,** what was my part?		

STEPS 6 & 7 – List of Character Defects

STEP 9 - Amends	STEP 8
	☐ Now ☐ Later ☐ Never

STEP 10

INVENTORY FORMS

Resentment (1) and/or Fear:	The Cause (Column 2)	Affects Our: (Column 3)
Person, Place or Thing		☐ Self-Esteem ☐ Security ☐ Ambitions ☐ Personal Relations ☐ Sex Relations ☐ Pride/Shame ☐ Fear
Ask Ourselves: ** (AA 67.3) * (AA 62.2)	Putting out of our mind the wrong others had done, we resolutely looked for our own mistakes... We admitted our wrongs honestly...** **STEPS 4** and/or **10 - (Column 4)**	
Where had I been selfish, self-centred or self-seeking?**		
Where had I been dishonest?**		
Where had I been frightened?**		
For what had I been responsible?**		
What decisions did I make based on self that later placed me in a position to be hurt?*		
When in the past did I make this decision? * (Earliest memory)		
Where was I wrong,** what was my part?		

STEPS 6 & 7 – List of Character Defects

STEP 9 - Amends	STEP 8
	☐ Now ☐ Later ☐ Never

COLUMN WORK

Resentment (1) and/or Fear:	The Cause (Column 2)	Affects Our: (Column 3)
Person, Place or Thing		☐ Self-Esteem ☐ Security ☐ Ambitions ☐ Personal Relations ☐ Sex Relations ☐ Pride/Shame ☐ Fear
Ask Ourselves: ** (AA 67.3) * (AA 62.2)	Putting out of our mind the wrong others had done, we resolutely looked for our own mistakes... We admitted our wrongs honestly...** **STEPS 4 and/or 10 - (Column 4)**	
Where had I been selfish, self-centred or self-seeking?**		
Where had I been dishonest?**		
Where had I been frightened?**		
For what had I been responsible?**		
What decisions did I make based on self that later placed me in a position to be hurt?*		
When in the past did I make this decision? * (Earliest memory)		
Where was I wrong,** what was my part?		

STEPS 6 & 7 – List of Character Defects

STEP 9 - Amends | **STEP 8**

	☐ Now ☐ Later ☐ Never

STEP 10

INVENTORY FORMS

Resentment (1) and/or Fear:	The Cause (Column 2)	Affects Our: (Column 3)
Person, Place or Thing		☐ Self-Esteem ☐ Security ☐ Ambitions ☐ Personal Relations ☐ Sex Relations ☐ Pride/Shame ☐ Fear
Ask Ourselves: ** (AA 67.3) * (AA 62.2)	Putting out of our mind the wrong others had done, we resolutely looked for our own mistakes... We admitted our wrongs honestly...** **STEPS 4** and/or **10** - **(Column 4)**	
Where had I been selfish, self-centred or self-seeking?**		
Where had I been dishonest?**		
Where had I been frightened?**		
For what had I been responsible?**		
What decisions did I make based on self that later placed me in a position to be hurt?*		
When in the past did I make this decision? * (Earliest memory)		
Where was I wrong,** what was my part?		

STEPS 6 & 7 – List of Character Defects				

STEP 9 - Amends	STEP 8
	☐ Now ☐ Later ☐ Never

MAINTAINING THE PROMISES...DAILY

COLUMN WORK

Resentment (1) and/or Fear:	The Cause (Column 2)	Affects Our: (Column 3)
Person, Place or Thing		☐ Self-Esteem ☐ Security ☐ Ambitions ☐ Personal Relations ☐ Sex Relations ☐ Pride/Shame ☐ Fear
Ask Ourselves: ** (AA 67.3) * (AA 62.2)	Putting out of our mind the wrong others had done, we resolutely looked for our own mistakes... We admitted our wrongs honestly...** **STEPS 4 and/or 10 - (Column 4)**	
Where had I been selfish, self-centred or self-seeking?**		
Where had I been dishonest?**		
Where had I been frightened?**		
For what had I been responsible?**		
What decisions did I make based on self that later placed me in a position to be hurt?*		
When in the past did I make this decision? * (Earliest memory)		
Where was I wrong,** what was my part?		

STEPS 6 & 7 – List of Character Defects

STEP 9 - Amends | STEP 8

☐ Now
☐ Later
☐ Never

STEP 10

INVENTORY FORMS

Resentment (1) and/or Fear:	The Cause (Column 2)	Affects Our: (Column 3)
Person, Place or Thing		☐ Self-Esteem ☐ Security ☐ Ambitions ☐ Personal Relations ☐ Sex Relations ☐ Pride/Shame ☐ Fear
Ask Ourselves: ** (AA 67.3) * (AA 62.2)	Putting out of our mind the wrong others had done, we resolutely looked for our own mistakes... We admitted our wrongs honestly...** **STEPS 4 and/or 10 - (Column 4)**	
Where had I been selfish, self-centred or self-seeking?**		
Where had I been dishonest?**		
Where had I been frightened?**		
For what had I been responsible?**		
What decisions did I make based on self that later placed me in a position to be hurt?*		
When in the past did I make this decision? * (Earliest memory)		
Where was I wrong,** what was my part?		

STEPS 6 & 7 – List of Character Defects			

STEP 9 - Amends	STEP 8
	☐ Now ☐ Later ☐ Never

COLUMN WORK

Resentment (1) and/or Fear:	The Cause (Column 2)	Affects Our: (Column 3)
Person, Place or Thing		☐ Self-Esteem ☐ Security ☐ Ambitions ☐ Personal Relations ☐ Sex Relations ☐ Pride/Shame ☐ Fear
Ask Ourselves: ** (AA 67.3) * (AA 62.2)	Putting out of our mind the wrong others had done, we resolutely looked for our own mistakes... We admitted our wrongs honestly...** **STEPS 4 and/or 10 - (Column 4)**	
Where had I been selfish, self-centred or self-seeking?**		
Where had I been dishonest?**		
Where had I been frightened?**		
For what had I been responsible?**		
What decisions did I make based on self that later placed me in a position to be hurt?*		
When in the past did I make this decision? * (Earliest memory)		
Where was I wrong,** what was my part?		

STEPS 6 & 7 – List of Character Defects

STEP 9 - Amends	STEP 8
	☐ Now ☐ Later ☐ Never

STEP 10

INVENTORY FORMS

Resentment (1) and/or Fear:	The Cause (Column 2)	Affects Our: (Column 3)
Person, Place or Thing		☐ Self-Esteem ☐ Security ☐ Ambitions ☐ Personal Relations ☐ Sex Relations ☐ Pride/Shame ☐ Fear
Ask Ourselves: ** (AA 67.3) * (AA 62.2)	Putting out of our mind the wrong others had done, we resolutely looked for our own mistakes... We admitted our wrongs honestly...** **STEPS 4 and/or 10 - (Column 4)**	
Where had I been selfish, self-centred or self-seeking?**		
Where had I been dishonest?**		
Where had I been frightened?**		
For what had I been responsible?**		
What decisions did I make based on self that later placed me in a position to be hurt?*		
When in the past did I make this decision? * (Earliest memory)		
Where was I wrong,** what was my part?		

STEPS 6 & 7 – List of Character Defects

STEP 9 - Amends	STEP 8
	☐ Now ☐ Later ☐ Never

COLUMN WORK

Resentment and/or Fear: (1)	The Cause (Column 2)	Affects Our: (Column 3)
Person, Place or Thing		☐ Self-Esteem ☐ Security ☐ Ambitions ☐ Personal Relations ☐ Sex Relations ☐ Pride/Shame ☐ Fear
Ask Ourselves: ** (AA 67.3) * (AA 62.2)	Putting out of our mind the wrong others had done, we resolutely looked for our own mistakes… We admitted our wrongs honestly…** **STEPS 4** and/or **10 - (Column 4)**	
Where had I been selfish, self-centred or self-seeking?**		
Where had I been dishonest?**		
Where had I been frightened?**		
For what had I been responsible?**		
What decisions did I make based on self that later placed me in a position to be hurt?*		
When in the past did I make this decision? * (Earliest memory)		
Where was I wrong,** what was my part?		

STEPS 6 & 7 – List of Character Defects			

STEP 9 - Amends	STEP 8
	☐ Now ☐ Later ☐ Never

STEP 10

INVENTORY FORMS

Resentment (1) and/or Fear:	The Cause (Column 2)	Affects Our: (Column 3)
Person, Place or Thing		☐ Self-Esteem ☐ Security ☐ Ambitions ☐ Personal Relations ☐ Sex Relations ☐ Pride/Shame ☐ Fear
Ask Ourselves: ** (AA 67.3) * (AA 62.2)	Putting out of our mind the wrong others had done, we resolutely looked for our own mistakes… We admitted our wrongs honestly…** **STEPS 4 and/or 10 - (Column 4)**	
Where had I been selfish, self-centred or self-seeking?**		
Where had I been dishonest?**		
Where had I been frightened?**		
For what had I been responsible?**		
What decisions did I make based on self that later placed me in a position to be hurt?*		
When in the past did I make this decision? * (Earliest memory)		
Where was I wrong,** what was my part?		

STEPS 6 & 7 – List of Character Defects			

STEP 9 - Amends	STEP 8
	☐ Now ☐ Later ☐ Never

COLUMN WORK

Resentment (1) and/or Fear:	The Cause (Column 2)	Affects Our: (Column 3)
Person, Place or Thing		☐ Self-Esteem ☐ Security ☐ Ambitions ☐ Personal Relations ☐ Sex Relations ☐ Pride/Shame ☐ Fear
Ask Ourselves: ** (AA 67.3) * (AA 62.2)	Putting out of our mind the wrong others had done, we resolutely looked for our own mistakes… We admitted our wrongs honestly…** **STEPS 4 and/or 10 - (Column 4)**	
Where had I been selfish, self-centred or self-seeking?**		
Where had I been dishonest?**		
Where had I been frightened?**		
For what had I been responsible?**		
What decisions did I make based on self that later placed me in a position to be hurt?*		
When in the past did I make this decision? * (Earliest memory)		
Where was I wrong,** what was my part?		

STEPS 6 & 7 – List of Character Defects			

STEP 9 - Amends	STEP 8
	☐ Now ☐ Later ☐ Never

STEP 10

INVENTORY FORMS

Resentment (1) and/or Fear:	The Cause (Column 2)	Affects Our: (Column 3)
Person, Place or Thing		☐ Self-Esteem ☐ Security ☐ Ambitions ☐ Personal Relations ☐ Sex Relations ☐ Pride/Shame ☐ Fear
Ask Ourselves: ** (AA 67.3) * (AA 62.2)	Putting out of our mind the wrong others had done, we resolutely looked for our own mistakes… We admitted our wrongs honestly…** **STEPS 4** and/or **10 - (Column 4)**	
Where had I been selfish, self-centred or self-seeking?**		
Where had I been dishonest?**		
Where had I been frightened?**		
For what had I been responsible?**		
What decisions did I make based on self that later placed me in a position to be hurt?*		
When in the past did I make this decision? * (Earliest memory)		
Where was I wrong,** what was my part?		
STEPS 6 & 7 – List of Character Defects		
STEP 9 - Amends		**STEP 8**
		☐ Now ☐ Later ☐ Never

MAINTAINING THE PROMISES…DAILY

COLUMN WORK

Resentment (1) and/or Fear:	The Cause (Column 2)	Affects Our: (Column 3)
Person, Place or Thing		☐ Self-Esteem ☐ Security ☐ Ambitions ☐ Personal Relations ☐ Sex Relations ☐ Pride/Shame ☐ Fear
Ask Ourselves: ** (AA 67.3) * (AA 62.2)	Putting out of our mind the wrong others had done, we resolutely looked for our own mistakes... We admitted our wrongs honestly... ** **STEPS 4 and/or 10 - (Column 4)**	
Where had I been selfish, self-centred or self-seeking?**		
Where had I been dishonest?**		
Where had I been frightened?**		
For what had I been responsible?**		
What decisions did I make based on self that later placed me in a position to be hurt?*		
When in the past did I make this decision? * (Earliest memory)		
Where was I wrong,** what was my part?		

STEPS 6 & 7 – List of Character Defects			

STEP 9 - Amends	STEP 8
	☐ Now ☐ Later ☐ Never

STEP 10

INVENTORY FORMS

Resentment (1) and/or Fear:	The Cause (Column 2)	Affects Our: (Column 3)
Person, Place or Thing		☐ Self-Esteem ☐ Security ☐ Ambitions ☐ Personal Relations ☐ Sex Relations ☐ Pride/Shame ☐ Fear
Ask Ourselves: ** (AA 67.3) * (AA 62.2)	Putting out of our mind the wrong others had done, we resolutely looked for our own mistakes... We admitted our wrongs honestly...** **STEPS 4** and/or **10 - (Column 4)**	
Where had I been selfish, self-centred or self-seeking?**		
Where had I been dishonest?**		
Where had I been frightened?**		
For what had I been responsible?**		
What decisions did I make based on self that later placed me in a position to be hurt?*		
When in the past did I make this decision? * (Earliest memory)		
Where was I wrong,** what was my part?		
STEPS 6 & 7 – List of Character Defects		
STEP 9 - Amends		**STEP 8**
		☐ Now ☐ Later ☐ Never

COLUMN WORK

Resentment and/or Fear: (1)	The Cause (Column 2)	Affects Our: (Column 3)
Person, Place or Thing		☐ Self-Esteem ☐ Security ☐ Ambitions ☐ Personal Relations ☐ Sex Relations ☐ Pride/Shame ☐ Fear
Ask Ourselves: ** (AA 67.3) * (AA 62.2)	Putting out of our mind the wrong others had done, we resolutely looked for our own mistakes… We admitted our wrongs honestly…** **STEPS 4 and/or 10 - (Column 4)**	
Where had I been selfish, self-centred or self-seeking?**		
Where had I been dishonest?**		
Where had I been frightened?**		
For what had I been responsible?**		
What decisions did I make based on self that later placed me in a position to be hurt?*		
When in the past did I make this decision? * (Earliest memory)		
Where was I wrong,** what was my part?		

STEPS 6 & 7 – List of Character Defects

STEP 9 - Amends	STEP 8
	☐ Now ☐ Later ☐ Never

STEP 10

INVENTORY FORMS

Resentment (1) and/or Fear:	The Cause (Column 2)	Affects Our: (Column 3)
Person, Place or Thing		☐ Self-Esteem ☐ Security ☐ Ambitions ☐ Personal Relations ☐ Sex Relations ☐ Pride/Shame ☐ Fear
Ask Ourselves: ** (AA 67.3) * (AA 62.2)	Putting out of our mind the wrong others had done, we resolutely looked for our own mistakes… We admitted our wrongs honestly…** **STEPS 4 and/or 10 - (Column 4)**	
Where had I been selfish, self-centred or self-seeking?**		
Where had I been dishonest?**		
Where had I been frightened?**		
For what had I been responsible?**		
What decisions did I make based on self that later placed me in a position to be hurt?*		
When in the past did I make this decision? * (Earliest memory)		
Where was I wrong,** what was my part?		

STEPS 6 & 7 – List of Character Defects			

STEP 9 - Amends	STEP 8
	☐ Now ☐ Later ☐ Never

COLUMN WORK

Resentment (1) and/or Fear:	The Cause (Column 2)	Affects Our: (Column 3)
Person, Place or Thing		☐ Self-Esteem ☐ Security ☐ Ambitions ☐ Personal Relations ☐ Sex Relations ☐ Pride/Shame ☐ Fear
Ask Ourselves: ** (AA 67.3) * (AA 62.2)	Putting out of our mind the wrong others had done, we resolutely looked for our own mistakes… We admitted our wrongs honestly…** **STEPS 4 and/or 10 - (Column 4)**	
Where had I been selfish, self-centred or self-seeking?**		
Where had I been dishonest?**		
Where had I been frightened?**		
For what had I been responsible?**		
What decisions did I make based on self that later placed me in a position to be hurt?*		
When in the past did I make this decision? * (Earliest memory)		
Where was I wrong,** what was my part?		

STEPS 6 & 7 – List of Character Defects

STEP 9 - Amends	STEP 8
	☐ Now ☐ Later ☐ Never

STEP 10

INVENTORY FORMS

Resentment (1) and/or Fear:	The Cause (Column 2)	Affects Our: (Column 3)
Person, Place or Thing		☐ Self-Esteem ☐ Security ☐ Ambitions ☐ Personal Relations ☐ Sex Relations ☐ Pride/Shame ☐ Fear
Ask Ourselves: ** (AA 67.3) * (AA 62.2)	Putting out of our mind the wrong others had done, we resolutely looked for our own mistakes... We admitted our wrongs honestly...** **STEPS 4 and/or 10 - (Column 4)**	
Where had I been selfish, self-centred or self-seeking?**		
Where had I been dishonest?**		
Where had I been frightened?**		
For what had I been responsible?**		
What decisions did I make based on self that later placed me in a position to be hurt?*		
When in the past did I make this decision? * (Earliest memory)		
Where was I wrong,** what was my part?		

STEPS 6 & 7 – List of Character Defects

STEP 9 - Amends	STEP 8
	☐ Now ☐ Later ☐ Never

MAINTAINING THE PROMISES...DAILY

COLUMN WORK

Resentment (1) and/or Fear:	The Cause (Column 2)	Affects Our: (Column 3)
Person, Place or Thing		☐ Self-Esteem ☐ Security ☐ Ambitions ☐ Personal Relations ☐ Sex Relations ☐ Pride/Shame ☐ Fear
Ask Ourselves: ** (AA 67.3) * (AA 62.2)	Putting out of our mind the wrong others had done, we resolutely looked for our own mistakes... We admitted our wrongs honestly...** **STEPS 4** and/or **10 - (Column 4)**	
Where had I been selfish, self-centred or self-seeking?**		
Where had I been dishonest?**		
Where had I been frightened?**		
For what had I been responsible?**		
What decisions did I make based on self that later placed me in a position to be hurt?*		
When in the past did I make this decision? * (Earliest memory)		
Where was I wrong,** what was my part?		

STEPS 6 & 7 – List of Character Defects

STEP 9 - Amends

	STEP 8
	☐ Now ☐ Later ☐ Never

STEP 10

INVENTORY FORMS

Resentment (1) and/or Fear:	The Cause (Column 2)	Affects Our: (Column 3)
Person, Place or Thing		☐ Self-Esteem ☐ Security ☐ Ambitions ☐ Personal Relations ☐ Sex Relations ☐ Pride/Shame ☐ Fear
Ask Ourselves: ** (AA 67.3) * (AA 62.2)	Putting out of our mind the wrong others had done, we resolutely looked for our own mistakes… We admitted our wrongs honestly…** **STEPS 4** and/or **10** - **(Column 4)**	
Where had I been selfish, self-centred or self-seeking?**		
Where had I been dishonest?**		
Where had I been frightened?**		
For what had I been responsible?**		
What decisions did I make based on self that later placed me in a position to be hurt?*		
When in the past did I make this decision? * (Earliest memory)		
Where was I wrong,** what was my part?		
STEPS 6 & 7 – List of Character Defects		
STEP 9 - Amends		**STEP 8**
		☐ Now ☐ Later ☐ Never

COLUMN WORK

Resentment and/or Fear: (1)	The Cause (Column 2)	Affects Our: (Column 3)
Person, Place or Thing		☐ Self-Esteem ☐ Security ☐ Ambitions ☐ Personal Relations ☐ Sex Relations ☐ Pride/Shame ☐ Fear
Ask Ourselves: ** (AA 67.3) * (AA 62.2)	Putting out of our mind the wrong others had done, we resolutely looked for our own mistakes… We admitted our wrongs honestly…** **STEPS 4 and/or 10 - (Column 4)**	
Where had I been selfish, self-centred or self-seeking?**		
Where had I been dishonest?**		
Where had I been frightened?**		
For what had I been responsible?**		
What decisions did I make based on self that later placed me in a position to be hurt?*		
When in the past did I make this decision? * (Earliest memory)		
Where was I wrong,** what was my part?		

STEPS 6 & 7 – List of Character Defects

STEP 9 - Amends		STEP 8
		☐ Now ☐ Later ☐ Never

STEP 10

INVENTORY FORMS

Resentment (1) and/or Fear:	The Cause (Column 2)	Affects Our: (Column 3)
Person, Place or Thing		☐ Self-Esteem ☐ Security ☐ Ambitions ☐ Personal Relations ☐ Sex Relations ☐ Pride/Shame ☐ Fear
Ask Ourselves: ** (AA 67.3) * (AA 62.2)	Putting out of our mind the wrong others had done, we resolutely looked for our own mistakes… We admitted our wrongs honestly…** STEPS 4 and/or 10 - (Column 4)	
Where had I been selfish, self-centred or self-seeking?**		
Where had I been dishonest?**		
Where had I been frightened?**		
For what had I been responsible?**		
What decisions did I make based on self that later placed me in a position to be hurt?*		
When in the past did I make this decision? * (Earliest memory)		
Where was I wrong,** what was my part?		

STEPS 6 & 7 – List of Character Defects			

STEP 9 - Amends	STEP 8
	☐ Now ☐ Later ☐ Never

536 MAINTAINING THE PROMISES…DAILY

COLUMN WORK

Resentment and/or Fear: (1)	The Cause (Column 2)	Affects Our: (Column 3)
Person, Place or Thing		☐ Self-Esteem ☐ Security ☐ Ambitions ☐ Personal Relations ☐ Sex Relations ☐ Pride/Shame ☐ Fear
Ask Ourselves: ** (AA 67.3) * (AA 62.2)	Putting out of our mind the wrong others had done, we resolutely looked for our own mistakes… We admitted our wrongs honestly…** **STEPS 4 and/or 10 - (Column 4)**	
Where had I been selfish, self-centred or self-seeking?**		
Where had I been dishonest?**		
Where had I been frightened?**		
For what had I been responsible?**		
What decisions did I make based on self that later placed me in a position to be hurt?*		
When in the past did I make this decision? * (Earliest memory)		
Where was I wrong,** what was my part?		

STEPS 6 & 7 – List of Character Defects			

STEP 9 - Amends	STEP 8
	☐ Now ☐ Later ☐ Never

STEP 10

INVENTORY FORMS

Resentment (1) and/or Fear:	The Cause (Column 2)	Affects Our: (Column 3)
Person, Place or Thing		☐ Self-Esteem ☐ Security ☐ Ambitions ☐ Personal Relations ☐ Sex Relations ☐ Pride/Shame ☐ Fear
Ask Ourselves: ** (AA 67.3) * (AA 62.2)	Putting out of our mind the wrong others had done, we resolutely looked for our own mistakes… We admitted our wrongs honestly…** STEPS 4 and/or 10 - (Column 4)	
Where had I been selfish, self-centred or self-seeking?**		
Where had I been dishonest?**		
Where had I been frightened?**		
For what had I been responsible?**		
What decisions did I make based on self that later placed me in a position to be hurt?*		
When in the past did I make this decision? * (Earliest memory)		
Where was I wrong,** what was my part?		

STEPS 6 & 7 – List of Character Defects

STEP 9 - Amends		STEP 8
		☐ Now ☐ Later ☐ Never

COLUMN WORK

Resentment (1) and/or Fear:	The Cause (Column 2)	Affects Our: (Column 3)
Person, Place or Thing		☐ Self-Esteem ☐ Security ☐ Ambitions ☐ Personal Relations ☐ Sex Relations ☐ Pride/Shame ☐ Fear
Ask Ourselves: ** (AA 67.3) * (AA 62.2)	Putting out of our mind the wrong others had done, we resolutely looked for our own mistakes... We admitted our wrongs honestly...** **STEPS 4** and/or **10 - (Column 4)**	
Where had I been selfish, self-centred or self-seeking?**		
Where had I been dishonest?**		
Where had I been frightened?**		
For what had I been responsible?**		
What decisions did I make based on self that later placed me in a position to be hurt?*		
When in the past did I make this decision? * (Earliest memory)		
Where was I wrong,** what was my part?		

STEPS 6 & 7 – List of Character Defects				

STEP 9 - Amends	STEP 8
	☐ Now ☐ Later ☐ Never

STEP 10

INVENTORY FORMS

Resentment (1) and/or Fear:	The Cause (Column 2)	Affects Our: (Column 3)
Person, Place or Thing		☐ Self-Esteem ☐ Security ☐ Ambitions ☐ Personal Relations ☐ Sex Relations ☐ Pride/Shame ☐ Fear
Ask Ourselves: ** (AA 67.3) * (AA 62.2)	Putting out of our mind the wrong others had done, we resolutely looked for our own mistakes... We admitted our wrongs honestly... ** **STEPS 4 and/or 10 - (Column 4)**	
Where had I been selfish, self-centred or self-seeking?**		
Where had I been dishonest?**		
Where had I been frightened?**		
For what had I been responsible?**		
What decisions did I make based on self that later placed me in a position to be hurt?*		
When in the past did I make this decision? * (Earliest memory)		
Where was I wrong,** what was my part?		

STEPS 6 & 7 – List of Character Defects

STEP 9 - Amends	STEP 8
	☐ Now ☐ Later ☐ Never

COLUMN WORK

Resentment (1) and/or Fear:	The Cause (Column 2)	Affects Our: (Column 3)
Person, Place or Thing		☐ Self-Esteem ☐ Security ☐ Ambitions ☐ Personal Relations ☐ Sex Relations ☐ Pride/Shame ☐ Fear
Ask Ourselves: ** (AA 67.3) * (AA 62.2)	Putting out of our mind the wrong others had done, we resolutely looked for our own mistakes... We admitted our wrongs honestly...** **STEPS 4 and/or 10 - (Column 4)**	
Where had I been selfish, self-centred or self-seeking?**		
Where had I been dishonest?**		
Where had I been frightened?**		
For what had I been responsible?**		
What decisions did I make based on self that later placed me in a position to be hurt?*		
When in the past did I make this decision? * (Earliest memory)		
Where was I wrong,** what was my part?		

STEPS 6 & 7 – List of Character Defects

STEP 9 - Amends | STEP 8

☐ Now
☐ Later
☐ Never

STEP 10

INVENTORY FORMS

Resentment (1) and/or Fear:	The Cause (Column 2)	Affects Our: (Column 3)
Person, Place or Thing		☐ Self-Esteem ☐ Security ☐ Ambitions ☐ Personal Relations ☐ Sex Relations ☐ Pride/Shame ☐ Fear
Ask Ourselves: ** (AA 67.3) * (AA 62.2)	Putting out of our mind the wrong others had done, we resolutely looked for our own mistakes… We admitted our wrongs honestly…** **STEPS 4 and/or 10 - (Column 4)**	
Where had I been selfish, self-centred or self-seeking?**		
Where had I been dishonest?**		
Where had I been frightened?**		
For what had I been responsible?**		
What decisions did I make based on self that later placed me in a position to be hurt?*		
When in the past did I make this decision? * (Earliest memory)		
Where was I wrong,** what was my part?		

STEPS 6 & 7 – List of Character Defects

STEP 9 - Amends	STEP 8
	☐ Now ☐ Later ☐ Never

COLUMN WORK

Resentment and/or Fear: (1)	The Cause (Column 2)	Affects Our: (Column 3)
Person, Place or Thing		☐ Self-Esteem ☐ Security ☐ Ambitions ☐ Personal Relations ☐ Sex Relations ☐ Pride/Shame ☐ Fear
Ask Ourselves: ** (AA 67.3) * (AA 62.2)	Putting out of our mind the wrong others had done, we resolutely looked for our own mistakes… We admitted our wrongs honestly…** **STEPS 4 and/or 10 - (Column 4)**	
Where had I been selfish, self-centred or self-seeking?**		
Where had I been dishonest?**		
Where had I been frightened?**		
For what had I been responsible?**		
What decisions did I make based on self that later placed me in a position to be hurt?*		
When in the past did I make this decision? * (Earliest memory)		
Where was I wrong,** what was my part?		

STEPS 6 & 7 – List of Character Defects

STEP 9 - Amends | STEP 8

	☐ Now ☐ Later ☐ Never

STEP 10

Chapter 6

The Principles

THE PRINCIPLES OF THE PROGRAM

The following are *"the Principles by which AA members recover"* [109] as we see them.

"AA's Twelve Steps are a group of principles, spiritual in nature, which, if practised as a way of life, can expel the obsession to drink (or, we believe, any obsession) *and enable the sufferer to become happily and usefully whole."* [110] *"The basic principles of AA, as they are known today, were borrowed mainly from the fields of religion and medicine."* [111]

When AA began there were six principles. Today, now that we have Twelve Steps, we believe there are twelve principles. *"We begin to see that the AA principles are good ones. Though we are still beset with much rebellion, we increase the practice of these principles out of a sense of responsibility to ourselves, our families, and our groups."* [112] These principles are the *"common denominators of all religions...potent enough to change the lives of men and women.* [113] It is nearly impossible to put these powerful principles created by the Steps into single words, but here is an attempt to do so.

The initial six comprised: **Defeat** (now our Step One); **Honest** self-survey (now our Step Four); **Confession** (now our Step Five); **Restitution** (now our Step Nine); **Conscious contact** with a Higher Power (now our Step Eleven) and **Service** (now our Step Twelve). These principles went with the original Six Steps. We consider the additional principles to be: **Open-mindedness** (Step Two); **Surrender,** (Step Three); **Willingness** (Step Six); **Humility** (Step Seven); **Forgiveness** (Step Eight); **Stewardship** (Step Ten).

THE PRINCIPLES OF THE PROGRAM

1) **Defeat** (Step 1)
   Here the acceptance of our powerlessness and the knowledge of our **defeat** are paramount. I cannot make it on my own. "We" begin a life-long process. **Ego deflation** is the removal of a belief in separation. We are not alone or separate. We must be clear that *"any life run on self is not worth living."*

2) **Open Mindedness** (Step 2)
   Step Two is the smallest beginning of a pattern of faith *and open-mindedness* that builds. First is *faith* in the program, where we see *a power greater than ourselves* at work. To be **O**pen Minded is the **KEY**.

3) **Surrender** (Step 3)
   When we walk through the doors of our first meeting, or even with our first call for help, something begins to happen. That "something" becomes clearer by the time of our decision in Step Three. We decided to **surrender** to, and *trust* in, the process of the Steps, *a power greater than ourselves*. The bottom line for **surrender** is the recognition that "I could be wrong."

4) **Honesty** (Step 4)
   It can be argued that each of these "Principles" is buried in all the steps; "**H**onesty" is the **KEY**. However, Step Four begins a lifetime of **honest self-survey**.

5) **Confession** (Step 5)
   Our AA journey begins with the *courage* to ask for help. For some of us this journey begins with our first meeting. For others of us when we ask for help from a sponsor, but certainly for all of us that *courage* is there by the time we begin the **confession** of our "short comings" in Step Five.

6) **Willingness** (Step 6)
   All our answers are found deep inside, **Willingness** is the **KEY**. We must be willing to go against the demands of our self-will to use the tools we have created to, we think, survive; our defects of character.

7) **Humility** (Step 7)
Step 7 reminds us to give up our attempts at fixing ourselves and turn it over to God, an act of **humility** and open-mindedness that most of us never understood.

8) **Forgiveness** (Step 8)
Forgiveness begins here when we release resentments and hurts, "real or imagined," becoming ready to make amends.

9) **Restitution** (Step 9)
Amend, means "to mend" our past behaviour. Our new found life long experience of "mending" and making **restitution** for our past (and not so past) actions begins on Step Nine. This is where the "promises" are received, giving us an experience of **freedom** never before experienced.

10) **Stewardship** (Steps 10)
The so-called "maintenance steps" of the program begin with Step 10, teaching us perseverance and **stewardship**. *Perseverance* is just plain "keep on, keeping on," where as **stewardship** is the learning of the necessity for daily maintenance of the "Promises." Dr. Bob said that *"We are stewards of what we have."* [114]

11) **Conscious Contact** (Step 11)
Now that we have a belief in a Higher Power we *"improve our conscious contact"* with that Power greater than ourselves through Prayer and meditation. This is where we find a wonderful source of **Conscious** enlightenment. Enlightenment can only come to a **conscious** mind. A greater **conscious contact** is the benefit of the *patient* use of daily prayer and meditation, as we give up our desire for instant gratification. We must "Let Go and Let God". We become more **conscious** of our beliefs, of our actions, and attitudes. And most importantly we become more and more God **conscious**, "a spiritual awakening."

12) **Service** (Step 12)
Our entire life, through the *"practice of these principles in all our affairs"* [115] becomes one of service, including our jobs, and our home life, everywhere. We learn the true meaning of the word *charity*, as we carry the message through **service** and become a beacon to others in AA. In Step Twelve it is made clear that we must *"give it away to keep it"*. *"Our real purpose is to fit ourselves to be of maximum service to God and the people about us."* [116]

The References

REFERENCES

The page number is before the decimal and paragraph number after.

---

[1] Alcoholics Anonymous – Page 133.1
[2] Pass It On—Bill Wilson and the AA Message – Page 299.2
[3] Language of the Heart – Page 98.2
[4] Best of the Grapevine – Page(s) – 171.7
[5] The Language of the Heart – Page 333.3
[6] Language of the Heart – Page 258.8
[7] As Bill Sees It – Page 95.1
[8] Daily Reflections Page 248.2
[9] Twelve Steps and Twelve Traditions – Pages 130-3 – British Edition – 1999
[10] Alcoholics Anonymous – Page 63.2
[11] Alcoholics Anonymous – Page 76.2
[12] Twelve Steps & Twelve Traditions – Pages 101-102 – British Edition –1999
[13] Alcoholics Anonymous – Page 88.1
[14] Alcoholics Anonymous – Page 85.2
[15] Alcoholics Anonymous – Page 88.1
[16] Twelve Steps & Twelve Traditions – Pages 105.2 – British Edition – 1999
[17] Alcoholics Anonymous – Page 59.4
[18] Twelve Steps and Twelve Traditions – Page 90.1 – British Edition
[19] Twelve Steps and Twelve Traditions – Page 112.1 – British Edition
[20] Alcoholics Anonymous – Page 84.3
[21] As Bill Sees It – Page 98.1
[22] Alcoholics Anonymous – Page 84.4 – 85.2
[23] Language of the Heart – Page 238.8
[24] Twelve Steps and Twelve Traditions – Page 49.1 – British Edition
[25] Alcoholics Anonymous – Page 265.1 – 4th Edition
[26] Alcoholics Anonymous – Page 64.2
[27] Language of the Heart – Page 239.6 – 240.1
[28] Language of the Heart – Page 239.6 – 240.1
[29] Twelve Steps and Twelve Traditions – Page 118.3 – British Edition
[30] Alcoholics Anonymous – Page 60.5
[31] Alcoholics Anonymous – Page 58.3
[32] Alcoholics Anonymous – Page 66.1
[33] Alcoholics Anonymous – Page 381.5 – 4th Edition
[34] Twelve Steps and Twelve Traditions – Page 51.4 – 52.1 – British Edition
[35] Daily Reflections Page 250.2
[36] Twelve Steps and Twelve Traditions – Page 117.2 – British Edition
[37] As Bill Sees It – Page 234.3
[38] Alcoholics Anonymous – Page 64.2
[39] The Language of the Heart – Page 321.5, 322.1-3
[40] Twelve Steps and Twelve Traditions – Page 91.2 – British Edition
[41] Twelve Steps and Twelve Traditions – Page 91 – British Edition
[42] Twelve Steps and Twelve Traditions – Page 92.2,3 – British Edition
[43] Experience, Strength, & Hope – Page(s) 255.2
[44] Experience, Strength, & Hope – Page(s) 330.3
[45] Alcoholics Anonymous – Page 417.2 – 4th Edition
[46] Twelve Steps and Twelve Traditions – Page 92.3 – British Edition

REFERENCES

[47] Twelve Steps and Twelve Traditions – Page 92.3,4 – 93.1 – British Edition
[48] Twelve Steps and Twelve Traditions – Page 94.4 – 95.1 – British Edition
[49] Living Sober – Page(s) 38.5,6
[50] Experience, Strength, & Hope – Page(s) 23.1
[51] Living Sober – Page(s) 38.8,9, 39.2,4,5,9
[52] Twelve Steps and Twelve Traditions – Page 93.1 – British Edition
[53] Twelve Steps and Twelve Traditions – Page 93.2 – British Edition
[54] Living Sober – Page(s) 40.8
[55] Twelve Steps and Twelve Traditions – Page 90.1 – British Edition
[56] As Bill Sees It – Page 58.1
[57] Twelve Steps and Twelve Traditions – Page 92.3 – British Edition
[58] *Re-written as a formula from the "Big Book" of* Alcoholics Anonymous Page 84.3 *the numbers and format are ours.*
[59] Alcoholics Anonymous – Page 84.4
[60] Alcoholics Anonymous – Page 67.4
[61] Alcoholics Anonymous – Page 68.3
[62] As Bill Sees It – Page 184.3
[63] Twelve Steps and Twelve Traditions – Page 93.3 – British Edition
[64] As Bill Sees It – Page 39.3
[65] Alcoholics Anonymous – Page 133.1
[66] Alcoholics Anonymous – Page 133.1
[67] Twelve Steps and Twelve Traditions – Page 91 – British Edition
[68] Twelve Steps and Twelve Traditions – Page 91.2 – British Edition
[69] Alcoholics Anonymous – Page 61.2
[70] Experience, Strength, & Hope – Page(s) 410.3,4
[71] Twelve Steps and Twelve Traditions – Page 97.2 – British Edition
[72] The Language of the Heart – Page 324.5
[73] Twelve Steps and Twelve Traditions – Page 97.2 – British Edition
[74] Twelve Steps and Twelve Traditions – Page 95.5 – 96.1 – British Edition
[75] Twelve Steps and Twelve Traditions – Page 96.2 – British Edition
[76] Alcoholics Anonymous – Page 86
[77] Came to Believe… – Page(s) – 26.4
[78] Alcoholics Anonymous – Page 529.3 – 4th Edition
[79] Alcoholics Anonymous – Page 86.2
[80] Alcoholics Anonymous – Page 84.3
[81] Alcoholics Anonymous – Page 84.4
[82] As Bill Sees It – Page 168.1
[83] Came to Believe… – Page(s) – 94.8 – 95.1
[84] Came to Believe… – Page(s) – 95.3
[85] Twelve Steps and Twelve Traditions – Page 91.2 – British Edition
[86] Alcoholics Anonymous – Page 59.3.5
[87] Alcoholics Anonymous – Page 72.2
[88] As Bill Sees It – Page 253.3
[89] Experience, Strength, & Hope – Page(s) 430.2
[90] Twelve Steps and Twelve Traditions – British Edition – Page 79.1
[91] Experience, Strength, & Hope – Page(s) 424.3
[92] Daily Reflections – Page 70
[93] Twelve Steps and Twelve Traditions – British Edition Page 95.2

REFERENCES

[94] DR. BOB and the Good Oldtimers – Page 105.1
[95] Alcoholics Anonymous – Page 58.3
[96] Alcoholics Anonymous – Page 58.3
[97] Best of the Grapevine – Page(s) – 128.2
[98] Experience, Strength, & Hope – Page(s) 40.3, 41.1
[99] Experience, Strength, & Hope – Page(s) 335.3
[100] Experience, Strength, & Hope – Page(s) 332.1
[101] Experience, Strength, & Hope – Page(s) 213.1
[102] Twelve Steps and Twelve Traditions – Page 53.4 – British Edition
[103] Experience, Strength, & Hope – Page(s) 330.3
[104] Experience, Strength, & Hope – Page(s) 214.2
[105] Think and Grow Rich – Napoleon Hill
[106] Alcoholics Anonymous – Page 62.2
[107] Twelve Steps and Twelve Traditions – Page 127.2 – British Edition
[108] DR. BOB and the Good Oldtimers – Page 158.2
[109] Twelve Steps and Twelve Traditions – Page 15.2 – British Edition
[110] Twelve Steps and Twelve Traditions – Page 15.3 – British Edition
[111] Twelve Steps and Twelve Traditions – British Edition – Page 16.4
[112] Language of the Heart – Page 302.2
[113] Pass It On—Bill Wilson and the AA Message – Page 128.1
[114] DR. BOB and the Good Oldtimers – Page 105.1
[115] Alcoholics Anonymous Page 60.1
[116] Alcoholics Anonymous – Page 77.1

REFERENCES

Also available from *HP* Publishing:

Meditation CDs	USA	UK
– Prayer of St Francis of Assisi	$ 16.95	£ 7.95
– Forgiveness Meditation – (available soon)	$ 16.95	£ 7.95
– Life's an Ocean – (available soon)	$ 16.95	£ 7.95

Books		
– Deep Soul Cleansing (text) Hardcover	$ 43.95	£ 22.50
– Deep Soul Cleansing (text) Paperback	$ 26.95	£ 13.95
– Deep Soul Cleansing – Workbook Paperback	$ 44.50	£ 22.95
– Maintaining the Promises – Daily Hardcover	$ 55.95	£ 27.95
– Maintaining the Promises – Daily Paperback	$ 32.95	£ 19.50
– 366 Daily Prayers – (available soon)	$ 24.95	£ 12.95
– Four Column Inventory Forms Only Paperback	$ 28.95	£ 14.50

Write for more information about upcoming Retreats and/or workshops or send your order to:

United Kingdom

HP Retreats

63 Shepherds Court
LONDON England
W12-8PW
44+(0)208-740-8567
www.hpretreats.org

United States

HP Publishing

1701 The Greensway
Building 1425
Jacksonville Beach FL 32250
1+ 904-543-0608
www.hppublishing.com

Orders are best made via the internet do to our busy travel schedule.

www.ingramcontent.com/pod-product-compliance
Lightning Source LLC
Chambersburg PA
CBHW020632300426
44112CB00007B/90